Acoustics of Empire

Acoustics of Empire

Sound, Media, and Power in the Long Nineteenth Century

Edited by

PETER MCMURRAY

AND

PRIYASHA MUKHOPADHYAY

OXFORD
UNIVERSITY PRESS

OXFORD
UNIVERSITY PRESS

Oxford University Press is a department of the University of Oxford. It furthers
the University's objective of excellence in research, scholarship, and education
by publishing worldwide. Oxford is a registered trade mark of Oxford University
Press in the UK and certain other countries.

Published in the United States of America by Oxford University Press
198 Madison Avenue, New York, NY 10016, United States of America.

© Oxford University Press 2024

Library of Congress Cataloging-in-Publication Data
Names: McMurray, Peter L., editor. | Mukhopadhyay, Priyasha, 1988– editor.
Title: Acoustics of empire : sound, media, and power in the long nineteenth century /
edited by Peter McMurray and Priyasha Mukhopadhyay.
Description: New York : Oxford University Press, 2024. |
Includes bibliographical references and index.
Identifiers: LCCN 2023056775 (print) | LCCN 2023056776 (ebook) |
ISBN 9780197553794 (paperback) | ISBN 9780197553787 (hardback) |
ISBN 9780197553817 (epub) | ISBN 9780197553824 | ISBN 9780197553800
Subjects: LCSH: Sound—Social aspects—History—19th century. |
Sound—Political aspects—History—19th century. | Sound in mass media. |
Communication—Social aspects—History—19th century.
Classification: LCC P96.S66 A33 2924 (print) | LCC P96.S66 (ebook) |
DDC 302.209/034—dc23/eng/20240311
LC record available at https://lccn.loc.gov/2023056775
LC ebook record available at https://lccn.loc.gov/2023056776

DOI: 10.1093/oso/9780197553787.001.0001

Contents

PART III. MUSICAL ENCOUNTERS

PART IV. SILENCE AND ITS OTHERS

Acknowledgments

A project of this nature is necessarily a collaboration with many people. First and foremost, we thank the contributors to this volume, who have produced exciting research and juggled deadlines through the Covid-19 pandemic, with all its challenges. It has been a privilege to work with them in this capacity. This book is the result of a series of workshops held at the Max Planck Institute for the History of Science (Berlin), Mahindra Humanities Center at Harvard University, and Corpus Christi College, University of Cambridge. This project grew out of initial conversations with David Trippett in the context of his European Research Council Starting Grant, *Sound and Materialism in the 19th Century* (2017–2022), which provided generous support for the workshops that followed, allowing these ideas to develop as an extended dialogue. That grant has also enabled Open Access publication, which we hope will allow this book to reach a much wider audience than it might otherwise. David's research team, including Melle Kromhout, Melissa Van Drie, Edward Gillen, and Stephanie Probst, provided an invaluable sounding board for these ideas, especially in the early stages of the project.

In addition to the authors whose contributions appear here, a number of other academics participated in these workshops in a variety of roles, including Viktoria Tkaczyk, Anindita Nag, Bernhard Siegert, and Xiaochang Li in Berlin; Jim Sykes, Glenda Goodman, Adam Mestyan, Carolyn Abbate, and Sugata Bose at Harvard; and Katharine Ellis, Nicholas Cook, Arthur Asseraf, Ariana Phillips-Hutton, Vanessa Paloma Elbaz, Rashel Pakbaz, Rumya Putcha, and Peter Asimov at Cambridge. Special thanks go to Birgitta Mallinckrodt (Max Planck), Steven Biel (Harvard), and Elaine Hendrie, Viktoria Lorenser, Sarah Wordsworth, Pilar Alonso, and Zeynep Kaçmaz Milne (Cambridge) for their organizational support, which was indispensable given the complexities of the project. A special mention needs to be made of Jim Sykes and Rumya Putcha (again) and Louise Meintjes for early and thoughtful conversations in envisioning the project. We also thank Sebastian Klotz at the Berlin Lautarchiv and Darcy Kuronen at the Museum of Fine Arts, Boston, for welcoming us into their collections.

We are grateful to Norm Hirschy, along with Lauralee Yeary, Laura Santo, Rada Radojicic, and the production team at Oxford University Press, who have helped guide this project through the complexities of publication. The book is stronger thanks to the peer reviewers, as well. In addition, Jacob Olley's assistance with copyediting has been an immense help. Any editorial mistakes that remain are our own.

The project has also benefited from support from the Philip Leverhulme Prize fund and the project, *Ottoman Auralities and the Eastern Mediterranean: Sound, Media and Power, 1789–1922*, selected as a European Research Council Starting Grant, funded by UK Research and Innovation (EP/X032833/1).

The chapters by Ziad Fahmy and James Q. Davies incorporate content previously published in: Ziad Fahmy, *Street Sounds: Listening to Everyday Life in Modern Egypt* (Stanford, CA: Stanford University Press, 2020) and James Q. Davies, *Creatures of the Air: Music, Atlantic Spirits, Breath, 1817–1913* (Chicago: University of Chicago Press, 2023). We are grateful to those presses for permission to reproduce that material here.

As a final note, we want to single out Melle Kromhout for particular thanks. He co-organized all the workshops with us and played an integral role not only in planning and holding these events, but in thinking through the conceptual framework, possibilities, and potential pitfalls of the project. This book, and the intellectual community that coalesced around it, owes much to his insight and energies.

Contributors

Alejandra Bronfman, State University of New York, Albany

Elleke Boehmer, University of Oxford

Hyun Kyong Hannah Chang, University of Sheffield

James Q. Davies, University of California, Berkeley

Faisal Devji, University of Oxford

Ziad Fahmy, Cornell University

Alexandra Hui, Mississippi State University

Nazan Maksudyan, Centre Marc Bloch, Berlin

Peter McMurray, University of Cambridge

Jairo Moreno, University of Pennsylvania

Projit Bihari Mukharji, Ashoka University

Priyasha Mukhopadhyay, Yale University

Sindhumathi Revuluri, Harvard University

Gavin Steingo, Princeton University

Benjamin Walton, University of Cambridge

Richard David Williams, SOAS, University of London

Introduction

Imperial Sounds, c. 1797

Peter McMurray and Priyasha Mukhopadhyay

In 1797, the London Missionary Society began organizing missionary expeditions to Tonga, Tahiti, and the Marquesas Islands. In written accounts of these voyages, told and retold in diaries, official reports, and histories, cuckoo clocks make a repeated appearance. According to the Missionary Society's account, the Tahitians and Tongans who encountered these clocks responded with "wonderous attention," a mix of terror, curiosity, and envy.[1] We learn that the local inhabitants of Tahiti, horrified that the missionaries did not feed the cuckoo, would offer it pieces of breadfruit and plantain to eat.[2] Some refused to be in the same room as it; others coveted the clock for themselves. In Tonga, locals imagined it to be a miniature panopticon, a trap to catch thieves. They invested it with spiritual and medical powers; the king of Tonga himself asked that it be brought to him on his deathbed in hopes of a miraculous cure.[3]

Accounts of the cuckoo clock and the responses it elicits draw on many of the now-hackneyed tropes used to describe the colonial encounter. Describing a scene of Bible reading in India in 1817, Homi Bhabha argues that printed English books were a material instantiation of colonial power, "signs taken for wonders" generating feelings of shock and awe.[4] Shoring up the scientific superiority of the white missionaries over the natives, the clock is also a symbol of colonial authority and discipline. The cuckoo clock became critical to the venture of the missionaries, who reveled in the public excitement and superiority they believed the technology conferred on them. In turn, the spectacle of the clock prompted feelings of inadequacy in the local population, many of whom "mutter[ed] out bitter reflections on their own country" and its ignorance of the "ingenious arts" of the Western world. The clock, as the unnamed Missionary Society author notes, "was not without its use."[5]

Peter McMurray and Priyasha Mukhopadhyay, *Introduction* In: *Acoustics of Empire*. Edited by: Peter McMurray and Priyasha Mukhopadhyay, Oxford University Press. © Oxford University Press 2024.
DOI: 10.1093/oso/9780197553787.003.0001

Later European accounts set the scene of the cuckoo clock a little differently. In recounting the missionary efforts of the late 1790s, William Brown's multi-volume *The History of Missions; Or, Of the Propagation of Christianity Among the Heathen, Since the Reformation* from 1814 focuses on the instrument's particular call:

> Having fixed up a cuckoo clock, it was viewed by the natives with the utmost astonishment, even before it was put in motion; but their wonder was increased a thousand-fold, when, on its being set a going, the bird came out, crying, "cuckoo, cuckoo." Such was their wonder, that, for some time, they could not take their eyes off it; then they looked at each other, dumb with astonishment, and at length withdrew in perfect amazement. The news of this wonderful curiosity, quickly spread over the whole island. It was reported the missionaries had got *Accoulair*, that is, "wood that speaks." The numerous visitors which it attracted completely occupied them from early in the morning, till late in the evening; and at length they multiplied so greatly, that it was necessary to refuse admittance to many of them.[6]

The Tongan '*Akaulea* (given by Brown as *Accoulair*) literally means "a plant that makes a sound," or more aptly, "speaking tree," referring to a sacred tree interposed between human and divine realms in Tongan mythology and capable of sonic mediation between them, a concept predating the arrival of Christian missionaries to the South Pacific.[7] Indeed, it was understood as a "superior means of communication" for shamans in western Polynesia, because "the tree was supposed to be able to summon whatever Hikule'o [an important deity in Tongan myth] required from the earth plane."[8] The concept highlighted a site of sonic mediation between the divine and the human. Accordingly, the cuckoo was not terrifying because these Tongans thought it was a Christian-like god-incarnate or that the wood itself was speaking. Rather, it seems they understood the clock and its utterance as a medium between multiple realms of power, sensation, and materiality. This, in turn, leads to the elicitation of different kinds of sonic responses to the clock among the Tongans, ranging from the loss of the ability to produce sound ("dumb with astonishment") to the rapid circulation of the news of this wondrous object, which, we are told, "quickly spread all over the whole island." In short, sound and its mediations—especially temporality, in this case of the cuckoo clock— play a central role in the colonial encounter, with these missionaries and locals conceptualizing that mediation in very different ways.

Like the English Bible reading in India, the cuckoo clock holds within it the seeds of what Bhabha has termed "colonial ambivalence."[9] The clock is not simply an object that consolidates colonial regimes of power; it is also the site at which they are actively dismantled. While the Missionary Society account from 1799 focuses on the potentials of exploiting the wonder of native subjects to proselytizing and disciplinary ends, a moment of fracture destabilizes that narrative in Brown's 1814 account. We are told that the Duatonga (i.e., the Tu'i Tonga), one of the highest ranking Tongan chiefs, asked for a clock as a gift, only to dismantle it immediately to see how it worked. Seeking help to put it back together again, he discovered that the missionaries were just as incapable of reassembling it as he was. It seems unveiling infrastructures has always been more glamorous than maintaining them. Brown summarizes the outcomes of the incident: "The circumstance lessened them [i.e., the missionaries] not a little in the eyes of the natives, and brought down upon them a great deal of ridicule; while, at the same time, it flattered the natural vanity of the Tongas [sic] who now prided themselves in the idea that they were at least as skilful as 'the men of the sky' [the missionaries]."[10] While Brown consistently asserts the moral superiority of the missionaries in his account, this moment is one of sonic disenchantment, as the power of the call of the cuckoo-clock is literally disassembled and replaced by the ridicule of the Tongans.

The clockness of these encounters is relevant here as well. This cuckoo clock was not the only timepiece to circulate during these years, or even to circulate as an object of sonic wonder. William Mariner, a teenage British sailor who lived in Tonga for four years (c. 1806–1810) after his ship, the *Port-au-Prince*, was attacked by Tongans, recounts another story of listening to timekeeping devices. A group of Tongans brought him a watch they had taken from the belongings of Fīnau 'Ulukālala, an important local chief who took Mariner into his custody. To demonstrate what it was, Mariner "took it from them, wound it up, put it to the ear of one of them," before passing it around the group: "It was applied in turns to their ears; they were astonished at the noise it made; they listened again to it; turned it on every side, and exclaimed 'mo-ooi' (it is alive!)."[11] Mariner eventually opened the watch to demystify it, only for it to get broken during the whole exchange. Like the missionaries, he was unable to reassemble the watch but was saved from the encounter by a Tongan who had spent time on a French ship and drew a massive diagram of a clock-face in the sand to explain to his compatriots its relationship to the sun. On another occasion, Mariner notes that at Fīnau's wedding, he and his wife presented the guest musicians with "an hour-glass, without either sand or stand."[12] These two brief examples suggest an ongoing intertwining of timekeeping devices and sound/music, as well as an accumulation of timekeeping devices in Tonga. As historian On Barak has argued for nineteenth-century Egypt, temporal regimes, as manifested through timekeeping devices, as well as communications technologies and transit systems, are a commonplace site of colonial struggle.[13] So these cuckoo clocks, watches, and hourglasses in Polynesia are neither surprising nor incidental.

This chapter is not a postcolonial history of the cuckoo clock, though the device certainly warrants a place in (yet-to-be-written) global histories of automata, musical instruments, and timekeeping devices of its era. Rather, as we have shown, the cuckoo clock introduces several key elements of the acoustics of empire in the long nineteenth century. For the 1790s missionaries, the cuckoo clock in the South Pacific foregrounds the superiority of Western technology. It generates humor from the disjunction between a familiar object and the unfamiliar perception of it by the Islanders. It mediates material transactions as both a commodity to be given away and as an object to draw Polynesian masses into the limited physical spaces controlled by the missionaries. It repels and attracts. It becomes a staged and intentional fetish, designed to displace animistic material cultures that may have existed with a tool of the "mechanic arts." Indeed, it becomes a kind of meta-fetish, a material distillation of the encounter of these two belief systems, itself distilled into a predictable set of social scripts that can and must play out between the colonizer and the colonized.

More broadly, we might conceive of these cuckoo clocks as part of a larger set of items that circulated around 1800 as part of Euro-American expansion around the globe, producing sound or otherwise generating some form of sonic encounter. We might call these things *imperial sound objects*, drawing on and expanding recent conversation in sound studies about "sound objects" more generally, such as James Steintrager and Rey Chow's groundbreaking 2019 volume. While pointing to the pioneering work of Pierre Schaeffer on the sound object, or *objet sonore*, they emphasize how modern sound and theories of sound (such as Schaeffer's) are "inseparable from the technological media of reproduction" of their time.[14] For Steintrager and Chow, "[t]he sound object was thus neither found nor captured. It was in part machine-made; in part, a construct of iterative perception."[15] Of course, the inextricable linking of sound and technology they propose looks quite different around 1800 or 1900 than it does in France after World War II where Schaeffer was composing, thinking, and writing. And crucially for our purposes, sound objects like the evangelizing cuckoo clocks are, again, imperial: they are built into circuits of power, colonizing, and exploitation.

Other such imperial sound objects might include Tipu's Tiger (sometimes "Tippoo's Tiger"), a musical semi-automaton depicting a wooden tiger pouncing on a British soldier, with a hand-cranked organ featuring eighteen distinct pitches embedded inside the tiger below a retractable lid. The tiger was commissioned by Tipu Sultan of Mysore in what is now southern India sometime in the 1780s or 1790s and was looted by the British when they defeated and killed Tipu Sultan in 1799. It now graces the Victoria and Albert Museum in London.[16] A few miles across town, the Rosetta Stone, another imperial sound object, if less obviously so, sits in the British Museum. Like Tipu's Tiger, the stone was a spoil of European conquest, discovered in Egypt in 1799 by Napoleon's army during his invasion and then seized by the British after they defeated Napoleon. While the stone's trilingual inscriptions do not produce sound per se, their decipherment was made possible by the recognition that "hieroglyphs recorded the sound of the Egyptian language" rather than representing it through ideograms.[17] We might also look to musical instruments as imperial sound objects: one of the contributors to this volume, James Davies, having previously made similar claims about Sir Stamford Raffles' commissioned gamelans as "instruments of empire,"[18] discusses the performance histories of the *ngombi* harp within the context of the transatlantic slave trade in his chapter here; and Sindhumathi Revuluri's chapter in this volume takes musical instruments in French museums as its point of departure. On the whole, what emerges is a network of sound objects being taken *by force* from colony to metropole or being deployed *as force* in the other direction, with the sonic dimensions of these objects producing new affective forms, ways of knowing, and coercion.

In short, regardless of how we read the Polynesians and their encounter with the cuckoo clock, the encounter itself underscores a routinely disregarded, if obvious, point: sound is not a neutral or even positive object in the way in which it has sometimes been valorized by its theorists and scholars.[19] European modernity, very much including imperial and colonial domination, may well have been visualist and ocularcentric at times; but it could just as well take sound and exploit its unique sensory qualities as well, even if unconsciously or, as it appears in this case, by means of decades of (mis)interpretation. Jonathan Sterne has suggested in his classic formulation of the "audiovisual litany" that these oft-repeated presumptions about sound's distinctness (and often its more positive associations) in contrast with the visual are not just false but part of a larger ideology of power.[20] Instances like the Tongan and Tahitian cuckoo clocks remind us that recovering the sonic from a traditionally visualist narrative does not ensure a felicitous political outcome. Indeed, as the utopianist dream of sound studies' liberatory capacity largely subsides and right-wing populisms spread around the globe, it may be more sensible to presume as a starting point that sound, like all other cultural phenomena, is complicit in racism, imperialism, and sexism, even as it also figures prominently in resistance to different modes of oppression.[21]

***

On Acoustics

The Tongans and the contradictory accounts of their encounter with the cuckoo clock encapsulate what we might call an *acoustics of empire* in the long nineteenth century: how sound and empire are intertwined in relationships of power and resistance. In this introduction and in the essays that follow, we explore the intersections of these two domains, of *acoustics* and of *empire*. We argue that these co-constitute and sustain one another in crucial ways that come into existence over the century following this cuckoo clock encounter in Tonga. By *acoustics* we mean not only the European (or Euro-American) science of sound as a subfield of physics, which had its heyday in the long nineteenth century thanks to figures like Fourier, Chladni, Helmholtz, and Rayleigh, as well as sound technologists like Scott de Martinville, Edison, and Bell. Rather, we take a broader, more global view of acoustics as a cultural technique that aims to articulate ways of knowing sound across different places and times. Such articulations of knowing may be explicit and discursive or tacit and rooted in forms of practice, embodied understanding, and tradition. In short, this cultural acoustics extends well beyond the teleological trajectory of European positivist science to include other forms of sound-knowledge rooted in other places, along the lines of what Steven Feld has called *acoustemologies*, a "knowing-with and knowing-through the audible,"[22] or what Tomie Hahn has called "sensational knowledge" of and through embodied experiences of sound.[23]

Furthermore, this book interrogates the ways that acoustics as an unmarked, Euro-American science is historically bound up in and predicated on the exclusion of other theories of sound from its disciplinary space. As an

allegedly objective form of physical science, acoustics traditionally has actively excluded these other cultural domains of sound knowledge, including
the sonic practices and techniques associated with religion, witchcraft, non-
Western music, and folk arts. We hope to conceive of acoustics through such
domains, not only to expand the remit of "acoustics" as such, but also to critique and deconstruct the exclusions already built into such categories of
knowledge. In a sense, these collective assertions across this volume about a
cultural acoustics that goes beyond Euro-American scientists and inventors
is a self-conscious response to the work of Gayatri Chakravorty Spivak
and Achille Mbembe in showing how the philosophy of figures like Kant,
Hegel, and others was bound up in and inextricable from the imperial politics and epistemologies of their day.[24] Put another way, the developments
of acoustics and its technological applications in the nineteenth century are,
again, "instruments of empire," shot through with the power relations and
political violence of their era. By the same token, as Euro-American science
circulated globally, its applications could be unpredictable, as seen in Projit
Bihari Mukharji's chapter in this volume on Ramendrasundar Tribedi's reception and reformulation of Helmholtz through traditional South Asian
linguistics and musical thought, and in Gavin Steingo's contribution on auscultation and "medical imposters" in southern Africa.

For the most part, the authors in this volume neither privilege nor avoid
"music," considering it one of many sound-rich phenomena that may constitute an acoustics of empire, alongside language, environmental sound, sound
technologies, noise, silence, embodied and physiological encounters with
sound, and so on. Thus, some authors like Sindhumathi Revuluri and Richard
David Williams are specifically interested in music and the histories of musicology, while others like Faisal Devji and Jairo Moreno focus on the absence
or rejection of sound as a meaningful presence in imperialism as well as
anticolonial struggles. For others, like Alexandra Hui and Nazan Maksudyan,
sounds produced by birds or street vendors readily blur distinctions between
"music" and non-musical sound. Often such distinctions were contested,
depending on who was listening and in what circumstances, as both Hyun
Kyong Hannah Chang and Benjamin Walton explore.

Finally, as the cuckoo clock example also reminds us, knowledge is not
independent of forms of inscription, or what Friedrich Kittler has called
"discourse networks" (*Aufschreibesysteme*; more literally, "writing-upon
systems").[25] The different written accounts cited here have clear biases
and constraints, and contrast with the rich oral traditions that Tongans

themselves might have of the period—traditions we touch on below. And in Tonga as in so many other places (such as in Bhabha's account of wondrous signs), writing itself became part of the colonizer's toolkit, if not necessarily in a single, universal way.

On Empire

If we are expanding the notion of *acoustics*, we think of *empire* here in a somewhat more limited, circumspect way, as the political, cultural, and social orders imposed by hegemonic powers (especially but not limited to European states) on other geographical spaces, typified by nineteenth-century imperial rule. This is not to dismiss more imaginative interpretations of empire (most notably that of Michael Hardt and Antonio Negri) or the urgency of addressing political oppression in a more general sense.[26] However, we focus on empire more narrowly both to foster a more unified conversation that otherwise spans a massive geography and to reflect on the role of sound in more overt political formations of empire. Just as we examine acoustics as a site of contestations of power, we also interrogate how empire and empires were constructed and maintained, as well as resisted, through sound, sonic practices, and sound technologies.

In exploring intersections of sound and empire, this volume is in close dialogue with (and indebted to) Ronald Radano and Tejumola Olaniyan's 2016 edited volume, *Audible Empire: Music, Global Politics, Critique.*[27] Their introduction, "Hearing Empire—Imperial Listening," opens with a poetic meditation on the potential pitfalls of revisiting *empire* as a concept:

> "Empire" is one of those wandering melodies of contemporary social and cultural analysis, a key word that seems to show up again and again, in any number of circumstances and settings. So oft-repeated and overrehearsed is "empire" that the term itself can appear, at times, imperial in character, and in its incessant display and repetition, it begins to take on qualities of abstraction. The obsessive iteration of empire (as with a related term, neoliberalism) leads to a loss of significance; its meaning comes to seem ambiguous, its power diminished.[28]

Radano and Olaniyan's volume is ultimately somewhat agnostic about empire's scope and definition, but the book gestures powerfully toward a confluence of music and global politics, particularly in the mid to late twentieth century. Building on that foundation, we seek in this volume to further that project in the context of the long nineteenth century, where empire has a more particular, if still quite expansive, set of meanings. However, like our colleagues in that volume (some of whom appear here as well), we see empire as a point of departure for a broader critical engagement with questions of sound and power.

Sound's role in the formation and maintenance of empire is multifaceted. A skeptic might argue that sound studies is, as ever, a decade behind visual studies, where similar discussions have long prevailed.[29] But sound's place in post/colonial archives is in many ways more ephemeral and less obvious than that of the visual; precisely for these reasons, it warrants further inquiry. Sonic archives, whether inscribed through written texts, photographs, or audiovisual media developed in the late 1800s, preserve a sense of affect, of space and durationality, of place and displacement, and again, of techniques of knowing the world—all of which generate singular forms of meaning in imperial contexts, often distinct from Western-centric narratives of sound technologies or Euro-American soundscapes.

And indeed, sound is well-suited to trouble distinctions between the universal and the particular, speaker and listener, subject and object, the archival and the ephemeral, and so on. The intertwining of acoustics and empire offers precisely this kind of troubling.

Listening to the Long Nineteenth Century

We deliberately restrict our historical and theoretical explorations to the long nineteenth century. To historians of empire, this choice may seem unsurprising, given that global imperial expansion came to its height through this period. By the end of the century, the "Age of Empire," as Eric Hobsbawm called it, had reached a fever pitch.[30] Moving in tandem with that imperial growth, sound and communications technologies became bound up with practices of establishing and maintaining empire, a theme taken up by many of the essays here. It is worth noting that the same age of empire—the long nineteenth century—also corresponds to a moment of disciplinary formation across the humanities and social sciences, of which the history of sound studies is a case in point. To us, it seems far from coincidental that so many of the academic disciplines with links to sound studies—music studies, anthropology, history, physics and acoustics, history of science, and literary studies—emerge and are consolidated during this same period of imperial expansion. Many of these disciplines, like musicology, ethnomusicology, anthropology, and acoustics (as a subfield within physics) drew explicitly on a peculiar mixture of audio technologies and the geopolitical terrain of the day. The phonograph, in particular, was employed in documenting sonic culture across a large geography enabled by political hegemony. Some key examples of these phonographic efforts included: Jesse Walter Fewkes's recordings of Native Americans beginning in 1890; the 1898 Torres Straits' expedition, with its emphasis on psychology, which manifested both in recording verbal practices and in attempts to document the psychoacoustic experiences of Torres Straits Islanders; and in the substantial archives of non-European music and language in Berlin with the Phonogramm-Archiv (founded 1900) and Lautarchiv (founded 1909, with dramatic expansions through recordings of prisoners of war during World War I).[31] Given how central phonographic practices and ideologies have been in narrating sound studies *and* modernity (or both, in the case of Kittler's "discourse network 1900"), one might reasonably ask whether the "soundscape of modernity," and by extension, sound studies, is permanently entangled with the colonial encounter in a way similar to ethnomusicology.[32]

By focusing on the long nineteenth century—instead of, say, a long twentieth century—*Acoustics of Empire* animates the relationship between sound and empire in the years before widespread audio recording. We aim to reconceive what constitutes sound and sound technologies in the nineteenth century beyond the scope of mechanical, electrical, or digital reproducibility. This is no easy task: how does one write about sound without a material, audio record of it? Doing so, especially beyond a Euro-American context, requires the study of archives that are unevenly preserved, scattered in libraries and collections around the world, and documented in multiple different languages.[33] The contributors to *Acoustics of Empire* draw their observations and conclusions from nineteenth-century sanitation reports, photography albums, musical transcriptions, ethnographic catalogues, missionary narratives, private notebooks, and medical textbooks, among other sources. They draw on archives of sensation, bodily practice, and cultural techniques. They not only present local histories of empire and sound; against the paucity of recorded traces of sound, they develop tools, methods, and innovative practices by which to study the phenomenon in its absence. In doing so, they also demonstrate how a notion of "sound technologies" might extend to include a whole range of communications media that may archive or index sound and sonic techniques, including telegraphy, silent film, and the stethoscope. Archival absence within an acoustics of empire is thus simultaneously both a technical and a geopolitical challenge, with an abundance of ostensible archival "silences" and gaps to be addressed.

Acoustics of Empire as Dialogue

The essays in *Acoustics of Empire* are the product of a set of year-long conversations at the Max Planck Institute for the History of Science in Berlin, Harvard University, and University of Cambridge. We assembled a set of contributors whose strengths would speak to each other. As co-editors, we bring different perspectives to the table: Peter as an ethnomusicologist working primarily on sound in the eastern Mediterranean and related diasporic communities, and Priyasha as a book historian working on colonial South Asia. The participants we brought together represent similarly varied disciplinary backgrounds. Some are established scholars of sound foraying into new geographies; others are historians and theorists of the postcolonial world surprised to find hidden sonic traces in their familiar archives. The emphasis on the nineteenth century has made several of our contributors think through the limits of their disciplines; ethnographers turning to historical questions have had to think through the ways in which their methods translate, or do not. Alongside debates in sound studies and postcolonialism, the essays draw on the study of visual culture, musicology and music theory, the history of the book, anthropology, science and technology studies, theology, political theory, and literary studies. Given that postcolonial sound studies is still very much a field under construction, we have been deliberate in allowing—even encouraging—methodological promiscuity, which we hope, in turn, will inspire and instruct readers of the collection.

In thinking of acoustics and empire as being closely intertwined, we see this project as resonating strongly with two different academic conversations. First, we engage with the recent flourishing of work on nineteenth-century sound and materiality, especially pre-dating the phonograph, that has taken hold in sound studies in the past two decades, including the work of Mark Smith, Jonathan Sterne, Veit Erlmann, Alexandra Hui, and Jennifer Lynn Stoever, to name a few.[34] Like these scholars, we seek to consider the particular technologies and techniques that give rise to changing modes of listening and also respond to them. More immediately, this book of essays was made possible by and in conversation with David Trippett's multi-year research project, *Sound and Materialism in the 19th Century*. In practical terms, Trippett's project offered generous support and a set of thematic frameworks (the nineteenth century, materialism) as a starting point. That rough chronology has proven productive (if sometimes archivally challenging), and the question of materiality (if not necessarily materialism) has remained a touchstone for the intersections of sound, sound technologies, and cultural practices that animate our work here. Our emphasis on a global sonic modernity beyond Europe, as well as the questions of imperial power associated with that more expansive geography, naturally lead to different conversations and ultimately a stance that is critical of the Western-centrism of much of sound studies. But we see that critique as a dialogue in which both strands (Euro-American sound studies, a more postcolonial approach) are crucial for the continued unfolding of historical sound studies.

Second, the book builds on and extends some of the themes developed in several important recent edited volumes on sound and the geographies of power, including *Audible Empire* (discussed above) and Gavin Steingo and Jim Sykes's *Remapping Sound Studies*, as well as monographs by Ana María Ochoa Gautier, Alejandra Bronfman, and Dylan Robinson.[35] Across these studies, sound and imperial power (understood broadly) are inextricably linked. In much of this work, sound is mostly accessible either through audio recording or ethnography (which may itself entail extensive use of audio). Our own emphasis in this volume on the nineteenth century, by contrast, not only challenges us as scholars to find new ways to construct arguments about sound in the absence of audio or ethnography; it also sets the stage for a critical re-evaluation of the very existence of these technologies and practices. In other words, if we fail to assess the ways the science of acoustics, phonography, and radio (among other acoustic cultural techniques), as well as scholarly disciplines of anthropology and musicology, are rooted in imperial histories, we run the risk of replicating those logics in our studies of later cultural moments. As such, this book resonates most strongly with Ochoa's *Aurality* and Bronfman's *Isles of Noise*, which both offer focused histories of auditory cultures in nineteenth-century Colombia and the early twentieth-century Caribbean, respectively.

We hope that this book builds on the provocative and important call by Steingo, Sykes, and the authors in their volume to *remap* sound studies (again, with a different set of historical aims and priorities). However, it also seems that there is a need to go further—to *decolonize* sound studies. In our conversations with the authors in this book over the past five years, this notion has repeatedly arisen. Dylan Robinson's urgent call for an indigenous re-configuration and re-theorizing of sound studies in his monograph *Hungry Listening* is suggestive of what such an approach might look and sound like. We hope that this volume might contribute to that process, as well.

Three Key Provocations

Despite being, at times, significantly different from each other, the chapters in *Acoustics of Empire* share a commitment to uncovering the intersections of sound, race, power, and empire, across different geographical contexts in the long nineteenth century. While the essays in each section of the book speak to each other in obvious, thematic ways, the book comes together as a whole to explore the following questions, posed to the contributors at the beginning of the project:

1. What would it mean for both sound studies and postcolonial/decolonial studies to think of sound and empire as not just plausibly connected, but rather as epistemic regimes that fundamentally co-constitute one another?

In many ways, this question restates some of our observations above. But we might trace out some of the implications and possibilities of such an under-standing by looking at scholarly examples that do precisely this, linking sound and postcolonial/decolonial studies. Some foundational texts that are frequently mentioned in these contexts include W. E. B. Du Bois's *The Souls of Black Folk*, with its recurring musical and poetic interludes of "sorrow songs" (spirituals), or Frantz Fanon's provocative essay, "This Is the Voice of Algeria," about radio during the Algerian independence movement.[36] Recent discussions of Sourindro Mohun Tagore, the Indian polymath and musician, in the context of global musicology, point to other possible histories of musicology—although, as Richard David Williams notes in his essay here (and elsewhere), what sets Tagore apart from his contemporaries may not (just) be his theorizing of musicology from an Indian perspective so much as the fact that he did so in English, making it more accessible to Euro-American scholars.[37]

We might also find traces of sound-centered thinking in key postcolonial texts. For example, Edward Said's writings on music, especially European art music, became well known in the later years of his career, but some of his most significant writings on postcolonial theory grapple with music and sound to varying degrees.[38] The best known example is arguably *Culture and Imperialism*, in which Said analyzes Verdi's opera *Aïda* as an instance of "empire at work"; but even more substantively, one of his key methodologies in the book, "contrapuntal reading," relies on polyphonic music as a metaphor for conceptualizing cultural relationships within and against empire.[39] Even as early as in *Orientalism*, Said shows an ongoing interest in questions of silence, both archivally and as a manifestation of political relations, and voice, especially in literary narrative, not to mention recurring mention of music as a site of Orientalism.[40] So too Gayatri Chakravorty Spivak: while "Can the Subaltern Speak?" only fleetingly deals with the question of a literal, physical voice, it reflects repeatedly on silence and silencing as forms of epistemic violence.[41]

Conversely, we might look to foundational texts in sound studies for moments in which sound is theorized from the outset through questions of race, power, and empire. For example, in the introduction to *In the Break: The Aesthetics of the Black Radical Tradition*, Fred Moten finds particular analytical purchase in the notion of the scream throughout the Black American experience from slavery to free jazz and funk as a way of conceptualizing timbres of the voice, histories of violence, and the limitations of utterance.[42] Questions of voice, race, power, and performativity are then taken up again in more recent but equally groundbreaking work by Nina Sun Eidsheim and Daphne Brooks, allowing a further refining of how sound and race have been historically co-constructed.[43] In a different vein, scholars like Tara Rodgers, Jonathan Sterne, and Mara Mills have foregrounded questions of gender and disability in sound studies, pointing to other crucial facets of the intertwining of sound and power.[44] And indeed, a more speculative history of sound studies might look back to a range of musicians and sound artists from the mid-twentieth century and beyond—Umm Kulthum, Sun Ra, Cecil Taylor, Pauline Oliveros, Annea Lockwood, the Association for the Advancement of Creative Musicians (AACM), Fela Kuti, Fairuz, King Tubby, Christine Sun Kim—whose work has not only exemplified a decentering of traditional forms of power within sound, sound art, and music, but who have articulated (whether in words or performance) a notion of sound and power being always already entangled.

2. In what ways might empires themselves be conceived of as media constellations in which political power, audiovisual techniques, transmission of natural resources/goods/bodies, and violent governmentality become interleaved with one another?

Thinking of empire as a form of media has a long history, dating back at least to Harold Innis's landmark 1950 book, *Empire and Communications*, which offers a sweeping theory about how empires rely on and are shaped (or even defined) by their communications media.[45] More recently, media historians such as Alejandra Bronfman and Nicole Starosielski have shown in more granular detail how radio broadcasting in the Caribbean and modern undersea cable networks, respectively, exemplify similar dynamics in roughly the past century.[46] Historians of empire such as Bhavani Raman and Miles Ogborn have, in turn, highlighted the particular dynamics of media practices such as writing and bureaucratic documentation.[47]

Building on these ideas, we conceive of media here as a constellation in which political power, audiovisual techniques, transmission of natural resources/goods/bodies, and state-sanctioned violence, all interact regularly in a kind of inseparable network. This means that we will expect to find sound and sonic media in some form or fashion across most any geopolitical formation, but also that sound (and by extension, sound studies) can never simply be excised from its cultural contexts and entanglements with power, and in this case, particularly with empire. In that sense, this book aligns itself with views articulated by Brian Kane emphasizing studies of auditory culture (i.e., sonic and auditory practices in their cultural contexts) over a more generic "sound studies," and, again, by Marie Thompson and Annie Goh in a special issue of *Parallax* highlighting sound as a situated, culturally-specific site of knowing, despite its ontological allures.[48]

Looping back to the cuckoo clock, it bears mention that these media need not be large objects or celebrated inventions like railways, telegraphy, or the phonograph, though all those media have deep entanglements with empire too. "Small media" can just as well play significant roles here, as we see, for instance, in the chapters in this volume by James Davies and Hyun Kyong Hannah Chang as musical notations structure a whole set of sonic encounters, or in Gavin Steingo's chapter, in which prevailing narratives in sound studies about (Western) modernity and the stethoscope are reshaped in colonial contexts. Indeed, at first glance some might not think of a cuckoo clock as a medium at all, and yet within these imperial media constellations, that is precisely the role it is made to play. Furthermore, as Alejandra Bronfman reminds us in her chapter on underwater telegraph cables, human labor—often conscripted or coerced—is required to produce, transport, maintain and repair such technologies, a challenge across many, if not all, media infrastructures, from the cuckoo clock to the railroad and beyond.

3. How do (or might) sound studies and imperial history deal with silence in their respective archives? What are the politics of excavating, transducing, or imagining voices (whether subaltern or otherwise) from sources that predate audio recording—or whatever other documentary technologies might be employed to inscribe those voices?

As with any archival project, but especially one focused on nineteenth-century empire, we have continually found ourselves asking: what kinds of archives exist and how might we best navigate the gaps and distortions that structure them? Those questions are probably relevant for most historical research, but the combined focus on sound and a cultural geography primarily outside Europe and North America has led to a distinctive set of archival "silences," both literal and figurative.

In terms of literal silences, the chapters in this book almost entirely work outside the domain of sound recordings. Since Walter Benjamin, the historical moment of "technical reproducibility" has marked an important threshold, and the same holds true for this book regarding the invention of the phonograph in 1877 in America and its eventual circulations more broadly. For instance, Jairo Moreno's contribution to this volume focuses on silent films during the Spanish-American War of 1898, and while sound recording did exist then, synchronizing it with film remained a challenge for decades to come. In Nazan Maksudyan's chapter, photography combined with music notation also creates a non-phonographic audiovisual object depicting Istanbul street vendors. And Alexandra Hui's chapter on starlings moves from a pre-phonographic into a phonographic era, but with a range of other forms of sonic transcription alongside. In most other pieces, writing about sound becomes the central archival medium, often revealing expansive discourses and other forms of documenting sonic experience, whether through newspapers, written treatises, or musical notation.

This heterogeneous set of materials partially helps address the challenges of more figurative silences too. And in some cases, as in the work of Ziad Fahmy, both in his chapter here and in his recent monograph about street sounds in modern Egypt, we find that archives exist but not necessarily where we might expect: for example, he has found public sanitation records to be a useful repository for noise complaints, a way into sound through government bureaucracy.[49] Alternatively, silence may simply be a preferred state, a kind of refusal of sound and its affective excesses, as Faisal Devji argues about Gandhi. In short, sound (and its significant absence) perennially haunts the colonial archive, sometimes documented by design, and other times as a kind of trace inscribed onto other materials. In the end, although sound as an acoustic phenomenon may dissipate much more quickly than a building, a painting, or even a census document, they are all subject to inevitable decay, even in the best of archival circumstances.

Voice and Empire 1800/1900

Perhaps a simpler way to describe the aim of this volume is that we hope to listen and attend to voices, literal and metaphorical, that have not typically been part of academic discussions of sound and sonic media. Sometimes these voices are more obviously audible; sometimes they require more complex or creative ways of hearing, as we listen for archival silences and absences. In such cases, hearing subaltern and other marginalized voices from the past may require the cultivation of new scholarly sources and tools—whether archival, linguistic, archaeological, technological, or otherwise—as well as a continued realignment of certain disciplinary orientations in the context of ongoing efforts to "remap" sound studies or conceive of it in global or planetary terms.

Having opened with an account of (and by) Europeans and their sound technologies in the Global South, we close this portion of our introduction by returning to Tonga and reflecting on the voices of two sonic artists (understood broadly), both indigenous Tongan women, whose lives bookend the nineteenth century: "Queen Tineh" or "Tiné," most likely Nanasipau'u, a high-ranking figure in Tongan society in the late 1700s; and Queen Sālote Tupou III, born in 1900, who ruled Tonga 1918–1965 and was a renowned poet and composer.

In 1793, the French naval explorer Antoine Bruni d'Entrecasteaux visited Tonga and met "Queen Tineh," as recounted by the naturalist Jacques Labillardière, who documented much of the trip. The prevailing view among modern scholars is that "Queen Tineh" was Nanasipau'u, a revered noble holding the title of Tu'i Tonga Fefine, or the elder sister of the Tu'i Tonga (paramount chief) of Tonga.[50] In the first meeting between the French crew and Tineh/Nanasipau'u and her entourage, music served as a kind of initial site of encounter, meditation, and perhaps resistance. After an exchange of gifts, the French wanted to see "what sensations the sounds of the voice, accompanied by the violin and the German guitar, would produce on these people" and were pleased to see "that this music was agreeable to them; but a few tunes played on a bird-organ, obtained plaudits still more expressive."[51] In turn, Nanasipau'u "ordered some young girls of her suite to sing," with one singing a kind of repeating melodic phrase, "apou lelley" (apō lelei; or "agreeable evening," in the text), with other girls following after her. Throughout the singing, the singers and some of the men in the entourage also danced and "beat time" with their feet or hands.[52] (Labillardière even gives a musical transcription of the brief tune.) The one-sided account limits what can be clearly understood here, but the Frenchmen appear to have seen this encounter as a chance for musical experimentation with guitars and a bird-organ (probably a *serinette*). In turn, the Tongan group, led by women, gently pushed back against such a unidirectional assertion of control through their own coordinated performance of music and dance.

On a later occasion, the French crew encountered Nanasipau'u herself singing, which Labillardière recounts as follows:

> Presently we arrived at the place where the Queen regularly held her court. . . . She was there giving a vocal concert, in which *Futtafaihe* [another of the principal chiefs] sang and beat time, which all the musicians followed with the greatest exactness. Some performed their part in it, by accompanying, with different modulations, the simple melody of the others. We now and then remarked some discordant notes, with which, however, the ear of these people seem very much gratified.[53]

This brief but remarkable account of a specific woman, Nanasipau'u, singing in the midst of European imperial expansion closes with interpretive ambivalence in Labillardière's comment about "discordant notes." On the one hand, the French listeners exhibit aural relativism, recognizing multiple aesthetic preferences and listening practices at play in the moment. On the other hand, Labillardière still insists that some notes are "discordant," a comment that suggests an air of objectivity and/or musicological expertise, but instead seems to reveal his inability to imagine musical intonation that differed from his European expectations. In short, we see a kind of informal acoustics of empire here, in which music acts as a medium of exchange, suggesting some form of commensurability between Tongan and French culture. Yet the modes of listening and subsequent interpretation assure, as in so many other domains, that European sonic techniques retain their primacy, at least in this telling. Nevertheless, the account of singing by Nanasipau'u—and on the previous occasion, by her attendant—offers a crucial sense of some of the women's voices that might allow a rethinking of music and sound globally at the beginning of the nineteenth century.[54]

This is true for the end of the century too, with the life and poetic practices of Queen Sālote. Born in 1900, she was renowned during her lifetime as the preeminent Tongan poet, a legacy that continues today.[55] As in many poetic traditions, distinctions between music, sound, voice, rhythm, and even dance begin to blur within Tongan poetry. In Sālote's case, she wrote poems, which were then often set to music, either by herself or by other musicians in her circles. Two examples of her poetry focusing on songbirds—in one case, as a symbol for humans, in the other, as a symbol for a clock—draw attention to some of the techniques of sonic resonance to be found in her poetry and point to the possibilities for traditional arts to play a role within (or against) an acoustics of empire.

The first poem is "Fakana'ana'a 'o Uiliami Tuku'aho" (Lullaby of Uiliami Tuku'aho), composed for her second son, Prince Tuku'aho, born in 1919. In it, the prince is compared to a red-tailed tropic bird (*tavake*) who flies throughout the Tongan islands, surveying sacred sites and listening to a lullaby (*fakana'ana'a*). It begins:

> 'Ofa he tavake tā mafua
> Na'e fakahifo 'e he la'aá
> 'O tamai ki he fetu'ufuká
> Kaloafu Tonga pe'i ke puna
> 'O 'omi e mahu 'o e fonuá
> Ke tu'ula 'i he Futu-ko-Vuná
> Pea mo e huni ko Vaiolá.
> 'E tavake toto pe'i ke na'á
> Ka ta ō 'o 'eva 'i Fakala'ā
> 'O fanongo ho fakana'ana'á
> Ko e le'o e fefine lakalaká.

> How I love this sustenance-seeking tropic bird
> That was born by the sun

> And fathered by the comet
> Oh fly, Kaloafu Tonga
> Bring me the affluence of the land
> Then perch at the Futu-ko-Vuna[56]
> And the *huni* called Vaiola.[57]
> Red-tailed tropic bird, be calm
> So we two can stroll down to Fakalaʻā
> And hear your lullaby being sung
> By the dancing maids.[58]

The poem continues, but already from these opening lines we see multiple elements that might figure into an acoustics of empire. From a media archaeological perspective, two elements stand out immediately. First, lullabies as a poetic genre (and the mother's voice more generally) act as a centerpiece for thinking about media, not unlike Friedrich Kittler's "discourse networks," which also begin with mothers' lullabies (albeit in a dramatically different cultural context).[59] And second, the listening itself becomes a recursive practice within the poetry: the poem's namesake, Uiliami Tukuʻaho, is meant to listen to a sung performance (that is, the lullaby as sung by, say, his mother) of a text that recounts another listening to a sung performance (that is, "the dancing maids" singing the same lullaby), though in this case the baby becomes a tropic bird, blurring the human/animal distinction.

The maids' performance is not identical, however; it is transformed from (just) a lullaby to a *lakalaka*, which (as the translation above suggests) entails not just singing but enacting a narrative through a collective dance ritual, featuring extensive use of arm gestures. *Lakalaka* itself emerged around the 1870s under the guidance of the chief of Tatakamotonga also named Tukuʻaho (d. 1897) as a reimagining of an earlier dance style, the *meʻelaufola*, within the confines of cultural constraints imported through Christian missionaries. One key change in the tradition was the loss of rhythmic instrumental accompaniment, such as that described in Labillardière. In any case, the allusion to *lakalaka* briefly but meaningfully gestures toward that colonial encounter with missionaries and the resultant changes in Tongan music, dance, and poetry. That quiet anticolonial narrative is further reinforced by the sonic mapping that takes place as the bird flies throughout the lullaby, with Sālote naming locations and objects that refer to genealogies of her own ancestors and their connections to indigenous chiefly lineages.[60] Those genealogies, while privileging a certain elite subset of Tongans, underscore the fact that although Tonga had been a British protectorate, it was never fully colonized, unlike most neighboring nations in Polynesia.[61]

As a final example of an acoustics of (and perhaps against) empire, Sālote's poem "Fuiva, Uasi e Fangatapu" (Fuiva, Clock of Fangatapu) brings us back to our initial confluence of clocks, birds, and sound. It begins, "The *fuiva*, clock of Fangatapu, is singing / Children, it is time to set sail" (*Ngā 'a e fuiva uasi e Fangatapu / Tamaiki kuo taimi 'a e folau*).[62] Melenaite Taumoefolau and Elizabeth Wood-Ellem clarify the bird/clock relationship here:

> The *fuiva* is a bird and Fangatapu is the area in front of the Palace. The poem suggests that the *fuiva* sang so regularly that the people at the Palace could keep time by it. Queen Sālote's words were sung to the tune of "Hang out your washing on the Siegfried Line," which is still a popular tune for Tongan brass bands. In later years the Queen gave the name Fuiva 'o Fangatapu to one of her bands.[63]

Later, the speaker in the poem shifts from listening to the *fuiva* bird and its temporal injunctions ("time to set sail") to listening to the environment, and especially the Angitoa trees planted around the royal palace in Nuku'alofa: "My heart is carried away when the Angitoa murmurs / Welcoming visitors to Nuku'alofa" (*Kāvea 'a e loto 'o ka lea e Angitoá / Tali 'eva e sola ki Nuku'alofa*). The poem then concludes with a statement of sensory desire "when the beloved is away": "Longing to see, yearning to hear / A trace of the wind blowing from the deep / Leaning shorewards so I may walk in contentment" (*Tangi ke sio pea holi fanongoa / Ma'ali he uini angi 'i he vahanoa / 'O falala mai ka u 'eva 'i he nonga*).[64] The passage highlights poetically both a desire to hear one's environment, or at least traces of it, and the impossibility of ever doing so fully.

If we can reorient this final sonic metaphor in Sālote's poetry, this "yearning to hear" that traces a "blowing from the deep"—whether across the ocean or around the globe—highlights the perils and potential of a venture such as this book. On the one hand, the perils: a dozen essays, even from the outstanding authors here, can hardly begin to do justice to the magnitude of such a global listening. Any attempt at a totalizing, global narrative of an acoustics of empire will necessarily replicate the same imperial tendencies we aim to critique; yet a piecemeal collection runs the risk of being rather arbitrary, making some historical periods or geographies central to its discussions, while omitting others entirely. "Yearning to hear" in this academic context has never ensured comprehension, and indeed, such desires have, under the guise of colonialism, often had a distinctly distorting effect.[65]

On the other hand, to hear (and to see) that the world extends beyond the metropole or the North Atlantic (or Bell Labs or the Gramophone Company), however obvious such a claim may be, invites and perhaps requires us to sit with the implications of that remapping of ideas and historical narratives about sound, hearing, technology, the audible environment, and power. We hope that the essays in this volume make a small contribution to that task at the intersection of sound studies and postcolonial/decolonial history.

Book Overview

In organizing this book, we have grouped essays into four broader themes that we hope will be useful in a range of contexts related to the study of sound, music, and media. These themes highlight what we see as some of the trenchant issues in the field of sound studies today. The following section gives a brief overview of the sections of the book and chapters in them.

1. Infrastructure and Cities

In recent years, "the doctrine of infrastructuralism," as John Durham Peters has phrased it, has come to the fore in sound and media studies, highlighting the underlying foundations and effaced labor that underpin any media network.[66] Empire is no different, though we pair infrastructure here conceptually with cities more generally as key aggregators and incubators of new infrastructural developments. Alejandra Bronfman's chapter, "Grappling All Day: Toward Another History of Telegraphy," foregrounds the human toll and toil of infrastructure in her account of laying telegraph cable in the West Indies in the late nineteenth century. These cables were meant to connect major cities across different islands, but laying cable required contending with the environmental challenges of working at sea, as well as illnesses that arose during the process. All told, the "transfer" of technology from the United States was hardly the frictionless diffusion technological histories sometimes presume. Nazan Maksudyan explores the sounds of Ottoman Istanbul through her chapter, "Encounter and Memory in Ottoman Soundscapes: An Audiovisual Album of Street Vendors' Cries." Her chapter particularly focuses on a photo album from around 1900 featuring Istanbul street vendors accompanied by musical notations (presumably transcriptions) of each vendor's unique call to potential customers. Reading alongside other contemporary accounts of street cries, she suggests a whole range of sonic encounters and circulations within the city, as well as a vivid sonic legacy in collective memories of city sound. Finally, Ziad Fahmy's "Listening to Infrastructure: Traffic Noise and Classism in Modern Egypt," considers changes to roads and transportation systems in Egyptian cities in the late nineteenth- and early twentieth-centuries and the accompanying sonic transformations. From eerily quiet tramways to painfully noisy automobiles, the urban sounds of this period invite reflection on municipal laws, modernization, and classism. His chapter concludes by considering these dynamics in the specific context of debates about the permissibility of electric horns on early cars.

2. Aural Epistemologies

As discussed briefly above, a key premise in much of sound studies, especially work intersecting with the history of science, has been that sound, and especially listening, functions as a site of cultivating and scrutinizing forms of knowing. As recent examples, Karin Bijsterveld's notion of "sonic skills" foregrounds techniques of "listening for knowledge" across a range of scientific domains, while Viktoria Tkaczyk, Alexandra Hui, and Mara Mills have argued that "the creation of modern aurality" emerges from ways of "testing *of* hearing and testing *with* hearing."[67] A lively feedback loop on this topic has emerged with music studies as well.[68] Several authors in this volume pose similar kinds of questions about aural epistemologies in the context of systems of knowledge that flourished in the Global South prior to or in dialogue with European imperial encounters. The entanglements between those multiple epistemologies, whether we understand them as being in competition, conflict, or dialogue, present an important opportunity for reconsidering how sound and knowledge are co-constituted in imperial contexts. In Gavin Steingo's chapter, "Colonial Listening and the Epistemology of Deception: The Stethoscope in Africa," he considers how auscultation, or listening via stethoscope, was taken up in colonial southern Africa. His chapter engages directly with Jonathan Sterne's concept of "audile technique," but rethinks it through the unexpected dynamics of colonialism. Whereas the stethoscope was used in Europe and North America to cultivate medical knowledge, its use in southern Africa was often bound up with "medical imposters" who lacked proper training and instead used the device as a tool for diagnoses unrelated to the listening techniques previously associated with auscultation. The chapter by Richard David Williams, "Epistemological *Jugalbandī*: Sound, Science, and the Supernatural in Colonial North India," similarly queries the reception of European medical science in a colonial context. In north India, a robust history of thought, pre-dating and extending into the colonial period, had long considered the interplay of music and medicine. The arrival of European science thus was an encounter of two competing and ultimately intertwined systems of sound knowledge, resulting in dialogue he suggests should be thought of as *jugalbandī*, a term from Indian classical music pairing two musicians in a kind of dialogue, rather than an external imposition against an imagined blank slate. Projit Bihari Mukharji takes the question of epistemological encounter in colonial South Asia in a different direction in his chapter, "Ramendrasundar Tribedi and a Sonic History of Race in Colonial Bengal." Tribedi (1864–1918) was a Bengali physicist and polymath who wrote extensively on language and race, in response to ongoing debates in comparative philology. Mukharji argues for a notion of "somatomimetic alphabetics" as a way of understanding Tribedi's work and its emphasis on the confluence of body, language, and sound as a site for reconciling traditional South Asian thought with the writings of physicist and acoustician Hermann von Helmholtz.

3. Musical Encounters

The site of encounter figures prominently in postcolonial studies, not so much as a crystallization of a moment of some imaginary "first contact" but rather as an ongoing process of interaction, with possibilities for exchange, negotiation, domination, exploitation, violence, or some combination of these outcomes. The chapters in this section all deal not just with sound but explicitly with music as a site and occasion of encounter across a range of temporal and geographic sites. Music has a complex and sometimes tenuous place within sound studies, but all of these chapters highlight aspects of music's mediation, whether through notation, the archival process, encounter with other (sometimes painful) sounds, or through the very particular mediations of academic study (i.e., musicology). James Davies opens the section with his chapter, "Cosmopoeisis: Stories Sung of the Equatorial Gulf of Guinea, 1817," which examines a musical encounter in that year. On that occasion, an unnamed, enslaved musician from central Africa sang and played the *ngombi* harp, a performance that was documented in writing and in a notated musical transcription by Sarah Wallis Bowdich, an English naturalist and explorer of Africa. Davies offers three distinct readings of this encounter, foregrounding questions of ecology, the transatlantic slave trade, and ideologies of race in analyzing it, ultimately highlighting how the global and the personal are intimately intertwined. Similarly invested in cross-cultural listening and its limitations, Hyun Kyong Hannah Chang's chapter, "Listening to Korea: Audible Prayers, Boat Songs, and the Aural Possibilities of the US Missionary Archive," moves away from the Atlantic toward a "trans-pacific listening." In particular, she assesses the usefulness of the archives of American missionaries as a source of documentation about Korean sonic practices, especially vocalization (including audible forms of prayer and singing), while situating that archive within a context of imperialism and proselytizing. She documents points of tension, such as whether Koreans were perceived to be singing Christian music "correctly," adaptation of musical materials, and geopolitical crisis due to Japanese imperialism. In a further discussion of voice(s) and archive, Benjamin Walton's chapter, "Listening through the Operatic Voice in 1820s Rio de Janeiro," situates the rise of Italian opera in Brazil within a broader acoustic geography. Looking at opera's reception in the period, he suggests that the operatic voice and its imagined potential for civilizing should be understood alongside the vocalizations of enslaved people at the same time as well as a broader urban "noisescape" in Rio de Janeiro. The institutionalization of opera in Brazil thus became, among other things, an attempt to cordon it off and insulate it, sonically and socially, from these other forms of vocality. The section then concludes with Sindhumathi Revuluri's chapter, "Ethnography and Exoticism in Nineteenth-Century France," which also explores the complex intersections of European art music with its global "Others," albeit from the perspective of the metropole and its musicological disciplines. Revisiting Edward Said's *Orientalism* and considering how it might have yet-unrecognized value for music studies, she re-examines nineteenth-century French musicology, especially foundational texts by François-Joseph Fétis and Julien Tiersot, along with Igor Stravinsky's *Rite of Spring*. These examples suggest that musical ethnography and exoticism are closely connected both to each other and to the broader venture of musicology in all its forms.

4. Silence and Its Others

As discussed above, silence may signify a range of meanings: an absence of sound; an absence of particular (unwanted) sound, such as noise; a silencing, usually through the exertion of force; a state or space of quiet, and perhaps contemplation; a refusal.[69] But much like concepts such as "music," "noise" and "listening," the particular valence of "silence" can shift dramatically from one cultural context to another. The chapters in this section grapple with silence of various kinds and its marked absence, exploring how silence and its absence may work to bolster or resist empire, or alternatively circulate around the globe in ways that are connected to but not coterminous with empire. Jairo Moreno's contribution, "The Anacoustic: Imperial Aurality, Aesthetic Capture, and the Spanish-American War," looks specifically at war films produced by the Edison Company during the 1898 conflict between Spain and America, especially in the context of the American invasion of Cuba. He coins the term "anacoustic" to characterize forms of silence, as in the Edison "Wargraph" films, in which silence is not the absence of sound so much as its potentiality or likeliness to have been present, a condition that encourages moviegoers to imagine "the real thing." He furthermore posits a concept of parasite-like "aesthetic capture" that extracts sensory meaning from the world and distributes it for consumption "at home." Alexandra Hui's chapter, "pēē ä wēē, an Outrageous Clatter, and Other Sounds of Acclimatization," examines global forms of acclimatization, particularly with birds, and the sonic and environmental consequences of such changes. She focuses specifically on the starling, which was introduced to the United States in the 1870s as part of a larger acclimatization movement (especially in Europe) and began to thrive to the point that many sought to curb its expansion. On top of this history of animal belonging (or lack thereof) and its sonic manifestations, she overlays a history of anti-immigration sentiments aimed at other humans who were deemed intrusive as well. Finally, Faisal Devji's succinctly-titled "Gandhi's Silence" considers silence as an overt and conscientious refusal of sound and its potential excess. The piece explores Mohandas K. Gandhi's skepticism of debate, noise, and democracy as an expression of voice, with Devji offering a political theorization of Gandhi's embrace of silence as a space devoid (at least as much as possible) of other forms of mediation, whether sensory or social. In Gandhi's lived experience, silence also became a way of reconciling one's own internal existence more transparently to the outside world as part of his "experiments" with truth.

The book then concludes with an afterword by Elleke Boehmer, "Sound in the Imperial Archive," that reflects on both the increased granularity a sound-based approach to empire might afford, as well as the challenges and historical realities that resist being listened to. She muses briefly on how poetry, an important set of sonic techniques that receives relatively little attention in this volume, might offer still further avenues for inquiring into the (sometimes barely) audible histories and acoustics of empire.

Notes

1. The Missionary Society (London, England), *A Missionary Voyage to the Southern Pacific Ocean, Performed in the Years 1796, 1797, 1798, in the Ship Duff, Commanded by Captain James Wilson* (London: Printed for T. Chapman, by T. Gillet, 1799), 229. The title page includes the following descriptive information: "Compiled from Journals of the Officers and Missionaries; and illustrated with Maps, Charts, and Views, Drawn by Mr. William Wilson, and engraved by the most eminent Artists, with a Preliminary Discourse of the Geography and History of the South Sea Islands; and an Appendix, including details never before published, of the Natural and Civil State of Otaheite; by a Committee appointed for the Purpose By the Directors of the Missionary Society. Published for the Benefit of the Society." Although geographically small, Tonga figures significantly in global/postcolonial histories of Polynesia and the Pacific. For two recent discussions, see Sujit Sivasundaram, "In the South Pacific: Travellers, Monarchs and Empires," in *Waves Across the South: A New History of Revolution and Empire* (Chicago: University of Chicago Press, 2020), 40–78, and Arcia Tecun and S. Ata Siuʻulua, "Tongan Coloniality: Contesting the 'Never Colonized' Narrative," *Postcolonial Studies* (2023; no volume/issue as of this writing), https://doi.org/10.1080/13688790.2022.2162353.
2. Missionary Society, *A Missionary Voyage*, 161.
3. Ibid., 227–228.
4. Homi K. Bhabha, "Signs Taken for Wonders: Questions of Ambivalence and Authority under a Tree outside Delhi, May 1817," in *The Location of Culture* (London: Routledge, 1994), 102–122.
5. Missionary Society, *A Missionary Voyage*, 227–229.
6. William Brown, *The History of Missions; Or, Of the Propagation of Christianity Among the Heathen, Since the Reformation*, vol. 2 (London: Longman, Hurst, Rees, Orme, & Brown, 1814), 368. Later editions were published in 1816 (first American edition) and 1854 (an expanded, three-volume edition).
7. We thank Lynn McMurray for his insight into these linguistic issues.
8. See Niel Gunson, "Tongan Historiography: Shamanic Views of Time and History," in *Tongan Culture and History*, ed. Phyllis Herda, Jennifer Terrell, and Niel Gunson (Canberra: Journal of Pacific History, 1990), 12–20, at 16–17; and Roger Neich,

"Tongan Figures: From Goddesses to Missionary Trophies to Masterpieces," *Journal of the Polynesian Society* 116/2 (2007), 213–268, at 255–256.

9. See Bhabha, *The Location of Culture*, 85–86.

10. Brown, *The History of Missions*, 368–369.

11. William Mariner, *An Account of the Natives of the Tonga Islands, in the South Pacific Ocean*, vol. 1, ed. John Martin (London: John Murray, 1817), 62–63.

12. Ibid., 169.

13. On Barak, *On Time: Technology and Temporality in Modern Egypt* (Berkeley: University of California Press, 2013).

14. James A. Steintrager and Rey Chow, "Sound Objects: An Introduction," in *Sound Objects*, ed. James A. Steintrager and Rey Chow (Durham, NC: Duke University Press, 2019), 1–19, at 8.

15. Ibid., 8.

16. See Susan Stronge, *Tipu's Tigers* (London: V & A Publishing, 2009).

17. British Museum, "Everything You Ever Wanted to Know about the Rosetta Stone," July 14, 2017, https://www.britishmuseum.org/blog/everything-you-ever-wanted-know-about-rosetta-stone, accessed January 1, 2023. Edward Said makes a similar point about the Rosetta Stone over forty years earlier. See Edward W. Said, *Orientalism* (New York: Pantheon Books, 1978), 140. See also Jed Z. Buchwald and Diane Greco Josefowicz, "Words and Sounds," in *The Riddle of the Rosetta: How an English Polymath and a French Polyglot Discovered the Meaning of Egyptian Hieroglyphs* (Princeton, NJ: Princeton University Press, 2020), 372–389.

18. James Q. Davies, "Instruments of Empire," in *Sound Knowledge: Music and Science in London, 1789–1851*, ed. James Q. Davies and Ellen Lockhart (Chicago: University of Chicago Press, 2016), 145–174.

19. Perhaps the classic example of this kind of phonophilia is the work of the World Soundscape Project, headed by R. Murray Schafer, though traces of an overt sound-positivity can be seen in more recent scholarship as well. For example, see Deborah Wong, "Sound, Silence, Music: Power," *Ethnomusicology* 58/2 (2014), 347–353 and Deborah Kapchan, ed., *Theorizing Sound Writing* (Middletown, CT: Wesleyan University Press, 2017). Our claim is not that such writing is inappropriate or necessarily inaccurate, but rather that such celebratory claims about sound should be held in dialogue with critical ones as well.

20. Jonathan Sterne, *The Audible Past: Cultural Origins of Sound Reproduction* (Durham, NC: Duke University Press, 2003), 14–16.

21. This claim echoes similar assertions by Marie Thompson and Annie Goh in a 2017 special issue of *Parallax*. See Marie Thompson, "Whiteness and the Ontological Turn in Sound Studies," *Parallax* 23/3 (2017), 266–282, and Annie Goh, "Sounding Situated Knowledges: Echo in Archaeoacoustics," *Parallax* 23/3 (2017), 283–304. For a roughly analogous argument in musicology, see Matthew Morrison, "Race, Blacksound, and the (Re)Making of Musicological Discourse," *Journal of the American Musicological Society* 72/3 (2019), 781–823.

22. Steven Feld, "Acoustemology," in *Keywords in Sound*, ed. David Novak and Matt Sakakeeny (Durham, NC: Duke University Press, 2015), 12–21, at 12. See also Steven Feld, "Waterfalls of Song: An Acoustemology of Place Resounding in Bosavi,

Papua New Guinea," in *Senses of Place*, ed. Steven Feld and Keith H. Basso (Santa Fe, NM: School of American Research Press, 1996), 91–135.

23. Tomie Hahn, *Sensational Knowledge: Embodying Culture through Japanese Dance* (Middletown, CT: Wesleyan University Press, 2007).

24. See Gayatri Chakravorty Spivak, *A Critique of Postcolonial Reason: Toward a History of the Vanishing Present* (Cambridge, MA: Harvard University Press, 1999) and Achille Mbembe, *Critique of Black Reason*, trans. and with an introduction by Laurent Dubois (Durham, NC: Duke University Press, 2017).

25. Friedrich A. Kittler, *Discourse Networks 1800/1900*, trans. Michael Metteer with Chris Cullens (Stanford, CA: Stanford University Press, 1990).

26. Michael Hardt and Antonio Negri, *Empire* (Cambridge, MA: Harvard University Press, 2000).

27. Ronald Radano and Tejumola Olaniyan, eds., *Audible Empire: Music, Global Politics, Critique* (Durham, NC: Duke University Press, 2016).

28. Ronald Radano and Tejumola Olaniyan, "Hearing Empire—Imperial Listening," in Radano and Olaniyan, *Audible Empire*, 1–22, at 1.

29. See, for example, Jocelyn Hackforth-Jones and Mary Roberts, eds., *Edges of Empire: Orientalism and Visual Culture* (Malden, MA: Blackwell, 2005); Priya Jaikumar, *Cinema at the End of Empire: A Politics of Transition in Britain and India* (Durham, NC: Duke University Press, 2006) and *Where Histories Reside: India as Filmed Space* (Durham, NC: Duke University Press, 2019); David Brody, *Visualizing the American Empire: Orientalism and Imperialism in the Philippines* (Chicago: University of Chicago Press, 2010); Lee Grieveson and Colin MacCabe, eds., *Empire and Film* (London: Palgrave Macmillan/British Film Institute, 2011); and Natasha Eaton, *Mimesis Across Empires: Artworks and Networks in India, 1765–1860* (Durham, NC: Duke University Press, 2013).

30. Eric Hobsbawm, *The Age of Empire: 1875–1914* (London: Weidenfeld and Nicolson, 1987).

31. On early phonographic ethnography, see Erika Brady, *A Spiral Way: How the Phonograph Changed Ethnography* (Jackson: University Press of Mississippi, 1999) and Roshanak Kheshti, *Modernity's Ear: Listening to Race and Gender in World Music* (New York: New York University Press, 2015).

32. Emily Thompson, *The Soundscape of Modernity: Architectural Acoustics and the Culture of Listening in America, 1900–1933* (Cambridge, MA: MIT Press, 2002).

33. Of course, considerable work has been done on historical sound studies that pre-date sound recording, which we discuss below. The challenge of doing so in tandem with a more global perspective lies at the heart of this book.

34. See Mark M. Smith, *Listening to Nineteenth-Century America* (Chapel Hill: University of North Carolina Press, 2001); Sterne, *The Audible Past*; Veit Erlmann, *Reason and Resonance: A History of Modern Aurality* (New York: Zone Books, 2010); Alexandra Hui, *The Psychophysical Ear: Musical Experiments, Experimental Sounds, 1840–1910* (Cambridge, MA: MIT Press, 2012); Jennifer Lynn Stoever, *The Sonic Color Line: Race and the Cultural Politics of Listening* (New York: New York University Press, 2016).

35. See Gavin Steingo and Jim Sykes, eds., *Remapping Sound Studies* (Durham, NC: Duke University Press, 2019); Ana María Ochoa Gautier, *Aurality: Listening and*

Knowledge in Nineteenth-Century Colombia (Durham, NC: Duke University Press, 2014); Alejandra Bronfman, *Isles of Noise: Sonic Media in the Caribbean* (Chapel Hill: University of North Carolina Press, 2016); and Dylan Robinson, *Hungry Listening: Resonant Theory for Indigenous Sound Studies* (Minneapolis: University of Minnesota Press, 2020). Two more recent volumes also have exciting resonance with this book: Emily Wilbourne and Suzanne G. Cusick, eds., *Acoustemologies in Contact: Sounding Subjects and Modes of Listening in Early Modernity* (Cambridge, UK: Open Book Publishers, 2021), and Georgina Born, ed., *Music and Digital Media: A Planetary Anthropology* (London: University College London Press, 2022). We see *Acoustics of Empire* as complementing the approaches taken in those volumes, with the overall efflorescence of these books as collective evidence of the timeliness and importance of these conversations.

36. W. E. B. Du Bois, *The Souls of Black Folk* (Chicago: A. C. McClurg & Co., 1903); Frantz Fanon, "This Is the Voice of Algeria," in *A Dying Colonialism*, trans. Haakon Chevalier (New York: Grove Press, 1965 [1959]), 69–97. Both Du Bois and Fanon are mentioned/included in Jonathan Sterne, ed., *The Sound Studies Reader* (Abingdon: Routledge, 2012).

37. Sourindro Mohun Tagore, *Universal History of Music, Compiled from Diverse Sources, Together with Various Original Notes on Hindu Music* (Varanasi: Chowkhamba Sanskrit Series Office, 1963 [1896]). On Tagore and his thought more generally, see Bruno Nettl, *Nettl's Elephant: On the History of Ethnomusicology* (Urbana: University of Illinois Press, 2010), 45–46; Richard David Williams, "Music, Lyrics, and the Bengali Book: Hindustani Musicology in Calcutta, 1818–1905," *Music and Letters* 97/ 3 (2016), 465–495; and Sagnik Atarthi, "Whither Musicology? Amateur Musicologists and Music Writing in Bengal," *Ethnomusicology Forum* 26/2 (2017), 247–268.

38. As an example of Said's writings on music, see Edward W. Said, *Music at the Limits* (New York: Columbia University Press, 2007). Said has enjoyed a mixed reception among musicologists, including both criticism for the Eurocentrism of his musical tastes and calls for more sustained engagement in music studies. As examples of these two respective approaches, see Wouter Capitain, "Edward Said on Popular Music," *Popular Music and Society* 40/1 (2017), 49–60, and Brigid Cohen et al., "Round Table: Edward Said and Musicology Today," *Journal of the Royal Musical Association* 141/1 (2016), 203–232.

39. Edward W. Said, *Culture and Imperialism* (New York: Knopf, 1993), especially "Discrepant Experience," 31–43, and "The Empire at Work: Verdi's *Aida*," 111–132.

40. Edward W. Said, *Orientalism* (New York: Pantheon Books, 1978), especially 86–95, on the Orient as a space of "silent obscurity," and 138–140, on (the West) causing the Orient to be transformed from a state of silence to being-spoken-of; 195–196, on authorial voice, and especially an idea of a "voice of Empire"; and on music, 118, on Mozart (as one example of Orientalism and the arts) and 186–187, on Kuchuk Hanem, an Egyptian dancer, courtesan and musician (as narrated in Orientalist literature).

41. "Can the Subaltern Speak?" was published in a number of forms, but the final iteration is Spivak's version in *Can the Subaltern Speak? Reflections on the History of an Idea* (New York: Columbia University Press, 2010), 21–78. For example, she summarizes

the core concern of her essay as the "historical silencing of the subaltern," 66, and calls for cultivating a methodology of *measuring silences*" to address gaps in historical archives, 48.

42. Fred Moten, "Resistance of the Object: Aunt Hester's Scream," in *In the Break: The Aesthetics of the Black Radical Tradition* (Minneapolis: University of Minnesota Press, 2003), 1–24.

43. Nina Sun Eidsheim, *The Race of Sound: Listening, Timbre, and Vocality in African-American Music* (Durham, NC: Duke University Press, 2019), and Daphne A. Brooks, *Liner Notes for the Revolution: The Intellectual Life of Black Feminist Sound* (Cambridge, MA: Harvard University Press, 2021).

44. See, for example, Tara Rodgers, "Toward a Feminist Epistemology of Sound: Refiguring Waves in Audio-Technical Discourse," in *Engaging the World: Thinking after Irigaray*, ed. Mary C. Rawlinson (Albany: State University of New York Press, 2016), 195–213; Jonathan Sterne, *Diminished Faculties: A Political Phenomenology of Impairment* (Durham, NC: Duke University Press, 2022); and Mara Mills, *Hearing Loss and the History of Information Theory* (Durham, NC: Duke University Press, forthcoming).

45. Harold Innis, *Empire and Communications* (Oxford, UK: Clarendon Press, 1950).

46. Bronfman, *Isles of Noise*, and Nicole Starosielski, *The Undersea Network* (Durham, NC: Duke University Press, 2015).

47. Bhavani Raman, *Document Raj: Writing and Scribes in Early Colonial South India* (Chicago: University of Chicago Press, 2012), and Miles Ogborn, *Indian Ink: Script and Print in the Making of the English East India Company* (Chicago: University of Chicago Press, 2007).

48. Brian Kane, "Sound Studies Without Auditory Culture: A Critique of the Ontological Turn," *Sound Studies* 1/1 (2015), 2–21; Thompson, "Whiteness and the Ontological Turn in Sound Studies," and Goh, "Sounding Situated Knowledges" (see footnote 21).

49. Ziad Fahmy, *Street Sounds: Listening to Everyday Life in Modern Egypt* (Stanford, CA: Stanford University Press, 2020).

50. Phyllis Herda and Billia Lythberg, "Featherwork and Divine Chieftainship in Tonga," *Journal of the Polynesian Society* 123/3 (2014), 277–300, especially 285–286. The name "Tineh" seems to be a corruption of the term *ta'ahine*, a more general term for a high-ranking female.

51. M. Labillardière, *An Account of a Voyage in Search of La Pérouse, Undertaken by the Order of the Constituent Assembly of France, and Performed in the Years 1791, 1792, and 1793 in the Recherche and Espérance, Ships of War, under the Command of Rear-Admiral Bruni D'Entrecasteaux*, vol. 2. (London: J. Debrett, 1800), 126.

52. Ibid., 126–127.

53. Ibid., 133.

54. For a different reading of this encounter and its potential sexual overtones, see Sivasundaram, *Waves Across the South*, 55–56.

55. On Queen Sālote's life generally, see Elizabeth Wood-Ellem, *Queen Sālote of Tonga: The Story of an Era 1900–1965* (Auckland: Auckland University Press, 1999). On her poetic and musical works, see *Songs and Poems of Queen Sālote*, trans. Melenaite Taumoefolau, ed. Elizabeth Wood-Ellem (Nuku'alofa: Vava'u Press, 2004).

56. Futu-ko-Vuna is a sacred site in the village of Lapaha in the eastern part of the island of Tongatapu associated with burial sites (*langi*) of the past principal chiefs.

57. *Huni* is a local flowering plant.

58. *Songs and Poems of Queen Sālote*, 205–206. Poems of Queen Salōte and their translations reproduced courtesy of Vavaʻu Press, Melenaite Taumoefolau, and Queen Nanasipauʻu Tukuʻaho.

59. Kittler, *Discourse Networks 1800/1900*, 25–69.

60. This practice of mapping-in-song in South Pacific contexts is reminiscent of Steven Feld's discussion of sung laments of the Kaluli of Papua New Guinea, in which Kaluli women narrate (through their song lyrics) a geographical route (*tok*) associated with a particular person. Steven Feld, "Weeping that Moves Women to Song," in *Sound and Sentiment*, 3rd ed. (Durham, NC: Duke University Press, 2012), 86–129.

61. On the history of *lakalaka* and its dis/continuities with the music depicted by Labillardière, see Adrienne L. Kaeppler, "Dances and Dancing in Tonga: Anthropological and Historical Discourses," in *Dancing from Past to Present: Nation, Culture, Identities*, ed. Theresa Jill Buckland (Madison: University of Wisconsin Press, 2006), 25–51.

62. *Songs and Poems of Queen Sālote*, 190.

63. Ibid.

64. Ibid.

65. On the distorting power of sonic desire, see Eric Lott, *Love and Theft: Blackface Minstrelsy and the American Working Class* (New York: Oxford University Press, 2013 [1993]), and Kheshti, *Modernity's Ear*.

66. John Durham Peters, *The Marvelous Clouds: Toward a Philosophy of Elemental Media* (Chicago: University of Chicago Press, 2015), 33.

67. Karin Bijsterveld, *Sonic Skills: Listening for Knowledge in Science, Medicine and Engineering (1920s–Present)* (London: Palgrave Macmillan, 2019). Viktoria Tkaczyk, Mara Mills, and Alexandra Hui, eds., *Testing Hearing: The Making of Modern Aurality* (New York: Oxford University Press, 2020), 2. Bijsterveld's book is part of a larger research project that has produced a wider body of research on related topics as well, available at sonicskills.org.

68. Within the domain of music history (i.e., unmarked, Euro-American "musicology"), see Davies and Lockhart, ed., *Sound Knowledge*, and David Trippett and Benjamin Walton, eds., *Nineteenth-Century Opera and the Scientific Imagination* (Cambridge, UK: University of Cambridge Press, 2019). As discussed above, ethnomusicologists and anthropologists of music/sound such as Steven Feld and Tomie Hahn have made similar arguments since the 1990s.

69. Ana María Ochoa Gautier, "Silence," in Novak and Sakakeeny, *Keywords in Sound*, 183–192.

PART I
INFRASTRUCTURE AND CITIES

1

Grappling All Day

Toward Another History of Telegraphy

Alejandra Bronfman

Figure 1.1 The Cuban cable—Landing the shore end at South Beach, near Fort Taylor, Key West. Sketched by Dr. J. B. Holder, *Harper's Weekly*, September 7, 1867.

According to its caption, the 1867 image by artist J. B. Holder portrays "The Cuban Cable, Landing at South Beach, Key West."[1] In the background are big sailing ships. It is the beginning of the age of steam, but these ships still rely on wind at least part of the time. There is also a building of some kind, flying a flag, perhaps a fort. In the mid-ground are two rowboats, full of people, probably men, who seem to be watching or overseeing the activity in the foreground. There, a man signals to the eight men who are pulling what we assume is the cable. Although it is presumably the focal point of all the

Alejandra Bronfman, *Grappling All Day* In: *Acoustics of Empire*. Edited by: Peter McMurray and Priyasha Mukhopadhyay, Oxford University Press. © Oxford University Press 2024. DOI: 10.1093/oso/9780197553787.003.0002 ships and all the people in the image, it is the least visible of all the objects. We cannot see the faces of the men who are pulling, either. They are doing the hard work of hauling the heavy and unwieldy cable to its landing spot, but their features are abstract. Although the caption tells us there is a beach, it is barely in the image. What takes up the most space in the image is the sea. The sea floats the ships, hides most of the cable, and remains calm enough for the rowboats to do their work, cooperating, for the moment, with the landing.

I begin with this image because it tells a story about the cable that brings labor and the sea itself into narratives about empire and technology. In this story, the water and the workers are more prominent than the cable itself. Unlike many historical accounts of telegraphy in which the technology is central, this image centers the sea. The image also reminds us of the labor that is obscured in scholarship on the subject. Like Bernhard Siegert's images of ships and cities as indicative of cultural techniques such as navigation and mapmaking, this image also alludes to practices that assisted and accompanied aspirations to modernity.[2] What this image directs us to, however, are the violent dimensions of those aspirations. In obscuring the workers it represents, it serves as a point of departure from which to explore the tragic poetics of infrastructure.[3] Telegraphy brought death, environmental degradation, and exploitation of labor to some, even as it meant connection and prosperity to others.

This chapter works to emphasize further the place of the environment and of labor in the story of the telegraph in the Caribbean region.[4] As Nicole Starosielski has observed, the undersea network of cables can be understood as entangled with social, political, and environmental conditions that enable its existence. These are often absent from histories of the telegraph, which mostly attend to moments of connection or of failure. Starosielski suggests instead an approach of media archaeology, which aims to "historicize the movements and connections enabled by distribution systems and to reveal the environments that shape contemporary media circulation."[5] This exploration of Caribbean telegraphy draws from that approach, lingering on the early phases of telegraphy and its colonial and imperial dimensions. It does so with particular attention to the aural and sonic dimensions of telegraphy. Jonathan Sterne has argued that telegraphy became a sonic medium, although it was not conceived as one, by virtue of the way people listened to the signals traveling through wires. This was part of the development of what he calls middle-class hearing practices, enabled by the commodification of sound and capitalist interests in reproducing and ultimately selling privatized listening spaces.[6] Certainly, this contributed to the possibility of faster communication and a world in which senders and recipients of messages were brought closer together with speed and efficiency.[7] But that applies mostly to the elite North American and European men, or their colonial counterparts, in whose interests the telegraph was built. From the vantage point of labor and the environment, however, thinking about aurality stresses the silences that were part of this process. The story of early telegraphy is also the story of all the sounds that were muzzled or ignored, or indeed, never captured in archives or documents mostly interested in the successes and accomplishments of its telegraph heroes. The emergence of nineteenth-century middle-class listening practices, supported by capitalism, the privatization of space and the commodification of sound, also depended, I argue, on the submerged sounds of labor, of entanglements with the environment, and of human loss and devastation, all necessary for the laying of the telegraph.

Historians of telegraphy have noted its relationship to empires.[8] For the most part, their emphasis has rested on the business of the telegraph as part of the extension of Europe and control over imperial space in India, Australia, or Southeast Asia. The politics of control over information, executed unevenly at best and laced with resistance, as Deep Kanta Lahiri Choudhury suggests, was crucial to the making of nineteenth-century empires. But as these histories center mostly on the British empire, they miss a messier process of telegraphy as it related to the waning Spanish empire and the nascent American one, which coincided in the Caribbean, colliding and affecting one another. The cable encountered distinct imperial trajectories as it unfolded in the Caribbean. Rather than proceeding along a single path, imperial time was fragmented and answered to a variety of imperatives. In this context, the so-called annihilation of time that has often described the impact of the telegraph misses the ways that it moved through and knit together distinct imperial temporalities.[9] The more southerly submarine cable had to contend with anticolonial revolution, antislavery mobilizations, and regimes of mixed free and unfree labor.

Shifting attention away from the Atlantic submarine cable to the Caribbean requires attention to the sea and environment, which behaved differently than in the North Atlantic. In the process of telegraphy's creation, the presence of the sea forced cable companies to reckon with vast expanses of uncharted oceans and relatively unknown islands. The water, the sea floor, mosquitoes, viruses, and even the sun made this a very different enterprise. In the Caribbean Sea, knowledge gained from the laying of the Atlantic telegraph was useless, and knowledge of the particulars of sea bottoms and coasts needed to be acquired rapidly. The most elusive part of the story is of the labor involved in laying the cable. Sailors, work crews, or hastily assembled groups of local laborers on different islands traveled with the cable, moved it from ship to water, searched for it when it broke, and ensured that it behaved as it was meant to. This is tucked away mostly in the footnotes of contemporary narratives. But it is worth remembering that the story of technological acquisition, so often linked to modernity, depended on the work of coerced labor in a region shaped by slave regimes and post-emancipation versions of unfree labor.

These stories suggest an alternative way to conceptualize the acoustics of empire. Thinking musically, James Davies writes of telegraphic communication as "an instrument of empire," thinking of it as a "contact instrument," variably facilitating entertainment, or violence, or scientific research.[10] Peter McMurray has pointed out the relationship among sound, law, and media, bringing these to bear on the Ottoman Empire and Islam.[11] Adding to this conversation, but turning away from an emphasis on the increased chatter that eventually sped through undersea cables and telegraph lines, this chapter listens instead for silences, misapprehension, the technological incapacity to transmit certain sounds, and miscommunication. The telegraph enabled unprecedented speed of communication, with sound playing an important role, both as a way of perceiving signal quickly but also as an index of the many sounds of destruction and death that it left in its wake. The aim of this chapter is not to try to recreate those sounds but rather to point to the ways they have been erased, forgotten, and heard but not heeded. The study of sound and media also requires an awareness of the silences that haunt our histories and historiographies. A media archaeology that conceives of telegraphy as a sonic medium leads straight into the workings of empire and its conscription of the sea, of labor, and ultimately of death to do its work.

The telegraphic enterprise yielded many contemporary accounts, so the archive of "telegraph tales" is rich with narrative texture. There is an "autobiography" of the submarine telegraph (1859) telling of its travails in getting funded and its ultimate achievement.[12] Sir Charles Tilston Bright, to whom the planning and execution of the Atlantic cable is often attributed, wrote "Submarine Telegraphs," and was the subject of *The Life Story of Sir Charles Tilston Bright, Civil Engineer* (1910), co-written by his son and brother.[13]

John Philip Edwin Crookes, a British engineer who traveled with the *Narva* on the Havana–Key West leg, wrote a stream of letters to his family, which his brother later published.[14] These texts dwell on the process of laying the equipment and include Bright's work on the extension of the International Ocean Telegraph Company (IOTC), for which they created the West India and Panama Cable Company and the Cuba Submarine Telegraph Company.[15] Together they open the possibility of re-reading the history of the telegraph. And while, as an 1899 review noted, they "leave a lot in the shadows" and raise many questions which may be impossible to answer, here I draw from them in order to put the most common refrains about telegraphy aside and work toward a new narrative.[16]

A Deadly Start

The Key West–Havana cable was the first leg of the International Ocean Telegraph, created to connect the United States and the Caribbean. The idea was floated by two separate parties in 1865, who were interested in building a connection between the United States and Europe, which could be completed by connecting the United States to Spain through Cuba. The Caribbean portion of the project, which was first proposed before the US Civil War but put on hold during the conflict, presumed the continuation of a booming trade with Cuban sugar.[17] From the perspective of both Spanish and American entrepreneurs, this was lucrative territory that would benefit from the same kind of communications infrastructure as the Atlantic cable had fostered further north. Of course, it was a complicated effort, and entailed acquiring the necessary landing permissions from the state of Florida's legislature and the government of Spain. In contrast to the Atlantic cable which might be narrated as a clear extension of British imperial might, connecting as it did the metropole with colonial Newfoundland, the Key West–Havana cable is a story of fringes: Florida's economy and infrastructure had suffered as a result of the Civil War, and the local government welcomed any opportunity for commercial development. Key West had only recently become part of Florida, but it was already populated with growing numbers of Cubans, many of them planning anticolonial armed uprisings.[18] Cuba was at the center of a Spanish political crisis in which the colonial Spanish government was clinging to power over one of its few remaining possessions. Its slave-holding, sugar-producing regime was still lucrative but faced challenges resulting from the ban of the slave trade in 1817 and an increasingly powerful anticolonial faction.[19] The initiation of a thirty-year-long series of conflicts was, in 1867, only a year away. The International Ocean Telegraph was to connect these places, beginning in Havana, where it would link to Spain via their existing telegraph system, through Key West, and then travel up through the center of the state and the east coast toward New York. Eventually it was to connect with other parts of the West Indies, including Jamaica, Puerto Rico, Dominica, Guyana, and Martinique.[20] All this would be subject to the whims of British, French, and Spanish colonial authorities, whose Caribbean possessions were in the midst of diverse processes of reckoning with post-emancipation and struggles for sovereignty.

When the cables surfaced and came ashore, their arrival was often met with dignitaries and celebrations, parties and glowing news reports of technological success. Engineer Philip Crookes's letters to his family began in this spirit. In language laden with unsurprising condescension, many anecdotes turned on British superiority. When they arrived in Havana, they met local officials: "There was the Captain-General of the island, who has absolute authority, subject only to the Home Government. He is said to be the ugliest man in Cuba, and he certainly is hideous." They were treated to organized celebrations: "In fact it was altogether a very gay spectacle, having a sort of resemblance to the Oxford and Cambridge boat race, in which we, however, were the heroes."[21] But he soon realized that laying the cable was an extended, slow-moving slog that dampened his confident tone. Not long into the process he learned that currents had pushed the ship far off course, causing a delay as they sought to return to their planned route. Soon after, the cable broke, forcing them to grapple for it.

Thus commenced one of the more frequent and time-consuming activities: searching the expansive sea bottom for the end of a cable: "[We] began our old work of grappling, with our old luck: Not one single time did we even hook anything that could be mistaken for a cable."[22] A grapnel looks like an anchor with more prongs attached; these have sharp ends and are meant to catch objects. Grappling means lowering the grapnel on a line and dragging it across the sea floor in the hopes of hooking a lost cable. Dragging a grapnel until it caught on something was not easy. It would have entailed fighting currents and a lot of guesswork as to where the cable might have ended up. If there was any kind of weather at all, it proved impossible. Moreover, sharp edges of coral continually cut the line, and the sea often swallowed grapnels and refused to relinquish the cable.

During this journey Crookes became attuned to the sounds that would help or hurt his project. The noises of cables breaking or paying out too quickly, of the wind and rain preventing the work, and of the machinery grinding away were the pervasive ones on these journeys. Crookes used them to guide his actions, or to gauge the urgency of a problem. In the early days of his work, unknown sounds triggered an anxious reaction: "In the testing-room I kept up the testing uninterruptedly, being startled every now and then by dreadful noises on deck, which put me in a cold perspiration for the safety of the cable."[23] The whine of mosquitoes also terrorized the expedition. Overwhelmingly, mosquitoes turned a misadventure into a lethal enterprise. Yellow fever plagued them from the beginning, as Philip noted in early letters.

The ship stopped briefly in Havana, which at the time had an outbreak of the disease.[24] Soon afterward, several men became ill. Tales of the disease began to pervade his letters home. Two months into the expedition, they had managed to lay one portion of the cable and lose four men. As he wrote on August 28, 1867, "Last night our remaining patient, the cook's lad, died, and was buried ashore with his messmates."[25] By September, they had finished laying the cable and were working their way through the multiple constraints of yellow fever, coal needs, and quarantine, necessary in order to get home: "We shall want more coals to get to New York, and cannot get them nearer than Havana; but if we go to Havana, they will put us in quarantine at New York." They had become frightened of Havana: "I do not think Mr. Webb would enter Havana if he could help it, as he has a wholesome horror of the place . . . as the harbour is certainly the focus of infection."[26] In fact, it may have been the ship itself that was the focus of infection. The relationship between yellow fever and its mosquito vectors had not yet been verified in scientific circles, but efforts to stop the spread of disease included scrubbing the ship down whenever possible.[27] As historian of the telegraph Bill Glover observed, "The cable tanks on the *Narva* would have contained standing water, a fertile breeding ground for mosquitoes, and Philip's belief that this was the center of infection on the ship was probably well-founded."[28] Although they are not explicitly in Crookes's account, perhaps we can speculate that the sound of telegraphy included the groans and calls of ill men, or the prayers, eulogies, and music considered appropriate for burials at sea.

The cables were intended to usher this part of the world into a version of modernity. As reported by the *New York Times*, Governor-General of Cuba Joaquin Manzano understood their arrival as crucial to the creation of wealth: "I celebrate this happy event, which, giving us more rapid communication, will powerfully contribute toward the development of our mutual interest and prosperity."[29] Ironically, it may have been the process of building the network that facilitated the deadly epidemics. The day after the exchange of celebratory messages, the *Times* reported 226 deaths from yellow fever, and 134 from smallpox, for the month of July in Havana. After losing half of his telegraph workers, Crookes also died of yellow fever, shortly before the expedition ended.[30]

Imperial Space and Time

Three years later, the project to extend communication continued, this time with links to other Caribbean islands. The Havana–Key West connection had proven lucrative, and the idea was to bring more islands into the commercial orbit. Charles Tilston Bright, the engineer who had led the Atlantic Cable enterprise, lent his expertise here, and his narrative moves through the Caribbean. As his *Life Story* suggests, laying the telegraph revealed and of necessity responded to the messy realities of imperial misrule. Their first stop was Cuba, where they were supposed to lay new lines between Batabano (already connected to Havana via landlines) and Cienfuegos, and ultimately to Santiago.[31] Initially, it was not the sea or coral that was understood to be a problem, but rather the incipient conflicts over independence and, for some combatants, the abolition of slavery. In 1870, when the extension began, Cuba was in the second year of what would turn into a ten-year struggle between Cuban insurgents and the Spanish colonial government.[32] Bright stepped into this scenario, noting that the "wild" land and inhabitants had forced a search for an alternative route: "The existing land lines through the wild interior worked badly at all times; but these were also constantly interrupted by the 'Cubanos' creoles, or born inhabitants, of the island, who were, proverbially, in a state of chronic revolt against the Spaniards' rule."[33]

To protect their lines from sabotage, which was a common insurgent strategy, Bright decided to lay submarine lines skirting the island rather than overland lines running across it.[34] Additionally, he encountered a context of fluctuating status and uncertainty for enslaved people. While Spain had in theory agreed to adhere to the British abolition of the slave trade by 1817, Cuban planters continued to demand and receive enslaved people through a variety of illicit routes. Facing higher prices for smuggled slaves, slave owners initiated efforts to increase the reproduction of their enslaved populations. As Sasha Turner has recounted for the case of Jamaica, this resulted in attention and care for pregnant enslaved women.[35] The ill-considered compromise law, the Moret Law, which freed unborn children while keeping their parents in bondage, passed that year, but does not seem to have been implemented, for Bright encountered efforts to reproduce enslaved populations in Cuba as well. As a visitor in Havana, he met a tobacco planter who named a cigar after him, and afterward, took him on a tour of his estate. There Bright and his brother noticed a "dozen detached cottages, given up to those slave-wives anticipating family increase. They were given no work to do, were looked after by a competent medical man, and had excellent food provided for them. Sir Charles and his brother were invited to serve as godfathers, and their names were given to a few of the already existing babies."[36] The Bright brothers left behind not only a telegraph line but also several Cuban namesakes of ambiguous legal personhood. One might imagine the future uttering of their names as aural markers of the entangled histories of telegraphy, empire, and enslavement.[37] As the colonial state grasped at what it could to maintain a slaveholding order, the telegraph had to work around and avoid contested space as well as the temporality of a slaveholding regime that looked to the past even as it planned for abolition. This was not the beginning of empire and not yet the end, but rather the middle of its unraveling.

The submarine cable traveled from war-torn Cuba to a recently subdued Jamaica, on the receiving end of efforts by the British to bring the island into its imperial orbit. The cable surfaced in Morant Bay in 1870, where a rebellion five years prior had ended in the slaughter of hundreds of Jamaicans and the imposition of centralized control. Where the partial extension of suffrage, in 1840, to some Jamaicans of African descent had resulted in a parliament controlled by the wealthy members of this group, this was dissolved and Jamaica was designated a Crown colony in 1866.[38] The rebellion also prompted colonial projects aimed at commercial development, to counter both recent British neglect of Jamaica in the face of declining sugar revenues, and incursions by the Americans, who saw opportunities in the business of bananas. 1870 was also the year that Lorenzo Dow Baker sailed his ship, the *Telegraph*, into a Jamaican harbor and sailed away with a bunch of bananas that he would sell in Boston. This enterprise would grow into the United Fruit Company, which eventually controlled vast regions of the Caribbean and Central America and was the first transnational company to implement vertical integration.[39] With these converging developments, Jamaica was once again of concern to the British, and they initiated infrastructural projects as well as putting resources into social welfare. Schools and roads intended to contribute to the civilizing mission also contributed to the expansion of large-scale agriculture at the expense of small landholders. A telegraph connection to ease communications over commerce suddenly made sense.[40]

Missionaries arrived as well, and the competition among Baptists, Methodists, and other groups turned fierce. Elite Jamaicans of African descent, many of whom were wealthy landowners, turned to the churches as a source of power. The Baptist church had defended enslaved and formerly enslaved Jamaicans against planters, and they had sought to expand their reach by engaging in missionary efforts to Africa, in which Black Jamaicans would spearhead the missionizing efforts in places like Fernando Po.[41] Though these had failed rather spectacularly, the local clergy seems to have remained hopeful that missionary work would eventually spread Christianity to African populations in these places. Charles Bright received a letter from one particular vicar who linked telegraphy to this missionizing impulse. He was the vicar of St. Thomas, in Morant Bay, and had this to say about the arrival of telegraphy, for which he was grateful:

> Within a brief period of five years of her political reconstruction, capitalists, men of genius, commercial men, and an enterprising galaxy of scientific men, have, with a wonderful combination, spent more money for the development of the resources of the island than has been done during any former government. . . . We further pray that the time may soon come when the shores of Africa will be visited by Telegraphy, and that as a continent with her varied nationality, contribute her share in the disbursement of the general outlay, and the knowledge of the "lord" cover the earth as the waters of the mighty deep.[42]

As an implicit critique of a colonial government that had allowed the island to languish and which many blamed for the social unrest and subsequent loss of political representation, the vicar's statement also aligns Jamaica's Black middle class with progress, science, and religion all at once. From his perspective, the telegraph was to serve as a tool for an empire of Christians of African descent. But—and here I speculate—if this vicar was indeed from Morant Bay, the brand of Christianity he and his congregation practiced may have been laced with myal, obeah, or other forms of polytheistic and animist spiritualities that had infused Baptist churches, particularly in that parish, recognized as a site of resistance. The 1860s Baptist revival had particularly promoted these complex spiritualities, and the vicar may have been speaking for them when he envisioned telegraphy as contributing not to a shrinking of space but rather to the expansion of territory for this particular form of worship.[43]

Exceedingly Troublesome Tortuous Passages

The work of laying the telegraph expanded, rather than shrank, marine space. Understanding the surface of the ocean floor was crucial to telegraphy, and marine life made its presence known. As Helen Rozwadowski has demonstrated, the laying of the Atlantic cable had prompted unprecedented research on the ocean floor and opened up the deep waters as spaces of scientific pursuits. She traces the eventual identification of the Atlantic plateau, and the ways scientific and popular writing interpreted it as a cooperative component of the enterprise of laying the cable. From the perspective of researchers, the ocean offered up a plateau for the cable to rest on, as if it desired to join the enterprise of telegraphic communication.[44]

Not so with the Caribbean Sea. Following Bright's account (which echoes Crookes's), the sea threw up frequent obstacles in the form of coral, sea creatures, and volcanic ridges that cut into the cables or prevented their paying out. Unlike the Atlantic, which scientists agreed merited research and study, the Caribbean seems to have remained outside of the purview of European scientists. Following Hans Sloane's eighteenth-century studies of the Caribbean Sea, which yielded objects and collections of things but not a mapping of the floor or an understanding of the ecosystems, the sea had not been made to yield its qualities to European scientists.[45] It was only after Bright's struggles with the sharp shallows of Caribbean coastlines that Alexander Agassiz began his research on coral. One of his expeditions launched in 1887 followed the telegraph's path, beginning with the Havana–Key West connection.[46]

The sea bottom became an actor in this drama, a particularly uncooperative one. Much of Bright's account of laying the West Indies leg of the cable is framed as a battle between the coral and his equipment. Bright compares the Caribbean Sea floor explicitly to the Atlantic, noting how much more difficult it was. Writing about a stretch between Puerto Rico and Jamaica, Bright observed that although only thirty miles off land, it "was in very deep water and on such a rough and rocky coral bottom that about forty grapnels and several grappling ropes were broken, and weeks passed before the cable could be recovered. It was a very different task to the comparatively easy grappling for the Atlantic lines, where the cable hook is readily drawn along the surface of the ground through soft ooze."[47] As he noted, the problem was that few observations of this particular stretch had been made, and those that did exist remained inadequate. The sounding technique that produced data five to ten miles apart "gave very little idea of the real state of things."[48] Gauging the depth of the sea was at this time accomplished by dropping a weighted wire or line and measuring the distance to when it hit the ocean floor. "Sounding" here did not refer to subsequent sonar technologies but rather to an earlier meaning referring to "water" or "sea." This sounding technique was difficult to accomplish, and its accuracy subject to the whims of currents, winds, and human error.[49] Moreover, apparently the Caribbean had not been a priority, and the measurements were few and far between. This was not known territory.

Despite the treacherous waters, a submarine cable was essential here in connecting Cuban cities Cienfuegos and Santiago as centers of production and export. Due to the war, landlines were too vulnerable to attack. Yet the cables were at the mercy not just of imperial politics, but also of coral-filled waters. Laying the Cuba Submarine Telegraph, noted Bright, proved "exceedingly troublesome, as the shallow and narrow channels of approach were composed of tortuous passages amidst coral reefs and rocky islets for some forty-five miles." He wrote to his wife, describing his experience laying the Cuban cable: "The charts are good for nothing"; and later, about the place he "hoped never to see again," as it had caused him "no end of trouble to get the cable right then, owing to the shallow water, rocks, squalls and troubles of every kind."[50] Indeed, the non-humans did not seem to want to cooperate at all. In addition to trouble with the coral, the sun itself was "knocking up the men very soon," and melting the gutta-percha, for which they struggled to maintain their ice supplies. Ice itself was hard to come by, as it entailed landing and telegraphing for it to be sent from Havana, from which there was only one train, in the morning.[51] Finally, like Philip Crookes three years earlier, they also struggled with illness. Bright noted that Cienfuegos at that moment was ravaged by yellow fever, cholera, and smallpox, and that he had forbidden his crew from landing there.[52]

The sea floor made its presence known off the coast of Jamaica as well, in another frustrating incident in which the cable parted, sank into the waters, and remained elusive while Bright's crew struggled for months to locate and raise it: "It required months of grappling and a very heavy outlay to raise the cable again, the bottom of the sea here (off Morant Point) being a nest of volcanic ridges interspersed with coral walls. The latter had a way of breaking grapnels, and occasionally, the still more precious grappling rope."[53] Troubles with the weather, and with the rocks and coral proved a frequent refrain in Bright's diaries and letters home. Even the sea creatures were a problem in this region: "Those West Indian cables have always given a deal of trouble, owing not only to the unfavourable character of the bottom, but also to frequent attacks at the hands, or rather the snouts, of saw and sword fishes, not to mention the teredo, previously referred to."[54]

Bright's attention was nonetheless drawn to some of the living creatures that they raised up with the grapnels, and he interpreted the path of destruction created by the grapnels as serving his desire for discovery and exploration. Either willingly or neglectfully oblivious to the damage wrought on fragile coral and sea life, he describes the dredged-up species with wonder and delicacy:

> After the weariness of eight or ten hours drifting without touching the cable, there was always something to look forward to when the hour or so of winding up had brought the grapnel on deck. First of all, the state of the prongs was a matter of interest. Then there was its companion, the six-foot swab, enveloping infusoria, coral and shells in its long tangles—collecting, like some octopus, whatever the prongs had detached. The number of unique specimens were secured in this way, including many varieties of the lovely network like lace of "venus bouquet holder" or the flower basket (euplectella) with numerous net coral cups, besides black coral and other varieties. The ooze consisted, as usual, of the microscopic skeletons of infusoria, globigerinae, diatomacae, etc.[55]

This may be the place to speculate about the cable's inability to hear the sound of the sea. Reefs and sea bottoms are noisy places, and scientists would eventually realize that listening to those noises was key to understanding ecosystems and gauging their health. No one intended that the dropped cables transmit those oceanic sounds, but it seems like a missed opportunity. What noises did a silenced, unconnected cable, resting on the floor and awaiting its "rescue" in order to become part of the infrastructure of business and commerce fail to transmit? The chirps and swooshes of the ocean floor went unheard and unheeded. These sounds only became objects of study later on in the twentieth century, with the appearance of hydrophones, bathyspheres, and changes in cable technology that allowed them to listen in on the sounds of the bottom of the sea rather than merely passing through it. As Rachel Carson put it, "Around the shorelines of much of the world, there is an extraordinary uproar produced by fishes, shrimps, [and] porpoises." Hydrophones had recorded "strange mewing sounds, shrieks and ghostly moans, the sources of which had not been traced."[56] In the early days of telegraphy, however, no one was listening.

The Question of Labor

Most elusive in the texts are the laborers who did most of the laying and grappling. If we circle back to the Key West–Havana connection, we might begin with the workers on the *Narva* itself. We learn of them only as they are dying. As Crookes wrote, they were differentially affected by yellow fever. It was specifically the telegraph workers who spent the most time working near the cable tanks, and who were most in peril: "All the cases of yellow fever we have had have been among the telegraph hands, and none among either the sailors or firemen. . . . Of the nineteen or twenty we had at first, five are now dead, and five very ill, one almost hopelessly so."[57] Although it was inadvertent, telegraph hands were put in direct danger as a result of this undertaking.

In the Caribbean context, the issue of labor became entangled with that of race. Paul Gilmore has argued that "telegraphic discourse of the antebellum period repeatedly returned to a racialized understanding of civilization, as most extensively illustrated in American racial science, to describe technology's role in the march of progress."[58] For Gilmore, the telegraph exemplifies the conquest of white power and privilege over the darker-skinned and presumably less civilized people of the world. At the same time, he argues that technology made it possible for some observers to "emphasize the disappearance of racial barriers defined in terms of bodily difference."[59] Turning from discursive representations to questions of labor and material infrastructure stresses the more exploitative dimensions of the process: while telegraphic communications may have erased visual racial barriers, the actual building of the telegraph depended on an entrenched system of racialized labor, and it did little to offer the presumed benefits of bringing the world closer together for most of the people involved in building it.

Mortality and the search for labor appeared frequently in Bright's account as well as Crookes's. But evidence of the workers themselves is fragmentary. If Crookes became more conscious of them as they fell ill and died, Bright's narrative relegates workers mostly to the footnotes. The body of the text notes that on December 12, 1870, they overcame bad weather and completed the Cuba–Puerto Rico leg. The municipality celebrated with a festive ball. On December 13 they resumed and found that they had "difficulty getting hands employed to transfer the cable."[60] The underlying reason does not make it into the body of the text, but rather resides in a footnote: "Owing to sickness and death, Bright was obliged to have recourse to native labour."[61] What was meant by "native labour" in this context can only be surmised. It may have referred to enslaved workers, as Puerto Rico formally abolished slavery in 1873. Most likely it was a combination of free and enslaved labor, as Puerto Rico's sugar industry was declining and demand for slaves had diminished in recent years. In any case, the workers were not particularly acquiescent. Indeed, Puerto Rico was also in the midst of its own anticolonial and antislavery conflicts. A short-lived uprising in 1868 had led to the promulgation, as in Cuba, of the Moret Law of 1870.[62] In this transitional period, workers, whether enslaved or free, may have been hard to come by and would have had little reason to cooperate. Moreover, Bright and his crew seemed inadequately prepared to interact with them in Spanish. He recorded in his diary that his crew had failed to communicate to "Spanish hands" adequate instructions to coil the cable. His own failure to anticipate encounters with people who spoke languages other than English became, in his eyes, the failure of the workers to do his bidding. They soon decided to turn instead to workers in St. Thomas, under Danish rule, in the hope that they would be more compliant. In this instance the process of laying the telegraph produced miscommunication rather than facilitating communication. The sounds of British crew members barking orders to uncomprehending workers in Puerto Rico, of attempted translations, or of workers speaking to one another or making efforts to speak to those who had hired them, are the lost sounds of the aurality of empire; the sounds the cable failed to transmit. When the Americans occupied Puerto Rico, they also struggled to impose the sound of English over Spanish, in classrooms and workplaces throughout the island. The efforts to dominate through language, as Ana María Ochoa Gautier points out, are at the heart of imperial gestures and definitions of "personhood."[63]

Even when they were on more solid linguistic ground in laying the connector between Anglophone Dominica and Antigua, they were not particularly welcomed by either the elite or workers. The Dominican elite, whose power was faltering in the wake of emancipation, did not necessarily regard a connection to the submarine cable as a positive development. As Joseph Boromé argues, the planter elite fought proposals of the telegraph, and "beneath hostile arguments lay the conviction that the telegraph would open up the island to capital and enterprise which would smash the 'power and patronage' of the local oligarchy, and, even more important, make resistance to federation impossible."[64] They may have found ways to block or disrupt the hiring process. In any case, Bright continued to express his discontent with workers, soon converted into a rather tired chorus: "work continuing very slowly, owing to the necessity of employing black labour."[65] Whether these laborers were from Dominica or Antigua he does not say, but it is not surprising that workers were not necessarily cooperative. Dominica had a long history of noncompliant labor. It had a large and powerful community of Maroons that had grown in numbers over the eighteenth century and waged successful battles with plantation owners and the colonial government until 1814, when many were killed or exiled.[66] When apprenticeship ended and emancipation formally began in 1838, many former slaves left their plantations and sought better conditions elsewhere, privileging access to land over wage labor.[67] So when Bright and his crew arrived in 1870, they encountered a place full of people working their plots of land, with possibly little interest in working for a telegraph company. From their perspective—mostly silenced—the cable signified wage labor at best, condescension and death at worst. The failure to translate here was perhaps less about English and more about the language of capitalism: the language of wages and supervisors, or appeals to modernity, efficiency, and direct contact with Europe may have fallen on uninterested ears. There was power in refusal to enter into relationships as wage laborers working for the interests of the state or empire rather than for themselves.[68]

To direct our attention to the sea and to the people who worked to lay submarine cables means to expand the range of sounds that made the acoustics of empire. The acoustics of empire must also include the piercing whine of mosquitoes, and of sick and dying men groaning or retching, or falling silent. There are voices trying to organize a workforce via translation or broken Spanish, and the sound of refusal, whatever form that took, and the missed sounds of sea life disrupted by intrusion. Taking this perspective also allows for thinking of telegraphy as moving through an expansive, rather than a shrinking space, and forcibly encountering empires at different stages of growth or unmaking, moving through a variety of temporal frames rather than annihilating time or producing a homogenous temporality. For the many who were not users or beneficiaries of the technology but who instead worked to ensure its creation, telegraphy did not sound like swift signals traveling through cables. It sounded like the wind blowing ships off course, snapped lines, sickness, arrogance, negotiation, refusal or revolt, and the dumping of broken bits from the sea onto a ship's deck.

Notes

1. *Harper's Weekly*, September 7, 1867.
2. Bernhard Siegert, "The Chorein of the Pirate: On the Origin of the Dutch Seascape," *Grey Room* 57 (2014), 6–23.
3. Brian Larkin, "The Politics and Poetics of Infrastructure," *Annual Review of Anthropology* 42 (2013), 327–343.
4. Jorma Ahvenainen, *The European Cable Companies in South America before the First World War* (Helsinki: Academia Scientarium Fennica, 2004); Simone M. Müller, *Wiring the World: The Social and Cultural Creation of Global Telegraph Networks* (New York: Columbia University Press, 2016); Dwayne R. Winseck and Robert M. Pike, *Communication and Empire: Media, Markets, and Globalization, 1860–1930* (Durham, NC: Duke University Press, 2007).
5. Nicole Starosielski, *The Undersea Network* (Durham, NC: Duke University Press, 2015), 15.
6. Jonathan Sterne, *The Audible Past: Cultural Origins of Sound Reproduction* (Durham, NC: Duke University Press, 2003), ch. 3.
7. Stephen Kern, *The Culture of Time and Space, 1880–1918* (Cambridge, MA: Harvard University Press, 2003); Wolfgang Schivelbusch, *The Railway Journey: The Industrialization of Time and Space in the Nineteenth Century* (Oakland: University of California Press, 2014 [1977]).
8. Deep Kanta Lahiri Choudhury, *Telegraphic Imperialism: Crisis and Panic in the Indian Empire, c.1830–1920* (London: Palgrave Macmillan, 2010); Müller, *Wiring the World*.
9. Kern, *The Culture of Time and Space*.
10. James Q. Davies, "Instruments of Empire," in *Sound Knowledge: Music and Science in London, 1789–1851*, ed. James Q. Davies and Ellen Lockhart (Chicago: University of Chicago Press, 2017), 145–174.
11. Peter McMurray, "The Revolution Will Not Be Telegraphed: Shari'a Law as Mediascape," in *Hearing the Crimean War: Wartime Sound and the Unmaking of Sense*, ed. Gavin Williams (Oxford, UK: Oxford University Press, 2018), 24–58.
12. Submarine Telegraph, *The Story of My Life* (London: C. West, 1859).
13. Edward Brailsford Bright and Charles Bright, *The Life Story of Sir Charles Tilston Bright, Civil Engineer, with which is incorporated the Story of the Atlantic Cable and*

the first Telegraph to India and the Colonies (London: Constable & Company, 1910); Charles Bright, *Submarine Telegraphs: Their History, Construction and Working* (London: C. Lockwood & Son, 1898).

14. John Philip Edward Crookes, *Letters from the Steamship Narva* (London: William Crookes, 1868), cited in http://atlantic-cable.com/Cables/1867Florida-Cuba/index. htm, accessed February 1, 2023.

15. Canter Brown Jr., "The International Ocean Telegraph," *Florida Historical Quarterly* 68/2 (1989), 135–159, at 155.

16. "Review, *The Life Story of the late Sir Charles Tilston Bright; with which is incorporated the Story of the Atlantic Cable and the First Telegraph to India and the Colonies*," *Nature*, October 26, 1899, 613.

17. Brian Pollitt, "The Rise and Fall of the Cuban Sugar Economy," *Journal of Latin American Studies*, 36/2 (2004), 319–348.

18. Antonio Rafael de la Cova, "Cuban Exiles in Key West During the Ten Years' War 1868–1878," *Florida Historical Quarterly* 89/3 (2011), 287–319.

19. Rebecca J. Scott, *Slave Emancipation in Cuba: The Transition to Free Labor, 1860–1899* (Pittsburgh, PA: University of Pittsburgh Press, 1985).

20. Brown, "The International Ocean Telegraph."

21. Crookes, *Letters from the Steamship Narva*, Letter to Jane, August 11, 1867.

22. Ibid., Letter to William, September 8, 1867.

23. Ibid., Letter to William, September 8, 1867.

24. War Department, Surgeon General's Office, *Report on Epidemic Cholera and Yellow Fever in the Army of the United States, During the year 1867* (Washington: Government Printing Office, 1868).

25. Crookes, *Letters from the Steamship Narva*, Letter to his mother, August 29 and September 1, 1867.

26. Ibid., Letter to William, September 8, 1867.

27. J. R. McNeill, *Mosquito Empires: Ecology and War in the Greater Caribbean, 1640–1914* (Cambridge, UK: Cambridge University Press, 2010).

28. Glover, cited in http://atlantic-cable.com/Cables/1867Florida-Cuba/index.htm.

29. Manzano to E. O. Gwynn, Mayor of Key West, August 21–24, 1867, cited in "The Havana Cable," *New York Times*, August 25, 1867.

30. Crookes, *Letters from the Steamship Narva.*

31. Bright, *Life Story*, 319.

32. Scott, *Slave Emancipation in Cuba*; Ferrer, *Insurgent Cuba.*

33. Bright, *Life Story*, 320.

34. This was a common strategy. See Starosielski, *Undersea Network*, ch. 1.

35. Sasha Turner, *Contested Bodies: Pregnancy, Childrearing and Slavery in Jamaica* (Philadelphia: University of Pennsylvania Press, 2017).

36. Bright, *Life Story*, 368.

37. I am grateful to Peter McMurray for making this point.

38. Thomas Holt, *The Problem of Freedom: Race, Labor and Politics in Jamaica and Britain, 1832–1938* (Baltimore, MD: Johns Hopkins University Press, 1992); Frederick

Cooper, Thomas Holt, and Rebecca Scott, *Beyond Slavery: Explorations of Race, Labor and Citizenship in Post-Emancipation Societies* (Chapel Hill: University of North Carolina Press, 2014).

39. Ansell Hart, "The Banana in Jamaica: Export Trade," *Social and Economic Studies* 3/2 (1954), 212–229; James Martin, *Banana Cowboys: The United Fruit Company and the Culture of Corporate Colonialism* (Santa Fe: University of New Mexico Press, 2018); Stephen Kinzer and Stephen Schlesinger, *Bitter Fruit: The Story of the American Coup in Guatemala* (Cambridge, MA: Harvard University Press, 2005 [1982]).

40. James Smith, "Empire and Social Reform: British Liberals and the 'Civilizing Mission' in the Sugar Colonies," *Albion* 27/2 (1995), 253–277.

41. Bela Vassady Jr., "Transplanting Prejudices: The Failure of the Baptist Experiment Using Jamaican 'Native Agents' in Fernando Po and Cameroons, 1841-1850," *Caribbean Quarterly* 25/1–2 (1979), 15–39.

42. Letter to Bright, n.d., n.a., cited in Bright, *Life Story*, 328–329. See also McMurray, "The Revolution Will Not Be Telegraphed" on yoking telegraphy to spirituality.

43. Vassady, "Transplanting Prejudices"; Emanuela Guano, "Revival Zion: An Afro-Christian Religion in Jamaica," *Anthropos* 89/4–6 (1994), 517–528; Rex Nettleford, "Freedom of Thought and Expression: Nineteenth Century West Indian Creole Experience," *Caribbean Quarterly* 36/1–2 (1990), 16–43.

44. Helen M. Rozwadowski, *Fathoming the Ocean: The Discovery and Exploration of the Deep Sea* (Cambridge, MA: Belknap Press, 2008).

45. James Delbourgo, "Divers Things: Collecting the World Under Water," *History of Science* 49 (2011), 149–185.

46. "Three Cruises of the Blake" [Review of *Three Cruises of the United States Coast and Geodetic Survey Steamer "Blake" in the Gulf of Mexico, in the Caribbean Sea and along the Atlantic Coast of the United States, from 1877 to 1880*, by A. Agassiz], *American Naturalist* 22/258 (1888), 516–517.

47. Bright, *Life Story*, 318.

48. Ibid., 367.

49. Sabine Hohler, "A Sound Survey: The Technological Perception of Ocean Depth," in *Transforming Spaces: The Topological Turn in Technology Studies*, ed. Mikael Hård, Andreas Lösch, and Dirk Verdicchio. Clio Online, https://www.clio-online.de/webr esource/id/webresource-25112, accessed February 1, 2023; James Poskett, "Sounding in Silence: Men, Machines and the Changing Environment of Naval Discipline, 1796–1815," *British Journal for the History of Science* 48/2 (2015), 213–232. https://www.rep ository.cam.ac.uk/bitstream/handle/1810/246193/OA1847_Sounding-in-Silence---Final-with-Figures---BJHS.pdf, accessed February 1, 2023.

50. Bright, *Life Story*, 322.

51. Ibid., 321.

52. Ibid., 323.

53. Ibid., 346.

54. Ibid., 361.

55. Ibid., 366–367.

56. Rachel Carson, *The Sea Around Us* (Oxford, UK: Oxford University Press, 2018 [1950]), 51. See also Starosielski, *Undersea Network*; Stefan Helmreich, "An Anthropologist Underwater: Immersive Soundscapes, Submarine Cyborgs and Transductive Ethnography," *American Ethnologist* 34/4 (2007), 621–641.

57. Crooke, *Letters from the Steamship Narva.*

58. Paul Gilmore, "The Telegraph in Black and White," *ELH* 69/3 (2002), 805–833, at 805–806.

59. Ibid., 806.

60. Bright, *Life Story*, 341.

61. Ibid., 341n2.

62. Sidney Mintz, "Labor and Sugar in Puerto Rico and Jamaica, 1800–1850," *Comparative Studies in Society and History* 1/3 (1959), 273–281.

63. Ana María Ochoa Gautier, *Aurality: Listening and Knowledge in Nineteenth Century Colombia* (Durham, NC: Duke University Press, 2014).

64. Joseph Boromé, "How Crown Colony Government Came to Dominica by 1898," *Caribbean Studies* 9/3 (1969), 26–67, at 45.

65. Bright, *Life Story*, 353.

66. Bernard Marshall, "Maronnage in Slave Plantation Society: A Case Study of Dominica, 1785–1815," *Caribbean Quarterly* 54/4 (2008), 103–110.

67. Michel-Rolph Trouillot, "Labour and Emancipation in Dominica: Contribution to a Debate," *Caribbean Quarterly* 30/3–4 (1984), 73–84.

68. On the power of refusal and silence, see Gaiutra Bahadur, *Coolie Woman: The Odyssey of Indenture* (Chicago: University of Chicago Press, 2014); Yannick Marshall, "An Appeal—Bring the Maroon into the Foreground in Black Intellectual History," *Black Perspectives*, June 19, 2020, https://www.aaihs.org/an-appeal-bring-the-maroon-to-the-foreground-in-black-intellectual-history/, accessed February 1, 2023.

2

Encounter and Memory
in Ottoman Soundscapes

An Audiovisual Album of Street Vendors' Cries

Nazan Maksudyan

Sait Faik, one of the greatest writers of short stories in Turkish, describes his itinerant merchant, "Cotton Candy Man" (*Ketenhelvacı*), as a curiosity.[1] At the beginning of the story, the narrator hears the cry of the cotton candy man from a distance: "*Vay ne güzel ketenhelvam!*" ("Oh, my cotton candy is so delicious!"). He thinks that, in 1942, under circumstances of war and scarcity, "cotton candy man is a fairy tale creature. And maybe he is the last of a dying breed; maybe cotton candy sellers will become extinct."[2] He goes on to exalt this itinerant merchant as a poet, as the cotton candy man was crying out, reciting little poems, apparently as part of his métier.[3] All of a sudden, the narrator burns with the desire to see him and talk to him. Following the direction of the voice, he comes across a roasted chestnut seller on his way. The latter says that the cotton candy man earns enough money to drink *rakı* every night. Finally, the narrator meets him and they talk a great deal. The man says he has been in this business for the past forty-two years—that is, since 1900. As a compliment, the narrator asks: "The cotton candy sellers are all poets, aren't they?" The man looks embarrassed and does not answer. Then, he says he will make another round before the next ferry comes and walks away reciting another poem:

> I am all skin and bone
> I tramp up and down the neighborhoods[4]

This short story has the richness to introduce the main themes of this chapter on the sonic presence of street vendors in nineteenth-century Ottoman soundscapes. First of all, the research is conceived as an auditory history

Nazan Maksudyan, *Encounter and Memory in Ottoman Soundscapes* In: *Acoustics of Empire*.
Edited by: Peter McMurray and Priyasha Mukhopadhyay, Oxford University Press. © Oxford University Press 2024.
DOI: 10.1093/oso/9780197553787.003.0003

tracing multiple encounters,[5] much like the encounter of the narrator with the seller in the story. Second, I emphasize that sound should be analyzed as a relationship between a listener and something listened to.[6] In the story, the narrator is fascinated by what was for him the voice of a rare poet passing by, whereas for the chestnut seller this was the sound of a habitual drinker. Focusing on street vendors' sonic practices, this chapter analyzes different listening habits and subjectivities along the lines of religion, class, language, ethnicity, gender, and other categories of difference. I stress the way cultural difference, especially intra-imperial difference, emerges in an urban soundscape like Istanbul. Thus, the soundscape is defined following Thompson, as "simultaneously a physical environment and a way of perceiving that environment," both as a world and "a culture constructed to make sense of that world."[7] I use the term, then, in the plural, as "soundscapes," taking into account multiple sensory experiences of a diversity of peoples.[8] Third, the chapter is based on four encounters and relations that itinerant sellers' cries delineate: migration (how rural migrants listened to Ottoman urbanites, and vice versa); multilingualism and diversity; human-nonhuman encounters; and the audibility of gender. Lastly, as Sait Faik's "Cotton Candy Man" suggests, there was a romantic fascination with the practice of itinerant merchants, due to their imagined "oriental" character and authenticity, as well as their anticipated extinction. In this way, a skinny, tired, poor old man could have been heard as a poet—and Sait Faik's insight underscored this irony.

The chapter contributes to recent scholarship on sound's uses and functions in Ottoman culture and society;[9] how Ottoman subjectivities, sociabilities, and power relations were reflected in the lives of sounds; and how sonic practices shaped Ottoman identities, bonded communities, and elevated or undermined power.[10] The chapter asks: if we could listen to the street vendors' cries, what traces of empire, environment, migration, diversity and gender might we hear?

An Audiovisual Album of Street Vendors' Cries

Aurality, as an "object" of historical enquiry, is elusive and its sources are dispersed. However, as Alain Corbin showed some three decades ago in his *Village Bells*, it is possible to work on novel questions of sound and sound perception on the basis of relatively traditional sources.[11] More recently, Nancy Hunt has suggested a new reading of the sources, old and new, through the senses, through fields of hearing and sound, to create an "acoustic register."[12] Ziad Fahmy, in his elaboration on Middle Eastern sound studies, has also stressed that many different forms of typical written sources (memoirs, letters, diaries, official documents, travelogues, literary sources) include records of what was heard.[13] This chapter also relies on typical written sources, including materials from the Ottoman archives, literature in different Ottoman languages, ego-documents, travelogues, scientific writings, newspapers, letters, diaries, legal documents, musical notation, and court records. It is also necessary to stress that visual sources from the period point to a crowd of street vendors. In innumerable photographs depicting Ottoman urban centers, streets and squares are populated by a multitude of different itinerant vendors at the same time. Assuming that they were all actively trying to sell their merchandise simultaneously, we can imagine their collective cries as a kind of polyphonic chorus that was part of an even broader urban polyphony. In this sense, the visual sources also hint at the vendors' impact on the soundscape.

The main source for this chapter is a unique and extraordinary audiovisual media object: an album of photos and musical transcriptions of street vendors' cries in Western staff notation, bringing to light the intersection of the visual and sonic. Every vendor category in the album is photographed and coupled with their typical "vending song," the "lyrics" written in transliterated Turkish and the name of the occupation in English. Twenty-three different occupational groups were documented in this album, featuring mostly (but not only) adult males, including a bread vendor, milkman, yogurt vendor, vegetable man, corn vendor, fishmonger, water carrier, fruit peddler, boot blacks (children), garbage collector, "bon marché" (silk man), and broom peddler (female, selling a different sort of broom). The sellers were photographed in the streets, in other words in the setting of their daily labors. We see them walking around the city with their merchandise and accompanying animals when relevant.

The original of the album was until recently kept in a personal archive in Istanbul, belonging to Rezan Benatar.[14] Formerly, it was part of Edward S. Sheiry's (1900–1980) estate (*tereke*). He was the head of the engineering department at Robert College in the 1930s. Sheiry is not the author of the album. Based on the outfits (and especially the kinds of headgear in the album), it is apparent that it was prepared in the late nineteenth or early twentieth century, before the 1920s.

Figure 2.1 "Where East and West meet—Istanbul." Opening page, "İstanbul'un sokak satıcıları—Street vendors of Istanbul" album, Salt Research, Photographs and Postcards Archive, https://archives.saltresearch.org/handle/123456789/195 592. Reproduced with permission.

The album opens with a panoramic view of Istanbul, presented with the caption, "Where East and West meet – ISTANBUL" (Figure 2.1), as the typical orientalist trope goes. The work can be considered a sort of Orientalist collection, like the so-called costume albums of different ethnicities or Ottoman palace servants.[15] Yet, the "collector" of this album was mainly interested in capturing the sound of Istanbul, along with the sights of street vendors.[16] Despite the brevity of the melody, he treated vending cries as musical sounds and he had the necessary education and experience to transpose these cries into musical notation. It is also necessary to note the collector's effort to put sounds into notes and words while transliterating the sound of a cry in a foreign alphabet/language. Without doubt, the musical notation reduces some of the sonic complexity of these calls. Some amount of information is presumably lost through transcription into the pitch and rhythmic structures of Western musical notation.[17] Despite the prevalence of the visual senses and representations of the "Orient" through paintings, photographs, and postcards, the existence of such sources emphasizes the interest in the auditory culture of the "East."[18]

Adhering to the conventions of the "city cries" genre, which became popular for the metropolitan cities of London and Paris in the early modern era,[19] this album represents the transfusion of this genre with Orientalist photography.[20] "Street vendors" were a popular topic for European as well as local Istanbulite photographers, and an especially successful postcard series in the Orientalist depiction of Constantinople in the second half of the nineteenth century.[21] The fascination with the practice of itinerant sellers appears to result from both its assumed peculiarity and its predicted extinction, as suggested by Sait Faik's story. Thanks to this Orientalizing bias, street vendor postcards, much like this album, refashioned a typical, and without a doubt unenviable, job for the newly migrated urban poor, as a quintessentially exotic, disappearing, and even romantic occupation. In that sense, the representation of street vending also makes visible a semi-colonial encounter with regards to how the Ottoman state, society, and culture were imagined, constructed, and depicted, both visually and audibly. The album could be considered part of this larger discourse and encounter, where European imperialism affects Ottoman life even though the empire was never technically colonized.

In the rest of the chapter, I will discuss how circulating sounds of vendors suggest cultural, political, and economic relations. After a brief discussion of mobility through urban space in general, I focus specifically on four encounters that are embodied through the sonic presence of street vendors and that shed light upon Ottoman subjectivities, social relations, and power relations. The first section delineates the aspect of rural-urban migration of street vendors, and thus focuses on social and economic relations. The second section examines the representation of multilingualism and diversity in the sonic practices of itinerant sellers. The next section sheds light upon the human-animal encounters that were inherent to the practices of street vendors. The final section focuses on the audibility of gender in street vendors' sounds. It is important to highlight the centrality of the *medium of documentation* for this research, namely the unique audiovisual booklet of street vendors' cries. The album invites us to contemplate especially the intersections of the visual and the sonic. The other *medium* that this chapter engages with is the street—as both the *stage* and the *channel* for urban sonic phenomena.

Each of the four parts opens with a vignette referring to a twentieth-century cultural and artistic product, offering insight into the persistence of the practices of itinerant sellers in post-Ottoman Turkey. These sensory recollections show how salient these urban sounds are in broader Turkish cultural representations and suggest some kind of collective memory of late Ottoman soundscapes. The presence of street vendor sounds in different formats—song, novels, film, journalistic interviews—also suggests a fascinating medium-focused question: what happens when cultural memory is preserved specifically in these different formats? What can a song embed that a photo cannot? The vignettes, in that sense, refer to the evocative nature of street vendors' cries, in reenacting the way intra-imperial differences emerge in urban soundscapes of Istanbul and persist in cultural memory.

Mobile Lives, Mobile Sounds

In a 1988 song by Barış Manço, a famous Turkish musician, singer, and songwriter with countless hits from the 1970s onwards, a guy is in love with a girl and wishes finally to confess his love to her. However, as he is about to hold her hand and open his mouth, he is interrupted by the echoing voice of the vegetable vendor calling from the streets: "*Domates, Biber, Patlıcan*" (also the title of the song; "Tomatoes, Peppers, Eggplants"). Even though the words awaken a colorful image in the listener's mind (with the vegetables' red, green, and purple colors), the guy feels like his entire world is going black:

> The streets echoed with this voice:
> "Tomatoes, peppers, eggplants."[22]

Manço's song intertwines the audio with the visual—there is the voice coming from the street and the world goes to black. He also describes the sound as if it were causing the streets themselves to vibrate and echo. The song is also ethnographic: the way he sings "*Domates, biber, patlıcan*" reflects how the vegetable sellers shouted—though his voice is a bit too loud. Yet, most importantly, the vendor's mobility is foregrounded by the song, with a silent moment suddenly broken with the arrival of the vegetable seller.

Itinerant sellers had a considerable impact on the Ottoman acoustic environment. Earwitness accounts stress that the cries of street vendors were quite dominant in the Ottoman soundscape. The 1871 *Handbook for Travellers in Constantinople* underscores that when a traveler first arrives in the city, he would be surprised by "the silence that pervades so large a capital." After all, the "only sounds" to be heard during the day were "the cries of bread, fruits, sweetmeats [*helva*], or sherbet, carried in a large wooden tray on the head of an itinerant vendor."[23]

Victor Eskenazi (1906–1987), a Sephardic Jew who spent his childhood in the early twentieth century in a neighborhood on the Golden Horn, noted in his memoirs that especially in morning hours, all kinds of "hawkers, offering an endless variety of merchandise, each with his own traditional and distinctive cry, would follow one another" down the street.[24] These included an Albanian who sold sheep's brains and feet, a yogurt man, a fishmonger, a vegetable and fruit vendor, tinkers, knife-grinders, lace-vendors, and also artisans who could mend or manufacture virtually anything on the spot. These were "the sights, the *cries* and the *turmoil*" on the street in the morning.[25] "The *toing and froing of street vendors* and the confusion would come to a standstill in the afternoon."[26]

Peddling was a ubiquitous extension of every kind of product and production. It was impossible to have a functioning system of buying/selling wares without mobile peddling, and so the "suppliers" had to be on the streets and cry out loud to sell their products. Most of the fruit and vegetable sellers, bread vendors, yogurt sellers, and innumerable others were itinerants, who carried and marketed fresh fruits and vegetables to the areas where they were to be sold.[27] According to the memoirs of Hagop Mıntzuri, who came to Istanbul in 1890 as a ten-year-old child to work as a peddler for his father's and uncle's bakery and worked there until 1907, bread was not sold in the bakery. No one would ever go to the bakery to buy bread. Grocers would not sell bread either. Instead, bread was taken to all the neighborhoods and to the suburbs, directly to the customers' doors.[28] Beşiktaş Square hosted a full crowd of street vendors, including a bread vendor, a broom peddler, a liver seller, a *helva* peddler (who would sell yogurt in summer), and a shoeshine boy.[29] Sinan Paşa Mosque in the square, which was visited twice a year by the Sultan, also attracted rosary sellers, scented oil sellers, blind people, and beggars.[30]

Considering that new communication infrastructures, such as wider roads, squares, cobbled streets, ferries, and trams, were limited to a few areas in the city, in many neighborhoods far from the tram lines and seashore, the sound of the street vendors must have been the most audible sound in residential areas.

Encounter 1: Migrating Shouts

In *Züğürt Ağa* (The Broke Landlord), a 1985 movie directed by Nesli Çölgeçen, a former *agha* (or rural landlord) who had owned a whole village in eastern Turkey is forced to migrate to Istanbul. Having no practical knowledge about urban life and no work experience, he tries to make a living in the city by doing various street vending jobs. He first tries selling tomatoes with a pick-up and amplifier, also using a microphone. Yet, he is incredibly shy about shouting out loud in the middle of urban Istanbul neighborhoods. He basically whispers "*Domatessss*," with a funny pronunciation of the "e" and a lisping "s." His former servant, now friend and helper, asks him to raise his voice, but he says it would disturb the quiet of urban people.[31] The movie is full of uncomfortable moments in the life of a rural migrant in a metropole, in his daily habits, attire, and interpersonal relations. The *agha* realizes that itinerant vending is a suitable occupation for migrants, but he has difficulty incorporating his own voice into the urban soundscape.

Like the *agha*'s story, one encounter that street vending reflects is between the urban and the rural: street vending was an urban profession that gave insight into the rural reality. The irregular and ambulant peddling of some well-known and easily sellable consumer goods at a small profit was an easily accessible "poor man's trade." A newly arriving and nonqualified rural migrant could expect to at least work as a street vendor and join the urban poor.[32] From the perspective of Ottoman guild structures, itinerant vendors were a threat and viewed as competitors from the eighteenth century onwards. Due to the growing population and the demand for affordable food, the number of itinerant sellers had increased in larger cities, especially Istanbul. The guilds often requested that the government carry out regular inspections of bakeries, workshops, commercial buildings, and bachelors' rooms (*bekar odaları*) to evict rural migrants, who lacked guarantors and membership in the guilds.[33]

What they peddled was also compartmentalized according to their places of origin, since generations followed one another to the city through locally-built networks of migration. The help of connections and the network of relatives and fellow townsmen already settled in the city were almost always a necessity. Mıntzuri's life story was a prototype of this rural-urban migration, and intergenerational and continuous mobility. He stressed that those from Pokr Armıdan (today Küçük Armutlu, Erzincan) had been coming to Istanbul for decades to work as bakers and bread vendors and he had no other chance to become anything else. Besides people from Armıdan becoming bakers, migrants with Central Asian backgrounds became *börek* sellers in Istanbul, one example of which is found in the album (Figure 2.2). Armenians from Muş would come to Istanbul and work as porters (*hamal*).

Figure 2.2 "Beoreg [*börek*] pedlar—Beoreg beoreg." "İstanbul'un sokak satıcıları—Street vendors of Istanbul" album, Salt Research, Photographs and Postcards Archive, https://archives.saltresearch.org/handle/123456789/195592. Reproduced with permission.

In Abdülaziz Bey's (1850–1918) *Âdât ve Merâsim-i Kadîme* (Ancient Customs and Rituals), the professions generally performed by those coming to Istanbul from various provinces were listed according to their places of origin. To name a few, those from Eğin would become butchers, wax producers (*balmumcu*), and coal sellers; those from Ioannina would sell grilled liver or tripe soup (*işkembe*) in the streets; those coming from Bar and Shkodra (Albania) would do vegetable and flower gardening; those coming from Safranbolu would sell pastry products (*börek*, *poğaça*); people of Kastamonu would sell traditional sweets (*helva* and *kadayıf*); and "Arabs" coming from "Ottoman Arabia" would sell hazelnuts and other sweets.[34]

In general, it was customary for occupational groups to "transfer" apprentice boys, children of 10–12, from their native villages. Therefore, numerous itinerant vendors were children or quite young boys. Three shoeshine boys figure in the album with their cry, "*Boyacı*" (Figure 2.3), as it was a common "occupation" for underage boys and little children. There are also other very

Figure 2.3 "Boot blacks—Boyadji [*boyacı*]." "İstanbul'un sokak satıcıları—Street vendors of Istanbul" album, Salt Research, Photographs and Postcards Archive, https://archives.saltresearch.org/handle/123456789/195592. Reproduced with permission.

young vendors in the album, such as the *helva* peddler (Figure 2.4) and *leblebi* (roasted chickpeas) vendor (Figure 2.5). As mentioned above, merchants of "luxury products," such as *helva* and *leblebi*, often had longer cries and in some cases little poems. These little poems, called *manzume*, constitute a fascinating oral literary genre. Several of these poems are recorded in literary or ethnographic works such as Abdülaziz Bey's *Âdât ve Merâsim-i Kadîme*. He notes that sometime in the nineteenth century, composing poetry had become almost like a hobby, such that even the street vendors composed their own poems pertaining to their product. Ramadan drummers, *boza* sellers, corn sellers, pudding (*muhallebi*) sellers, beggars, and cotton candy sellers would walk the streets, reciting the poems they had composed to attract customers.[35] Indeed, they would sell more goods this way. As much as children would love listening to them and buying their sweets, the adults were also quite interested in the performance and would say: "Look, here is so-and-so, let's go listen to this." The poem of the pudding seller would read as:

Figure 2.4 "Helva pedlar—Helva, helva." "İstanbul'un sokak satıcıları—Street vendors of Istanbul" album, Salt Research, Photographs and Postcards Archive, https://archives.saltresearch.org/handle/123456789/195592. Reproduced with permission.

> My pudding is creamy / It shines on plates / Those who praise it are quite right / Little gentlemen, come and get it
>
> My pudding is sugar in milk / Pulls money out of pockets / But somehow is worthy of praise / Little gentlemen, come and get it . . .[36]

These rural migrants brought their special clothing and head gear from their places of origin, and the colors of shirts and vests and cuts of their pants were usually explained at great length along with their selling cries in earwitness accounts. In addition to clothing and head gear, the presence of local dialects is also discernible in the sounds of the street vendors, who frequently had rural origins. Mıntzuri was warned a number of times that he should no longer "speak like a villager" and had to learn an urban style of speaking, a more complex linguistic register. This included speaking in a much quieter voice and using different vocabulary for several words. He gives a number

Figure 2.5 "Leblebi vender—Leblebidji [*leblebici*]." "İstanbul'un sokak satıcıları—Street vendors of Istanbul" album, Salt Research, Photographs and Postcards Archive, https://archives.saltresearch.org/handle/123456789/195592. Reproduced with permission.

of examples of local expressions he used. He began saying *hee* instead of *evet* for "yes," *yoh* instead of *hayır* for "no," *ecük* or *bir pırtık* instead of *biraz* for "a little."[37] Mıntzuri also notes that the way the language was spoken in the city was quieter than that of the countryside. In his *Istanbul Memoirs*, he recounts an anecdote from his very first day in the city in 1890. When he and his father were passing by the Dolmabahçe Palace, he asked if the sultan lived there. Suddenly, he was scolded by his father, saying: "Do not talk loudly. They talk slowly here. You are not in the village anymore."[38]

Encounter 2: Acoustics of Multilingualism

Yeşim Ustaoğlu's 1999 movie, *Journey to the Sun* (Güneşe Yolculuk), which is set in Istanbul, tells the story of Mehmet, a young man whose job is to find leaks in the water pipes below the ground. He uses a long brass rod he places on the pavement, listening through it to catch the rumbles. The rod becomes a magic tool, as Mehmet discovers an entire world his senses alone could not detect: he can hear turmoil under the streets but not above them. Then he meets Berzan, a Kurdish man and a street music vendor, who is constantly harassed by the authorities for selling Kurdish music cassettes in his cart in Eminönü. Mehmet's friendship with Berzan teaches him about ethnic violence and persecution. He experiences the suppression of Kurdish identity and of the Kurdish language, while his German-born girlfriend freely tells him, "Ich liebe dich."[39] *Journey to the Sun* gives a voice to the Kurds who were unable to speak out for most of Turkey's republican history. The brutal silencing of the Kurdish language since the 1920s constitutes a clear rupture from the multilingual urbanity of the Ottoman period.

The second issue that the sonic practices of itinerant vendors raises—and which appears repeatedly in *Journey to the Sun*—is the acoustics of multilingualism. Research on the practice of street vending not only provides a glimpse of the sonic lives of streets, it also opens up a discussion on the presence of empire in the lives of sounds. Multilingualism, in the form of communication in more than one language, was widespread in Ottoman cities.[40] The coexistence of different ethnicities, religions, and languages, at least in urban centers, offered an Ottoman imperial experience to the ear. Cities such as Istanbul, Smyrna, Salonika, Beirut, or Aleppo were referred to as the "Babel of languages,"[41] where many languages could be heard and many inhabitants were multilingual. In Ottoman Salonika, at least four languages were commonly used in daily life: Ladino, Greek, Turkish, French (the principal language of the local press).[42] Quadrilingual cities or regions could also be found in Macedonia and in Smyrna.[43]

For Edmondo de Amicis (1846–1908), writing in the nineteenth century, Galata Bridge was the beating heart of the city of Constantinople and embodied this "Babel." He described the bridge as "one continuous tramp and roar, a concert of exotic sounds, of guttural notes, incomprehensible aspirations and interjections."[44] It was "the Babel of sounds," bringing to the ear all possible languages and a wide range of low and high pitched sounds:

> Above the babel of sounds made by all this multitude one hears the *piercing cries of the Greek news-boys*, selling newspapers *in all languages* under heaven, the *stentorian tones of the porters, loud laughter* of the Turkish women; the *infantile voices of the eunuchs*; the *shrill falsetto* of a blind beggar reciting verses from the Koran; the *hollow-resounding noise of the bridge*

itself as it sways under this multitude of feet; the bells and whistles from a hundred steamboats.[45]

The notated street vendor album contains cries only in Turkish. However, there is overwhelming evidence that other languages were used to sell products in the streets. Eskenazi noted that fishmongers, whose selling cry was "*Balık*," like the one in the album, were usually Sephardi Jews and they would mostly speak Ladino, and sometimes Greek. The vegetable and fruit vendor in Eskenazi's neighborhood, who came right after the fishmonger, was Greek and would announce his various commodities on sale "with precise and particular modulations, in demotic Greek."[46] The Turcoman artisan, originating from Chinese Turkestan, "would utter in Ladino a strange sing-song call 'Adobar cinis . . . Adobar cinis,' meaning he could repair porcelains and ceramics."[47]

Mıntzuri remembers a little Greek vending boy, crying like "*O bakkal isirte*." He did not know what he was saying or what he was selling, but he assumed this boy had to shout in Greek to the women from Greek households, as they did not speak any Turkish.[48] De Amicis also noted that it was possible to hear selling cries in several different languages, including Armenian, Greek, Turkish, Italian, French, and more:

> At every step some fresh cry assailed the ear: Turkish porters yelling, "Sacun ha!" (Make room!); Armenian water-carriers calling out, "Varme su!"[49] and the Greek, "Crio nero!" Turkish donkey-drivers crying, "Burada!" venders of sweetmeats, "Scerbet!"[50] newsboys, "Neologos!" Frankish cab-drivers, "Guarda! Guarda!"[51]

In Recaizade Mahmut Ekrem's *Araba Sevdası* (Love of Cars, 1896), there is a newspaper boy's selling cry and interaction with a customer revealing the usage of three different languages—Turkish, French, and Greek—in the course of a very short conversation. It opens with a list of newspapers the boy is selling:

- "*La Turquie, Courrier d'Orient, Ceride-i Havadis, Vakit, Manzume-i Efkâr!*"
- "*Gazeteci! Gazeteci! Donnez-moi un Courrier d'Orient!*" ("Paperboy! Give me a Courrier d'Orient.")
- "*Oriste!*" ("Here you are!")

- *"Combien?"* ("How much?")
- *"Un gurush."*
- *"Un piastre?"*
- *"Malista ..."* ("Yes ...")[52]

The paperboy, selling newspapers in French (*La Turquie, Courrier d'Orient*), Turkish (*Ceride-i Havadis, Vakit*), and Armeno-Turkish (*Manzume-i Efkâr*) is most probably a Greek, since he answers automatically in Greek when he says *"Oriste!"* and *"Malista!"* The buyer speaks mostly French, but also Turkish, when he addresses the newspaper seller with the Turkish term *gazeteci*. This scene illustrates the linguistic diversity that characterized everyday life in the capital (and many other cities) of the Ottoman Empire. The mixing of several languages was also practiced often by the vendors themselves. Alka Nestoroff's letters from 1907 refer to an itinerant yogurt seller yelling *"Jaurt, jaurt, freski jaurt!"*[53] and an offal seller shouting *"Linguo cervello, cervello linguo!"*[54] She noted that combining different dialects and foreign expressions together in their shouts and having a special jargon was specific to street vendors.[55] In other words, street vendors' sonic presence in urban spaces complemented Ottoman multilingualism with their selling cries.

Previous research on "Ottoman cosmopolitanism" has focused largely on the bourgeoisie of the port cities, and their liberal and multicultural ideals.[56] Scholarship on multilingual and multicommunal links in urban centers and dynamic interaction between different ethnic, religious, and regional groups has also stressed the development of an "Ottoman identity" beyond particularities. These works focus on how a multilingual press and civil society facilitated the exchange of ideas, expectations, and political demands among the urban middle classes.[57] More recently, "cosmopolitanism" has been used more cautiously due to its bias towards elite interactions between different ethnic and religious communities and its disregard for conflict.[58] Works on "conviviality" stress heterogeneous and interacting communities beyond the middle classes that have complex, contextualized, and variable relationships with their neighbors.[59] The cries of street vendors also invite us to reconsider the multilingualism of the Ottoman peoples beyond the bourgeoisie and attest that urban inhabitants of lower and migrant classes also embodied this multilingualism.[60]

Encounter 3: Humans and Animals

The *boza* seller, Mevlut, in Orhan Pamuk's *A Strangeness in My Mind* (Kafamda Bir Tuhaflık, 2014) wanders "the poor and neglected cobblestone streets" by night, selling his *boza* from door to door. His selling cry— "*booozaaaa,*" "*İiiyiii booozaaaa . . .*"—usually arouses stray animals, also on the streets, and barking dogs circulate along with his *boza* shouts. The packs of dogs that follow him in the darkness of the city usually appear to him as a menace and a threat. Mevlut thinks they can sense his fear and so might attack him. He is convinced that "street dogs watched him at night from cemeteries and empty lots."[61] The *boza* seller's story not only brings into light non-human mobility and sonority in urban streets, but also highlights the contrast between the perception of sounds during the day and the night.

Thus the third encounter emphasized through the sonic practices of street vendors is the intermingling of human and non-human animal sounds in urban space. Sounds expose dualistic conceptions that divide "us" from "them." Dichotomies such as rural versus urban, Oriental versus European, native versus foreign, colony versus empire, and human versus non-human became especially exaggerated in listening practices. Sounds of animals are often heard (and listened to) with reference to loudness/noise against silence, implying an essential difference between humans and nonhumans.[62] The circulation of street vendors within urban spaces often coincided with the circulation of thousands of stray dogs and cats, newly introduced horse-pulled trams after the 1870s, and crowds of pigeons in mosque courtyards, squares, and other open spaces. The sonic presence of itinerant sellers, in that sense, often intermingled in urban space with animal sounds.

First of all, it was common for certain itinerant sellers to have accompanying animals, specifically donkeys and horses. In the album, the bread vendor (Figure 2.6) and *ipekçi* (silk product seller) have donkeys, while the water carrier (Figure 2.7) and garbage collector have horses. As such, their everyday sonic practices were intimately coupled with their animals' noises. According to the memoirs of Mıntzuri, a Macedonian vegetable seller, Lazo Curo, would always appear in the central marketplace of Beşiktaş with the loud sounds of his horses as if a caravan was approaching: "*Cangıl, dungıl, dangıl, dungul.*"[63]

As might be expected, an itinerant seller with an animal was perceived as a pair, and the inhabitants of neighborhoods would recognize and have a connection with them both. In his *Ancient Customs and Rituals*, Abdülaziz Bey mentions a pudding seller, Mehmet Ağa, who made his donkey a part of his

Figure 2.6 "Bread vender—Ekmekdji [*ekmekçi*]." "İstanbul'un sokak satıcıları—Street vendors of Istanbul" album, Salt Research, Photographs and Postcards Archive, https://archives.saltresearch.org/handle/123456789/195592. Reproduced with permission.

famous performance. Apparently, Mehmet Ağa had several poems, based on his complaints about his donkey. He would accept money to recite these poems, which children eagerly listened to, such as the following:

> Let me talk about my donkey / I don't know what I will do / Give it to him and I'll go / That's the kind of donkey I have

> My donkey is reluctant / Sometimes naughty / Throws his saddle and blows like the north wind / That's the kind of donkey I have.[64]

Moreover, stray animals often followed itinerant sellers, depending on the attractiveness of the product. Albanians who typically sold sheep's brains and feet were especially popular for cats, as noted in many accounts and depicted on postcards (Figure 2.8). As stressed by innumerable accounts (including Pamuk and his *boza* seller), however, thousands of stray dogs figured most

Figure 2.7 "Water carrier—Haidé soodji [*hayde sucu*]." "İstanbul'un sokak satıcıları—Street vendors of Istanbul" album, Salt Research, Photographs and Postcards Archive, https://archives.saltresearch.org/handle/123456789/195592. Reproduced with permission.

prominently in the soundscape of Ottoman cities. Dr. A. Neale claimed in 1806 that there were 10,000 of them in the city, while Albert Smith raised the number to 80,000 in 1852 (Figure 2.9).[65] Along with cats and birds, dogs were fed by the inhabitants of the city, who gave them food and water. Urban spaces were literally occupied by dogs, lying and sleeping in the middle of a street, in search of the kindness of strangers who would feed them. Even though they were targets of random human cruelty and state-ordered extermination, the dogs were mostly considered useful by the inhabitants, since they served as street sweepers and natural composters to collect the garbage and leftovers of households.[66]

The neighborhoods of the city were owned by different gangs of dogs, each with its own district. They would attack or expel strange animals coming from other neighborhoods, as trespassers on their own territory. Mıntzuri noted that "if a dog from the neighborhood of Kılıçali appears in the neighborhood of Paşa, all the dogs of the neighborhood would

Figure 2.8 "Souvenir of Salonica—Itinerant dealer," Postcard of an offal seller with a cat, Cats Museum in Kotor, Montenegro. Reproduced with permission.

Figure 2.9 "Group of dogs in the Grande Rue de Péra [İstiklal Caddesi], Salt Research, Photographs and Postcards Archive, https://archives.saltresearch.org/handle/123456789/99487. Reproduced with permission.

rise and bark." People's ears would be assaulted by the barks of dogs and they would shout angrily, "*Bre sus!*" ("Shut up!").[67] Since the dogs had divided the city into districts, each controlled by one pack under a leader, they were responsive to strangers and would warn the neighborhood of intruders. Therefore, they were also considered as aides to the guards and nightwatchmen. They were assumed to "guard the houses and streets at night."[68]

The sonic relationship between street vendors and animals was further intensified by the fact that criticisms of barking dogs and sellers' cries were often coupled with discussions about urban noise. The visibility and voices/ noises of stray animals, as well as itinerant sellers, appear as a nuisance in a number of late nineteenth- and early twentieth-century accounts.[69] Meftun Bey, for instance, the main character in the novel *Şıpsevdi* (Emophilia,1911) by Hüseyin Rahmi Gürpınar, was an overly Westernized caricature, who would constantly complain about "the beating of the stick of the *mahalle* nightwatchman in the streets at night; dogs barking; the sounds of *boza* sellers following close on each other's heels."[70] In an article that appeared in *Servet-i Fünun* (*Wealth of Sciences*), the famous literary and scientific magazine of the period, introducing Julia Barnett Rice's "The Society for the Suppression of Unnecessary Noise" (1906), the author listed the unbearable sounds in Istanbul. He stressed that many itinerant merchants were harassing people "by shouting as much as they can" ("*sesleri çıktığı kadar bağırarak*"), just to earn a little bit of money; cartwrights were hanging rattles around the neck of their horses; the bells and horns of the trams were constantly making noise; and the whistles of the steamers were used gratuitously.[71]

Servet-i Fünun's Rice piece should be seen in light of the global circulation of knowledge and scientific discussion on the noise of modern cities. The Ottoman public was also following developments on the subject. Despite the emergence of an awareness of the side-effects of noise, Ottoman municipal regulations did not entail relevant regulations, as shown by documents and complaints in the Ottoman archives.[72] Nineteenth-century criticism of street sellers was mostly concentrated on the smell and dirtiness (*koku ile pislik*) caused by rotten fruits and vegetables that food sellers threw away here and there.[73] The main concern of the city administrators was not the noise, but sanitary order, hygiene, and the prevention of diseases. The street vendors were often accused of selling non-sanitary food and drinks.[74] The other frequently raised concern about the omnipresence of street sellers in the city was their abundance (*kesret*)—just like stray animals—such that they were accused of blocking the pedestrian traffic even in large avenues.[75]

Noise legislation also reveals a great deal about the changing sounds of modernity. Which sounds were considered noise? Which sounds, on the other hand, were desirable, and according to whom? In the case of Istanbul, anti-noise regulations were established only after the 1930s, prohibiting, along with other things, the street vendors' cries. However, to what extent these laws were enforced in Turkey remains unclear.

Encounter 4: The Audibility of Gender

The great novelist Yaşar Kemal (1923–2015) made a series of journalistic interviews with poor, migrant street children in 1975 for the daily newspaper *Cumhuriyet*. The only girl that he interviewed was Zilo, the twelve-year-old daughter of a Kurdish migrant porter, who left home to escape her stepmother's cruelty. Sleeping in empty lots, parks, and sometimes her aunt's cellar, she started selling bird food in the courtyard of Yeni Cami (New Mosque). The passersby would buy fodder to throw to the birds of the mosque as a good deed.[76] Kemal thought this tiny girl had a velvet voice, the voice of a woman's warmth and affability. Before long she had "regular customers," and men would sit on the stairs of the mosque, stare at her, and sigh longingly from morning to evening. Due to constant harassment, she decided pickpocketing and collecting scraps were safer. Kemal's writing on Zilo sheds light on the gendered layers of subordination in urban streets and the ways sound became part of those gender dynamics. The audibility of women's voices in the streets was typically curtailed by age, social status, and the dictates of morality.

In a similar manner, gender manifested itself vocally in the cries of street vendors more generally. The album contains only one woman, a broom peddler (*çalı süpürge*). The photograph shows a relatively old woman (Figure 2.10). As will become clearer in this section, Ottoman female itinerant sellers were most likely older women. This was possibly determined by the dictates of urban sexual geography, in which the freedom to roam the streets was a male freedom. For women, however, it was only the lower classes and older women who could have a public presence without concerns about honor and shame. There were other common products peddled predominantly by women, such as fabrics (*bohça*), handkerchiefs (*mendil*), lace products

Figure 2.10 "Broom pedlar—Tchalu supurge [*çalı süpürgesi*]." "İstanbul'un sokak satıcıları—Street vendors of Istanbul" album, Salt Research, Photographs and Postcards Archive, https://archives.saltresearch.org/handle/123456789/195 592. Reproduced with permission.

(*ipek*), and flowers. These women, who also acted as matchmakers, were often invited into the houses to open their bundle and show the variety of their wares.[77]

Among the itinerant vendors that visited his neighborhood in the Golden Horn, Eskenazi lists only one female, the boiled corn vendor, an old woman. In contrast to those who came in the morning to sell daily necessities (such as the fishmonger or the fruit vendor), she would come in the afternoon about teatime, to sell a "luxury" with a "subdued call." It is interesting that he depicts the sound of this woman seller as "subdued," as opposed to other more "acute sounds" or "characteristic and colorful cries," such as "the shriek of the Albanian who sold sheep's brains and feet," or the "deep-voiced call of the peasant who sold yoghurt," or the "raucous call issued from the parched throat of a robust Kurd" selling melons.[78] Why was the corn seller's shout heard as "subdued," as opposed to male cries defined as a "shriek" or a "deep-voiced call"? Was it because she was old? Or was it simply because she was a woman?

In Abdülaziz Bey's *Ancient Customs and Ceremonies*, he refers to a specific group of female street vendors, selling stuffed wine or cabbage leaves (*yaprak dolma, lahana dolma*), a certain sweet made with sesame (*susam*), and tea biscuits (*kurabiye*).[79] These were older black women, former slaves manumitted through marriage or old age, yet impoverished by the passing of their spouses or masters. They lived in difficult circumstances in bachelor rooms in Arasta (Eminönü), Salmatomruk, Karagümrük, and Çukurbostan (Fatih).[80] They strived to make a living by making and selling *dolma* or *susam*. These women wore a chador, tying an outer belt in their waist. They would have a headscarf wrapped around their necks, and would tie a colored kerchief (*yemeni*) called *kaşbastı* under and over it. They would then carry the basket of *susam* in their hands and the *dolma* pot on their heads and go out into the street.

For their *dolma* business, they would choose areas where many artisans and bachelors frequented, such as the gates of the Grand Bazaar, especially the bazaar door on the "Kaşıkçılar" side of Bayezid Mosque. They would put the *dolma* pot on a stool they brought with them, sit next to it, and solemnly wait for customers without making any particular sound. In order to sell *susam*, on the other hand, they had a different sonic strategy. They would go to the women's side of bathhouses in the Bazaar area or to houses where they had heard that weddings were taking place. As the following example shows, their interaction with women customers was completely different. They would act in a more informal, witty, and intimate manner. They used to make jokes to attract the attention of women and children:

"Hey, I sold *susam* to your mother as well, did you forget the nanny (*dadı kadın*)?"
"Come on, nanny has brought *susam*."[81]

Street selling practices also facilitated public or semi-public encounters between (selling) men and (buying) women. Mıntzuri's memoirs give a number of examples as to how male vendors interacted with their female customers. These scenes often contain eroticizing tropes, exaggerating the aspect of desire in the interaction, but nevertheless give some sense of the ways sound mediated these interactions. Non-Muslim women they encountered did not hesitate to open the doors or converse with the sellers.[82] Eskenazi also noted that after "the sharp cry" of the fishmonger ("*balık*"), the Jewish housewives in their neighborhood "would rush to their windows and a colorful exchange of scurrilous wit would ensue during their bargaining."[83] Due to the rules of seclusion, the business with Muslim households or Muslim neighborhoods were different. Itinerant merchants carried out their transactions from outside in the street. They would shout their selling cries at the door. If there was a man or a boy in the house, they would come out. If not, then women would do the shopping. The main customers of street vendors in residential areas were mostly women. Hagop's friend Yusuf, the broom peddler, would always "listen to the female voices coming from beyond latticed windows." Sometimes a door would open slightly and he would hear the voice of a woman, who was hiding and careful not to be seen. When she called him, "Broom peddler, come!" he would run to the door. As a norm, women would interact with the vendors from behind doors and windows without being seen. Mıntzuri tried to guess the identity of the woman with whom he was interacting by her voice. Was she young, middle-aged, or old? Was she white or black? Was she a female slave (*halayık*) or an adopted girl (*besleme*)? However, in some households, women did not even speak in an audible voice ("*duyulabilecek tonda konuşmazlar*"). It seemed to him that they were even hiding their voices ("*seslerini bile gizlerlerdi*"). Their light whispers made it difficult to understand if they wanted two, three, or four loaves of bread.[84]

As part of the discussion of the audibility of gender within Ottoman soundscapes, one also comes across frequent references to the voices of eunuchs. They were at times referred to as "infantile," and at other times as reflective of the "gentility of their manners," as "insinuating, clear, and sonorous,"[85] and at yet other times as "hoarse."[86] When referring to "the infantile voices of the eunuchs" in his description of the Babel of the Galata Bridge (as quoted above), de Amicis was also underlining the audibility of gender more generally in the streets of Istanbul.[87] Reserving an entire section of his book for the eunuchs, de Amicis claimed that these mutilated men, "belonging to neither sex," were to be seen in every corner of Istanbul. Encounters with them, as an audible experience, were perceived as a disturbing realization of the gendered regime of slavery in the empire:

> These unfortunates are to be met at every street-corner, just as they are encountered on every page of history. . . . And the same way in Constantinople: in the midst of a crowded bazaar, among the throng of pleasure-seekers at the Sweet Waters, beneath the columns of the mosques, beside the carriages, on the steamboats, in kaiks [boats], at all the festivals, wherever people are assembled together, one sees these phantoms of men,

these melancholy countenances like a dark shadow thrown across every aspect of gay Oriental life.[88]

These observations by de Amicis, while crude and reductive in many ways, point to the complex, intersectional bodies and identities that could be heard and seen throughout Istanbul as crucial pieces of the economies of empire.

Conclusion

All traces of the past are transient in a certain way, and sounds maybe even more so. Past sounds and the experiences that individuals have had with them have naturally disappeared. Still, auditory historians try to reconstruct past sonospheres and listening experiences from essentially silent sources. The effort to listen to Ottoman soundscapes requires the mediation of contemporary observers. This chapter on the sonic practices of street vending relies on a rare audiovisual album with notated cries of street vendors. The History Foundation (*Tarih Vakfı*) in Turkey published the album as a small booklet for the January 2018 (no. 289) issue of *Toplumsal Tarih* (Social History) with the support of Irvin Cemil Schick. The Foundation also commissioned a YouTube video of the album, where notated vendors' cries are vocalized by Hami Ünlü, Yasemin Göksu, and Aydan Çelik.[89] It is interesting that this multimedia album almost demands a medium like YouTube—created more than a century later—both to document its visual and sonic dimensions and to allow it to circulate beyond the place/time it was created.

In this chapter, I have drawn on literary descriptions of the street vendors' sonic practices—rich accounts of both Europeans and locals contained in archives, letters, memoirs, travel writing, and ethnographic collections—analyzing different listening habits and subjectivities defined by cultural differences. On the one hand, the *peaceful sound* of the *ezan*, the *melancholic silence* of the Golden Horn, the *wild barking* of the dogs, and the *joyful cries* of the street vendors have all been typical Orientalist stereotypes to describe the soundscape of Istanbul. Further listening, on the other hand, complicates the picture. Listening to the sounds of itinerant vendors brings into focus a range of social encounters, highlighting histories of urban-rural migration, a multilingual street life, human-animal relations, and the selling cries of women vendors. The sonic traces of street vendors' presences—as evidenced by nineteenth-century accounts as well as novels, films, and other media from the twentieth-century, and even YouTube videos today—gesture toward histories of the empire and intra-imperial difference, offering an affective reminder of the cultural, political, and economic relations of Istanbul's past.

Notes

This work was supported by the research project: Ottoman *Auralities and the Eastern Mediterranean: Sound, Media and Power, 1789–1922*, selected as a European Research Council Starting Grant, funded by UK Research and Innovation (EP/X032833/1).

1. Sait Faik Abasıyanık, "Ketenhelvacı," in *Tüneldeki Çocuk* (Istanbul: Yapı Kredi Yayınları, 2016), 7–11.
2. Ibid., 7: "*Ketenhelvacı bir masal mahlukudur. O da göçüp gittikten sonra belki ketenhelvacıların nesli tükenecek.*"
3. Ibid., 8: For example, "*Fakirin halinden anlar fakir. / Benden ketenhelvası alan hanım, çakır. / Kapıdan bir tane daha çıkarsa / Kara gözlüm / Kutum kalacak tamtakır.*" And shortly thereafter: "*Kimseler bilmedi. / Gözüm yaşım silmedi. / Oğlum sekiz, torunum yedi. / Ben kazandım o yedi. / Vay ne güzel ketenhelvam!*"
4. Ibid., 11: "*Kaldım bir kemik bir deri, / Volta vurdum mahalleleri.*"
5. Ana María Ochoa Gautier, *Aurality: Listening and Knowledge in Nineteenth-Century Colombia* (Durham, NC: Duke University Press, 2015), 75; Gavin Steingo and Jim Sykes, "Introduction: Remapping Sound Studies in the Global South," in *Remapping Sound Studies*, ed. Gavin Steingo and Jim Sykes (Durham, NC: Duke University Press, 2019), 21.
6. Steven Connor, "Rustications: Animals in the Urban Mix," in *The Acoustic City*, ed. Matthew Gandy and B. J. Nilsen (Berlin: Jovis, 2014), 16–22; Ochoa Gautier, *Aurality*, 33, 63, 74; Alejandra M. Bronfman, *Isles of Noise: Sonic Media in the Caribbean* (Chapel Hill: University of North Carolina Press, 2016), 6; Steingo and Sykes, "Introduction," 17.
7. Emily Thompson, *The Soundscape of Modernity: Architectural Acoustics and the Culture of Listening in America, 1900–1933* (Cambridge: MIT Press, 2004), 132.
8. John M. Picker, *Victorian Soundscapes* (Oxford, UK: Oxford University Press, 2003); John M. Picker, "Soundscape(s): The Turning of the Word," in *The Routledge Companion to Sound Studies*, ed. Michael Bull (London: Routledge, 2018), 147–155.
9. Adam Mestyan, "Upgrade?: Power and Sound during Ramadan and 'Id al-Fitr in the Nineteenth-Century Ottoman Arab Provinces," *Comparative Studies of South Asia, Africa and the Middle East*, 37/2 (2017), 262–279; Adam Mestyan, "Sound, Military Music, and Opera in Egypt during the Rule of Mehmet Ali Pasha (r. 1805–1848)," in *Ottoman Empire and European Theatre*, vol. 2, *The Time of Joseph Haydn: From Sultan Mahmud I to Mahmud II (r. 1730–1839)*, ed. Michael Hüttler and Hans Ernst Weidinger (Vienna: Hollitzer, 2014), 539–564; Nina Ergin, "Ottoman Royal Women's Spaces: The Acoustic Dimension," *Journal of Women's History* 26/1 (2014), 89–111.

10. For a similar discussion, see Richard Cullen Rath, *How Early America Sounded* (Ithaca, NY: Cornell University Press, 2005).

11. Alain Corbin, *Les cloches de la terre: Paysage sonore et culture sensible dans les campagnes au XIXe siécle* (Paris: Albin Michel, 1994).

12. Nancy Rose Hunt, "An Acoustic Register: Rape and Repetition in Congo," in *Imperial Debris: On Ruins and Ruination*, ed. Ann Laura Stoler (Durham, NC: Duke University Press, 2013), 39–66.

13. Ziad Fahmy, *Street Sounds: Listening to Everyday Life in Modern Egypt* (Stanford, CA: Stanford University Press, 2020); Ziad Fahmy, "Coming to our Senses: Historicizing Sound and Noise in the Middle East," *History Compass* 11/4 (2013), 305–315; Ziad Fahmy, "An Earwitness to History: Street Hawkers and Their Calls in Early 20th-Century Egypt," *International Journal of Middle East Studies* 48/1 (2016), 129–134; see also Chapter 3 in this volume.

14. Recently, a copy of the album has been added to the online collection of SALT Research Archives, https://archives.saltresearch.org/handle/123456789/195592, accessed February 1, 2023.

15. Such albums were prepared as early as the early modern era by European diplomats to the Ottoman court. Famous examples include the Ralamb, Luyken, and Brindesi albums. During the nineteenth century, the Ottoman sultans started to officially sponsor and produce them. During the reign of Sultan Abdülaziz, photographs comprised an integral part of the Turkish pavilions at the 1867 (Paris) and 1873 (Vienna) World Expositions, for which albums of Ottoman "ethnicities" and costumes were produced. Abdülhamid II's photographic albums followed the same tradition. Ayshe Erdoğdu, "The Victorian Market for Ottoman Types," *History of Photography* 23/3 (1999), 269–273; Wendy M. K. Shaw, "Ottoman Photography of the Late Nineteenth Century: An 'Innocent' Modernism?" *History of Photography*, 33/1 (2009), 80–93.

16. On the collector, see note 89. A contemporary example that seeks to capture the sound of Istanbul was Fatih Akın's *Crossing the Bridge: The Sound of Istanbul*, which had strong orientalist tropes as well. See Nazan Maksudyan, "Bir, İki, Üç, Kaç İstanbul? Fantazi, Nostalji, Ütopya," in *Bir Kapıdan Gireceksin: Türkiye Sineması Üzerine Denemeler*, ed. Umut Tümay Arslan (Istanbul: Metis, 2012), 159–166.

17. Stefan Helmreich, "Transduction," in *Keywords in Sound*, ed. David Novak and Matt Sakakeeny (Durham, NC: Duke University Press, 2015), 222–231.

18. David Gramit, "Orientalism and the Lied: Schubert's 'Du liebst mich nicht,'" *19th-Century Music* 27/2 (2003), 97–115; Edward W. Said, *Culture and Imperialism* (London: Chatto and Windus, 1993), 134–157; Paul Robinson, "Is Aida an Orientalist Opera?" *Cambridge Opera Journal* 5/2 (1993), 133–140; Edward W. Said, *Musical Elaborations* (New York: Columbia University Press, 1991); Ralph P. Locke, "Cutthroats and Casbah Dancers, Muezzins and Timeless Sands: Musical Images of the Middle East," *19th-Century Music* 22/1 (1998), 20–53.

19. Dozens of its kind were produced especially for the metropolitan cities of London and Paris in the early modern era. For further information, see Karen F. Beall, *Cries and Itinerant Trades: A Bibliography/Kaufrufe und Straßenhändler. Eine Bibliographie* (Hamburg: Ernst Hauswedell, 1975).

20. Ali Behdad notes the importance of "the Orient" in the development of photography as a new form of representation. Ali Behdad, *Camera Orientalis: Reflections on Photography of the Middle East* (Chicago: University of Chicago Press, 2016).

21. Here one should note that Orientalist photography was not a production solely of Europeans, but was a new mode of representation produced through cultural encounters. Behdad, *Camera Orientalis*, 7.

22. "*Bu sesle sokaklar yankılandı / Domates, biber, patlıcan.*" For the music video of the song (though not featuring street vendors), see https://youtu.be/mmcy_woJmyM, accessed February 1, 2023.

23. Anon., *Handbook for Travellers in Constantinople: The Bosphorus, Dardanelles, Brousa and Plain of Troy* (London: John Murray, 1871), 66.

24. Victor Eskenazi, *Beyond Constantinople: The Memoirs of an Ottoman Jew* (London: I. B. Tauris, 2016), 11.

25. Ibid., 13.

26. Ibid., 14.

27. Cem Behar, *A Neighborhood in Ottoman Istanbul: Fruit Vendors and Civil Servants in the Kasap İlyas Mahalle* (Albany: State University of New York Press, 2003), 43.

28. Hagop Mıntzuri, *İstanbul Anıları (1897–1940)*, trans. Silva Kuyumcuyan (Istanbul: Aras, 2017), 54.

29. Ibid., 31.

30. Ibid., 35.

31. For a short clip of this scene, see https://youtu.be/xPoxw47DoGw (after 1:00), accessed February 1, 2023.

32. Behar, *A Neighborhood in Ottoman Istanbul*, 115.

33. Fariba Zarinebaf, *Mediterranean Encounters: Trade and Pluralism in Early Modern Galata* (Berkeley: University of California Press, 2018), 176–177.

34. Abdülaziz Bey, *Osmanlı Âdet, Merasim ve Tabirleri: Âdât ve Merâsim-i Kadîme, Tabîrât ve Muâmelât-ı Kavmiyye-i Osmâniyye* (Istanbul: Tarih Vakfı Yurt Yayınları, 1995, [1910]), 140.

35. Ibid., 451.

36. Ibid., 453: "*Muhallebim kaymaklıdır / Tabaklarda revnaklıdır / Medhedenler pek haklıdır / Küçük beyler gelin alın / Muhallebim süde şeker, / Paraları cepten çeker / Her nedense medhe değer / Küçük beyler gelin alın . . .*"

37. Mıntzuri, *İstanbul*, 91.

38. Ibid., 128.

39. For a short synopsis of the movie, see https://www.europeanfilmawards.eu/en_EN/film/journey-to-the-sun.5517, accessed February 1, 2023.

40. Johann Strauss, "Linguistic Diversity and Everyday Life in the Ottoman Cities of the Eastern Mediterranean and the Balkans (Late 19th–Early 20th century)," *The History of the Family*, 16/2 (2011), 126–141.

41. Ibid. While Strauss notes that Ottoman cities were often a Babel of different tongues and dialects, the number of languages spoken was limited in number, changing according to geography. In the capital, the main languages were Turkish, French, Greek, Armenian, and Ladino. In the Arab provinces, Arabic was the dominant language in nearly all cities.

42. Mark Mazower, "Salonica between East and West, 1860–1912," *Dialogos: Hellenic Studies Review* 1 (1994), 104–127; Mark Mazower, *Salonica: City of Ghosts* (London: Harper Collins, 2004).

43. Jouko Lindstedt, "Multilingualism in the Central Balkans in late Ottoman times," in *In Search of the Center and Periphery: Linguistic Attitudes, Minorities, and Landscapes in the Central Balkans*, ed. Maxim Makartsev and Max Wahlström (Helsinki: Helsingin yliopisto, Nykykielten laitos, 2016), 51–67; Sibel Zandi-Sayek, *Ottoman Izmir: The Rise of a Cosmopolitan Port, 1840–1880* (Minneapolis: University of Minnesota Press, 2012).

44. Edmondo de Amicis, *Constantinople*, vol. 1, trans. Maria Hornor Lansdale (New York: Merrill and Baker, 1896 [1877]), 49.

45. Ibid., 55. Emphasis added.

46. Eskenazi, *Beyond Constantinople*, 11.

47. Ibid., 12–13.

48. "I also didn't understand what he said. Yes, '*bakkal*' [meaning 'groceries'], but what did '*o*' and '*isirte*' mean? To whom was he shouting; what was he selling? Doors also remained closed and there was no one on the streets. I used to ask him, but he wouldn't answer; he kept walking and cried out in such a way I thought he was crying. Much later I noticed he was calling out to the houses. Like him, the Greek women of the Paşa neighborhood [*mahalle*] didn't know Turkish." Mıntzuri, *İstanbul*, 89.

49. This is actually a cry in the Turkish language, meaning "Anybody want water?" ("*Var mı su?*").

50. This word is not transliterated correctly; it is more meaningful as sherbet (*şerbet*), which was a sweetened fruit juice.

51. de Amicis, *Constantinople*, 89.

52. Recaizade Mahmud Ekrem, *Araba Sevdası* (Istanbul: İnkılâp, 1985), 110. Cited in Strauss, "Linguistic Diversity and Everyday Life," 126–127.

53. A corruption of the Italian word *fresco* (fresh).

54. Corruptions of the Italian words *lingua* (tongue), and *cervello* (brain).

55. Klara Volarić, ed., *The Istanbul Letters of Alka Nestoroff* (Bonn: Max Weber Stiftung, 2015), 35.

56. Edhem Eldem, Daniel Goffman, and Bruce Masters, *The Ottoman City between East and West: Aleppo, Izmir, and Istanbul* (Cambridge, UK: Cambridge University Press, 1999); Marc Baer, "Globalization, Cosmopolitanism, and the Dönme in Ottoman Salonica and Turkish Istanbul," *Journal of World History* 18/2 (2007), 141–170.

57. Michelle U. Campos, *Ottoman Brothers: Muslims, Christians, and Jews in Early Twentieth-Century Palestine* (Stanford, CA: Stanford University Press, 2010). See also Julia Phillips Cohen, *Becoming Ottomans: Sephardi Jews and Imperial Citizenship in the Modern Era* (Oxford, UK: Oxford University Press, 2014; Vangelis Constantinos Kechriotis, "The Greeks of Izmir at the End of the Empire: A Non-Muslim Ottoman Community between Autonomy and Patriotism" (PhD dissertation, Leiden University, 2005); Bedross Der Matossian, *Shattered Dreams of Revolution: From Liberty to Violence in the Late Ottoman Empire* (Stanford, CA: Stanford University Press, 2014).

58. Will Hanley, "Grieving Cosmopolitanism in Middle East Studies," *History Compass* 6/ 5 (2008), 1346–1367; Ulrike Freitag and Nora Lafi, eds., *Urban Governance under the Ottomans: Between Cosmopolitanism and Conflict* (London: Routledge, 2014).

59. Ulrike Freitag, "'Cosmopolitanism' and 'Conviviality'? Some Conceptual Considerations Concerning the Late Ottoman Empire," *European Journal of Cultural Studies*, 17/4 (2014), 375–391; Nora Lessersohn, "'Provincial Cosmopolitanism' in Late Ottoman Anatolia: An Armenian Shoemaker's Memoir," *Comparative Studies in Society and History* 57/2 (2015), 528–556.

60. Edhem Eldem has noted that prostitutes, petty criminals, and barkeepers were highly mobile and carriers of cosmopolitanism. Edhem Eldem, "The Undesirables of Smyrna, 1926," *Mediterranean Historical Review* 24/2 (2009), 223–227. Malte Fuhrmann has also written about the presence of lower migrant classes in Ottoman port cities and the emergence of a particular type of sociability and public sphere in taverns and pubs. Malte Fuhrmann, "Down and Out on the Quays of Izmir: 'European' Musicians, Innkeepers, and Prostitutes in the Ottoman Port-Cities," *Mediterranean Historical Review* 24/2 (2009), 169–185.

61. "*Geceleri sokak köpeklerinin mezarlıklardan, boş arsalardan kendisini sandığından daha da çok seyrettiklerini de yazıyı okurken anlamıştı.*" Orhan Pamuk, *Kafamda Bir Tuhaflık* (Istanbul: Yapı Kredi Yayınları, 2014), 80.

62. Ochoa Gautier, *Aurality*, 74.

63. Mıntzuri, *İstanbul*, 31.

64. Abdülaziz Bey, *Osmanlı Âdet*, 454: "*Eşeğimden bahsedeyim / Bilmem elinden nideyim / Ona verin de gideyim / Böyle benim eşeğim var. / Eşeğim bana nazlanır / Bazı defa haylazlanır / Semer atar poyrazlanır / Böyle benim eşeğim var.*"

65. Albert Smith, *A Month in Constantinople* (Boston: Bradbury & Guild, 1852), 64.

66. For more on Istanbul's stray dogs, see Cihangir Gündoğdu, "The State and the Stray Dogs in Late Ottoman Istanbul: From Unruly Subjects to Servile Friends," *Middle Eastern Studies* 54/4 (2018), 555–574; Irvin Cemil Schick, "İstanbul'da 1910'da Gerçekleşen Büyük Köpek İtlâfı: Bir Mekân Üzerinde Çekişme Vakası," *Toplumsal Tarih* 200 (2010), 22–33.

67. Mıntzuri, *İstanbul*, 74.

68. Anon., *Handbook for Travellers in Constantinople*, 117.

69. For a European account, see Smith, *A Month in Constantinople*, 64: "*The yelping, howling, barking, growling, and snarling, were all merged into one uniform and continuous even sound, as the noise of frogs becomes when heard at a distance. For hours there was no lull. I went to sleep, and woke again; and still, with my windows open, I heard the same tumult going on: nor was it until day-break that anything like tranquility was restored.*" Emphasis added.

70. Hüseyin Rahmi Gürpınar, *Şıpsevdi* (Istanbul: Everest Yayınları, 2015 [1911]), 67.

71. Anon., "Madam Rays ve Sokak Gürültüleri," *Servet-i Fünun* 33/851, August 15, 1907.

72. A series of documents focuses mostly on the prohibition against using church bells. Ottoman Christians were only allowed to use the *semantron*, a wooden board pounded by a wooden hammer. Prime Ministry's Ottoman Archives (Başbakanlık Osmanlı Arşivi, hereafter BOA), HR.MKT., 132/57, 12.01.1856; BOA, C.ADL., 66/ 3952, 04.09.1868; BOA, DH.TMIK.M., 43/57, 20.11.1897.

73. BOA, A.MKT.MHM., 189/99, 31.07.1860; BOA, DH. MKT., 2006/6, 28.09.1892.

74. BOA, DH. MKT., 732/38, 04.07.1903.

75. BOA, A.MKT.NZD., 310/23, 04.04.1860; BOA, A.MKT.MHM., 450/100, 28.03.1873; BOA, DH. MKT., 2659/27, 16.11.1908.

76. "*Zilo, Polisi Kırk Günlük Yoldan Görse Hemen Tanıyıverir Bu Allah Vergisidir . . .*," *Cumhuriyet*, September 23, 1975.

77. Abdülaziz Bey, *Osmanlı Âdet*, 106.

78. Eskenazi, *Beyond Constantinople*, 10–11.

79. Abdülaziz Bey, *Osmanlı Âdet*, 321.

80. Ibid., 321, 371.

81. Abdülaziz Bey, *Osmanlı Âdet*, 321: "*Hu, ben senin anana da susam sardım, dadı kadını unuttun mu? Haydi bakalım mam dadı susam getirdi.*"

82. Mıntzuri, *İstanbul*, 45.

83. Eskenazi, *Beyond Constantinople*, 10.

84. Mıntzuri, *İstanbul*, 45–46.

85. Jane Hathaway, *The Chief Eunuch of the Ottoman Harem: From African Slave to Power-Broker* (Cambridge, UK: Cambridge University Press, 2018), 152.

86. Hathaway cites Sir Richard Francis Burton's claim that Beshir Agha's "hoarse voice inspired awe and respect, thus contributing to an authoritative aura." Jane Hathaway, *Beshir Agha: Chief Eunuch of the Ottoman Imperial Harem* (New York: Oneworld Publications, 2012), 21.

87. de Amicis, *Constantinople*, 55.

88. Ibid., 181–182.

89. https://youtu.be/JE2RK0VuQE0, accessed February 1, 2023. Based on a recent discovery by Els Curry, student at the Faculty of Music at the University of Cambridge, there is another copy of the album at the Skilliter Centre for Ottoman Studies, Newnham College, Cambridge. The archival box containing the album was donated by Amanda Beart and includes letters of the family, photographs, and postcards. According to the Skilliter collection, including a family history by Beart, the albums were originally made by an Alfred W. Sellars (great uncle of the donor). The Sellars family was connected to Robert College and had long resided in the Bebek area. According to a 1950 article, "Alfred Sellars of Bebek, Istanbul" was still a resident of the city in 1934–1935 and took photographs of the Hagia Sophia after a storm carried away the conical roofs of the two eastern minarets. See William Emerson and Robert L. van Nice, "Hagia Sophia and the First Minaret Erected after the Conquest of Constantinople," *American Journal of Archaeology* 54/1 (1950), 28–40, at 31. Beart's book and other objects in the archival box state that a copy of the album had been given to a "local museum in Bebek." I assume this copy was part of the Robert College Museum and later found its way into Edward S. Sheiry's estate, and then passed to Rezan Benatar.

3

Listening to Infrastructure

Traffic Noise and Classism in Modern Egypt

Ziad Fahmy

Let's walk together through a great modern capital, with the ear
more attentive than the eye, and we will vary the pleasures of our
sensibilities by distinguishing among the gurglings of water, air and
gas inside metallic pipes, the rumblings and rattlings of engines
breathing with obvious animal spirits, the rising and falling of
pistons, the stridency of mechanical saws, the loud jumping of
trolleys on their rails, the snapping of whips, the whipping of flags.
We will have fun imagining our orchestration of department stores'
sliding doors, the hubbub of the crowds, the different roars of railroad stations, iron foundries, textile mills, printing houses, power
plants and subways.

—Luigi Russolo, *The Art of Noises* (1913)[1]

In his 1913 manifesto "The Art of Noises" ("*L'Arte dei rumori*"), Luigi
Russolo, an Italian painter and self-proclaimed "futurist," describes the
sonic implications of a modernizing early-twentieth-century city. To
Russolo, the final purpose of his project was to capture and distill the new
modern noises of the city and reuse them to compose and produce music
for his audiences. He in fact invented all kinds of machines and instruments
to approximate and duplicate the everyday clanks, gurgles, and vibrations
of the city. Thus, according to Russolo, the main "characteristic of noise is
to brutally bring us back to life," but his purpose as a futurist artist was to
capture, reconstruct, and combine distillations of these noises to produce
music.[2] To what degree Russolo was successful in his endeavors is of course
outside the scope of this chapter, but what is intriguing and relevant is his
position as a listener and "observer" in a key transitional period in urban
history, where the very perception, feel, sound, appearance, and smell of

Ziad Fahmy, *Listening to Infrastructure* In: *Acoustics of Empire*. Edited by: Peter McMurray and Priyasha Mukhopadhyay,
Oxford University Press. © Oxford University Press 2024. DOI: 10.1093/oso/9780197553787.003.0004

the city were rapidly changing. In writing his manifesto in 1913, Russolo no doubt remembered a time in the near past when the city sounded very differently, and he must have noted the dramatic change that took place in towns and cities in just a couple of decades. This auditory transformation, which Russolo lived through, must have made a tremendous impression not only on him, but on his entire generation. The international press coverage Russolo received and the tremendous success he achieved as a "futurist" artist was, in part, a testament to these changes and to the need to rationalize and explain them.[3]

At the turn of the twentieth century, as Russolo has eloquently described, the sounds of modernity came roaring through, becoming "integral to the phenomenon of modernity itself."[4] These sounds, emanating from a host of new electrical and gasoline- and steam-powered machines, eventually and unevenly transformed the soundscapes of the streets in urban Egypt. The acoustics of wide streets and large squares differed from those of the small alleys of the older, more traditional urban areas, as broader streets allowed for mass congregations of commuters, pedestrians, and merchants. As the streets were converted from packed earth to paved cobblestone and later asphalt, the sounds of animal and wheeled traffic also changed.[5] Newer and wider streets and boulevards allowed for louder wheeled vehicles, from mule- and horse-drawn carts and carriages in the nineteenth century to motorcycles and automobiles in the twentieth century and beyond. Starting in the late 1890s, electric tramways became fully operational, and came to dominate public transportation in Cairo, Alexandria, and Port Said for almost half a century. Soon after, the spread of automobiles, buses, and motorcycles, with their roaring engines, honking horns, and gasoline aromas, sensorially added to the new cacophonies and smells of the city.

This chapter begins by documenting some of the traffic and infrastructural changes taking place in the streets, while broadly surveying the impact this may have had on a wide spectrum of Egyptian society. All the while, I will highlight the changing sounds of city traffic and the resulting hubbub taking place in these new urban spaces. Early in the twentieth century, the sounds of modernity, as fetishized above by futurists like Russolo, were viewed positively as a novel sign of "progress," but as cities became louder, many among the elite and the upwardly mobile middle classes began to complain about the incessant "noise."[6] This was certainly the case in Egypt, as various noise laws began to proliferate by the 1920s and 1930s. As I reveal in this chapter, many of these noise laws were classist, in that they explicitly blamed most noise violators as being lower class, and by association, silencing "noise" meant silencing the poor and the working class. To paraphrase Jennifer Stoever, there was a clear sonic class line generated and continuously articulated in elite and middle-class discourses about Egypt and the Egyptian streets.[7]

Using a sensory approach to examine the streets allows for a more micro-historical examination of everyday people's interactions with each other and helps us evaluate the impact of the various street-level technological and infrastructural manifestations of modern Egyptian life. In the process, the chapter addresses the sensory politics of sound and "noise," and critically examines the intersection of state power with street life as the state attempted to control the sounds of the streets. Just as importantly, it accounts for the growing middle classes as they set out to sensorially differentiate themselves from working-class Egyptians. The first few decades of the twentieth century were marked by increasingly modernist bourgeois sensibilities, calling for quieter streets and advocating for the silencing of working-class street sounds, including traffic noise. At the time, most of Egypt's print media advocated for the de facto civilizational uplift of everyday Egyptians, while lecturing the "loud" urban masses on the necessity of a more "civilized" silence. In fact, as this chapter demonstrates, most discussions about sounds and noise were infused with class anxieties, civilizational shaming, and judgmental dualities concerning changing definitions of taste, class, and modernity.

Carriages, Cars, and Tramways: City Traffic and the Changing Sounds of the Road, 1850s–1940s

> Everything is changed! Alexandria, at present, is filled with carriages—private carriages and hired carriages, which closely resemble our cabs.
>
> —Gabriel Charmes (1883)[8]

In the eighteenth century, wheeled horse- and mule-drawn coaches and carts were almost nonexistent in Egypt. It was not until the mass construction of wider and straighter roads, starting in the mid-nineteenth century, that wheeled vehicles began to proliferate in Egypt's urban streets.[9] As much wider streets were built starting at mid-century and beyond (see Figure 3.1), horse- and mule-drawn coaches and carts became a common sight in Cairo and Alexandria (see Figure 3.1).[10] Horse-drawn cabs were initially used only by wealthy Egyptians and foreigners, becoming more affordable to the middle classes as their numbers increased by the end of the nineteenth century. In the meantime, donkey- and mule-drawn carts, which were also used to transport goods, would become the transport of choice for lower- and lower-middle-class Egyptian men and women.

Later in the century, mule- or horse-drawn omnibuses were introduced in Cairo, Alexandria, and the Canal cities, and they became popular with most Egyptians who could not afford coaches. By 1932, Egyptian roads supported more than 50,000 of these animal-powered carriages. Over two-thirds of these vehicles were used in Cairo and Alexandria alone (see Table 3.1).[11]

It is important to note that these numbers only reflect the vehicles that were registered and licensed by the government. The actual figure was likely much larger.

It is not hard to imagine the sonic implications of these rapid, seismic shifts in transportation technology alone. The proliferation of wheeled animal-drawn vehicles undoubtedly changed the sounds of the streets. The sounds from simple dirt roads were muffled, macadam roads were louder, and cobblestone streets were louder still, producing a more unique clacking/rumbling sound. As asphalt-paved roads became more common in the 1920s, the sounds from carriages and automobiles also changed.[12] Wooden wheeled carts and coaches had unique creaking sounds as they rolled by in the street. These sounds, however, would drastically change depending on the type of road surface they traversed, and on the speed that these vehicles traveled. Also depending on the speed of the vehicles, the sounds of galloping horses or mules added to the din, along with the occasional cracks of the driver's whip.[13] In the early days of private coaches, a *sayis* (usually a boy or a young man) would walk or run ahead of the coach to warn and move pedestrians and other traffic out of the way. According to John Chalcraft, employing a *sayis* was still a standard practice in the 1870s.[14] Also, most of the horses, mules, and donkeys pulling these vehicles had small bells jingling loudly, mainly to alert pedestrians and other vehicles of their presence. When necessary, the cab or cart driver would yell out to warn others of his impending approach and, as I examine in more detail elsewhere, nonverbal vocalizations were common. These included whistling, hissing, tongue and cheek clicking, and in some cases cart drivers beat a stick against their cart, loudly producing drumming sounds to alert pedestrians.[15]

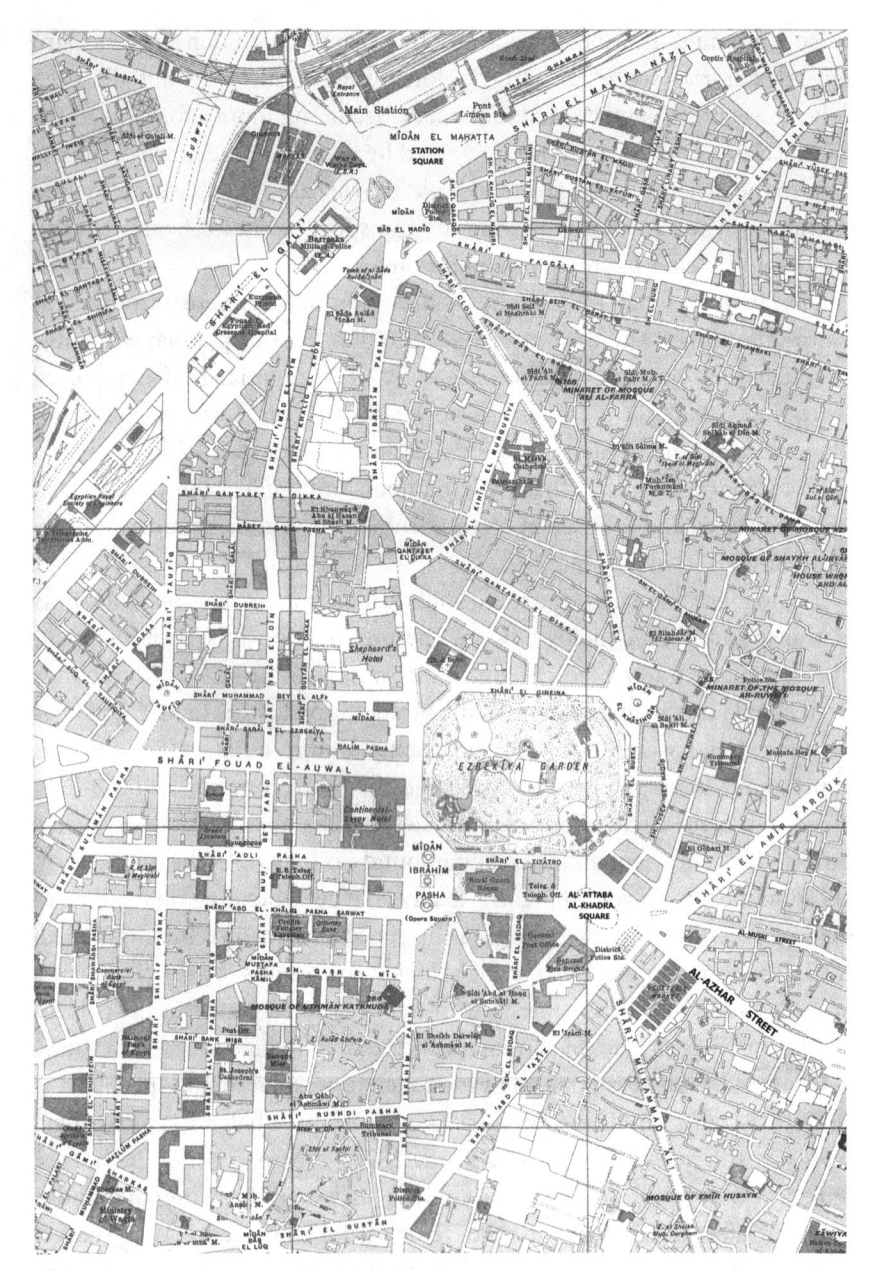

Figure 3.1 Cairo's roads and squares (circa 1947). Adapted from *Maslahit al-Misahah* (Cairo: Survey of Egypt, 1950).

Table 3.1 Licensed animal-drawn vehicles in Egypt.

	Cairo	Alexandria	Total in Egypt
Horse-drawn carriages (cabs)			
1891	-	1,516	-
1916	1,586	2,199	-
1921	1,321	1,666	-
1932	732	1,320	3,332
1936	1,009	1,143	3,826
1947	698	943	3,322
1953	386	747	3,244
Flatbed carts/wagon (*Arabiyyah karro*)			
1891	-	1,935	-
1906	-	3,357	-
1916	11,289	3,038	-
1921	9,000	9,391	-
1932	23,074	13,642	46,566
1936	13,470	10,092	39,222
1947	30,000	4,605	51,619
1953	23,176	5,106	49,056

It is important to note that even before automobiles, the sounds of hundreds of carriages and carts drawn by horses, mules, and donkeys were quite loud and noticeable "keynote" sounds that typify most urban areas.[16] In fact, as Hillel Schwartz has shown, early automobiles were initially "welcomed in the cities as soon as they had rubber tires, with the expectation that they would be quieter than horses clattering and cartwheels rumbling over cobblestone or concrete."[17] The ubiquity and all-immersing sounds of carts and carriages were especially noticeable when for whatever reason this traffic stopped. This was the case in Egypt during the 1919 Revolution, when the majority of the transportation sector in Cairo and Alexandria went on strike. In the spring of 1919, newspaper reporters remarked on how quiet the city had become. This is how a correspondent for the newspaper *al-Ahram* described the sounds of Cairo during the morning of March 18, the day after carriage and cart drivers went on strike: "Cairo used to wake up every morning to the creaking noise of carriages and other animal drawn carts. But this intimate and familiar sound was missing yesterday, as all cabbies and carriage drivers went on strike."[18]

This growing number of carts and carriages began to compete for road space with electric trams and bicycles in the late nineteenth century and motor vehicles at the turn of the twentieth, all of which of course added to the soundscape of the streets. Although sidewalks were plentiful in the newly built parts of Cairo, in the more populous traditional areas, sidewalks were at a premium (if they were available at all) and pedestrians had to share the streets with all of the above-mentioned wheeled vehicles. In some parts of the city, they also had to deal with passing electric trams. This reality necessitated the extensive and constant reliance on intentional and unintentional auditory signaling and notifications, be it in the form of bells, galloping horses, whistles, horns, engine sounds, or the human voice.[19] To the initiated ear of a local resident, all these sounds were a part of a sonic vocabulary that was innately and subconsciously familiar, allowing easy and intuitive navigation of the streets. However, when new and unfamiliar vehicles were thrown into the mix, it took some adjustment before the senses were recalibrated to the size, speed, "behavior," and sounds of these vehicles. That was certainly the case with trams and motor vehicles, which, in the first few years of their introduction to traffic streams, presented different challenges to pedestrians and coachmen.

The Silence of the (Killer) Trams

> Alexandria seemed a capital city. In the trim garden nurses were rolling their prams and children their hoops. The trams squashed and clicked and rattled.
>
> Lawrence Durrell, *Justine* (1957, from *The Alexandria Quartet*)[20]

Trams are obviously not silent. When their heavy cars moved along the tracks, they "squashed and clicked and rattled," as British author Lawrence Durrell described in *Justine*, the first novel in his Alexandria Quartet. There was also a perpetual buzzing sound produced as the metal rod pantograph on top of the tram grazed the overhead electrical wires. However, relative to trains and automobiles with their loud steam and internal combustion engines, the sounds that trams made as they raced through the streets seemed minimal. Also, in a loud and busy urban environment, it could be difficult for many to hear an approaching tram. In one of the frequently quoted anecdotes about early tramways in Cairo, Egyptian children serenaded the first tramway run in August 1896 by repeatedly chanting "*al-'afrit*" ("the ghost").[21] It is important to point out that these children had most certainly seen trains before, as by that time trains had been operating in Egypt for almost a half century. Therefore, the *al-'afrit* chants likely reflected the relative silence of the tram in comparison to steam locomotives, and not the fact that the "ignorant" native children believed that the horseless tram magically propelled itself along the tracks.[22] Nevertheless, seeing and hearing the electric tram for the first time must have been an altogether novel experience. This new experience is somewhat recaptured and comically made light of, by a popular folk (children's) song that circulated shortly after the introduction of the electric tram in Egypt:

> *Al-Kahraba'iyya, al-kahraba'iyya / Til 'it tigri 'alah al-Manshiyya*
> *Al-Kahraba'iyya mashiyya kuwayis / Wa'afuha 'and Khamis*
> *Wa Khamis wa'if mitayyis / Kab al-bamiyya 'alla al-mulukhiyya*
> *Al-Kahraba'iyya nihas fi nihas / Wa'afuha 'and 'Ilyyas*
> *Wa 'Ilyyas wa'if mihtas / Kab al-bamiyya 'ala al-qulqas*

> The electric car, the electric car / It rushed through to Manshiyya
> The electric car is running well / But when it stopped in front of Khamis
> Khamis froze up and stared / And spilled his okra in his *mulukhiya* [soup]
> The electric car is made of pure brass / But when it stopped in front of
>   Elias
> Elias stood there stupefied / And spilled his okra in his *qulqas* [taro stew][23]

When trams were first introduced to Alexandria, Cairo, and Port Said, they had frequent collisions with carriages, carts, and pedestrians; some were fatal. Predictably, the relative silence of the trams was identified as one of the key reasons for some of these inevitable accidents and deaths. Journalists, commentators, and legislators tried to find varying ways of projecting noise to alert pedestrians to oncoming electric trams.[24] At the time, sensationalistic newspaper headlines about the dangers of the tram abounded. Some no doubt were nationalistic and were influenced by the fact that the foreign-owned tramways were primarily crushing Egyptians.[25] Yet vilifying the electric tramways was in fact common around the globe at this time. For example, because of similar safety concerns, in 1900, many Parisians apparently called tramways the "murderous tramways" and "tramways of death."[26]

In Egypt, alarmist press coverage of tramway accidents led to some political action. In a letter dated February 7, 1898, from Umar Lutfi, the president of Majlis Shurah al-Qawanin, (Legislative Council) to the President of Majlis al-Nuzzar (Council of Ministers), Lutfi complained that something had to be done about the high rates of tramway accidents in Cairo. The letter begins by announcing that on Thursday, February 3, 1898, the legislative council met to discuss "the grave dangers and painful accidents caused by the tramway company," which according to the council, has led to "the killing of some and the injury and maiming of countless others." It attributes these accidents to the lack of safety procedures and the apparent exhaustion of the tramway operators and workers, who according to the council were forced to work "sixteen hours straight, which leads to tired and inattentive workers, causing these accidents." The rest of the letter suggests that the government should stipulate that the tram company install sonic warning devices, have its agents warn people in the streets, and limit the trams to only two connected cars. When neither Lutfi nor the Majlis received a response to their first letter, the entire legislative council met on April 21, 1898, and wrote up another letter admonishing the minister for not responding: "There are many innocents that are killed, children orphaned, and women that are widowed. This is despite the fact that we have previously warned the government about this issue. We urge you to act in order to remedy the situation."[27]

Not much was done when it came to reducing the working hours of tram operators. This would lead, in part, to a long history of strikes and labor activism by tram workers in Egypt.[28] However, because of this uproar, tramway companies in Egypt and elsewhere devoted some time and effort to figuring out ways to sonically warn pedestrians and improve tram safety. Tram horns and bells were employed more regularly, but in the early days of the tram, accidents were inevitably more frequent, as pedestrians were not yet adapted to the pace and sound of the trams. To be sure, decades before, there was a similar outcry by many over trains crushing people and more often farm animals.[29] Whereas trains, which were introduced to Egypt a half a century earlier, mostly operated outside of city centers and did not have to deal with city traffic, trams operated in the middle of crowded urban areas and took a bit of getting used to.[30] Also, unlike trains, which for the most part have their tracks completely separated from other traffic, many tramways in Egypt have to share the roadways with pedestrians and other wheeled traffic, including automobiles, which would soon be introduced into the cacophonous traffic mix. To be sure, as automobile numbers began to increase during the first two decades of the twentieth century, complaints about the dangers of cars

Table 3.2 Registered motorized vehicles in Cairo
and Alexandria, 1904–1921.

	Cairo	Alexandria
1904		
Total vehicles (1904)	-	18
1911		
Total vehicles (1911)	-	155
1916		
Private vehicles	745	263
Taxis/buses/trucks	192	24
Private motorcycles	457	168
All vehicles (1916)	1,394	455
1921		
Private vehicles	1,944	1,372
Taxis/buses/trucks	497	267
Private motorcycles	930	390
All vehicles (1921)	3,371	2,029

Note: These figures do not include government- or military-owned vehicles.

and trucks would also increase (see Table 3.2). Unlike trams, whose main problem for the authorities was their relative silence, automobiles would soon be deemed too loud. Whereas at the end of the nineteenth century the Egyptian government required trams to install and use louder horn and bells to warn pedestrians, by the late 1920s automobile drivers were being ticketed for excessively honking the horn.[31]

Loud and Smelly Motor Vehicles

I decided recently to ride in a motorized omnibus in order to experience something new. So, I went to a bus stop and rushed to sit in one of the empty seats. As soon as I sat down, the driver began to move a metal rail next to his leg and I immediately heard this awful sound, smelled this disgusting smell, and felt vibrations reverberate in every part of my body. It was as if I, and all the other passengers experienced a sudden illness. However, I remained seated, thinking that I am simply not used to riding this vehicle. Finally, as the machine started moving, billowing smoke, rumbling loudly, while the hated smell of gas began to spread, I prayed for God's help. It was at that moment that the conductor arrived and I bought from him a ticket to the end of the line. . . . Immediately afterwards, the automobile veered towards the left as I fell on top of the man sitting next to me and we both fell on a third passenger and all three of us leaned towards the fourth. If it wasn't for the safety barrier we would have all been goners . . . We continued in this state of affairs for a while. Every time the bus leaned towards the right we all leaned towards the right, when the driver turned left all of us swayed towards the left. It was as if we were all participating in a Sufi *zikr* [ritual prayer]. This continued until we arrived at Cairo Train Station. As I stepped out of this machine, I proceeded to curse all motor vehicles, their inventors, and their manufacturers.

—Fathi 'Azmi (*Al-Dik*, June 17, 1908)[32]

This excerpt was from a June 1908 newspaper article titled "The Worst Invention to Appear in the Twentieth Century," and it is specifically describing one of the early "motorized omnibuses" in Cairo, which was probably operated by the Société des Automobiles et Omnibus du Caire (SAOC) or the Cairo Public Motor Car Service.[33] *Al-Dik* (*The Rooster*) was a weekly satirical periodical, so we must read the words of Fathi 'Azmi in context.[34] Despite 'Azmi's exaggerated prose, this satirical, multisensory, and embodied critique of motor vehicles provides a glimpse of the relative novelty of experiencing an automobile or bus for the first time. It also comically relates the auditory and sensory overload experienced by many who first encountered automobiles. 'Azmi's flamboyant account, with its descriptions of the foul smells of gasoline exhaust, loud vibrating engine sounds physically reverberating people's bodies, and the inevitable touching of passengers who are crowded in an enclosed space, gives a vivid embodied narrative of what would soon become the everyday reality of urban dwellers everywhere. However, in 1908, when 'Azmi wrote the above satire, automobiles were still rare in Egypt. The entire city of Alexandria for example had only 173 motor vehicles. By the second decade of the twentieth century, the numbers and sounds of automobiles, trucks, buses, and motorcycles began to grow exponentially, creating unexpected traffic and infrastructural problems (see Table 3.2).[35]

As the twentieth century roared on, the mounting number of motor vehicles put an unexpected strain on all the preexisting road, traffic, and policing institutions. As early as 1920, police officials in Cairo and Alexandria were already complaining about increased motor vehicle traffic. Describing Cairo, the Interior Ministry report for 1920 declared: "The difficulty of adequately controlling the traffic in the city is largely increased by the growing number of motor-cars on the streets. It will not be easy to effect any great improvement in this respect until heavier penalties can be inflicted on persons contravening the traffic regulations than are possible under the present law."[36] Also in Alexandria, according to the same report, "the number of motor-car licenses during 1920 is nearly double that of 1919 with a consequent increase in the difficulty of controlling traffic in the city."[37] Of course, in hindsight this apparent panic by some of the authorities over the number of automobiles in 1920 seems rather quaint as motor vehicles numbers skyrocketed in the next few decades (see Table 3.3).[38] By the late 1920s, motorized taxis would replace horse-drawn coaches as the new transport of choice for the middle classes, with more of the upper classes buying their own chauffeured automobiles.

For better or worse, just like in the rest of the world, Egypt's roads and traffic police were not ready or equipped to deal with this rapid and unexpected rise in the number of motor vehicles, and they would continue to play catch-up for years to come. The total number of motor vehicles in Egypt reached around 21,000 in 1927, 31,000 in 1936, and more than tripled to around 103,000 in 1954.[39] The environmental, cultural, and economic impact of this traffic explosion affected all Egyptians on a fundamental level. As I examine in the rest of this chapter, the hubbub of this new motor traffic and its increasingly loud electric horns, along with the noises radiating from trams, animal-powered traffic, and thousands of pedestrians and passengers, created a vibrant yet cacophonous soundscape characterizing all Egyptian cities.

Classism, Civilizational Shaming and Controlling Motor Vehicle Horn Noise

Every effort has been made to reduce noise to a minimum. The number of contraventions for excessive use of electric horn or klaxon drawn up during the year show an increase of approximately 1,000, in figures for 1936, while thousands of warning letters have been sent to owners in the cases of first offense.

Annual Report of the Cairo City Police[40]

Table 3.3 Licensed motorized vehicles in Egypt, 1925–1954 (non-government-owned).

	Total in Egypt (Approx.)
1925	
Private cars	7,661
Taxis	3,739
Trucks	1,246
Buses	848
Motorcycles	3,456
All vehicles (1925)	16,950
1936	
Private cars	20,771
Taxis	4,152
Trucks	2,794
Buses	1,103
Motorcycles	1,909
All vehicles (1936)	30,729
1946	
Private cars and taxis	30,948
Trucks and buses	9,497
Motorcycles	3,602
All vehicles (1946)	44,047
1954	
Private cars	58,808
Taxis	12,221
Trucks	15,156
Buses	5,331
Motorcycles	11,634
All vehicles (1954)	103,150

Tramways, trains, and the steady increase in motor vehicle traffic dramatically transformed the soundscape and decibel levels of Egyptian cities and towns. As I examined above, just like with the early introduction of trains and tramways, the Egyptian press printed alarmist articles covering "killer cars" and "death under the wheels," as pedestrians recalibrated their senses in order to share the road with much faster and heavier vehicles. The lack of sidewalks in many of the poorer urban areas also exacerbated this problem. For this reason, during the first two decades of the twentieth century, car horns were regarded as necessary for alerting pedestrians and avoiding accidents.[41] Not surprisingly though, as the number of motor vehicles increased, car horns in particular added disproportionately to the cacophony of the cities and were increasingly viewed as a nuisance in need of regulation. In the 1920s, Egyptian driver's licenses had a small bilingual (French/Arabic) booklet—printed by the Egyptian Royal Automobile Club—listing 15 driving rules and regulations (see Figure 3.2). Rule 9 in the booklet deals directly with excessive honking of the horn: "Only use the horn when absolutely necessary and do not use the horn continually and unreasonably."[42]

By the mid-1930s, the government drew up more anti-honking regulations and instituted monetary fines in order to limit "noise by instruments of warning," by ticketing the "excessive use of electric horn or klaxon."[43] However, by the government's own account, these measures—applied in 1936—were not very effective, since "fines of P.T. 5 and P.T. 10 did not make drivers respect the law."[44] Five to ten piasters for excessively honking the horn may have been a deterrent for taxi drivers, but for private car owners who could afford a car in 1930s Egypt, the fine was simply not enough to curb the noise.

Figure 3.2 An Egyptian driver's license with attached traffic rules book.

The increased level of noise was frequently noted in the press starting in the early twentieth century, but by the early 1930s newspaper articles were increasingly alarmist about the emotional, psychological, and physical dangers of the growing cacophony of Egyptian cities. A November 1933 article, for example, declared that "everything about living in the capital (Cairo) is cacophonous and disturbingly exhausting [*muqliq lil-Raha*]. For living in Cairo is akin to living in a factory where steel is constantly being pounded."[45] Car horns in particular were increasingly viewed as a nuisance and the Egyptian press was filled with articles and editorials describing the problem and possible solutions. Increasingly, these newspaper articles unfavorably compared the level of noise in Egypt with Europe. In the summer of 1934, after new car horn laws were implemented in London, banning the use of the electric horn at night, the Egyptian press immediately lobbied for similar laws to be put into effect in Cairo.[46] In another article printed in October 1935, the bold-print title declared, "Street Noise: A Problem that was Solved in Europe. Is There any Hope of Fixing this Issue in Egypt?"[47] Street noise was not, of course, eliminated in Europe, but the Egyptian press typically compared the Egyptian streets unfavorably to those in the West, with the inevitable conclusion that reforms must be made to follow the Western example. This sort of civilizational shaming was common at the time as it was the tactic of choice for Egyptian newspapers.

These recurring civilizational comparisons were usually classist, as very often the blame for the noise was almost exclusively directed at the Egyptian masses. The above-mentioned October 1935 *al-Ahram* editorial, for example, startlingly blames the incessant use of car horns not on the drivers, but on Cairene pedestrians—most of whom could not afford to buy a car or even to pay a taxi fare in the 1930s. According to the article, pedestrians "disregard their own safety by illegally crossing the streets from non-designated areas and without properly paying attention to car traffic," leading automobile drivers to incessantly honk their horns.[48] The article concludes by sanctimoniously declaring that car horns can be eliminated and entirely banned, only after we "educate pedestrians on all the nuances of pedestrian traffic laws and the legal consequences of ignoring them."[49]

Classism and patronizing civilizational uplift were also at the heart of a novel discussion concerning car horns in the late 1930s. Using the European streets once again as the prototypical model to emulate, debates arose in the Egyptian press about following London's lead and replacing the loud electric car horn with the older hand-squeezed (leather) bulb horn.[50]

As these discussions were about to be enacted into law, the well-connected Royal Automobile Club of Egypt (RACE) launched a coordinated campaign attacking the proposed law. As the name implies, the Automobile Club was sponsored by the Egyptian royal family, and most of its members were wealthy car enthusiasts. Since its official founding in 1924, it had an outsized role in lobbying for Egyptian traffic and automobile policies. It printed a magazine, informational booklets on cars and traffic laws, and as I examine later, it even sponsored informational short films and cartoons encouraging "proper" driving etiquette.[51] In January 1938, *al-Ahram* reprinted an article that was published earlier in the official magazine of the automobile club. Using the typical civilizational discourse that was common at the time, the article is titled: "Moving Backwards or Regressing for a Quarter of a Century: The Royal Automobile Club Challenges the Outlawing of Electric Horns." Despite agreeing that the streets are becoming too noisy, and that "drivers go overboard with their use of the electric horn and a large majority of them use it unnecessarily and repeatedly," the article urges the government to not apply the proposed law.[52] After declaring the proposed law absurd, the article sarcastically pronounces that if we were to "ban the electric horn and replace it with the leather blowhorn that was commonly used a quarter of a century ago . . . why not ban the use of automobiles and motorcycles altogether and return to the exclusive use of donkeys, carriages and horse-drawn carts."[53] The rest of the article returns to the same trope we have seen, of civilizational shaming and then blaming Egyptian pedestrians and even "street children," for the entire car horn problem:

> They suppose that Cairo can follow the example of Paris, London, Brussels, and Rome.
>
> However, the obvious difference is that pedestrians in Europe are accustomed to following the rules and are careful to not put themselves in harm's way. Here however, the situation is entirely different, for street children attack the streets face-first, climbing on tramways illegally and disembarking from them quickly in order to avoid the ticket inspectors. They also play soccer and other games in the middle of the streets as if completely unaware of their surroundings. They also ride on their bikes scurrying here and there, never keeping on the right-hand side of the road. Pedestrians cross the streets disregarding the flow of traffic and at times stopping in the middle of the streets, almost always avoiding the sidewalks. . . . In almost all

of those cases it is not practical to use these old manual air horns with their limited range and lower volume.[54]

The Automobile Club–sponsored article then bizarrely concludes that it was the Egyptian drivers that were daily risking their lives and "exposing themselves to danger, as they did their level best to avoid collisions with these reckless boys [playing in the street], oblivious bicyclists blocking traffic, or ignorant pedestrians."[55] There is evidence to suggest that lobbying by the Automobile Club was successful, as a compromise of sorts was reached. Later that year, a fourteen-page booklet titled "Traffic Rules in Cairo: Directives to Preserve Public Security" was printed by the Egyptian traffic police. The booklet lists sixteen traffic rules and regulations directed at "pedestrians, automobile, motorcycle, and bicycle drivers."[56] Five of the sixteen rules directly address noise and noise-making, and rule 7 specifically bans "truck, commercial vehicle, bus, taxi, and motorcycle drivers" from using the electric horn, as they are "only allowed to use the normal leather [non-electric] horn."[57] Private car drivers, on the other hand, are "allowed to use a low-volume electrical horn during the permissible hours, but only if they do so without causing a ruckus or hubbub [*dagig aw 'agig*]."[58] Considering that most private car owners in 1930s Egypt were financially well-off, the above directives clearly privilege the rights of the elites. Rule 8 seems to bizarrely corroborate this class distinction, by specifically urging private car drivers to not use their car horns late at night "after returning from the opera, or after an evening out at the cinema or a casino/dance hall."[59]

Aside from legal regulations and enforcement of car horn violations, a continuing and steady stream of newspaper editorials and commentary about traffic noise and excessive use of car horns issued from the Egyptian press. With an ever-increasing number of Egyptians attending movie theaters, in 1939 a short public service animated film, sponsored and produced by the Royal Automobile Club of Egypt, used humor to shame Egyptian drivers into limiting their use of car horns. The cartoon, titled "*Mafish Mukh*" ("Brainless"), ran for only a minute and a half and featured the cartoon character Mishmish Effendi (Mr. Apricot), who was already well known to Egyptian cinema audiences (see Figure 3.3). Created and filmed by Frenkel Productions, Mishmish Effendi cartoons regularly played during previews and intermissions in cinemas throughout Egypt.[60] The new cartoon effectively made its anti-noise message through humor and vernacular dialogue, voiced by comedian and monologist Ahmad Mitwali. After loudly

Figure 3.3 Mishmish talking to the other driver. Frenkel Brothers, *Mafish Mukh* (1939).

demonstrating the noises of Cairene traffic, the film introduces Mishmish driving his car and stopping at a red traffic light. Mishmish is visibly disturbed as an impatient driver behind him incessantly honks his car horn. Mishmish then speaks up to the honking driver: "What's the use of beeping the horn? There are no pedestrians walking in front of you!" When the driver does not respond and continues to honk his horn, the exacerbated Mishmish yells out, "Man . . . can't you tell that it's a red light and not a person that you're beeping at!" At the end of the cartoon a written message appears: "Do not use the car horn unnecessarily!" (*"La tasta'mal al-Klaksun bidun Da'"*).[61]

Vital to the messaging of this short cartoon is the verbalization, pronunciation, and tone of Mishmish as contrasted with that of the loud driver. There is a clear class and educational distinction represented in the ways they speak the Egyptian vernacular. Although both have a Cairene accent, Mishmish clearly sounds like an educated "modern gentleman," whereas the man honking the horn responds to Mishmish in a stereotypically low-brow Cairene Arabic. This mediated lower-class voice, as spoken by the loud, car-horn-beeping character, associates loudness, yet again, with classless or "lower-class" behavior. It is unlikely that the Mishmish Effendi cartoon had much of an effect on the ubiquity of car horn noises in Egypt's urban streets, yet it highlights the changing sonic realities of cities in the 1930s, while revealing changes in middle-class sensibilities and discourses about noise.

Conclusion

From the late nineteenth to the mid-twentieth centuries, the very materiality of the streets and the physical spaces above and below them changed. Metal tramway tracks and asphalt ran through the streets, allowing for new, often louder, transportation vehicles; pipes carrying water and gas ran underground; and electrical and telephone wires ran above and below, bringing with them transformative sounded technologies that were unimaginable just decades before. These new infrastructural arteries were (and still are) vitally connected to the social fabric of the city, as they changed how everyday people sensorially, economically, and socially connected with their immediate environment. For a time, these new electric and motor-powered vehicles coexisted with animal-powered carts, creating what must have seemed like a symphony of sounds and movements. Soon, however, this rapid growth in vehicular traffic pressured the infrastructural limits of Egypt's roads and forever changed how everyone sensorially experienced public space.

The level of social, economic, and sensory interaction in early twentieth-century city streets was unprecedented, as people physically experienced and negotiated these new transportation technologies and thousands of other people on a daily basis. The scope of these new, larger spaces produced an entirely different sensory experience from the more traditional enclosed urban quarters, where residents knew each other by face, voice, and most likely even by name. Adding to the auditory and visual disorientation of these large, crowded squares are a plethora of smells from engines, gasoline, various vended foods and drinks, and the ever-present aroma of horse and donkey dung which inevitably filled the air. For those riding in a busy tram or bus, physically touching other passengers completes what must have felt like a continual, multisensory bombardment.[62]

As discussed in the introduction, early in the twentieth century, the novel sounds of modernity were universally portrayed as a positive indicator of progress, but by the 1920s there was a palpable critical shift, as many of these sounds were viewed as potentially harmful and in need of controlling and silencing. To be sure, a big part of this shift was due to the increase in the loudness of these noises as the number of loud machines drastically increased. However, as I have shown in this chapter, a critical component to this shift was unabashedly classist. The more everyday people began to use these buses, trams, motorcycles, and automobiles, the easier it was for the elites and upwardly mobile middle classes to blame the "noise" problem on the urban masses. Newspapers at the time were replete with modernizing Egyptians preaching to the masses about how loud and vulgar they were and the need for more "civilized" silence. Bizarrely enough, this classism was reflected in discourse about excessive car horn noises. Despite the fact that cars in the 1920s and 1930s were predominantly owned and operated by well-off Egyptians, the blame for excessive car horn noises was placed squarely on working-class pedestrians and even street children, who were accused of wrongly and "irrationally" crossing the streets and forcing automobile drivers to use their horns. In many ways, this selective weaponization of modernizing discourses about loud "lower-class" noises, and the blaming of most street and traffic noise on working-class pedestrians, reflected the anxieties of the growing, upwardly mobile middle classes attempting to distinguish themselves from the Egyptian masses. These classist and dehumanizing discourses were rationalized somewhat by giving the self-declared modernizers a clear directive to educate and uplift their fellow citizens to follow the traffic rules and hence reach an "acceptable" level of civilization.

Notes

Parts of this chapter appear in Ziad Fahmy, *Street Sounds: Listening to Everyday Life in Modern Egypt* (Stanford, CA: Stanford University Press, 2020). Reproduced with permission of Stanford University Press.

1. Luigi Russolo, *The Art of Noises: Futurist Manifestos, 1913* (New York: Something Else Press, 1967), 7.
2. Ibid., 9–10.
3. For more on early twentieth-century futurism and Russolo and his music, see Jacques Attali, *Noise: The Political Economy of Music*, trans. Brian Massumi (Minneapolis: University of Minnesota Press, 1985), 136; and Gavin Williams, "A Voice of the Crowd: Futurism and the Politics of Noise" in *19th-Century Music* 37/2 (2013), 113–129. For a more direct connection between Italian futurism and Egypt, see Nadine Wassef, "Mafarka Before Being a Futurist: The Intimate Egypt in the Writings of F. T. Marinetti," in *Mediterranean Modernism: Intercultural Exchange and*

Aesthetic Development, ed. Adam Goldwyn and Renee Silverman (London: Palgrave Macmillan, 2016), 29–50.

4. Richard Cullen Rath, "Hearing American History," *Journal of American History* 95/2 (2008), 417–431, at 431.

5. Hillel Schwartz, *Making Noise: From Babel to the Big Bang and Beyond* (New York: Zone Books, 2016), 22.

6. For more on this reclassification of modern noise from a sign of progress to a nuisance, see Emily Thompson, *The Soundscape of Modernity: Architectural Acoustics and the Culture of Listening in America, 1900–1933* (Cambridge, MA: MIT Press, 2002), 116–168.

7. My examination of class distinction using noise and sound politics emulates the success of sound studies scholars who have examined American racism and race formation using the racial politics of sound. See much of Mark Smith's writings and, more recently, the work of Jennifer Lynn Stoever and Nina Sun Eidsheim. Jennifer Lynn Stoever, *The Sonic Color Line: Race and the Cultural Politics of Listening* (New York: NYU Press, 2016); Nina Sun Eidsheim, *The Race of Sound: Listening, Timbre, and Vocality in African American Music* (Durham, NC: Duke University Press, 2019); Mark M. Smith, *How Race Is Made: Slavery, Segregation, and the Senses* (Chapel Hill: University of North Carolina Press, 2006).

8. Gabriel Charmes, *Five Months at Cairo and in Lower Egypt* (London: Bentley Press, 1883), 21.

9. John T. Chalcraft, *The Striking Cabbies of Cairo and other Stories: Crafts and Guilds in Egypt, 1863–1914* (Albany: State University of New York Press, 2005), 59–60; On Barak, "Scraping the Surface: The Techno-Politics of Modern Streets in Turn-of-Twentieth-Century Alexandria," *Mediterranean Historical Review* 24/2 (2009), 187–205, at 192.

10. For more on the road and track infrastructure of twentieth-century Egypt, see Fahmy, *Street Sounds*, 81–98.

11. Ministère des finances, Direction de la statistique, *Annuaire statistique de l'Egypte 1920* (Cairo: Imprimerie Nationale, 1921), 138; Ministère des finances, Direction de la statistique, *Annuaire statistique de l'Egypte 1921–1922* (Cairo: Imprimerie Nationale, 1923), 77; Ministère des finances, Direction de la statistique, *Annuaire statistique de l'Egypte 1935–36* (Cairo: Imprimerie Nationale, 1938); Ministère des finances, Direction de la statistique, *Annuaire statistique de l'Egypte 1951–54*. (Cairo: Imprimerie Nationale, 1956), 265–266.

12. For an analysis of the acoustical properties of different road surfaces, see C. Michael Hogan, "Analysis of Highway Noise," *Water, Air and Soil Pollution* 2 (1973): 387–392.

13. For a closer examination on how road sounds can be a type of local auditory knowledge, see Fahmy, *Street Sounds*, 31–40, and Nicole Dietrich, "Berlin Sounds: Audible Cartography of a Formerly Divided City," in *Germany in the Loud Twentieth Century: An Introduction*, ed. Florence Feiereisen and Alexandra Merley Hill (Oxford, UK: Oxford University Press, 2011), 95–110.

14. Chalcraft, *The Striking Cabbies*, 61.

15. Fahmy, *Street Sounds*, 26–31.

16. See R. Murray Schafer, *The Soundscape: Our Sonic Environment and the Tuning of the World* (Rochester, NY: Destiny Books, 1994 [1977]), 3–14.

17. Schwartz, *Making Noise*, 22.

18. *Al-Ahram*, March 19, 1919.

19. Fahmy, *Street Sounds*, 29–31.

20. Lawrence Durrell, *Justine* (New York: E. P. Dutton & Co.), 236.

21. *Ministry of Public Works: Annual Report for 1899* (Cairo: Government Press, 1900), 270; *Al-Muqatam*, August 1, 1898. Cited in Muhamad Sayyid Kilani, *Tram al-Qahirah: Dirasah Tarikhiyya, Ijtima'iyya, Adabiyya* (Cairo: Matba'it al-Madani, 1968), 14.

22. For a different analysis of this incident, see On Barak, *On Time: Technology and Temporality in Modern Egypt* (Berkeley: University of California Press, 2013), 100.

23. This is my translation from Bahija Sidqi Rashid, *Aghani Misr al-Sha'biyya* (Cairo: Matba'it al-Anglu al-Misriyya, 1982), 10–11. Rashid offers an English translation, though in order to keep the rhyming quality of the piece, that translation somewhat changes the intended meaning of the song's original lyrics.

24. Recently, in the early days of hybrid and electric automobiles, a similar argument was made.

25. For more on the sensationalism of the press with regard to this issue, see Barak, *On Time*, 82.

26. Peter Soppelsa, "Urban Railways, Industrial Infrastructure, and the Paris Cityscape, 1870–1914," in *Trains, Culture, and Mobility: Riding the Rails*, ed. Benjamin Fraser and Steven D. Spalding (Lanham, MD: Lexington Books, 2012), 128–129.

27. Egyptian National Archives, DWQ 0075-015839 (1898). Letters from Umar Lutfi Ra'is Majlis Shurah al-Qawanin to the president of Majlis al-Nuzzar .

28. See Joel Benin and Zachary Lockman, *Workers on the Nile: Nationalism, Communism, Islam, and the Egyptian Working Class, 1882–1954* (Cairo: Cairo University Press, 1998).

29. Barak, *On Time*, 56–60.

30. The Cairene tramway system transported almost 10 million passengers yearly in 1899, over 51 million passengers in 1909, 82 million passengers in 1920, and reached over 178 million passengers in 1950. Fahmy, *Street Sounds*, 89–93.

31. Fahmy, *Street Sounds*, 103–107.

32. *Al-Dik*, June 17, 1908. Quoted in Kilani, *Tram al-Qahirah*, 18.

33. Roland Dussart-Desart, "The Cairo Tramways: Africa's Greatest Tramway Network, Part 1," *Journal of Modern Tramway and Light Rail Transit* (May, 1991), 160–169, at 165. The Cairo Public Motor Car Service was created by the Cairo Tramway Company, specifically to compete with the SAOC. These early buses were small ten- to fourteen-passenger "motorized omnibuses."

34. *Al-Dik* was owned and edited by a writer and translator named Fathi 'Azmi, and according to the Egyptian National Library Periodical Index, was in circulation for only one year (1907–1908). See *Dar al-Kutub al-Misriyya: Fihrist al-Dawriyat al-'Arabiyya alati Taqtaniha al-Dar* (Cairo: Dar al-Kutub al-Misriyya), 1996.

35. Ministère des finances, Direction de la statistique, *Annuaire statistique de l'Egypte 1912* (Cairo: Imprimerie Nationale, 1912), 474; Ministère des finances, Direction de la statistique, *Annuaire statistique de l'Egypte 1916* (Cairo: Imprimerie Nationale, 1916), 208; Ministère des finances, Direction de la statistique, *Annuaire statistique de l'Egypte 1920* (Cairo: Imprimerie Nationale, 1921), 138; Ministère des finances, Direction de la statistique, *Annuaire statistique de l'Egypte 1921–1922* (Le Caire: Imprimerie Nationale, 1923), 77; Ministère des finances, Direction de la statistique, *Annuaire statistique de l'Egypte 1922–1923* (Cairo: Imprimerie Nationale, 1924), 475.

36. British National Archives, FO 141/586/4. *Ministry of the Interior Report for the Year 1920.*

37. Ibid.

38. Department of Overseas Trade, *Report on the Economic and Financial Situation of Egypt, Dated June, 1925* (London: Published by his Majesty's Stationary Office, 1925), 39–40; Ministère des finances, Direction de la statistique, *Annuaire statistique de l'Egypte 1935–36* (Cairo: Imprimerie Nationale, 1938); Ministère des finances, Direction de la statistique, *Annuaire statistique de l'Egypte 1951–54* (Cairo: Imprimerie Nationale, 1956), 265–266; Overseas Economic Surveys, *Egypt: Economic and Commercial Conditions in Egypt* (London: His Majesty's Stationery Office, 1948), 25.

39. These figures do not include government-owned vehicles. See Department of Overseas Trade, *Report on the Economic and Financial Situation of Egypt, Dated June, 1927* (London: Published by his Majesty's Stationary Office, 1927), 43; Ministère des finances, Direction de la statistique, *Annuaire statistique de l'Egypte 1935–36.* (Cairo: Imprimerie Nationale, 1938); Ministère des finances, Direction de la statistique, *Annuaire statistique de l'Egypte 1951–54.* (Cairo: Imprimerie Nationale, 1956), 265–266.

40. Ministry of the Interior, *Annual Report of the Cairo City Police for the Year 1937* (Cairo: Government Press in Bulaq, 1938), 47.

41. Barak, "Scraping the Surface," 198.

42. Egyptian Driver's License (1928), author's collection. See Figure 3.2.

43. Ministry of the Interior, *Annual Report*, 47.

44. Ibid.

45. *Al-Ahram*, November 1, 1933.

46. *Al-Ahram*, August 30, 1934.

47. *Al-Ahram*, October 26, 1935.

48. Ibid.

49. Ibid.

50. *Al-Ahram*, October 9, 1937.

51. Fahmy, *Street Sounds*, 103–107.

52. *Al-Ahram*, January 4, 1938.

53. Ibid.

54. Ibid.

55. Ibid.

56. Bulis Misr, *Nizam al-Murur bil-Qahirah: Ta'limat li-hafz al-Amn al-'Am* (Cairo: Hikimdar Bulis Misr, 1938), 1; see also *al-Ahram*, June 8, 1938.

57. Misr, *Nizam al-Murur bil-Qahirah*, 3.

58. Ibid.

59. Ibid.

60. The Frenkel family (of Belarusian Jewish origins) created Frenkel Brothers Productions in Egypt in the mid-1930s. In 1914, the six brothers moved to Egypt from Jerusalem as children along with their family. They created the first regular cartoon production in Egypt, using entirely Egyptianized characters and themes. Mishmish Effendi became their most popular cartoon character, after the short cartoon "*Mafish Fayda*" ("There Is No Use") debuted in 1936 and played in theaters for at least a couple of years. About a dozen "Mishmish Effendi" cartoons were made. See *Al-Sabah*, May 14, 1937; and Ahmad al-Hadari, *Tarikh al-Sinima fi Misr: al-Guz' al-Thani, 1931–1940* (Cairo: al-Hay'a al-Misriyya al-'Ammah lil-Kitab, 1989), 305.

61. See *Mafish Mukh*, Frenkel Brothers, 1939. https://www.youtube.com/watch?v=rzUk ep3Xifw, accessed March 1, 2023.

62. See for example Fahmy, *Street Sounds*, 107–119.

PART II
AURAL EPISTEMOLOGIES

4

Colonial Listening and the Epistemology of Deception

The Stethoscope in Africa

Gavin Steingo

French physician René-Théophile-Hyacinthe Laennec invented the steth-oscope in 1816, and he wrote an important treatise on the instrument three years later.[1] Although the instrument was ubiquitous in European medical practice by the end of the nineteenth century, the details of its introduction into the Cape Colony are sketchy at best. What we know is due only to incidental mentions in the biographies of "great men." David Livingstone likely employed a stethoscope in southern Africa from 1841 until his return to the UK in 1857.[2] Several decades later, Arthur Conan Doyle is said to have "lifted his stethoscope out of its case" after a decade of not practicing medicine in order to volunteer for the British imperial forces in the Second Boer War.[3] Despite the paucity of details surrounding the stethoscope's journey to southern Africa, what is immediately evident is the close association between the instrument's use and British imperial confrontation. Indeed, Cecil John Rhodes was sent *to* southern Africa in his teens after his doctor performed a stethoscopic examination on him and determined that the future arch-colonialist would be better off in the Cape's moderate clime.[4]

The history of the stethoscope in Europe and North America, by con-trast, has received a great deal of scholarly attention.[5] This scholarship is less about the history of the device than the historical developments it enabled. Most notably, Jonathan Sterne suggests that Laennec's invention was part of a much larger movement toward "audile technique," that is, a modality of *rational and focused listening characteristic of modern bourgeois European*

Gavin Steingo, *Colonial Listening and the Epistemology of Deception* In: *Acoustics of Empire*. Edited by: Peter McMurrayand Priyasha Mukhopadhyay, Oxford University Press. © Oxford University Press 2024. DOI: 10.1093/oso/9780197553787.003.0005 *subjectivity*. Sterne elucidates the concept by identifying six primary features, two of which are particularly important for the purposes of this chapter:

1. Listening gets articulated to notions of science, reason, and rationality . . .

and

5. Techniques of listening are based in and described through a language of mediation. Audile technique is premised on some form of physical distance and some mediating practice or technology. . . .[6]

As Sterne's careful adumbration of the concept elucidates, audile technique needs to be understood in a broad and flexible way. Brian Kane observes that the concept encompasses many intersecting dynamics: cognitive, affective, institutional, technological, and cultural.[7]

For scholars of sound, the notion of audile technique has been particularly useful because it suggests that listening is just as susceptible to rationalization as vision. As Sterne puts it, "As there was an Enlightenment, so too was there an 'Ensoniment.' A series of conjunctures among ideas, institutions, and practices rendered the world audible in new ways and valorized new constructs of hearing and listening. . . . Through techniques of listening, people harnessed, modified, and shaped their powers of auditory perception in the service of rationality."[8] This is a fact often overlooked by many historians, who conceptualize the rationalization of listening as a kind of "becoming visual" of the ear, rather than simply a redeployment of audition as such.[9] There is nothing inherently rational nor irrational about any sense organ. Rather, the rationalization and separation of these senses is shot through with historical dynamics, including those documented by Kane.[10]

The work of Sterne and Kane, among others, inscribes sound and listening within a broader conventional narrative of European modernity. This conventional narrative is exemplified by the work of Michel Foucault, who famously argued that the birth of clinical medicine meant nothing less than "the opening up of the concrete individual, for the first time in Western history, to the language of rationality, that major event in the relationship of man to himself and of language to things."[11] A signal achievement of sound studies in the past two decades has been to show that the ear, no less than the eye, was instrumental in this process, "reconstructing," as Sterne writes, "the living body as an object of knowledge."[12]

While recent work on the history of sound and listening has offered important insights into European and North American contexts, those insights cannot be easily generalized.[13] We have every reason to doubt the narrative—everywhere implied, if not stated explicitly—that the rationalization of the ear in nineteenth-century Europe gradually "globalized," first to North America and then to the rest of the world. This chapter shows that colonial medical practice in southern Africa has a very different story to tell. Focusing on late nineteenth- and early twentieth-century colonial southern Africa, I suggest that the deployment of European listening technologies led equally to new forms of knowledge and new forms of deception. Particularly in colonial medical practice, deception proliferated in the form of medical imposters—that is, con men and women without training who acted like doctors and nurses, and who pretended to listen to the signs of the body while making (fake) diagnoses. The stethoscope in particular was often associated with such fakery, a fact that led to mystification of the instrument and to an association of auscultation with African "superstition." By considering the stethoscope and medical listening in the colonial context, a series of novel issues emerges.

Indeed, Britain's colonial territories in southern Africa were plagued by uncertainty and epistemological instability, particularly where European medical practice was most robust. I show that in addition to increased rationalization and efficiency, imperialism produced acoustic deception, counterfeiting, and illusion. This leads me to a broader meditation on knowledge and modernity. As Ackbar Abbas notes, "running alongside the dialectic of Enlightenment is a *dialectic of deception*, which requires a radical rethinking of knowledge and epistemology."[14] I take a cue from Abbas's insight that "knowledge and deception do not form a simple opposition," and that—in certain instances—"deception can be a form of knowing," which means that there can be "an epistemology of deception alongside an epistemology of truth."[15]

This chapter therefore makes a twin intervention into the history of sound and the acoustic. First, I consider colonial cases rather than limiting my analysis to the metropolitan center. Second, I introduce a dose of critical theory to mediate the historical analysis of sound, which is often excessively historicist. The story told in this chapter runs counter to the conventional one in fields as diverse as sound studies and the history of medicine. Rather than becoming articulated to science and reason, in colonial southern Africa listening was entangled with violence, skullduggery, and dissimulation.

Medical Practice in the Colonies

In many ways, the history of colonial medicine in southern Africa resembles that in other British colonies. The deployment of doctors to, and the setting up of medical institutions in, the Cape served several interrelated purposes. For one thing, it was part of Britain's "civilizing process"[16]—a way to maintain a strict distinction between Europeans and "native heathens," on the one hand, and a powerful tool for conscripting "natives" into European dispositions, on the other.[17] As Shula Marks comments about British colonialism in nineteenth-century southern Africa, "Western medicine was clearly part of the contest for hegemony."[18]

For example, the establishment of a hospital in a new British territory near King William's Town in the 1870s was designed with the explicit mandate of destroying local Xhosa healing practices, to persuade "Natives" toward "civilization and Christianity," and to "drive the witchdoctor out of the field."[19] And in 1895, to provide another example, the British *Nursing Record & Hospital World* reported receiving a "most interesting letter" from one "Miss Wild, Matron of the Grey Hospital, King William's Town, Cape Colony." In this letter were enclosed "two photographs, the one of a witch doctor, the other of the Grey Hospital which was erected by Sir George Grey for the purpose of breaking the belief of the natives in witch doctors by placing skilful [sic] medical and surgical treatment within their reach, free of charge."[20] Note that the assumed aim of the Grey Hospital is *not* the free provision of medical aid; rather, this provision was offered "*for the purpose* of breaking the belief of the natives."[21]

As the second example indicates, medical work in the colonies was not complete without a dispatch back to the metropolitan center. Colonial dispatches made good use of photographic representation as a way to intertwine claims to objective knowledge with colonial desire. A similar preoccupation with the panoramic gaze is evident in exhibitions of the colonial period. In the early twentieth century, the Queen of England herself was "delighted" by a missionary exhibition focused on comparing and contrasting "the equipment of the witch doctor and that of the missionary who brings to the relief of quack-ridden millions the latest results of medical and surgical skill."[22] The Wellcome Historical Medical Museum (founded in 1913) likewise made a point of contrasting "the hideous effigies of witch doctors" with the lineage of Western medicine: "the great Greek physician, Hippocrates," "Ambrose Paré, the great French surgeon," "Joseph Priestly, who discovered oxygen about 1765, and many others."[23] In brief, one important aspect of colonial medical practice was the way it *performed* and *displayed* itself during the battle for ideological hegemony.

But medical practice in Britain's southern colonies was also spurred by practical motivation. After the discovery of diamonds (in the 1860s) and gold (in the 1880s), southern Africa went from a colonial backwater to a valuable global asset. In this new context, medical men and women—doctors, nurses, and apothecaries—were required for the health and vitality of those working the mines. A clear illustration of the relationship between medical practice and mining is the famous smallpox outbreak of 1882. Although the disease was widespread in Cape Town and had already made its way as far north as Mozambique, the colonial elite was desperate to prevent an outbreak in the areas surrounding Kimberley's diamond mines. And yet, smallpox reached Kimberley in late 1883, as recorded by four physicians on examining a group of migrant workers newly arrived from Mozambique. Those same four physicians soon reversed their diagnoses, however, claiming instead that the symptoms they observed were evidence of another illness entirely. As one witness later recounted, on arriving in Kimberley he encountered "a number of lads running about and offering little pink slips of paper to the people passing along the streets. On descending from the coach, which had pulled up in front of the Post Office on the market square, I was offered one of these slips. I was very puzzled on reading it, to see the words to this effect: 'The disease at Felstead's farm [on the outskirts of Kimberley] is not smallpox, it is a bulbous disease of the skin allied to pemphigus.'"[24]

The entire operation was a cover-up, supported and bankrolled by Kimberley's wealthy. Hans Sauer—whose words in the previous paragraph document the beginnings of the conspiracy—was the physician in charge of the epidemic in the region. He had traveled to Kimberley to investigate when he encountered the "lads" with their pink slips. Sauer was skeptical of the slips and continued his investigation, but at the entrance of the Kimberley Hospital he was treated coolly and refused entry—at least initially. Having forced his way into the wards by threatening police action, Sauer found a situation of extreme neglect. No attempt at isolation had been made, in part because hospital staff were still denying the presence of smallpox. In the mortuary, Sauer came across a case where a doctor had administered a tracheotomy—a procedure completely useless for treating smallpox, and which Sauer deemed "needless, and verging on criminality."[25]

Sauer called this episode the "greatest scandal in the long and honourable history of the British Medical Association."[26] Indeed, covering up the epidemic was a carefully planned conspiracy that required the complicity of much of Kimberley's white population. As Buss and Buss observe, there was a "fear that if an epidemic of smallpox became common knowledge in the town, the native workers in the diamond mines would pack up at once and leave with the result that the whole of South Africa would be ruined, to say nothing of a good number of millionaires living in Kimberley who had their entire fortunes sunk in the mines."[27] Sauer found, in fact, that the same doctors denying the presence of the illness had vaccinated some patients in secret.

One response to the scandal was to establish much stricter medical regulatory bodies. It was largely because of the Kimberley smallpox incident that the British Medical Association inaugurated its first branch in South Africa.[28] Just as significantly, 1891 saw the first legislation for the registration of qualified nurses under the Cape Medical and Pharmacy Act.[29] This was not just the first nursing registration in the Cape—it was the first time official registration for nurses had been legislated anywhere in the world. It is worth dwelling on this for a moment, especially since it forms such an integral— and in some ways exceptional—part of the history of colonial medicine in South Africa. In some ways, registration might be understood as a technique akin to stethoscope listening (we may be tempted to dub it a "cultural technique" in the parlance of post-Kittlerian media theory).[30] Like audile technique, registration conjoins the domain of science with the domains of health and law. In other words, it *articulates* the body with notions of rational knowledge and ordering. And, like audile technique, registration is a form of *mediation*, in the "extreme" sense that even when a nurse comes into direct contact with a patient, that tactile relation is made possible—and, indeed, mandated—by the bureaucratic machinery of a legislative body. And there is a third, peculiar sense in which registration is akin to audile technique: both function quite differently in the colony from the metropolitan center.

Shula Marks notes that in addition to its status as a global "first," the registration of nurses in South Africa was also atypical because it met such little resistance. Marks writes:

> In contrast to the situation in late nineteenth-century England where many doctors felt threatened by the registration of nurses and midwives, and where Florence Nightingale herself opposed their registration, in the

Cape Colony the self-consciously British doctors seem to have seen the new cadres of "lady nurses" as fitting "helpmeets" and appropriate adjuncts to their own newly acquired status. The majority of English-speaking, British-trained, white, middle-class, male doctors worked among the affluent patients in the urban areas, and had little to fear from female competition, while the small number of untrained nurses and midwives, who may have felt threatened by registration, lacked the power and influence to make their voices heard.[31]

Marks also points to a more specific reason that nursing registration may have happened in South Africa some three decades before the United Kingdom: the singular figure of Henrietta Stockdale. Stockdale is a legendary figure in contemporary South African nursing, as I learned a few years ago when I conducted formal interviews with nurses and midwives in Cape Town, Johannesburg, and Tshwane for a different project.[32] Often referred to as the "South African Florence Nightingale" (a title that is somewhat ironic considering Marks's observation in the above quotation), Stockdale was an exceptionally charismatic figure who had a close personal relationship with many of the Cape Colony's most important figures. Of particular note, Stockdale worked closely with both Cecil John Rhodes and Leander Starr Jameson (the famous doctor and protagonist of the "Jameson Raid").

It was none other than Henrietta Stockdale who barred Hans Sauer's entry into the Kimberley Hospital during the smallpox epidemic of 1882–1883. Sauer recounts the interaction in detail in his memoir, describing how Stockdale "flatly refused" his initial attempts to examine the clinic.[33] With this context in mind, Charlotte Searle's observation that Sister Henrietta enjoyed a "truly collegial relationship with the medical practitioners in the country" and that she had a "rare partnership with the great business, political, medical and religious leaders of the day" must be read with more than a hint of irony.[34] As Marks points out, Stockdale—like much of the white South African nursing sisterhood—was unabashedly pro-imperial.[35]

A few larger points can be gleaned from the preceding discussion. First, at least in the realm of medical practice, the Cape Colony cannot be viewed merely as a belated or mimetic version of what had already happened in the metropolitan center. Instead, developments in the colonies (such as a nursing register) happened *first* in the colony and were later imported back to the center. This was not only the case in medicine. To provide just two other examples: Kimberley had electricity several years before London did; and Johannesburg's electricity grid was integrated before London's.[36]

Second, power was operationalized in a fundamentally different manner in the colonies from the metropolitan center. The colonist did not merely "exploit" the black population, as much as he lived "on the native as one might live on the fruit of wild trees."[37] Rosalind Morris notes that in colonial and apartheid-era South Africa the procedures associated with Foucault's notion of biopower were "implemented only partially, and primarily for white populations."[38] "Black miners were treated as expendable," she continues, "and received relatively little biopolitical investment. They worked until illness made them, from the mine company's perspective, useless, at which point the miners were abandoned to fate."[39] In contrast to the biopower theorized by Foucault, the apartheid state acted according to a logic of *superfluity*, in which black life was considered excessive and "constituted wealth that could be lavishly spent."[40] This explains the response to the smallpox epidemic in Kimberley. The cabal of magnates and medical practitioners did not attempt to *save* African workers, even for selfish reasons like compelling them to work more. Rather, Jameson, Stockdale, and the others, concocted a full-scale conspiracy whose only aim was to not let the secret out. They treated black laborers as superfluous bodies that could be lavishly spent.

A third point is that the drive toward regulation and legislation was undermined by what many at the time viewed as proliferating *imposters*. Once the line between "official" and "unofficial" nurse had been drawn, those falling under the latter category were left with few options. Prior to the legislation, by contrast, many women worked in various "nursing" capacities without official qualification. But increased legislation also led to increased counterfeiting. By 1896, an author for the *South African Medical Journal* would complain that "the country is absolutely overrun with ignorant imposters, who dress and masquerade as nurses, many being barely able to read."[41]

What, in this particularly volatile context, becomes of Foucault's dictum that medical practice in the nineteenth century meant "the opening up of the concrete individual, for the first time in Western history, to the language of rationality, that major event in the relationship of man to himself and of language to things"?[42] As Sauer observes, the only time a body was "opened up" during the Kimberley smallpox scandal was for a totally useless tracheotomy.[43] The language deployed in Cape colonial medical practice, meanwhile, was often anything but "rational." Diseases were invented on the spot to suit the needs of colonial elites (recall the "bulbous disease of the skin allied to pemphigus"). Medical treatment was more a matter of jockeying for power and maintaining order in the colony than anything else. Medical practice was deployed as a form of deception based on an economic model of "superfluity." At least when it came to the lives of "Natives," medical rationality was largely jettisoned.

Metropolitan Auscultation

If we have good reason to doubt the applicability of conventional analysis to the African colonial case, how then might we analyze the deployment of medical practices, especially those associated with listening and the ear? To answer this question adequately, it is necessary to more fully flesh out how auscultation was conceptualized in the metropole.

To some extent, mediate auscultation is simply a generalization of a far older practice—percussing—in which a physician knocks on a patient's skin in order to ascertain the density of what lies beneath. As Peter Szendy suggests, "auscultation does not proceed by tapping blindly around, like percussion does: it stops at some points on the surface in order to *overpunctuate* them, by dividing their stigmatic unity, by listening to *more than one sign in one point*."[44] Laennec commented about mediate auscultation that one can "hear in the same point the heartbeat, the breathing, various rattles, the gurgling in the bowels."[45]

But the true medical "innovation"—at least in Foucault's terms of rationalization and "opening up" the body—was less a shift from percussing to auscultation than the introduction of an instrument to *mediate* sound between a patient's body and the doctor's ear. Mediate auscultation, through the deployment of an instrument such as the stethoscope, had myriad advantages over its unmediated counterpart (what Laennec began referring to as *immediate* auscultation). To name just a few: mediate auscultation cuts out unwanted sounds potentially contributed by the face during immediate auscultation; a stethoscope is nimbler than the human head and neck and can thus reach places on a patient's body that the human ear by itself cannot; it was far more socially acceptable in early nineteenth-century Europe for a doctor (usually male) to apply an instrument to a patient's body (especially a female patient) than to touch the patient directly with his face. One final important advantage was that immediate auscultation was considered "disgusting" (on

physical and moral grounds). Foucault takes disgust to be the major determining factor of mediate auscultation, writing that the stethoscope acts as a
"solidified distance" between doctor and patient.[46]

Laennec's earliest device was nothing more than a rolled-up piece of paper
applied to the patient's chest. He initially called his instrument simply *le
cylindre* (the cylinder) before coming up with "stethoscope," derived from
the classical Greek words for "chest" and "examine."[47] The binaural stethoscope familiar to us today was only put into practice in 1851 (even though it
had been proposed two decades earlier).[48] Many other "stethoscopic" devices
have been developed since, including ones intended for specific purposes.[49]

And yet, Laennec's most important insight was arguably less the invention
of the stethoscope itself than the principle behind it.[50] The full significance of
the stethoscope (and of mediate auscultation) can only be fully apprehended
when one acknowledges medical practice prior to the entrenchment of em-
pirical medicine in nineteenth-century Europe. Although knowledge of
human anatomy through direct inspection of corpses goes back to the sixteenth century, physicians relied mostly on patients' verbal accounts for their
diagnoses up until the beginning of the nineteenth century. Sterne writes
that in the nineteenth century,

> audile diagnosis shifted from a basis in intersubjective speech between
> doctor and patient to the objectification of patients' sounds—in mediate
> auscultation, patients' voices existed in relation to other sounds made by
> their bodies, rather than in a privileged relation to them. Speaking patients
> with mute bodies gave way to speaking patients with sounding bodies.[51]

This transformation implies a more general shift from an earlier "privileging
of the mouth, voice, and speech as the most important sonic location on
the [human] body to a diffusion of bodily sounds to be apprehended and
sorted out in the ear."[52] The voice became one contender among many for
the trained auditor's attention. The interesting point here is that although
it was thought that bodily sounds might potentially mislead doctors, it was
also maintained that such sounds could not be *deceptive*, since according to
theorists of the time the only sound capable of speaking an untruth was the
human voice.[53] And so, the centrality of the voice in medical diagnosis was
displaced, but without fully dislodging its singular claim to the very specific
kind of truth that can tell a lie.

Unlike the human voice, the heart did not declaim truths (or falsehoods) as much as emit sound that—if listened to correctly—was beyond reproach or doubt. The heartbeat came to be heard in terms of a Western ideology that Cimini and Moreno call the *sonic fiduciary*, a notion that joins "faith" and "fidelity" through those words' shared root in *fides*.[54] According to this ideology, sonic perception, especially when divorced from speech and language, "always already believes that *it* senses and *in* what it senses."[55] But this ideology relies on the fiction that medical knowledge can be severed from larger social worlds—a situation in which the heart is attended to *directly*, or a situation in which mediate auscultation produces, ironically, unmediated access to the functioning of the heart. If these pretenses were sustainable in Britain, they were not in the colonial context.

Auscultating the Periphery

To be sure, many ideas and beliefs were carried from Britain to its colonies. For example, an 1886 article in the *Journal* (a periodical published in Grahamstown), noted baldly that medicine is indeed a progressive science, presenting as evidence the stethoscope "which has made it as easy to detect a damaged heart or an inefficient lung as a broken leg."[56]

But references to stethoscopes are more often to fraudulence and deception than to the victories of science. These references increase around the turn of the twentieth century, when frontier development around Johannesburg was at its peak. In the last decade of the nineteenth century, most accusations of fraudulence against medical professionals concerned nurses. Recall, for example, the article from the *South African Medical Journal* that laments: "The country is absolutely overrun with ignorant imposters, who dress and masquerade as nurses, many being barely able to read."[57] A debate raged in medical and news periodicals about the establishment of proper authenticating insignia for registered nurses. All of this took place against the backdrop of an apparent ubiquity of "pirate nurses" in the late nineteenth century. After 1900, accusations of fakery were targeted increasingly at phony doctors in the Johannesburg area. For those con men pretending to be doctors, the stethoscope proved a handy tool. Indeed, simply being in possession of a stethoscope seemed to signal the genuine identity of a doctor. Hence, an article about a fraudulent doctor notes specifically that the man "had a stethoscope in his possession."[58] A slightly later article titled, "Man Said to Have Posed as Doctor" focuses on the possession and fake use of a stethoscope.[59]

The many cases of stethoscope fakery throughout the southern colony (but particularly in Johannesburg) were connected to multiple other forms of dissimulation. Crime reports from this period are littered with references to dubious promissory notes, forged "mine tickets,"[60] and the sale of fake medicine. Hence, while this chapter focuses primarily on stethoscopes, I would argue that duplicity in a variety of forms is a constitutive feature of nineteenth- and twentieth-century colonial cities. Kirsten McKenzie notes, for example, that the life of the most important surgeon and medical personality in early nineteenth-century Cape Town, one James Barry, was plagued by rumor and alleged dissimulation. "Although Barry's life was punctuated by scandals," writes McKenzie, "none matched the furor that erupted after his death, when the servant who laid out Dr Barry's body claimed that it was that of a woman and that she had borne a child." Stated generally: "In colonial cities people could be other than what they seemed."[61]

In Johannesburg, a particularly significant incident concerned a substance called "Lungsava" (to be pronounced "lung saver," I would imagine) that was targeted at those miners suffering from respiratory illnesses. In this case, one Charles Henry Stevens was accused of having "wrongly practiced or performed an act which specially belonged to the calling of a medical practitioner by medically examining John Eugene Durant, by making him undress, measuring and sound [sic?] his chest with his fingers, and diagnosing his complaint, prescribing the use of a medicine called 'Lungsava,' and receiving as payment certain promissory notes."[62] Stevens told the patient that part of his lung was gone and could be "rebuilt" by taking Lungsava.

In this case, it was not the stethoscope itself that was used to deceive. As mentioned in the above quote, Stevens used his fingers to measure and sound (that is, percuss) the chest. The same article does, however, note that Stevens "sometimes used his fingers and sometimes a stethoscope" for diagnostic purposes. But the issue was not only pretending to be a doctor by virtue of owning a stethoscope. The fakery, it seems, was more a matter of claiming knowledge of the size and functioning of inner organs. This, indeed, is what Foucault meant by the "opening up" of the body. But Stevens, to be sure, did nothing of the sort, and his "examinations" were mere ploys to sell Lungsava. (One can only wonder, then, about an affidavit submitted by a miner in which he thanks Lungsava for pulling him "out of the grave.")[63]

The case of Stevens illustrates clearly the asymmetry of power between physician and patient that has lasted until today. And the stethoscope adds a certain mystifying element to the otherwise fairly self-evident practice of audition, since the user of the stethoscope alone knows what he or she hears. Indeed, the stethoscope is probably the first example of an entirely private auditory experience, of an experience in which a single auditor has access to a particular sound.[64]

There is some evidence that con-doctors used the mystification of the stethoscope and of private listening against unwitting patients. For example, one such individual "examined the heart and lungs" of an African patient and "told her to say 'ninety nine' as fast as she could."[65] Now, the instruction to utter "ninety-nine" was a common one in early twentieth-century medicine. In general terms, it is part of a practice known as whispered pectoriloquy, in which the patient is asked to whisper a word or short phrase during stethoscopic examination in order to amplify lung consolidation. (If the lung is healthy, the whispered word will be heard only faintly. If there is fluid in the lung due to pneumonia, for example, then that fluid will transmit the whispered word loudly to the physician's ear.)

While it is possible that the African patient mentioned above understood this (or at least part of it), I think it is far more likely that the entire performance—the fake stethoscope examination, the whispered word, and so on—was part of the con. My interpretation of the scene described as somewhat mystified is bolstered when we recognize a dose of mystification is at work even in contemporary whispered pectoriloquy, which is a somewhat antiquated but still known practice. Indeed, the choice of the word "ninety-nine" comes from a German physician who found that *neunundneunzig* produced significant resonance in the chest, but when translated into English this resonance is lost.[66] Few doctors, either today or in the nineteenth century, seem to know this, however. "Ninety-nine," then, is more like a religious incantation than an aid to auscultation. One can only wonder what the word meant to the con-doctor and African patient in 1906.

From the perspective of sound studies, whispered pectoriloquy ("speaking from the chest") is an intriguing form of vocalization. The practice invites us to consider how the unmediated "truth" of the body's sound (the brute resonance of the lungs) becomes entangled with linguistic (non-)meaning. It also invites us to further broaden the repertoire of sounds we might profitably study, as for example in recent work on breath and whispering.[67]

In another case, a fraudulent doctor examined an African woman's "chest and used certain things which he pressed against her body and held the other part to her ear."[68] Here, the con man mystifies the instrument—or rather, "uses" it performatively—in a very paradoxical way: he makes a diagnosis by pressing the "other part" to the patient's own ear.

In early twentieth-century southern Africa, medical practice was riddled with problems, in large part because of the perceived gulf between metropolitan center and colonial periphery. It is not surprising, then, to find a very interesting article speculating on the invention of telephonic auscultation:

> The day when the medical man will sit in his London consulting room and examine patients hundreds of miles away by telephone is brought nearer by an invention which makes heart-beats distinctly audible over many miles of wire. This is the telephone relay, an instrument for magnifying sound, invented by Mr Sidney Brown. Used with an electric stethoscope, it has already enabled a doctor in the Isle of Wight to hear the heart-beats in a lady in London.[69]

The interest of this instrument for the patient in the colony is precisely that she or he can bypass local examination by subjecting the body directly to the "ear" of the metropole. If metropolitan medicine had opened up the human body to rationalization, and if the colony was "overrun by imposters," then the dream of a telephone relay would save the day. A magical lung saver indeed.

Unfortunately, we know very little about how colonial doctors at the time felt about mediate auscultation. Most of my evidence about stethoscopes and medical listening comes from newspaper article reporting on legal cases. A 1968 article notes that "South African medical literature is almost devoid of references to early stethoscopes."[70] The author is probably correct that the earliest *medical* paper to discuss stethoscopes is R. Schaffer's "The Misleading Stethoscope" from 1942. (It seems we will need to add yet another "shepherd" to the sound studies canon!) Although Schaffer's paper falls outside the historical scope of this chapter, it is nonetheless instructive since it captures something of the thinking about mediate auscultation leading up to the moment of its writing.

Unlike the vast majority of texts written in Britain or the United States, Schaffer's displays a striking ambivalence towards the stethoscope. "While extremely valuable, in the ears of the few," he writes, the stethoscope

becomes a snare and a delusion in the ears of the many. It has come to oc-
cupy far too important a place in the general scheme of things, and is now
considered so indispensable that a learned Appeal Court in this Province of
Natal has ruled that it would be unreasonable to suggest that a Zulu witch-
doctor should be allowed to carry on his trade without the assistance and
guidance of such a valuable instrument.[71]

Schaffer's complaint here concerns a confusion between the power of medical knowledge, on the one hand, and a mere physical device, on the other. He
suggests that stethoscopes themselves have become invested with so much
value, that even a "Zulu witch-doctor"—for him, the example par excellence
of irrationality—will soon be using them.

Reading further, one wonders whether Schaffer really believes that
stethoscopes can ever be "extremely valuable" (even if restricted to the "ears
of the few"). Perhaps thinking of those con men who trade in mystification
rather than the deployment of rationalized audile technique, Schaffer notes
the following about a novel "electrical contraption":

> The proud owner of it will be able to tune this device so as to reproduce
> his patient's heart sounds in either a major or a minor key and at any
> volume desired. The effect must be tremendous. No wonder the Zulu
> witch-doctor wants to add the stethoscope to his bones and to his other
> charms.[72]

Evoking the tired cliché of a "witch-doctor's" bone throwing, Schaffer again
emphasizes the association between certain kinds of mediate auscultation
and superstition. Towards the end of the article, he continues the association: "It is not my intention to suggest that the stethoscope should be entirely
abolished. The more elaborate models should, of course, be sent to museums,
and the more ornate ones will, no doubt, be bought by Zulu witch-doctors."[73]
By the end of Schaffer's paper it is unclear whether he believes that there is
any value in the instrument at all. Perhaps his faith in the instrument was finally broken by the many pirates, imposters, and con men. Distance from the
metropole—and, by extension, from the seat of rationality and science—only
made matters worse.

It remains unclear what the author has in mind regarding the auscultative
harmony of "heart sounds in either a major or a minor key."[74] (How would
it even be possible to transform the primarily rhythmic phenomenon of a

heartbeat into a harmonic one?) Even so, we have already noted that the body, when heard via mediate auscultation, has something of a polyphonic interior: heartbeat, breathing, various rattles, and a gurgling in the bowels, as Laennec put it. If, for European and North American physicians, the aim was to not be *misled* by the crossing of voices (to extend the musical metaphor further still) in this panoply of sound, in the southern colonies audition was a far more hazardous endeavor. There, various modes of deception impinged upon the clinical encounter, and competing knowledge systems led further to epistemological entropy.

An article titled "Will There Be a Witch-Doctor Boom in the Twentieth Century?" in the *South African Medical Journal* takes the "witch-doctor" analogy further.[75] In the article, mediate auscultation seems not to even be a real consideration, which leads the author to associate auscultation (of the "immediate" variety) with disgust, as Foucault would later document. "No unprejudiced man can doubt," he writes, "that, under certain circumstances, for instance, when the subject for examination is very smelly—a not extravagant hypothesis—that bone-throwing is preferable to auscultation and other old-fashioned methods of ascertaining the existence of disease."[76] The author takes a very patronizing attitude towards "witch-doctors," but is also charmed by their "innocence" (an old colonial trope, to be sure). The author emphasizes that the "witch-doctor" is "not always a *conscious* imposter" (my emphasis), in the sense that he *believes* the inventive and usually spurious chains of causation he uses for his practice. (The author provides as an example the apparent belief that snipping wooly socks will produce a snowstorm.) While the author finds this understanding of causation dubious, he emphasizes that even the British medical man cannot rule out *any* connection between seemingly unconnected events. "It would be only a very bold or a very foolish man who would assert that there would be none," he writes.[77] Returning to the question posed in its title, "Will There Be a Witch-Doctor Boom in the Twentieth Century?," the article concludes: "The coming century will certainly see a revival of mysticism. Then will the long-despised and neglected witch-doctor have his innings." If major Africanists like Adam Ashforth and Peter Geschiere are to be believed, the author named only as "M.O.M" in the *South African Medical Journal* was proved right.[78] Ashforth in particular has argued that witchcraft increased exponentially in the last decade of the *twentieth* century, thus illustrating once again that rationality and modernity do not move like straight arrows into the future.

Concluding Thoughts

This chapter has shown how medical practice in southern Africa diverged from the narrative of progressive rationalization that has become part of "sound studies." I want to emphasize that deception was a crucial vector in colonial epistemology. The stethoscope, in other words, was capable of more than simply misleading people, as Sterne notes of the Euro-American context. It was able to deceive people in large part because in southern Africa the sound of the heart (which by itself can mislead but not deceive) had not been sufficiently severed, via audile technique, from the wider cornucopia of sounds and sights: the voices of lying con-doctors, the muffled "ninety-nines" of whispered pectoriloquy, the powerful image of the stethoscope itself—of what the instrument represented to both colonialists and "Natives."

The stethoscope participated in a larger framework of dissimulation that we have every right to term deception. And the Enlightenment or the Ensoniment, on this score, is less the path toward rationality than the dialectical interplay of knowledge and deceit. If careful listening does not bring us closer to the truth of modernity, it nonetheless reveals a torsion at the heart, as it were, of the empire's acoustics.

Notes

I would like to thank Peter McMurray and Priyasha Mukhopadhyay for thoughtful comments on an earlier draft of this paper. I am also grateful for conversations with the following individuals: Hyun Kyong Hannah Chang, Nicholas Cook, Ziad Fahmy, Alexandra Hui, Nazan Maksudyan, Jairo Moreno, Rumya Putcha, Sindumathi Revuluri, Joel Steingo, Leonard Steingo, Elizabeth Tolbert, and David Trippett.

1. René-Théophile-Hyacinthe Laennec, *De l'Auscultation Médiate ou Traité du Diagnostic des Maladies des Poumons et du Coeur* (Paris: Brosson & Chaudé, 1819).

2. He apparently irked his examiners when he insisted on using a stethoscope during his final examination in Glasgow, a year before his departure for the Cape. Many have interpreted this incident to mean that the efficacy of the stethoscope was not widely accepted c. 1840, at least not in the United Kingdom—see, for example, Jean Comaroff, "The Diseased Heart of Africa: Medicine, Colonialism, and the Black Body," in *Knowledge, Power, and Practice: The Anthropology of Medicine and Everyday Life*, ed. Shirley Lindenbaum and Margaret Lock (Berkeley: University of California Press, 1993), 305–329; Sjoerd Rijpma, *David Livingstone and the Myth of African Poverty and Disease: A Close Examination of His Writing on the Pre-Colonial Era* (Leiden: Brill, 2015). Colonial newspapers did occasionally mention stethoscopes,

for example, the brief item, "Genezing van die Tering," *Kaapsche Grensblad* [Grahamstown], May 1, 1845, 3.

3. "Lifting up his stethoscope" is, of course, a figure of speech. But considering Conan Doyle's interest in and known deployment of the instrument, it is safe to say that he probably did take his stethoscope with him. See Sarah LeFanu, *Something of Themselves: Kipling, Kinsley, Conan Doyle and the Anglo-Boer War* (Oxford, UK: Oxford University Press, 2020), 1.

4. George Dunea, "Cecil John Rhodes: The Man with a Hole in His Heart," *Hektoen International: A Journal of Medical Humanities*, Winter 2018 <https://hekint.org/2018/12/18/the-man-with-a-hole-in-his-heart/>, accessed January 1, 2023.

5. Stanley Joel Reiser, *Medicine and the Reign of Technology* (Cambridge, UK: Cambridge University Press, 1978); Jens Lachmund, "Making Sense of Sound: Ausculation and Lung Sound Codification in Nineteenth-Century French and German Medicine," *Science, Technology & Human Values* 24/4 (1999), 419–450; Jonathan Sterne, "Mediate Auscultation, the Stethoscope, and the 'Autopsy of the Living': Medicine's Acoustic Culture," *Journal of Medical Humanities* 22/2 (2001), 115–136; Jonathan Sterne, *The Audible Past: Cultural Origins of Sound Reproduction* (Durham, NC: Duke University Press, 2003).

6. Sterne, *The Audible Past*, 93–94.

7. Brian Kane, "Sound Studies Without Auditory Culture: A Critique of the Ontological Turn," *Sound Studies* 1/1 (2015), 2–21.

8. Sterne, *The Audible Past*, 2.

9. Ibid., 127.

10. Kane, "Sound Studies Without Auditory Culture."

11. Michel Foucault, *The Birth of the Clinic: An Archeology of Medical Perception*, trans. A. M. Sheridan Smith (New York: Pantheon, 1973), xiv. Foucault is a prime example of someone who understood the rationalization of listening as a kind of "becoming visual" of the ear. Sterne (*The Audible Past*, 127) writes: "Foucault performs some interpretive gymnastics in order to locate mediate auscultation as a subspecies of the gaze."

12. Sterne, *The Audible Past*, 99.

13. See also Gavin Steingo and Jim Sykes, eds., *Remapping Sound Studies* (Durham, NC: Duke University Press, 2019).

14. Ackbar Abbas, "Adorno and the Weather: Critical Theory in an Era of Climate Change," *Radical Philosophy* 174 (2012), 7–13, at 10; my emphasis.

15. Ibid., 13.

16. Norbert Elias, *The Civilizing Process*, trans. Edmund Jephcott (New York: Urizen Books, 1978 [1939]); Bill Ashcroft, *Post-Colonial Transformation* (London: Routledge, 2001).

17. Talal Asad, "Conscripts of Western Civilization," in *Dialectical Anthropology: Essays in Honour of Stanley Diamond*, ed. Christine Ward Gailey (Gainesville: University of Florida Press, 1992), 333–351.

18. Shula Marks, *Divided Sisterhood: Race, Class and Gender in the South African Nursing Profession* (New York: St. Martin's Press, 1994), 79.

19. Marks, *Divided Sisterhood*, 79. Marks gets the part about the witch doctor from the Cape House of Assembly, G.64-'77, *Annexures to Votes and Proceedings*, King William's Town, Grey's Hospital, report of the superintendent of the Native Hospital, for the year 1876, p. 1. See Marks, *Divided Sisterhood*, 237n5.

20. "Royal British Nurses' Association," *Nursing Record & Hospital World*, Jan. 5, 1895, 5.

21. Ibid; my emphasis.

22. "Outside the Gates," *British Journal of Nursing*, 48 (June 22, 1912), 499.

23. "The Wellcome Historical Medical Museum," *British Journal of Nursing*, 59 (November 17, 1917), 319.

24. Hans Sauer, *Ex Africa* (London: Geoffrey Bles, 1937), 71–72.

25. Ibid., 86.

26. Ibid., 74.

27. W. M. Buss and Vincent Buss, *The Lure of the Stone: The Story of Henrietta Stockdale* (Cape Town: Howard Timmins, 1976), 73.

28. Buss and Buss, *The Lure of the Stone*, 79.

29. Marks, *Divided Sisterhood*, 113.

30. See Bernhard Siegert, *Cultural Techniques: Grids, Filters, Doors, and Other Articulations of the Real*, trans. Geoffrey Winthrop-Young (New York: Fordham University Press, 2015).

31. Marks, *Divided Sisterhood*, 114.

32. Gavin Steingo, "Listening as Life: Sounding Fetal Personhood in South Africa," *Sound Studies* 5/2 (2019), 155–174.

33. Sauer, *Ex Africa*, 84.

34. The quote is from Searle's 1984 "Henrietta Stockdale Memorial Lecture." As cited in Marks, *Divided Sisterhood*, 224n117.

35. Marks, *Divided Sisterhood*, 41.

36. On Kimberley, see Sauer, *Ex Africa*, 34; on Johannesburg, see Renfrew Christie, *Electricity, Industry, and Class in South Africa* (Albany: State University of New York Press, 1984).

37. Hannah Arendt, *Origins of Totalitarianism* (New York: Harcourt, 1968 [1951]), 190.

38. Rosalind Morris, "The Miner's Ear," *Transition* 98 (2008), 96–115, at 110.

39. Ibid.

40. Achille Mbembe, "Aesthetics of Superfluity," in *Johannesburg: The Elusive Metropolis*, ed. Sarah Nuttall and Achille Mbembe (Durham, NC: Duke University Press, 2008), 37–67.

41. *South African Medical Journal* 4, part 5 (September 1896), 123–125, at 125. The quote appears in the "Nursing" section, edited by Walter T. Harris (author not named).

42. Foucault, *The Birth of the Clinic*, xiv.

43. Sauer (*Ex Africa*, 86) notes that the procedure had been done allegedly "with the object of allowing air to get into the lungs." Considering that the doctors at Kimberley seemed to have known the problem was smallpox all along, my reading of Sauer here is that those who performed the tracheotomy later *claimed* that they did it for the purpose of allowing air into the lungs. My evidence for this (aside from the larger context) is that Sauer himself says that the procedure was criminal.

44. Peter Szendy, "The Auditory Re-Turn (The Point of Listening)," in *Thresholds of Listening: Sound, Technics, Space*, ed. Sander van Maas (New York: Fordham University Press, 2015), 18–29, at 22.

45. Laennec, *De l'Auscultation Médiate*, 23; as quoted in Szendy, "The Auditory Re-Turn," 22.

46. Foucault, *The Birth of the Clinic*, 164. This paragraph is based largely on Sterne's *The Audible Past*. Future research would do well to examine how "disgust" played itself out in the highly racialized colonial context.

47. Sterne, *The Audible Past*, 104.

48. Ibid., 111.

49. M. Donald Blaufox, *An Ear to the Chest: An Illustrated History of the Evolution of the Stethoscope* (Boca Raton, FL: Parthenon, 2005).

50. Sterne, *The Audible Past*, 102.

51. Ibid., 117.

52. Sterne, "Mediate Auscultation," 127.

53. Ibid.

54. Amy Cimini and Jairo Moreno, "Inexhaustible Sound and Fiduciary Aurality," *boundary 2*, 43/1 (2016), 5–41, at 7.

55. Ibid., 37; original emphases.

56. "The Science of Medicine," *The Journal* [Grahamstown], July 24, 1886, 3.

57. *South African Medical Journal* 4, part 5 (September 1896), 123–125, at 125.

58. "Medical Prosecution: Rivera in Court," *Rand Daily Mail* [Johannesburg], June 27, 1908, 8.

59. "Man Said to Have Posed as Doctor," *Rand Daily Mail*, April 30, 1915, 5.

60. These were basically employee punch cards. See *Rand Daily Mail*, February 2, 1916, 8.

61. Kirsten McKenzie, *Scandal in the Colonies: Sydney and Cape Town, 1820–1850* (Melbourne: Melbourne University Press, 2004), 3. The complexities of Barry's transgender identity in the context of nineteenth-century Cape Town have been widely documented. For an excellent discussion and references to other texts, see Erin Johnson-Williams, "Silencing 'Savage' Soundscapes: Hearing C-Section Births in the British Imperial Records," *Women and Music*, 26 (2022): 101–124.

62. "Lungsava in Court: Stevens Sentenced," *Rand Daily Mail* [Johannesburg], October 23, 1907, 5.

63. Albert Kerby, "Lungsava v. What the Miners Say: Persecution or Prosecution?" *Rand Daily Mail*, October 23, 1907, 5.

64. I would like to thank David Trippett for this idea.

65. "Court of the Eastern Districts," *The Journal* [Grahamstown], April 21, 1906, 4.

66. Such, at least, is William Dock's oft-cited argument. See Dock's "Examination of the Chest: Advantages of Conducting and Reporting It in English," *Bulletin of the New York Academy of Medicine*, 49/7 (1973), 575–582, at 579.

67. Ashon T. Crawley, *Black Pentecostal Breath: The Aesthetics of Possibility* (New York: Fordham University Press, 2016); John Mowitt, "Like a Whisper," *differences* 22/2–3 (2011), 168–189.

68. "How Women Are Duped," *Rand Daily Mail*, January 15, 1919, 3.

69. "Heartbeats Heard by Telephone," *Mafeking Mail and Protectorate Guardian*, June 24, 1910, 3.

70. S. Levin, "The Venerable Stethoscope," *S.A. Tydskrif vir Geneeskunde* 42/10 (1968), 232–234, at 232.

71. R. Schaffer, "The Misleading Stethoscope," *South African Medical Journal* 16/22 (1942), 400–401, at 400.

72. Ibid.

73. Ibid.

74. Ibid.

75. M.O.M., "Will There Be a Witch-Doctor Boom in the Twentieth Century?" *South African Medical Journal* 1/5 (1893), 89.

76. Ibid.

77. Ibid.

78. Adam Ashforth, *Witchcraft, Violence, and Democracy in South Africa* (Chicago: University of Chicago Press, 2005); Peter Geschiere, *The Modernity of Witchcraft* (Charlottesville: University of Virginia Press, 2009).

5

Epistemological *Jugalbandī*

Sound, Science, and the Supernatural in Colonial North India

Richard David Williams

In 1885, the Bengali musicologist Krishnadhan Bandyopadhyay (1846–1904) published his cutting-edge treatise on the theory and practice of music, the *Gītasūtrasār* (*Quintessence of Music*).[1] In his introduction, Krishnadhan proposed a radical approach to the epistemology of sound. He first acknowledged that music was the ancient lore of humanity ("*saṅgīt manuṣyajātir prācīnatam bidyā*") and then perfunctorily described the classic explanations for the divine origins of music.[2] Here, he was summarizing the established Indic traditions that articulated how sound had emanated from God—in this case, Shiva—which was how pre-colonial musicologists, especially those writing in Sanskrit or Classical Hindi (Brajbhasha), conventionally began their treatises. Even Krishnadhan's Muslim contemporaries, writing in Urdu, paid homage to these associations between sounds and Hindu gods in their own works. However, Krishnadhan then advocated for a new line of enquiry: "Now, having first given up all these mythological narratives and having adopted a logical and rational path, let it be seen how music originated" ("*ekṣaṇe ai sakal paurāṇik bibaraṇ parityāg kariýa nyāý o jukti path abalamban pūrbbak dekhā jāuk, saṅgīter utpatti kirūp*").[3]

Krishnadhan supported his position by invoking the English-language research of the Anglo-Indian scholar Augustus Willard (*Treatise on the Music of Hindostan*, 1834), as well as Charles Burney (*A General History of Music*, 1789), to argue that approaches borrowed from linguistics (*bhāṣātattvabit*) could explain how ancient music had evolved along with language. He summarized this perspective, and then grounded the production of music in animal biology:

Richard David Williams, *Epistemological* Jugalbandī In: *Acoustics of Empire*. Edited by: Peter McMurray and Priyasha Mukhopadhyay, Oxford University Press. © Oxford University Press 2024. DOI: 10.1093/oso/9780197553787.003.0006

From this it is known that music is the natural religion of living things. Accordingly, the famous zoologist, the most respected Darwin, has said that through sexual selection [*maithunik nirbbācan*] (sekśuẏ́yāl silekśan) the sounds of living creatures slowly changed by means of reproductive development [*jananbikāś*] (ibholyusan) and, propelled by necessity, this resulted in the physiological voice. In fact, living creatures attract females through vocal sounds, and there is a particular need for the voice to be appealing. This voice excelled most in the practice of humankind. It resulted in the various disciplines of vocal music, instrumental music, and so on.[4]

Krishnadhan's willingness to break with tradition extended to the minutiae of his treatise, in which he maintained that adopting Western staff notation was the best way forward for Hindustani classical music.[5] While other Bengali musicologists were also exploring the possibilities of notation, Krishnadhan's attitude gestured to his manifesto for sound as universal, intelligible, and open to what he considered a rational and analytical mode of study.

Across the nineteenth century and around the world, circles of scholars were fashioning a universal approach to sound and pursuing a musical history for humankind.[6] Krishnadhan's own acquaintance, Sourindro Mohan Tagore (1840–1914), had developed his own global histories of music, inspired in part by earlier European scholars, most notably Charles Burney (1726–1814).[7] Beyond musicology, questions about sound and phonology were being articulated through new vocabularies: in poetics, Sourindro Mohan's famous cousin, Rabindranath Tagore (1861–1941), wrote about the aural textures of the Bengali language, and created neologisms to accommodate his ideas, including *dhvanyātmak* ("soul in the sound") for onomatopoeia, as Projit Mukharji describes in his chapter in this volume.[8] Figures like Sourindo Mohan have received more scholarly attention in recent years, and have been positioned in global conversations.[9] This is not incidental: Sourindro Mohan wrote extensively in English and directly addressed conversations happening on the other side of the world, so he can readily be included in histories of European music and sound. But do these European histories and debates automatically turn "global" because they found conversation partners in India? Sourindro Mohan, like many Indian intellectuals of his time, was highly multilingual and pursued other lines of enquiry in Bengali and Sanskrit. His conversation partners in those language arenas, who chose not to write in English, have largely been forgotten in the "global" histories we write today.

Although musicologists like Krishnadhan Bandyopadhyay or Sourindro Mohan Tagore were engaging with developments in European research and scholarly practice—from sexual selection to staff notation—their ideas do not add up to a total epistemic rupture, or a total colonization of South Asian knowledge systems. Instead, elements of European science were reworked and embedded in longstanding, precolonial intellectual traditions about the nature of sound and music. Looking across a range of genres, and languages, this chapter examines moments of enquiry into the physics and experience of sound, and considers points of continuity, transition, and departures into new directions. Far from a single arena of global debate, nineteenth-century books, manuscripts, and newspapers in Indian languages indicate an enormous diversity of ideas, arguments, and sonic practices, many of which intersected with ideas from Europe, but selectively and often unexpectedly.

This chapter begins by reviewing how nineteenth-century Indian scholars discussed music and the nature of sound by drawing upon pre-colonial models. Moving outside of musical literature, I listen for echoes of sonic practices in books relating to medicine, healing, and divination, in order to consider the relevance of early modern understandings of sound and the body in the age of competing booksellers and doctors. Finally, I examine how French history and British philosophy became entangled with Hindustani music and tantric hymnology. I argue that these entanglements gesture to what I term an epistemological *jugalbandī*—borrowing a term in Hindustani music for a creative dialogue—that is, a contrapuntal, selective, and adaptive conversation between knowledge systems. I suggest this term challenges us to rethink how we discuss global flows of ideas under colonialism, without flattening the textures of local arenas and vernacular languages.

Pre-colonial Ontologies of Sound

When colonial-era writers recorded their reflections on the nature and physical properties of sound, or considered why music can have profound effects on the listener, they were joining a long line of South Asian scholars and musicologists who had been considering these questions for centuries.[10] Sanskrit intellectuals wrote densely theoretical treatises under the rubric of *saṅgīta-śāstra*, canonical knowledge relating to the performing arts, especially music.[11] As Krishnadhan noted much later, many of the classical works began with a consideration of primordial sound (*nāda*) and the relationship between sonic structures and the divine. The intellectual discipline of *saṅgīta-śāstra* continued and flourished under the Mughal empire, when, from the seventeenth-century onward, writings proliferated in Persian—as *'ilm-i mūsīqī*, "science of music"—and courtly vernaculars, especially Brajbhasha (classical Hindi).[12] Each generation of treatise writers was in conversation with their predecessors: some were very traditional, and systematically recalled established theory, while others were more radical and cutting-edge.

Far-reaching changes in the languages, literary forms, genres, and material media that were deemed appropriate for conversations about aesthetics had significant implications for writing about music. Over the mid-nineteenth century, Indo-Persian gave way to Urdu, and while Brajbhasha musical literature continued to be read, fewer poet-scholars wrote new works on music in that dialect, in line with a larger sea-change toward different forms of Hindi and new styles of poetry.[13] As the Persian treatise and the Brajbhasha poem were phased out, the nineteenth century saw a wealth of new treatments of music in Urdu, (Khari Boli) Hindi, and Bengali, including instrument manuals, essays, and music histories, alongside reorientations of older genres like the treatise or songbook.[14]

A particularly rich example is an Urdu study of music, Mardan Ali Khan's *Ghunca-yi Rāg* (*Bouquet of Music*, 1863). Khan's distinctively opinionated voice comes through as he examines the theory and history of north Indian music and surveys contemporary developments in instrumentation and dance. He situates the study of music within the intellectual sciences (*'ulūm-i maʿqūl*) and describes his own book as a "selective compendium" (*intekhāb mukhtaṣar*), prepared over a lifetime.[15] He relates information he has sourced from other works of scholarship, but also anecdotal knowledge (*'ilm-i khabar*) and the ideas learned from salon-type assemblies of musicians and listeners (*'ilm-i majlis*), including life-stories and "accounts of nobles, lords, blessed Sufis, and pure ones."[16] These threads can be tied together around a specific topic, as in his introduction to the legendary source of the *sur*, a musical "note" or the essential unit of "sound":

> The sound of a given *sur* is like such-and-such a creature. But there is a great variety among them, and the impression and constitution of each and every *sur* has been established. Some have written about the seven nostrils of the phoenix's beak. This is a famous mountain creature. The name of this creature in Arabic is *kuknus* or *kaknus* or *qaqnus*, and in Persian *ātish-zan*

["combustible"], and in Hindi they say *dīpak-lāṭ* ["lord of the flame"]. This comes from the combination of *dīpak*, meaning lamp-light, and *lāṭ*. It is well known that this is a solitary creature; it has no partner. In its youth, it becomes lustful, and collects together a pile of rubbish around itself, and dances like a peacock in heat. At that time, a beautiful sound comes out of its beak, in which there are seven nostrils, and a lamp-like light appears. Then, as a result of this, the pile instantly burns up into ashes, the phoenix itself burns up and becomes a fire, and from those ashes, by the knowledge of the omnipotent and perfect Creator, an egg comes out—then the creature is born out of this twenty days later. This is how it reproduces. God is most wise. The above picture is evidence.[17] When Hazrat Muhammad Gaus Gwaliori, whose miracles are famous, honored Tansen by meeting with him and giving him initiation, he revealed an abundance of hidden things, and showed him the course of this creature's lust. The aforementioned Miyan (Tansen) thought about the *sur dīpak* in connection to this. Actually, *dīpak rāga* had this same undesirable power.[18]

This passage conveys many of the larger themes in Mardan Ali Khan's scholarship. The phoenix allows him to draw connections between musical structures (the seven notes of the scale) and "natural" phenomena (the seven nostrils) and to convey how patterns in sound reflect the larger patterns of creation. His outline of the word for "phoenix" in Arabic, Persian, and Hindustani echoes other sections of the book, where he relates conceptual histories, explaining how an idea has been analyzed by generations of Muslim scholars, and transmitted through the circuits between Arabia, West Asia, and South Asia. The phoenix story, like other legends in the book, ultimately reveals God's miraculous designs. Khan gestures to implicit authorities and evidence: facts and opinions are "famous," "well-established," or confirmed by clear diagrams. This approach extends to his relating the authoritative oral transmission behind the stories, in this case the most celebrated musician of all time, Tansen, and his Sufi master. The single anecdote about the miraculous origins of the seven notes therefore sweeps across the western Indian ocean and through the centuries, tying the divine creation to historical celebrities and to the everyday practice of living musicians.

Many twentieth-century ethnomusicologists have discussed how musicians continue to collect stories about the miraculous qualities of particular *rāgas*,[19] and Daniel Neuman suggests that "the most articulate expression of the power of music is revealed through anecdotes, assertions, and stories about the magic potential of rāgs."[20] Mardan Ali Khan referenced *rāga* Dīpak, and later discussed the famous story of how Tansen caused a conflagration by performing it before the Emperor.[21] Early modern musicologists, poets, and painters had explored the idea that Dīpak could start fires, either literally or in the form of a fever within the body. In the hands of a master, Dīpak's power was miraculous, but it was also "undesirable" (to repeat Mardan Ali Khan's term) and dangerous, and there is a suggestion that these associations had made Dīpak unpopular and less likely to be performed as early as the seventeenth century.[22] Another Urdu music treatise, the *Maʿdan al-Mūsīqī* (*Mine of Music*) (written from the 1850s but first published 1925), also noted that because Dīpak could produce these fires,

> singing of this Raga was banned and its place given to the Khat Raga.... This is how our forebears described the effects of various Ragas. In fact the above Ragas were able to produce the prescribed power in those days. But now these effects have totally disappeared. Instances of Ragas captivating the minds of the listeners or making them weep, etc., are to be found even today.[23]

The power of Dīpak is not denied here but is relegated to a former age when musicians were able to perform miracles. Dīpak did not disappear entirely, but it is conspicuously absent in many otherwise comprehensive surveys of *rāga* from the nineteenth century.[24] This might be because people were wary of its heat, but also because it had acquired recognition—through word of mouth and the printed page—as the terrible fire-inducing *rāga*, which meant that to perform it *without* producing a flame was a sure sign of lackluster ability. By the end of the nineteenth century, it was a mark of gnostic prestige for musicians to know this solemn *rāga*. Neuman was told by a musician that although he knew how to perform Dīpak, he chose not to: "If you sing *Dīpak* rāg in a house regularly it will be bad for the house, it will be destroyed. If you play it for eleven days you feel it in your body. My eyes will start burning. I'll get pimples and boils."[25] Significantly, even when a musician says he does not (rather than cannot) sing Dīpak, by invoking the theory of sonic power of *rāga*, he lays claim to possessing the requisite skills to perform a miracle through his music.[26]

Dīpak was the most famous example of music's power, but it was not unique. Ideas about specific powers that were recorded in early modern music treatises continued to be reported by word of mouth in the mid-twentieth century:

> Kedar (rāga) melodies were taught by prison wardens and their assistants to those prisoners who were able to pay an adequate remuneration to the music teacher. If, by chance, the singing of Kedar did not melt the stones of the prison walls, the teacher would say that the rendition of the rāga was not absolutely correct.[27]

There are different dimensions to the distinctive powers of the rāgas, including factors like time of day. (Kaufman also recalled a conversation from 1934 that seemed to prophesy the Second World War as a consequence of Western musicians' performing compositions at wholly inappropriate timings.)[28] While the effective properties of music are primarily associated with rāga, musical structures like vocal ornaments were also considered powerful. In his memoirs, the celebrated musician Alladiya Khan (1855–1946) recalled how the dhrupad artist Behram Khan (d. 1878) had made a joke at the expense of khayāl singers; outraged, Mubarak Ali Khan (d. 1880)

> sang such a forceful taan [a fast vocal ornament characteristic of the genre] that because of its force, all the four legs of the cot broke and it crashed. . . . Mubarak Ali said, "If one sings a forceful gamak taan, he would die spitting blood. Such is the singing of the khayalia." Indeed, it was a taan of that kind. All fell silent.[29]

These examples indicate how the esoterica of music theory and pre-colonial philosophies of sound continued to resonate across the colonial period: ideas enshrined in the treatises of musicologists working in royal courts circulated through to the twentieth century, and impacted on the repertoires, self-fashioning, and life-stories of professional musicians. At the same time, the intellectual study of music and sound was far from static: these examples do not indicate an Orientalist fantasy of the superstitious musician. Pre-colonial studies of sound acknowledged the idea that musicians could wield miraculous powers through their craft, and musicologists invoked a variety of disciplines and theological worldviews to make sense of where sound came from and how it impacted the embodied self. As the infrastructures and contexts supporting musical scholarship changed over the nineteenth century, new generations of scholars engaged with older musical lore in new directions, resulting in a range of sonic epistemologies, from Mardan Ali Khan's phoenix to Krishnadhan Bandyopadhyay's Darwinism. This diversity can be interrogated further by looking beyond musical scholarship, to consider the place of sound in literature on the medical body.

Music and Medicine, Exorcism and Ears

Many early modern intellectuals thought of music and medicine as conversant disciplines. In the realm of Indo-Persian music treatises, Katherine Schofield has shown how seventeenth-century authors considered the influences of planetary bodies and bodily humors—drawing extensively on sources on Unani physiology—in their treatment of music's effects on the human system, and drew correlations between *rāgas* and the four elements and humors.[30] Certain scholars took a complementary interest in musicology and medicine; for example, Maharaja Pratap Singh (r. 1776–1803) of Jaipur, himself a lyricist and musician, commissioned one Hindi treatise on music, (*Saṅgītasāra* [*Essence of Music*], c. 1799) and another (in Hindi and Sanskrit) on medicine (composed in Hindi as the *Amṛt Sāgar* [*Ocean of Nectar*], and in Sanskrit as *Pratāp Sāgar* [*Pratap's Ocean*]). This medical treatise drew on canonical Sanskrit authorities (i.e., the *Caraka* and *Suśruta* compendia), but that is not to say it was treated as an old-fashioned relic.[31] It received renewed interest in the late nineteenth century, when it was published in at least eleven different versions between 1864 and 1878 alone.

A later edition of the *Amṛt Sāgar*, from 1891, is a multilayered work: the edited Hindi text has been augmented with lithograph illustrations of human anatomy, organs, cross-sections of a womb containing twins, and the complete human skeleton. These images appear at the front of the book, alongside diagrams of pots, jars, and vessels being heated in laboratory-style arrangements. These images, which appear without labels or captions, excite the reader's attention with the promise of contemporary science, before progressing to the text itself, a digest of classical Ayurvedic principles. This was not seen as an incongruous alignment: diagrams of muscles and tendons sat quite comfortably alongside discussions of the permeable, humoral body.[32] For example, fevers induced by ghost possession could be treated with mantras, apotropaic *añjana* (medicinal collyrium), and *tantra*:

On the attributes of the one in whom a fever has arisen from being struck
by a ghost:
>   Becoming agitated in their body
>   Sometimes laughing, sometimes weeping, sometimes trembling,
>   Their mind never still: know that a ghost has entered them.
On the effort to drive the ghost away:
>   Tying them up and scolding them, and applying mantra, *yantra*, and
>   *tantra*, and destroying them they are driven away bit by bit—everyone
>   has written the proofs of this.
On the mantra to cast out a ghost:
>   "aum ham him hun" drives out the ghost.[33]

This was the first in a series of effective mantras, which came with
accompanying instructions for how to use additional tools, such as peacock feathers. These authoritative techniques thus combined sonic utterance
(*mantra*), diagrams of power (*yantra*), and ritual instruments (*tantra*). The
pervasive presence of mantras and incantations throughout medical and therapeutic literature in the late nineteenth century qualifies the idea that printing
medical texts was a symptom of an imported modernity, grounded in a disen-
chanted worldview. The continuing relevance of mantras gestures to popular
assumptions about the efficacy of the utterance, the ability to impose one's will
on biological or spiritual matter through the medium of sound, and the place
of audition as a receptive gateway for gaining access to the patient's internal
constitution.[34] The ears in effect provided a keyhole to unlock the self. This
physiology drew on a long-established tradition of the porousness of the yogic
body, which had multiple "doors," that is, points of access and manipulation.[35]

What if the ears themselves were compromised? The *Amṛt Sāgar* listed
thirty-two illnesses of the ear: twenty-eight from the *Suśruta* Ayurvedic
compendium, and four from *Carak*. It then considered a selection in detail:

On ringing in the ears: when Wind is trapped in someone's earhole, and
then in that man's ear many sounds are resounding, beginning with the
bherī drum, *mṛdaṅg* drum, and conch, they call this "ringing in the ears"
(*karṇanād*).

On tinnitus: when Wind, Bile, and Phlegm become trapped in someone's
ear, and in their ear there is a cough-like sound of splitting open bamboo—
they call that illness "tinnitus" (*karṇakṣveḍ*).[36]

The reader is then led through a series of treatments (*jatan*, pp. 313–316), beginning with:

> the juice of green ginger mixed with rock salt and oil—taking all of these together and heating them a little, pour them into the ear; then earache, ringing in the ears, and deafness and tinnitus (*kān kī pīṛ karṇanād aur baharāpan aur karṇākṣveḍ*)—all these illnesses will be removed.[37]

In my translations, I have kept the distinction between the conditions known as *karṇanād* and *karṇakṣveḍ* by translating them as "ringing in the ears" and "tinnitus" respectively, but this raises a challenge that numerous scholars working in sound studies have underlined.[38] Projecting English phrases and modern medical terms backward in time poses problems. Today, practitioners and scholars of Ayurveda may see both terms as equally referring to tinnitus.[39] However, Mark M. Smith has stressed that people made sense of the sounds they experienced using comparisons from their own world: just as soldiers in the American Civil War heard bullets and thought of buzzing bees or swarming insects,[40] the theorists of Ayurveda considered how people heard sounds without external causes, and described those sounds in terms of specific drums, the conch, cough- or sneeze-like wrenching sounds, and the ripping of bamboo.

The selection of instruments in the description of these auditory conditions is revealing, as they had particular connotations in divination. Nineteenth-century readers continued to consider destiny as entangled with the human body and its sonic environment. A popular Sanskrit divination manual, the *Pañcasvarāsya* (*The Five Vocalisations*) of Prajāpati (pre-1625), which had many Hindi commentaries that continued to circulate in manuscript form into the mid-nineteenth century, laid out the methods of *svar vijñān*, "breath knowledge."[41] The practitioner was advised to exhale and sound out syllables, and then diagnose their meanings by consulting a prescribed chart. The sonic textures of the breathed, uttered syllables, drawn upward and outward from the inner constitution, could reveal larger truths and generate knowledge.[42] This attentiveness to the sound and movement of the breath was part of a larger set of sonic omens, including divination by listening to animals and birds, which were often discussed in nineteenth-century guides to medicines.[43]

The production of printed books in Hindi escalated dramatically mid-century and jostling publishers stressed how their products could provide a diverse toolbox for self-regulation and management.[44] So much is apparent from works like the *Amar Binod Bhāṣā* (*Amar's Vernacular Delight*, 1884), another medical handbook that reformatted pre-colonial lore for the contemporary book market. This was a Hindi (Brajbhasha) adaptation of the medical sections in the famous Sanskrit encyclopedia, the *Amarakoṣa*, edited for ease of use. The subtitle read:

> [A book] in which the causes of disease are described from the definitions of the Glossary [i.e., the *Amarakoṣa*], covering in every matter the treatment of all diseases by means of medicine, mantra, *yantra*, and so on—and, from the definitions of astrology, a complete understanding of mortality.[45]

In this manual, sonic practices were included both as treatments (i.e., healing mantras) and omens, as in the section on *śakuna-parīkṣā*, or how to identify auspicious signs for embarking on a journey:

> *bheri, mṛdang*, and *mardal* sound sweet
> > maid and calf are running
> a pair of fish, curds cooking
> > a priest comes to speak, with a *tilak* on his face . . .
> *vīṇā, bher*, and conch give so much delight
> > the king goes with a courtesan
> all these and more are all good signs
> > when you encounter them, set off from your home
> he whose front door the doctor (*vaidya*) visits
> > will never again suffer from an illness in this lifetime.[46]

It is unclear what was meant by these three drums—*bher* or *bheri*,[47] *mṛdang*, and *mardal*—sounding sweet (*mṛdu*), or why a *bher* might be paired with a conch and *vīṇā*, or whether the readers of this book understood what they were expected to listen out for. However, this kind of prescription indicates how print did not simply provide a platform for disseminating either "modern" or European ideas: some nineteenth-century readers clearly enjoyed the new opportunity to engage with older systems of sound knowledge. Listening practices were wide-ranging—from the sigh of the breath to the calls of birds—and were not thought of as a separate domain but fed directly into the shared techniques of healing and divination.

These books circulated alongside other kinds of self-help manual, which took an entirely different approach, such as *Kaṇṭhasudhāranbidhi*

(*Treatments for Improving the Voice*, 1886) by Saiyid Gulam Husen, a *ḍākṭar* based in Gurgaon.[48] Music and medicine converged here too, but Husen's priority was to recommend chemical preparations for the health and maintenance of singers' voices. In his preface, Husen followed the familiar model of many other self-help books, by describing how he had helped a friend who was struggling to sing the *Rukmaṇī Maṅgal* (a song associated with wedding celebrations) by applying a medication (*auṣadhī*) to his throat. His friend benefitted from it immensely and, we are told, implored the reluctant Husen to write a book for treatments for when you lose your voice ("*galā baiṭhne kā ilāj*"). Instructions appeared in Hindi, while ingredients were written (in lithograph) both in Devanagari and a cursive Roman script—e.g., "*kār boneṭ āf ye moniuā 4 gren*—Carbonate of ammonia gr 4"[49]—perhaps to clarify the intended meaning or to assist the book user when they went to source their chemicals. The book also provided a brief introduction to the anatomy of the throat—beginning with how there were two distinct "paths" (*mārg*) for eating-drinking and breathing, and two cords (*ḍoriyāṅ*), and so on—which Husen attributed to the saying of the *ḍākṭar*s. In his explanation of how the voice can become hoarse, he discussed the problems facing singers in terms of biological matter, the movement of air, exertion, and changes with age. He also suggested that certain practices, like drinking alcohol, could damage the voice. Husen prioritized the *ḍākṭarī* model, but also briefly outlined how *hakīm*s and *vaidya*s (i.e., Unani-Tibb and Ayurvedic physicians) would explain hoarseness too.[50]

Reading these materials together gestures to a range of popular understandings of how the body operated. Non-specialists and specialists alike listened to both the workings of the body and its sonic environment and understood the human body as physically and spiritually malleable, vulnerable both to sonic instruments like a mantra, an auditory omen, or a chemical compound. Intellectually, music and medicine sat on a continuum of knowledge and self-regulation. Ideas and substances from Europe could be brought into the mix but did not automatically displace traditional techniques and theories. In the following section, I consider further how we might conceptualize these subtle forms of reconfigured knowledge.

Epistemological *Jugalbandī*

Conversations about the nature of sound and its effects on the body were unfolding across different genres and languages, and a number of writers drew on an eclectic range of theoretical frameworks and European sources to develop new ways of thinking through old traditions about sound. Rather than replacing or subordinating local knowledge systems, unfamiliar materials from European languages were invoked as authoritative opinions, in order to provide evidence and support for Indian ideas. This eclectic approach to reinforcing indigenous concepts of sound and metaphysics is quite different from "diffusionist" models of colonial intellectual history, and speaks to the ongoing debate about vernacular modernities.[51] In the realm of colonial-era musicology, it has often been taken for granted that Indian scholars changed the way they wrote about music, having digested the methodologies and biases of English Orientalist scholars, especially William Jones. However, I have argued elsewhere that this kind of historiography has been overly dependent on Anglophone sources and reformist literature. By taking the vast vernacular archive of sources about music into account, the picture becomes much more complicated: European ideas—when they were considered relevant—were not systematically imported to the absolute detriment of pre-colonial music theory.[52] In certain cases, it is perhaps more helpful to read the archive in terms of what I term an epistemological *jugalbandī*. In classical music, the *jugalbandī* (lit. "to tie a pair") is a form of duet between two well-matched solo vocalists or instrumentalists.[53] In the context of scholars attempting to make sense of sound and explain its power, we find works that are neither a neat translation of European ideas nor a reiteration of pre-colonial lore: instead, the writers tie together different epistemologies, appealing to a universal sense of sound. Here, I will briefly comment on two Bengali examples from the 1870s to 1880s that exemplify this eclecticism.

Nabinacandra Datta was a scholar of music based in Calcutta, who was part of a community of amateur musicians and enthusiasts that collected around the prolific musicologist, Sourindro Mohan Tagore and his academy, the Bengal Music School (est. 1871). Taking inspiration from Tagore and Kshetramohan Goswami (1813–1893), who took a directing role at the School, Nabinacandra wrote a guide to classical *rāgas* in 1872, using Goswami's favored notation system. On the title-page of this hefty work (307 pp.), the *Saṅgītaratnākara*, Nabinacandra gave his study an English subtitle, *The Art and Science of Hindu Music*, and advertised his other books, on astronomy and agriculture.

From his introduction, it appears that Nabinacandra was writing in harmony with a number of other music enthusiasts associated with Tagore's circle, who bemoaned what they saw as the stagnation of musical progress in India.[54] Music had not realized its full potential, he argued, because of people with "impure tastes" ("*asādhu rucir prabhābe*") who did not appreciate the intricacies and the profound power ("*asāmānýa śakti*") of "pure" music ("*pabitrabhāb*"). Evidence of this power could be traced throughout world history, for example:

> At one time, King Henry IV of Denmark expressed his desire to test the power of music, and commanded a singer: "You boast that your own compositions will de facto drive their performer insane—demonstrate this to me today!" The singer, following the king's command, commenced such unprecedented music that there and then the king himself was driven insane, and four or five nearby individuals lost their lives and perished. Once Caliph Umar was quelling a rebellion and gave the order to behead the prisoners. A Persian singer was among them. He told the king that he desired to sing a song, and if the king permitted it then he would fulfil his heart's desire. The king consented. He sang such a sweet tune that Umar granted him his life and, upon his request, the lives of the other prisoners.[55]

It is unclear precisely where Nabinacandra acquired these anecdotes, but he may have been mis-reading Jean-Jacques Rousseau's (1712–1778) *Dictionary of Music* (c. 1765). Rousseau retold two fables together: one about Eric, King of Denmark, who was driven into a frenzy by music and murdered his finest servants, and another about the musician Claudin, in the court of Henri III of France, whose rendition of the Phrygian mode excited a courtier to take up arms before the king, before Claudin calmed him down again with the Hypophrygian mode.[56] Nabinacandra appears to have conflated the two stories (and added to the confusion by misreporting Henri III as Henry IV). Rousseau had considered several tales in this vein, to explore the power of music over "the affections of the soul" and "the marvelous and almost divine effects which the Ancients attribute to *Music*."[57] Like Rousseau, Nabinacandra collated a range of stories around these common themes, and passed seamlessly through Denmark, the Caliphate, the court of Murshidabad in Bengal, and then onto the French Revolution:[58]

> At the time of the French Revolution, a song was composed called the Marseillaise Hymn [*mārselis him*]. Wherever that song struck, the people there would give up their everyday business and taking up swords would

set forth for the cause of war with eastern Austria and Prussia. In the end, under Napoleon's command, that army conquered almost all of Europe. Many such examples of Music's wondrous, bewitching power could be collected. The Father of the Universe, the treasury of compassion, has revealed his limitless greatness by making this kind of ineffable, concrete connection between our sense of hearing and sound [*śabder sahita śrabaṇeindriẏer eirūp anribbacanīẏa sambaddha nibaddha kariẏā*].

Theories about the metaphysical effects of sound and legends about music's miraculous powers were nothing new to Indian scholars, but Nabinacandra repositioned local figures—like the Bengali tantric singer Ramprasad Sen—in a global history of sonic power, where music could rob the individual of their sanity, right injustices, and even change the political destiny of Europe. Nabinacandra's discussion of the Marseillaise hymn is very similar to those of many English writers,[59] but his research is interlaced with Hindu theology, revolving around the Father of the Universe (Biśvapitā, elsewhere Lord of the World, Jagdīśva) and expressed through a specific vocabulary for describing a sacred "wondrous, bewitching power" ("*adbhut mohinī śakti*"). In particular, *mohinī śakti* was a familiar term in Vaishnava religious tradition, gesturing to the feminine energy within God that is responsible for the enchanting and illusory world of perception. Therefore, tropes borrowed from Rousseau and Napoleon were deployed as rhetorical strategies to think through the categorical sense organs (*indriẏa*), divine energy (*śakti*), and sacred sound (*śabda*).

Nabinacandra's essay at the start of a book of *rāga* notations was typical for his time: many Bengali music editors liked to begin their performance-oriented books with intellectually stimulating introductions. A case in point is Kailascandra Simha's *Sādhak Saṅgīt* (*Worshipper's Music*, 1885), a tantric hymnbook. This was designed for goddess worship, both in terms of providing an appropriate song repertoire, and examining the sonic techniques for accessing the deities through meditation and the activation of the body's *cakra*s.[60] To support these endeavors, Kailascandra included an introduction to the six *cakra*s, and the truth of the Goddess as the primeval energy (*śakti*) of the universe. Like Nabinacandra, he pulled European intellectuals into the conversation, making a direct reference to the essays of Herbert Spencer (1820–1903)—"There is an Infinite and Eternal Energy from which everything proceeds" (cited in English)—as an example of non-Hindu scientists acknowledging the reality of the Goddess, even without the insights of devotion (*bhakti*).[61]

These two Bengali authors were not merely reiterating ancient ideas about sound and the sacred. Of course, they were speaking to a long-standing intellectual tradition, using familiar categories and theological principles, and had not radically changed the terms (literal words and larger concepts) of the discussion. However, their printed medium, colonial readership, and social position as urban gentleman-scholars colored their studies and marked a departure from the work of earlier generations of professional musicologists and theologians. In particular, their reading habits and engagement with non-Indian history, trends in Anglophone writing about music, French legends, and British philosophy gave them the ingredients to compose a *jugalbandī* of European and South Asian reflections on sound.

They represent a quite distinct approach to that taken by writers like Krishnadhan Bandyopadhyay, from the start of this chapter, who acknowledged Hindu ideas about the origins of music but found Darwin's evolutionary theory was more convincing. It is important to remember that Krishnadhan was originally part of Nabinacandra's musical community, and had worked closely with Kshetramohan Goswami of Bengal Music School fame, before a series of disagreements led them to parting company.[62] Krishnadhan did not engage European voices as confirmation of Indic ideas but instead asked his readers to change their assumptions about the sonic universe, appealing to a different kind of modernity from the version cultivated by Nabinacandra and other neo-traditionalists.

Looking beyond music and Bengal, and moving westward to Bihar, it is apparent that Krishnadhan was not alone in his warm embrace of European science as an alternative to *śāstra* lore. One especially intriguing window onto the kinds of conversations happening around the science of sound comes from an Urdu work on acoustics, thermodynamics, and optics, *'Ilm-i āvāz o garmī o roshnī* (*Knowledge of Sound, Heat, and Light*, 1871). This was a composite text of essays and even newspaper columns on the physics of soundwaves, some of which were incorporated into the body of the book complete with the lithographed headings of the Patna-based newspaper *Chasma-yi 'Ilm* (*Fountain of Knowledge*). The editor may have been one Sohan Lal, who printed a treatise on heat from the same press.[63] Here, sound was explained in terms of the physics of waves and vibrations, presented through digestible prose and neatly annotated diagrams of soundwaves, resonating tuning forks, and a concise illustration of the anatomy of the human ear.[64] This last image, which showed bones and membranes in cross-section, was a reproduction ultimately derived from a drawing by William

Bagg for John Quain's (1796–1865) *Elements of Anatomy* (first published 1835).[65] The *Elements of Anatomy* gave a description of the "tympanum or drum" in the middle ear,[66] which is labelled in the Urdu lithograph as "*kān kā ḍhol*," the "*ḍhol* [a specific variety of drum] of the ear."[67] The prose is economical and less ornamental than my previous Bengali examples, but this writer was also conscious of his readers' response to this new information about how their bodies were operating without their knowledge. Following an explanation of how the eardrum responds to soundwaves, he observed:

> This is an astonishing mystery (*'ajīb bhed*), the likes of which cannot be solved. But it is well established that what we call seeing or hearing, and the activity in the brain (*jo 'aml dimāgh men*), is one and the same thing. That which is outside of the brain is a wave (*lahar*) or a variety of motion (*cāl*).[68]

Works like this book, or the newspaper columns dedicated to scientific findings, gesture to the excitement these Urdu writers and journalists experienced as they worked through guides to human anatomy and physics textbooks. Curating and re-presenting this material around the themes of "sound, heat, and light" was partly a way to think through the different aspects of waveforms, but also, I suggest, to ground physics and biology in the tangible realm of experience and sensation. The science enthusiasts of Patna were asking their readers to reconsider the underlying structures of their world, their senses, and their bodies. This demanded rethinking the mechanics of how they listened, but also the philosophy and enchantment of their conceptual universe, setting aside notions of primeval *nāda* or humors in deference to reverberating waves and eardrums.

***

How does the north Indian-language archive shed light on the landscape of intellectual engagement with music and sound under colonialism? While many of the authors I have examined were from elite communities, and were at ease with developments in European history, science, and philosophy, others were not; in particular, re-workings and new editions of pre-colonial texts, and continuities between manuscripts and printed books, gesture to larger arenas of listeners, musicians, physicians, astrologers, and journalists, who were engaging with the theory and practice of sound. The esoterica of musical metaphysics were not necessarily obscure, and the persistent trope of the fiery dangers of Dīpak gestures to the ongoing relevance of ontologies of sound throughout the colonial and post-colonial period. However, these ideas were not unchanging or timeless either, and transformed alongside the structures of mediation and interpretation. Even before the advent of recording technology, the possibilities of the book industry, print journalism, notation, and the reproduction of schematic diagrams influenced the ways in which discussions about sound unfolded. However, the influence of colonial technologies was not straightforward: diagrams of the dissected eardrum circulated alongside images of the seven-nostriled phoenix, and both were used as supporting "evidence" for the author's own knowledge system. While the illustrated ear served a similar function in the *Elements of Anatomy* and the *'Ilm-i āvāz*, the same cannot be said of Herbert Spencer's appearance as an unwitting devotee of the tantric goddess.

I have attempted to make sense of certain thinkers in terms of an epistemological *jugalbandī*, since the overall picture is one of diversity and creative adaptation. Ideas and practices from Europe were selectively deployed and refashioned, outright ignored, collated alongside local or older knowledge systems, or used to overhaul the *śāstra*s altogether. How can this multifaceted landscape of intellectual enquiry and sonic practice be incorporated meaningfully into a global history of sound in the nineteenth century? I suggest that the archives should caution us when we position non-European writers who responded directly to contemporary European discussions about music as the only type of "global" intellectual. Europe's explicit conversation-partners were only one element in the larger landscape of nineteenth-century reflections, and by concentrating too narrowly on Anglophone voices we risk closing our ears to the textures of music and sound in colonial South Asia.

Notes

1. While Anglophone scholarship conventionally associates "musicologist" with the growth of *Musikwissenschaft* in nineteenth-century Europe, in this article the term refers to scholars engaged with the systematic and canonical epistemology of music that developed in the South Asian context.

2. See Richard David Williams, "Music, Lyrics, and the Bengali Book: Hindustani Musicology in Calcutta, 1818–1905," *Music and Letters* 97/3 (2016), 465–495; Sagnik Atarthi, "'Whither Musicology? Amateur Musicologists and Music Writing in Bengal," *Ethnomusicology Forum* 26/2 (2017), 247–268.

3. Krishnadhan Bandyopadhyay, *Gītasūtrasār* (Koch Bihar: Rajakiya Press, 1885), i. All translations are my own unless attributed otherwise.

4. Ibid., ii. See Charles Darwin, *On the Origin of Species by Means of Natural Selection*, 5th edition (London: John Murray, 1869), 559.

5. On debates about notation in this period, see Charles Capwell, "Musical Life in Nineteenth-Century Calcutta as a Component in the History of a Secondary Urban Center," *Asian Music* 18/1 (1986), 139–163, especially 148–150.

6. See James Q. Davies, "Instruments of Empire," in *Sound Knowledge: Music and Science in London, 1789–1851*, ed. James Q. Davies and Ellen Lockhart (Chicago: University of Chicago Press), 145–174.

7. On Tagore's musicology, see Williams, "Music"; Charles Capwell, "Marginality and Musicology in Nineteenth-Century Calcutta: The Case of Sourindro Mohun Tagore," in *Comparative Musicology and Anthropology of Music: Essays on the History of Ethnomusicology*, ed. Bruno Nettl and Philip V. Bohlman (Chicago and London: University of Chicago Press), 228–243.

8. Hanne-Ruth Thompson, *Bengali* (Amsterdam: John Benjamins), 317.

9. Bennett Zon, *Evolution and Victorian Musical Culture* (Cambridge, UK: Cambridge University Press, 2017), 78–114.

10. For a comprehensive discussion of Sanskrit writings on sound, see Annette Wilke and Oliver Moebus, *Sound and Communication: An Aesthetic Cultural History of Sanskrit Hinduism* (Berlin: De Gruyter, 2011). On Sanskrit music treatises see Emmie te Nijenhuis, *Musicological Literature* (Wiesbaden: Otto Harrassowitz, 1977).

11. Jonathan Katz, "Music and Aesthetics: An Early Indian Perspective," *Early Music* 24/3, 407–412, 415–420.

12. Emmie te Nijenhuis and Françoise "Nalini" Delvoye, "Sanskrit and Indo-Persian Literature on Music," in *Hindustani Music: Thirteenth to Twentieth Centuries*, ed. Joep Bor, Françoise "Nalini" Delvoye, Jane Harvey and Emmie te Nijenhuis (New Delhi: Manohar, 2010), 35–64; Richard David Williams, "Reflecting in the Vernacular: Translation and Transmission in Seventeenth- and Eighteenth-Century North India," *Comparative Studies of South Asia, Africa and the Middle East* 39/1 (2019), 96–110; see also Katherine Butler Schofield, *Music and Musicians in Late Mughal India: Histories of the Ephemeral, 1748–1858* (Cambridge, UK: Cambridge University Press, 2023).

13. Allison Busch, *Poetry of Kings: The Classical Hindi Literature of Mughal India* (New York: Oxford University Press, 2011), 202–239.

14. Allyn Miner, "Enthusiasts and Ustāds: Early Urdu Instructional Books," unpublished paper; Williams, "Music."

15. M. M. A. Khan, *Ghunca-yi Rāg* (Lucknow: Naval Kishor, 1863), 2–3.

16. Ibid., 2.

17. This description is accompanied by an illustration of the phoenix with seven nostrils.

18. Ibid., 13–14.

19. An early reference in English scholarship is A. H. Fox Strangways, *The Music of Hindostan* (Oxford, UK: Clarendon Press, 1914), 155.

20. Daniel M. Neuman, *The Life of Music in North India: The Organization of an Artistic Tradition* (Chicago: University of Chicago Press, 1990), 66.

21. Khan, *Ghunca-yi Rāg*, 61.
22. Katherine Ruth Butler Brown, "Hindustani Music in the Time of Aurangzeb," (PhD dissertation, SOAS University of London, 2003), 177, 187, 196–197; Walter Kaufmann, *The Ragas of North India* (Bloomington: Indiana University Press, 1968), 53.
23. As translated in Karam Imam and Govind Vidyarthi, trans., "Melody through the Centuries," *Sangeet Natak Akademi Bulletin* 11–12 (1959), 6–14, 13–26, 33, 49–58, at 8.
24. Example notations given in Alain Daniélou, *The Rāga-s of Northern Indian Music* (London: Barrie and Rockliff, 1968), 253–255.
25. Neuman, *Life of Music*, 66.
26. See Richard David Williams, "The Rāg that Burned down Delhi: Music and Memory Between 1857 and 1947," *Cracow Indological Studies* 23/1 (2021), 197–217.
27. Kaufmann, *Ragas*, 13.
28. Kaufmann, *Ragas*, 18.
29. Alladiya Khan, Amlan Das Gupta, and Urmila Bhirdikar, trans., *My Life: As Told to His Grandson Azizuddin Khan* (Calcutta: Thema, 2000), 46.
30. Brown, "Hindustani music," 189–201.
31. On colonial and modern Ayurvedic medicine, see Rachel Berger, *Ayurveda Made Modern: Political Histories of Indigenous Medicine in North India, 1900–1955* (London: Palgrave Macmillan, 2013); Dagmar Wujastyk and Frederick M. Smith, *Modern and Global Ayurveda: Pluralism and Paradigms* (Albany: State University of New York Press, 2008); Projit Bihari Mukharji, *Doctoring Traditions: Ayurveda, Small Technologies, and Braided Sciences* (Chicago: University of Chicago Press, 2016).
32. Ayurvedic medicine builds on the doctrine of three humors (*tridoṣa-vidyā*), that is, Wind (*vāta*), Bile (*pitta*), and Phlegm (*kapha*).
33. Pratap Singh, *Amṛt Sāgar* (Delhi: Hindu Press, 1891), 30.
34. On mantra, see André Padoux, "Mantra," in *The Blackwell Companion to Hinduism*, ed. Gavin Flood (Oxford, UK: Blackwell, 2005), 478–492.
35. Monika Horstmann, "Managing the Senses in Sant Devotion," in *Exploring the Senses: South Asian and European Perspectives on Rituals and Performativity*, ed. Axel Michaels and Christoph Wulf (New Delhi: Routledge, 2014), 78–92.
36. Singh, *Amṛt Sāgar*, 311.
37. Ibid., 313.
38. For an overview, see Mark M. Smith, "Echo," in *Keywords in Sound*, ed. David Novak and Matt Sakakeeny (Durham and London: Duke University Press, 2015), 55–64.
39. Hemangi Shukla and Nileshkumar Chabhadiya, "A Clinical Study on the Concept of *Karnanada* and *Karnakshved* with Special Reference to Tinnitus," *International Ayurvedic Medical Journal* 5/3 (2017), 705–10.
40. Mark M. Smith, *The Smell of Battle, the Taste of Siege: A Sensory History of the Civil War* (New York: Oxford University Press, 2014), 48.
41. For example, Prajapati, *Pañcasvarāsya* (unpublished Sanskrit and Hindi manuscript), Wellcome Collection, London, MS Hindi.144.

42. *Svar vijñān* is still practiced today although, anecdotally, it generally appears to be understood as a therapeutic rather than divinatory technique.

43. For example, Madan Pal, *Nighaṇṭa Bhāṣā Nāgarī* (*Herbology in Hindi*) (Lahore: Mustafai Press, 1890), 149–152.

44. On the implications of vernacular printing for medical literature, see Seema Alavi, *Islam and Healing: Loss and Recovery of an Indo-Muslim Medical Tradition, 1600–1900* (London: Palgrave Macmillan, 2008); Mukharji, *Doctoring Traditions*; and Kavita Sivaramakrishnan, *Old Potions, New Bottles: Recasting Indigenous Medicine in Colonial Punjab (1850–1945)* (Hyderabad: Orient Longman, 2006).

45. *Amar Binod Bhāṣā* (Lucknow: Nawal Kishore, 1884).

46. Ibid., 9.

47. *Bherī* might refer to a double-headed barrel-drum made of copper (according to the early thirteenth-century *Saṅgītaratnākara*) or a kettledrum. In Nepal, *bherī* is also the name of a trumpet.

48. On *ḍāktarī* medicine see Mukharji, *Doctoring Traditions*.

49. Saiyid Gulam Husen, *Kaṇṭhasudhāranbidhi* (Agra: Mumtaziya Press, 1886), 33.

50. Ibid., 6–7; for parallels in Bengali, see Mukharji, *Doctoring Traditions*, 78–79.

51. For example, Partha Chatterjee, *Our Modernity* (Rotterdam: SEPHIS, 1997); Gyan Prakash, *Another Reason: Science and the Imagination of Modern India* (Princeton, NJ: Princeton University Press, 1999).

52. Williams, "Music."

53. Neuman, *Life of Music*, 92.

54. Lakshmi Subramanian, "The Master, Muse and the Nation: The New Cultural Project and the Reification of Colonial Modernity in India," *South Asia* 23/2 (2000), 1–32.

55. Nabinacandra Datta, *Saṅgītaratnākara* (*Ocean of Music*) (Calcutta: Sucharu Press, 1872), iv.

56. Jean-Jacques Rousseau, *Essay on the Origin of Language and Writings Related to Music*, ed. and trans. John T. Scott (Hanover: University Press of New England, 1998), 442. Rousseau's source seems to be *Chamber's Cyclopedia* (London, 1741–3), 591n89. The original source of the King of Denmark tale was perhaps Saxo Grammaticus, *Danorum regum heroumque historiae* (*History of Danish Kings and Heroes*) (Paris, 1514). See Stephen Rose, *The Musician in Literature in the Age of Bach* (Cambridge, UK: Cambridge University Press, 2011), 136n88. The King of Denmark tale was included in an Armenian music treatise by Minas Bžškean (1777–1851) in 1812, most likely drawing on Rousseau's dictionary. I am grateful to Jacob Olley for this information.

57. Rousseau, *Essay*, 442–443.

58. Datta, *Saṅgītaratnākara*, v.

59. Compare with Joseph Mainzer, writing in 1848: "Have we not witnessed the *Marseillaise Hymn*, wherever it was heard, exciting indescribable enthusiasm: the workmen quitting their shops, abandoning wife and children, and running in their shirt-sleeves to swell the ranks of the republican army? Deeds, which seemed beyond human power, were accomplished whenever the Marseillaise was struck up." Joseph

Mainzer, *Music and Education* (London: Longman, Brown, Green, and Longmans, 1848), 31.

60. Kailascandra Simha, *Sādhak Saṅgīt* (Calcutta: Victoria Press, 1885), 15. See Richard David Williams, "Playing the Spinal Chord: Tantric Musicology and Bengali Songs in the Nineteenth Century," *Journal of Hindu Studies* 12 (2019), 319–338.

61. Simha, *Sādhak Saṅgīt*, 3n.

62. Williams, "Music," 484; Atarthi, "Whither musicology?"

63. See also Sohan Lal, *Garmī kā Bayān* (*Exposition on Heat*) (Patna: Faiz-i Amm, 1875).

64. *'Ilm-i āvāz o garmī o roshnī* (Patna: Faiz-i Amm, 1871), 4.

65. E.g., William Sharpey, Allen Thomson and John Cleland, eds., *Quain's Elements of Anatomy*, 7th edition, vol. 2 (London: Longmans, Green and Co., 1867), 740, fig. 495. It is unclear which edition was available to the author(s) of *'Ilm-i āvāz*. It is also possible that this image had been reproduced in another work, which in turn became the source-text for *'Ilm-i āvāz*.

66. Ibid., 744.

67. *Kān kā ḍhol* is still used in Hindi today, though *kān kā pardā* (ear-membrane) is more common.

68. *'Ilm-i āvāz*, 4.

6

Ramendrasundar Tribedi and a Sonic History of Race in Colonial Bengal

Projit Bihari Mukharji

The history of race in South Asia—perhaps even globally—is intimately tied to the history of language. It was Sir William Jones's adumbration of the discipline of comparative philology, based upon his acquaintance with classical Sanskrit works in eighteenth-century Calcutta, that catapulted the word "Aryan" to global prominence. Comparative philology did much more than simply put the comparative study of languages on a new scientific footing. It also "radically reordered existing ideas about the relations among different nations or races of peoples," "created new knowledge of such interrelationships in the deep past," even when no memory of such interrelationship was preserved in extant classical literatures, and "became a new key to ethnological history."[1]

The history of violence, bigotry and xenophobia that unspooled later around the global history of that once linguistic and later racial category of the Aryan is too well known to bear repetition here.[2] But what exactly was "language" in this history? Jonesian comparative philology, with its framing of language-as-grammar, had itself emerged by displacing an earlier practice of "comparative vocabularies," which had imagined language-as-vocabulary.[3] Language-as-grammar has proven to be a resilient framework and even today remains popular in many circles.[4] Yet, this is unquestionably a very partial view of language. David Samuels and Thomas Porcello point out that while the English word "language" has all too often been conceptualized as a "conceptual entity," it has never really managed to divorce itself from the "mechanisms of its material embodiment as a socially circulating sound."[5] In other words, there is a persistent tension between the conceptual and the descriptive thrusts of "language." As Benjamin Steege has pointed out, even the mode of knowledge that is imagined as being closest to sound, that is, acoustics, eventually developed a conceptual framework that

Projit Bihari Mukharji, *Ramendrasundar Tribedi and a Sonic History of Race in Colonial Bengal* In: *Acoustics of Empire.* Edited by: Peter McMurray and Priyasha Mukhopadhyay, Oxford University Press. © Oxford University Press 2024. DOI: 10.1093/oso/9780197553787.003.0007 entirely eschewed the sonic and rendered spoken language as a series of energy waves.[6] The long genealogy testifies to both the historical marginalization of the socially embodied sonic aspects of language as well as the sheer difficulties in developing scientific frameworks that are capable of holding the sonic and social aspects of language together with the formal and cognitive ones.

Moreover, any attempt to conceptualize language as both grammar and sound is immediately confronted by the shallowness of the historical archive at its disposal. After all, it has been possible to preserve grammatical rules in texts for much longer than it has been possible to archive human speech-sounds. Comparative philology's debt to Sanskrit texts on grammar and, through them, to the usually upper-caste scholarly authors who produced these grammars is well established.[7] The deeper pasts of languages, as a result, remain captive to the silent prejudices of purely textual archives.

These insights about the troubling marginalization of the sonic aspects of language, as well as its consequent indebtedness to textual archives of ("racialized") privilege, might seem to be informed by the recent advances in sound studies scholarship. Yet, remarkably, they have a longer history in the thought of a Bengali physicist and polymath, Ramendrasundar Tribedi (1864–1918) at the cusp of the nineteenth and twentieth centuries. Tribedi developed a conceptual framework for mapping South Asian racial histories through language-as-embodied-sound, a framework that was both innovative and radical not only for its own time, but arguably even for our own. Rather than a standalone scientific schema that would further reify racial categories, Tribedi's ideas were part of a concrete project for guiding the translation of modern scientific works from European languages into Bengali. Tribedi worked with sound from within a deeply racialized, colonial context to appropriate the egalitarian promise of science and modernity. Recovering Tribedi's ideas from historical oblivion is therefore not just a matter of adding another quirky voice to an essentially European story, but rather a matter of looking back at a precocious historical figure for both inspiration and conceptual resources by which to intervene in contemporary debates around sound, language, and race.

Part of that conceptual inspiration is engendered in the ways in which Tribedi transformed each of these key terms within his theoretical framework. "Sound," for him, was dually anchored in social ecologies and alphabetics. "Language" was the onomatopoeic relationship that connected these dual roots of sound. And race, itself constantly read into and out of caste, was for Tribedi what marked the distance between language-as-sound and language-as-grammar or -text. Tribedi's theorizations, which I call "somatomimetic alphabetics," operated by constantly defamiliarizing key conceptual resources he harvested from more cosmopolitan intellectual networks. In what follows, I describe this somatomimetic alphabetics and sonic world within which Tribedi developed it.

Language as a Sonic Archive

It would be impossible to understand Tribedi's ideas about language without locating them within a history of entanglements between race and language in colonial India. As we have already seen, the conception of language-as-grammar had arisen in the late eighteenth century and, from its very inception, had been intimately entangled with the histories of raciology. Theories of racial superiority were developed in direct conversation with the supposed sophistication of the grammar of the language of a race. In the United States, for example, such debates fed directly into the politics around the Indian Removal Act of 1830.[8]

Though the so-called "race-language scale" that pegged racial rank to grammatical sophistication was widely contested by the mid-nineteenth century, it still had influential supporters in the second half of the nineteenth century. Charles Darwin, for one, invoked this scale in an attempt to rebut opponents who sought to prove divine creation. Reasserting the link between race and language, Darwin cited examples of peoples otherwise considered backward who nonetheless had sophisticated and beautiful languages.[9] As Romila Thapar points out, the Aryan theory which conflated race and language, in general "had the support of rationalist groups opposed to the Church, and supportive of Enlightenment thinking."[10] The work of linguists such as Max Müller on classical Sanskrit in the period between 1849 and 1874 further consolidated this kind of "rational" Aryanism.[11]

By the end of the nineteenth century, however, Darwinians had begun to move conspicuously away from Darwin's own invocation of a race-language scale. This was enabled, so argues Gregory Radick, by the direct and indirect influence of Horatio Hale from the 1880s onward on the emerging discipline of anthropology. Hale himself had trained in the 1840s within an anthropological tradition defined by the influence of J. C. Pritchard, a committed champion of the underlying unity of humankind.[12]

Though challenged and largely dismantled by Tribedi's time, the equations of race and language still had a hoary and respectable pedigree in Victorian scientific circles. What was more distinctive in South Asia was the way the race-language scale then mapped onto a caste scale. The higher the caste, it was alleged, the more Aryan it was and hence the closer its affinity with Sanskrit. Müller's work provided an authoritative framework whereby the Aryans were seen to be "fair-complexioned Indo-European speakers who conquered the dark-skinned *dasas* of India." The *Arya-varna* and the *dasa-varna* mentioned in the *Rigveda* came to thus be understood as two opposing racial groups, "differentiated particularly by skin colour, but also by language and religious practice."[13] The dark-skinned indigenes, according to Müller, were of Scythian origin, whom he called Turanians, and they did not speak Sanskrit. What segregated the conquering race from the conquered was the institution of caste. The upper castes, and particularly the Brahmins of modern times, were said to be descended from the Aryans, whilst the "untouchables" and tribals were descended from the Dasas.[14]

Müller's views were widely disseminated in India and soon taken up by a range of different actors. Texts by Christian missionaries, such as John Muir's *Original Sanskrit Texts* (1858–1863) and John Wilson's *Indian Caste* (1877), used the combination of language and race to explain caste oppression in terms of Aryan conquest. Subsequently, this position was taken up and further radicalized by lower-caste intellectuals like Jyotiba Phule (1827–1890). In Phule's telling, the lower castes were the true inheritors of the land that had been forcibly snatched from them by the Aryan conquerors, whose descendants were the modern-day upper castes.[15] A number of upper-caste social and religious reformers, such as Keshab Chandra Sen, Bal Gangadhar Tilak, and Swami Dayanand Saraswati, also appropriated the casted version of Aryan theory and put it to their own use. Tilak, for instance, suggested that European Aryans had in fact fallen from their glorious common inheritance, while the upper-caste Indian Aryans had in fact preserved the original, superior civilization through the conquest of the non-Aryans.[16]

By the late nineteenth century, as nationalism began to emerge as an organized political and cultural force in South Asia, Aryanism was further appropriated and repurposed. Since the early nationalists were largely drawn from the middle classes and were both mostly upper caste in origin and exposed to European theories such as Müller's, the upper-caste version of Aryanism was smoothly incorporated into Indian, mostly Hindu, nationalism.[17] The result was a fourfold linkage structured as Sanskrit = Aryan race = upper-caste Hindus = Indian nation. Within this structure of Indian nationalism, the lower castes and the non-Hindus were progressively marginalized from the nation's body politic.

Whereas Dalit radicals like Phule and upper-caste nationalists like Tilak both adopted a version of the Aryan theory that emphasized opposition and conflict, a different version of the theory emerged amongst nationalist intellectuals who were more attuned to the issues of social justice. Especially prevalent in Bengal, this position contrasted the capacity of the caste system to assimilate difference and construct a more inclusive society that was in clear contrast to the problems of race and racism in the West. These intellectuals argued that whereas the history of race and racism in the West had led to the absolute exclusion or extermination of conquered groups, the mechanism of caste had in fact provided a way for the conquered and the conqueror to live side by side and gradually integrate their cultures within a unified system. This position was particularly popular amongst Bengali intellectuals such as Subhas Chandra Bose and, somewhat earlier, Tribedi's close friend and Nobel-laureate, Rabindranath Tagore.[18]

Tribedi too worked within this latter tradition. He embraced the language of "Aryans" and "non-Aryans" and wrote of their coexistence. Yet, he also sought a way to recover the historical contributions of the underprivileged descendants of the so-called non-Aryans. Furthermore, unlike Tagore, Tribedi did not state that the coexistence had been devoid of friction or conflict. Indeed, he explicitly accepted historical conflict between castes.[19] Far from romanticizing caste as a mechanism for integration, he also explicitly criticized the modern caste system as a perversion of what had existed in ancient times. Instead of any structural and altruistic logic, Tribedi argued that the modern system of caste had evolved out of the need for sequestering technical knowledge in localized, guild-like units within an overall racialized hierarchy inaugurated by Aryan conquest. But these interests, he firmly believed, were in the process of being dismantled by new institutions such as the railways, telegraph, technical schools, etc.[20] He ended his essay on caste by eloquently reminding his readers that the poor working classes in India, in their work ethic, selflessness, and skill, though doomed to remain anonymous, were in fact comparable to an Isaac Newton or a Michael Faraday.[21]

Whereas most intellectuals who spoke of "assimilation" usually thought of it as a process of "incorporation" whereby non-Aryans took on Aryan language and customs, Tribedi emphasized the reverse. In fact, Tribedi argued that the Sanskrit language, which was intimately tied to claims of Aryan racial superiority, was itself radically transformed by non-Aryans. Writing about Bengali, the language spoken in the then-imperial capital of Calcutta, Tribedi argued that while its alphabet was undoubtedly indebted to the Aryan progenitors of Sanskrit, its sonic aspects had been radically transformed by non-Aryans. This transformation was clearly audible in the many onomatopoeic words prevalent in Bengali. He wrote that, "The specialty of these onomatopoeic words is that they are mostly autochthonous (*deshaja*). We cannot find their roots in Sanskrit. Being autochthonous they carry the odor of their non-Aryan origins on their bodies. The linguistic scholars of this country, who have established their scholarly credentials by the exclusive study of the Aryan tongue, cannot bear that body odor."[22]

Carrying on in the same personifying vein, Tribedi wrote that, notwithstanding the snootiness of the classical scholars, "Lady Sanskrit-language, that old Aryan lady (*briddha arjya sanskrita-bhasa thakurani*), in the course of time, has digested numerous such words." Any perusal of Sanskrit dictionaries (*koshagrantha*), especially a comparison of older and later dictionaries, would amply testify to this process of absorption.[23] Even more importantly, Tribedi argued that, whatever may be the case in Sanskrit, in colloquial Bengali such onomatopoeic words were so important that to suppress them would make it impossible for Bengalis to converse altogether.[24] Drawing upon an earlier essay by Tagore, he referred to these onomatopoeic words as *dhwanyatmak sabda*, that is, "sonic-souled words."[25] Their history could not be mapped through texts and grammars. Instead, it had to be sought in the very sounds themselves.

Tribedi's basic categorization of words was not entirely novel. Sanskrit grammarians writing within the tradition of *vyakarana* had long divided words into *tatsama* and *tadbhava* words. The former were those that retained a recognizable Sanskrit root (*dhatu*) in its original form but added a different termination. The latter were those where the root itself had been transformed. There were a further set of residual words whose roots could not be recognized at all. These were called *desya* (country), *gramya* (rustic) or *antardesya* (foreign).[26] What Tribedi did was merge the *tadbhava* and the *desya* together and distinguish them from the *tatsama* words. Moreover, *vyakarana* already had within it a robust discipline of *pratisakhya* or phonology which determined the actual pronunciations of these words. Tribedi, however, rejected the applicability of this Sanskrit phonology and insisted that Bengali had its own phonology that was discernible in its own distinctive sounds. He did this in part by redefining the notion of *vyakarana* itself as being much more than simply the study of word roots, as he said it was in classical Sanskrit.[27]

Tribedi's major innovation was his emphasis on sound. His insistence that the sonic-souled words held the key to a true, authentically Bengali linguistic identity made the sounds themselves the basis rather than the instantiation of any grammatical exegesis. He repeatedly stressed that unlike the learned people who spoke a polished and therefore Sanskrit-bound Bengali, the unlettered and rustic classes spoke a truer Bengali. Therefore, it was their speech that should illuminate a new authentic grammar of the language.[28] Grammar could, in his view, only model the spoken sounds, not determine them.

This interest in spoken language further allowed Tribedi to open up a historical project to recover the proper phonological and grammatical rules of Bengali by tracing its historical antecedents in the spoken language of various subaltern classes. He located both the Sanskrit-derived *tatsama* and *tadbhava* words and the underived *deshaja* words within an emphatically demotic history. Of the Sanskrit-derived words, Tribedi pointed out that some scholars argued that these were not derived from the high Sanskrit of classical grammarians, but rather from a demotic form of the language. Regarding the non-Sanskrit words, he writes: "Perhaps they are Sanskrit words that have been so deformed that now they can no longer be recognized." But it might also be, he points out, that these words have been adopted from "non-Aryans, Mughals, Dravidians or any other primitive inhabitants of this land." He continues: "With the Aryan conquest, the existence of these people has been assimilated to the Aryans, [but] perhaps the investigation of the languages of the lower classes (*nimnasrenir lok*), or the languages of those forest- and mountain-dwellers will reveal the origins of many authentic Bengali words."[29]

Tribedi argued that extant grammars of Bengali were unworkable because they derived from the textual history of Sanskrit and not the demotic history of spoken sounds. Bengali schoolchildren, he lamented, were learning an entirely misleading grammar grounded in this historical misunderstanding. Any reliable grammar for him had to be based upon a historical inquiry into changed pronunciations and not just etymological roots.[30]

Pushing this line of reasoning further, Tribedi posited that sound and meaning were intimately connected. Drawing on a quotation attributed to the classical Sanskrit poet Kalidasa, he wrote that the relationship between sound and meaning was akin to the intimacy of the god Shiva and his consort

(*Hara-Gauri sambandha*), but that the origins of this intimacy lay buried in history.[31] Meaning was not derived from word roots that led back to the textual archive of Sanskrit, but rather from the actual pronunciations whose most authentic registers were to be found in the everyday speech of the subaltern classes. Language, for Tribedi, became a sonic archive. Unlike colonial linguistics, which had been grounded in grammar, script, and text, Tribedi approached lay speech, particularly of the rural working classes, as a sonic archive from which the history and identity of a language would emerge. This archive would allow him to draw the outlines of a language that owed much more to the historic genius of subaltern, unlettered, and non-Aryan groups than the Sanskrit *pandits* of yore.

Somatomimetic Alphabetics

Notwithstanding the breadth of Tribedi's oeuvre, writing only a year before his demise he was explicit that it was in his theories of language and sound that he felt he had been able to offer something truly original.[32] As we have seen, at the heart of Tribedi's theory was a history of sonic transformations of Sanskrit words. The alterations, he argued, had primarily affected the vowels, but since the consonants contained vowel sounds within them, these too had become modified. Moreover, it was the mechanism by which each of these altered consonants made its characteristic sound that held the key to its meaning. These sounds, he argued, mimicked the sounds that we encounter in the world around us. As a result, the meanings of the words, through the actual bodily mechanism of pronunciation, linked the sounds constituting the words back to those contexts in which the sounds were originally encountered. This is also why, in his scheme, the *dhwanyatmak* or sonic-souled words were so central to the Bengali language and its extra-Sanskritic history. The meanings of these words arose directly by a "law of association" that connected our bodily mechanisms for uttering that sound with the way the sound was originally encountered.

Bengali consonants are usually arranged in rows of four letters each. Tribedi argued that all of the four letters in any given row were uttered in a broadly similar way, but that as one moved from left to right along the row additional vowel sounds were added to the basic sound. Directly invoking Helmholtz's work on the pronunciation of vowels, he essentially described each consonant as a "combination tone." Once again, he visually illustrated with a chart how the basic tone for each row was successively magnified across the row.

The bulk of Tribedi's discussion involved going through the entire set of Bengali consonants and discussing each letter in the light of his theory. He described, for instance, how the onomatopoeic call of a duck (*pyank-pyank*), the slushy mud at the bottom of village ponds (*pank*), and insects (*ponka*) all began with the *p* sound. Explaining this, he wrote that this was because the *p* sound in Bengali required the expulsion of air from between pursed lips, similar to the way in which one plays the flute. Thus, all those words for which the sound is produced by the expulsion of air by force from a hollow cavity, such as a duck's call, slushy mud at the bottom of a pond, etc., and even the onomatopoeic sound said to be made by the flute (*pon*), begin with the consonant *p*.[33]

Since the very next letter to follow *p* in the Bengali alphabetical row is *ph*, Tribedi continued that it was basically the same tone added to an extra vowel sound. Hence, the expelled air needed to produce the sound was more forceful. Its associations too were therefore with other similarly more forceful sounds produced through the forcible expulsion of air. The blowing out of a fire was therefore called *phun*, or the hissing of a snake called *phonsh*, and so on.[34] In other words, Tribedi was describing the ways in which the embodied mechanism for producing a particular sound itself retained a memory of a quintessentially rustic Bengali lifeworld. This retention operated by the bodily movements necessary for uttering the sound themselves mimicking a range of material and environmental sounds. This is what I will call "somatomimetic alphabetics."

Peter McMurray has recently proposed using the term "alphabetics" to designate "the interplay between letters as a written, or at least writable, sign system that gives rise to sonic performance as well as a set of sonic transcriptions."[35] Tribedi's investments in the pronunciations of the Bengali alphabet are clearly comparable to the Quranic pronunciation techniques that are the subject of McMurray's theorizations. Tribedi's conception of the relationship between the somatic mechanisms for the vocal production of such pronunciations and its socio-historical environment as one of actual mimesis, however, is unique. The mirroring of the environment through bodily movements for vocalization that Tribedi outlines is, I would suggest, best captured by the phrase "somatomimetic alphabetics."

Tribedi's fundamental understanding of sound was rooted in two intellectual currents. On the one hand were the writings of the German scientist Hermann von Helmholtz. On the other was a body of Sanskritic sciences, mostly Vaishnava lore, Nyaya philosophy and Sanskrit *vyakarana* (grammar). By braiding elements from these two intellectual sources, Tribedi conceived of sound in terms of "waves" and their production in terms of "vibrations." He commenced his elaborate discussion of sonic-souled words with "a few words about the origin of sound" (*dhwanir utpatti sambandhe dui-chariti katha*) and invoked the well-known Vaishnava myth according to which, upon hearing the sound of Lord Krishna's flute, the women of the village would be so overcome that they would immediately run to meet him. He asked why the *pandits* are unable to explain how sound (*dhwani*) came to be thus associated with joy (*ananda*) and even madness (*unmadana*), even though such a nexus was self-evident, "otherwise the entire discipline of music would have been pointless."[36] From here, he proceeded to give a basic description of the physics of sound.

Taking his cue from the example of Krishna's fabled flute, he wrote that, "when one plays a flute, the air trapped within the flute vibrates (*kampiya uthe*). These vibrations then exit the flute and give rise to waves (*dheu*) in the air outside. The waves push against the ear (*dhakka deye*) and repeatedly beat against the nervous mechanism (*snayujantre punah punah aghat kare*) there. Immediately there arises a perception of sound (*dhwanir bodh*)."[37] Tribedi then proceeded to describe the importance of the frequency of sound waves and their relation to the perception of sound. He stated that if the frequency of waves was less than 200 waves per second, or greater than one hundred thousand waves per second, we would not be able to perceive any sound. It is only within this range that audible sound would be produced. Moreover, it was the frequency that determined whether the sound would be perceived as a soft (*komol*) sound or a sharp (*tiyar*) sound. The higher the frequency, the sharper the sound and the lower the frequency the softer the sound.[38]

He followed up the explanation with another brief exposition using the *tanpura*, a stringed instrument. Indeed, he would go on to further elaborate the nature of the sound wave (*sabda-taranga*) in much greater detail and with graphic visual illustrations, using this latter example of a *tanpura*, in another set of essays published posthumously in 1926. In these latter essays he further explained the components of the sound waves, such as wavelength (*urmi*), wave motion (*taranga-gati*), crests (*matha*), troughs (*kol*), phase difference, etc.[39] Interestingly, although Tribedi's example referred to a stringed musical instrument, the visual illustrations he used deployed consonants of the Bengali alphabet to make his point.

Julia Kursell has described Helmholtz's vowel research as the production of "sound objects." These objects were heard under specific circumstances, using particular instruments and models, but then also made to persist so that they could be made into stable objects of investigation. Such sound objects emerged, Kursell argues, in the post-Kantian context where the objects of perception were reconceptualized as objects produced by the physiological mechanisms of hearing.[40] Tribedi explicitly drew upon the research of Helmholtz. He also referred explicitly to Helmholtz's mechanical apparatuses for breaking down "physical" sounds into their simpler constituent tones as well as recombining them.[41] In fact, he also invoked a range of other scientific instruments, such as telephones, phonographs, and vacuum pumps, to establish the reality of sonic vibrations.[42] But were Tribedi's "sound objects" identical to Helmholtz's?

I would argue that they were not: both because the actual technologies of inscription, most conspicuously the Bengali consonants, were distinct, and because Tribedi also drew upon a set of older terms and ideas available in Sanskrit and Bengali phonology to produce his sound objects. The organization of the alphabet into rows and columns and the claim that every consonant in the same row was essentially the same basic sound augmented by extra vowel sounds, themselves described as a breath (*prana*), a half-breath (*alpaprana*), a double-breath (*mahaprana*) and, eventually, a still more powerful breath (*ghosh*) that helped move from one row to the next, were all drawn from Sanskrit phonology.[43] The sound that Tribedi heard and the sound that he inscribed as a stable object that could be further investigated drew upon a combination of Helmholtzian and *vyakarana*-derived conceptual and mechanical tools. Even the use of such South Asian musical instruments as the *tanpura* attests to the specificity of Tribedi's sound objects.

In fact, Tribedi also alluded to a South Asian tradition of conceptualizing wave forms. Referring specifically to the philosophical tradition of *Nyaya-shastra*, he wrote: "The books of the *Nyayashastra* have clearly stated that just as dropping a vessel in a pond creates ripples, so too do ripples generated by an object give rise to sound-perception when they strike our hearing."[44] This invocation was, however, not unequivocal. He also pointed out that much of the classical Sanskrit understanding of waves was built on the imagination of a subtle and ethereal substance (*akash*) which was distinct from air. "Their inference," Tribedi asserted, "was incorrect."[45] Instead, he adapted the Nyaya view of waves to the Helmholtzian view.

Amongst the most significant differences between Helmholtz's physiological enquiries and Tribedi's, however, was the latter's almost complete lack of interest in the physiology of listening. Whereas Helmholtz was deeply interested in the physiology of listening, Tribedi's main interests were in the physiology of speaking.[46] His discussions of the physiology of audition were brief and standard, whereas the discussions of the physiology of speaking were elaborate and innovative. Whether this was a result of accents produced by the *vyakarana* and *pratisakhya* traditions is difficult to tell. But it is certainly another point of clear contrast between Tribedi and his inspiration.

Notwithstanding such differences, one key shared concern for both Helmholtz and Tribedi was how to refigure the relationship between subject and object. In Tribedi's case, this also became an opportunity to link the Bengali-speaker to a specifically local history, geography, flora, and fauna. In seeking these associations, he described a slew of objects, creatures, and features that typified a Bengali village. The village ponds, ducks, bulbuls, *boro* paddy, the drone of mosquitoes, and characteristic local vegetables such as *barbati* and *puni sak* all served to link the Bengali-speaker's "speech mechanism" (*bagajantra*) back to the land, its culture, and its history. The subject was thus reconstituted as one that mirrored the historical geography within which it was engendered through language. Voicing became an occasion for somatomimesis.

Tribedi's Sonic World

One of the questions that remains is why and how Tribedi selected the elements he drew from his intellectual resources for his theories of sonic language. Clearly, he neither took everything from Helmholtz's program nor the totality of the *vyakarana* or Nyaya frameworks. To understand the pattern of his selections, I will argue that we need to return to Tribedi's own "sonic world."

Alexandra Hui writes about Helmholtz having "fashion[ed] a sonic world around himself that made his theory of sound sensation possible."[47] This "sonic world," in Hui's formulation, does not pre-exist as a stable and already-formed sonic milieu. Rather, it was actively constituted by the social and aesthetic choices that Helmholtz made and the musical instruments he surrounded himself with. In Helmholtz's case, the sonic world was engendered at two interacting levels. First was his own deep personal involvement with music, including playing music for himself and his close interactions with musical instrument makers such as the New York piano-maker, Theodore Steinway. Second was his participation within a "liberal professional taste public." This particular taste public gave Helmholtz both an appreciation for "classical music" and inspired him to cultivate music listening as a contemplative, serious aesthetic practice, rather than a purely affective entertainment.[48]

Tribedi's sonic world too was actively constituted by his social and aesthetic choices. Music, of course, played an important role in Tribedi's discussions as well. As we have seen, he repeatedly invoked the *tanpura* as the exemplary musical instrument through which he explained his musical tones. Indeed, the instruments he invokes in themselves evoke a particular musical culture. In the absence of the kind of fulsome archive that has permitted historians to reconstruct Helmholtz's sonic world in detail, these invocations serve as clues into Tribedi's musical engagements. In an essay on musical instruments (*badyajantra*), he divided them into four classes, namely stringed instruments (*beenajantra*), wind instruments (*benujantra*), drums (*patahajantra*), and bell-metal instruments (*kangshyajantra*). In the first class he mentioned the sitar and the violin (*behala*). Amongst wind instruments he referred to the flute, particularly the bamboo flute, and the clarinet.[49] Later, in discussing Helmholtz's experiments, he further mentioned the organ and the pipe.[50] For these two instruments, however, he did not mention any specific instruments, discussing them only in generic terms.[51] This is clearly a highly selective engagement. If we momentarily leave aside the new European instruments, namely the violin and the clarinet, we essentially have references to only three musical instruments. Two of these, the *tanpura* and the sitar, are clearly associated with South Asian traditions of "classical" or "art" music. And, in fact, even the violin had already been absorbed into South Asian musicological treatises by 1844, over half a century before Tribedi's writing.[52] All this clearly suggests a classicist accent as at least one of the primary constituents of Tribedi's sonic world.

Throughout the nineteenth century, the city of Calcutta and Bengal more generally had emerged as one of the pre-eminent locations for the cultivation, performance, and reflection on Hindustani music. Richard David Williams has described how, with the decline of the northern centers of imperial Mughal culture, the new British capital in Calcutta and its new elites came to claim and refigure Hindustani music. Bengal was disengaged from its somewhat peripheral position at the fringe of a Persianized, Mughal, and

Hindustani (i.e., northern South Asian) cultural and epistemic world, and positioned as a privileged site for erudite Hindustani music. This transition was engendered in a proliferation of new musicological texts in Bengali which downplayed the historical importance of north Indian and mostly Muslim musicians, and in Williams's words "Banglafied" Hindustani music.[53]

Locating Tribedi in relation to these developments gives us a new understanding of the choices he made in framing his somatomimetic alphabetics. The Bengali engagement with Hindustani music was not framed preeminently in terms of a clash between empire and nation. Instead, it played out as a "conversation across regions of the subcontinent, doubtless shaped by the change in fortunes of Delhi and Calcutta as capitals of the old and new empires."[54] The motivation therefore was to constitute Bengal as a relatively autonomous space that, whilst not closed off from influences from the north or indeed elsewhere, was actually a privileged and self-contained cultural unit, a position which, of course, bears remarkable similarity with Tribedi's position on language.

Indeed, looking closer at the Bengali musicological tradition that emerged by the late nineteenth century, one finds further resonances with Tribedi's arguments. One of the most influential of these musicological works was Krishnadhan Bandyopadhyay's *Geetasutrasara* (Quintessence of Music, 1885). Bandyopadhyay "reframed classical theory, with a long essay on acoustics described in modern scientific terms, situating the development of human sound, communication, and speech in the context of human evolution and the biological development of the throat."[55] Though Bandyopadhyay's invocations of the *"pranitattwabid* Darwin *mahodaya"* ("zoologist Mr. Darwin") and his theory of "sexual selection" as an explanation for the emergence of music may not have appealed to Tribedi, Bandyopadhyay's emphasis on the physiology of speech clearly anticipated Tribedi's own selective appropriation of Helmholtz.[56]

Indeed, some of Bandyopadhyay's formulations bear striking similarities with the way Tribedi later approached the issue of linguistic sounds. While discussing the vexed issue of rival notation systems for Hindustani music, something that had divided Bengali musicologists of the day, Bandyopadhyay fell back on the analogy of the relationship between the written and spoken language. He wrote that, "[i]rrespective of meaning, language requires innumerable [different] pronunciations, yet the alphabet cannot even signal a hundredth portion of these."[57] Once again, this position is precisely the starting point from which Tribedi built his argument about language, namely that the spoken language already exceeds the written one and that difference is located in pronunciation.

Finally, Bandyopadhyay's adoption of the European system of musical notations with Bengali alphabets was first proposed in a manual on sitar playing. Not only did Tribedi's invocations of mainly stringed instruments, and especially the sitar, seem to mirror this practice, but indeed the latter's clear statements about accepting foreign, including English, terms so long as the pronunciations fitted with Bengali phonology (something I will discuss further in the last section) evinces the same cosmopolitan attitude.

At a more general level, Tribedi's engagement with classical music might also have putatively inspired his view of the human voice as a form of choreographed performance that was sculpted by one's immersion in a specific socio-historical and ecological milieu. As Amanda Weidman's fascinating account of "playback" singers in southern India has shown, the "Western cultural imagination" of the voice as a "guarantor of truth and self-presence" clearly needs to be recognized as a provincial, Euro-American figuration of the "voice" that has limited analytic force in South Asia.[58] Careful and prolonged training, recognition of the materiality of the voice, technological mediation, performativity, and the interplay of reproduction and creativity that constitute "voicing," all serve to unyoke "voice" from any naturalized derivation from truth and self-presence. It is, of course, crucial to recognize that Weidman's specific examples, despite being from the same broad region, are very different from Tribedi's sonic world. Playback singing is not "classical" music and Hindustani classical is not Carnatic ("South Indian") classical music.[59] Yet I think some of the general points she makes are equally applicable to Hindustani vocal music in nineteenth-century Calcutta. The sheer emphasis on training the voice, voicing, performance, and so on would all serve to underline just how much sculpting went into the articulation of the voice, something that Tribedi then extended beyond the musical context to everyday speech.

Tribedi's sonic world, however, was not exclusively constituted by the Banglafied culture of erudite Hindustani music. In it we also hear the strains of the bamboo flute, especially through the repeated evocations of the myth of Krishna and his flute. This image of Krishna-as-cowherd playing his bamboo flute is a redolent one. On the one hand it evokes the Vaishnavite religious tradition that was particularly prominent in Bengal.[60] On the other hand, it also became one of the stock images in Bengali romanticism, which, by the turn of the twentieth century, was particularly invested in a bucolic image of the Bengali village.[61] Both of these trajectories, which congealed in the image of Krishna's flute, came together in the poetry of Tribedi's close friend and collaborator, Tagore.

How far any actual bamboo flute featured in Tribedi's sonic universe is difficult to tell. But there is an enormous amount of evidence of the friendship of Tagore and Tribedi and their mutual influence on each other. Tagore's poetry certainly formed part of Tribedi's sonic world. Through it a particular religio-political outlook, which has variously been called "humanist" and "universalist," also became accessible to Tribedi. We know that Tribedi not only admired Tagore's poetry, but in fact enjoyed hearing him recite his own writing. Indeed, one of Tribedi's biographies includes an anecdote in which, on his deathbed, he asks his friend to recite the letter Tagore had recently written renouncing his knighthood in protest against a colonial massacre at Jallianwala Bagh. According to the biography, Tribedi finally slipped out of consciousness while listening to his friend recite Tagore's letter.[62]

Translating Science

Tribedi's sonic world helps us understand his theory of somatomimetic alphabetics and its political investments. But his elaborate discussions of Bengali phonology and racial history were not intended to be idle theories. They were conducted with a concrete purpose in mind. His reflections and research had been occasioned through his work on a committee set up by the Bangiya Sahitya Parishad (Bengali Literary Association) at its annual meeting in February 1909 at Rajshahi. The committee was established in response to a call for a comprehensive plan for translating scientific terms made by the eminent essayist and historian, Rajanikanta Gupta. It was made up of eighteen members and initially presided over by the famous Bengali chemist, Sir P. C. Ray. Ray's selection as the head of the committee itself signaled the importance and urgency of the subject. One of the foremost South Asian scientists of his era, Ray was also a chemist of international standing. That he was a chemist was particularly important since the need to standardize chemical nomenclature, in the wake of the standardization of the periodic table, was one of the most pressing reasons for a comprehensive plan and systematic approach for the translation of Western scientific terms into Bengali.[63] This is precisely what the committee was tasked with doing.[64]

While this was not the first attempt to translate modern scientific terminology into Bengali or other South Asian languages, it was a qualitatively
much more robust effort than what had been attempted before.[65] Not only
were eminent men of science with international intellectual connections,
such as Ray, directly involved; the efforts had also been authorized by the
foremost intellectual body that, in some ways, sought to provide a single
unified platform for all Bengali intellectual aspirations. Notwithstanding
the eventual failure of the committee to devise a single, workable plan for
translating modern scientific terms into Bengali, its existence is crucially important for our discussion.

That the effort, despite its promising start, eventually failed, was itself a
consequence of precisely the political investments in Tribedi's work that
I have outlined above. Soon after its creation, P. C. Ray, the president, with two
of the younger members published an independent set of recommendations
limited only to chemical terms, a result of his disagreements with Tribedi
and others on the committee. This undermined the committee's combined
recommendations, rendering them redundant.

Ray's own recommendations are themselves revealing. He essentially
proposed creating new chemical terms by drawing on Sanskrit words and
roots. This was not surprising, since at precisely this time he was working
on his *History of Hindu Chemistry*. For Ray, the past was in Sanskrit and the
knowledge was clearly "Hindu"—a category that was already simultaneously
acquiring anticolonial and exclusionary national connotations. Labeling
chemical knowledges of the past as essentially "Hindu" and Sanskrit, Ray
was also connecting this past to the racial category "Aryan."[66] Indeed, in one
place in his *Hindu Chemistry* Ray wrote: "As Aryan conquerors began to
settle in India and came into frequent contact with aborigines, they had unconsciously to imbibe some of the gross superstitions of the latter, and thus
in course of time a superstructure of monstrous growth sprang up, ready to
swallow even the purer and more orthodox creed."[67] Patently, Ray valorized a
pure Aryan past, devoid of all corrupting influences of non-Aryans. Nothing
could be further from how Tribedi conceptualized contact between "Aryans"
and "non-Aryans."

In sharp contrast to Ray's pursuit of an unadulterated Sanskritic Aryanism,
Tribedi pointed out that even the ancient Sanskrit writers had borrowed a
number of Greek and Latin terms in their scientific treatises. He argued further that no one language monopolized science at the time: "The French may
believe that their language will soon be universally accepted, the English may

hope that their language will soon be universal, but none of these hopes is likely to be realized soon. We also hear of efforts to create an artificial universal language of science, but the realization of that too seems distant."[68] Thus, all languages had to rely on other languages. There was nothing wrong or shameful in this. Eschewing any narrowly nationalist anti-colonialism, Tribedi wrote further that "we have entered into a relationship with the Western nations. The knowledge they had acquired through much effort has thereby been laid open in front of us. If we wish we can acquire this tremendous wealth of knowledge for ourselves. There is no place here for personal, communal or national conflict or opposition. . . . We must approach the Western nations with the same spirit of humility with which the novice used to approach the guru in ancient times."[69]

According to Tribedi, translations, especially of scientific terminology, had to proceed with a view to clarity and precision of meaning. For this, it was crucial to keep the actual sounds rather than the mere roots of the words in mind. Since he understood meaning to be generated through a "law of associations" with the actual sound or pronunciation of the word, he advocated an open-ended approach to scientific terminology that would be premised upon the sonic rather than the textual.

A racio-linguistic past that was shaped more by non-Aryans and outsiders authorized Tribedi to propose a future grounded in cosmopolitanism and racial equality, rather than hierarchies. His views may have been utopian, but they were clearly orthogonal to the conservative nationalism of Ray. In contrast, his view of national—and perhaps even racial—identity was an open-ended one that was flexible, fungible, and functional. Indeed, notwithstanding his emotional commitment to Bengal and Bengali, his own family were relatively recent migrants to the region. His surname was not a common Bengali one and his family traced its roots to the Bundelkhand region in central India, far away from Bengal. They had migrated to Bengal in the trail of Mughal armies but having settled there, they had quickly adopted the local language and become fully Banglafied. Indeed, several of his ancestors had written books in Bengali.[70] Moreover, Tribedi himself was keenly interested in this history of his family and even wrote about it.[71] This personal history might have made him more willing to conceptualize a past and future where migration and exchange could take place without erasure or marginalization of subordinate groups and their contributions.

Whatever may have been the deeper reasons for Tribedi's positions, what is indubitable is that placing his ideas about somatomimetic alphabetics back into the context of the work on the committee for translating scientific terms and his disagreements with Ray clarifies the specific political resonances of his ideas. It shows that his was not yet another abstract set of intellectual reflections on racio-linguistic histories. Rather, it was a concrete attempt to find a scientific way of acknowledging the past contributions of racialized subalterns within a highly racialized nationalist milieu. Moreover, this acknowledgment itself was in turn deployed to authorize a cosmopolitan, open-ended approach to future scientific work.

Conclusion

Recent years have witnessed something of an explosion of studies on the language of science and, even more so, on scientific translations.[72] Much of this has focused on language-as-script or language-as-text. While recent scholarship in sound studies is certainly trying to add a soundtrack to this earlier body of work, such efforts seem rather novel and unprecedented. In Tribedi's theory of somatomimetic alphabetics, however, we have a clear precedent for a framework that simultaneously approaches language as sound and seeks to implicate those sounds in concrete sociohistorical contexts. The apparent precocity of his ideas, however, seems much less out of place once we locate him within his own sonic world and recognize the specific view of the future that his narrative about the past authorized.

More generally, Tribedi's interventions demonstrate that once we move out of the narrow European canon of sound sciences, there are much more ambitious attempts to conceptualize the relationships between language, race, the past, and the future. These attempts not only had their ears to the ground, but also sought to understand the sound-making human body in ways that went beyond the Kantian idealism that held so much of contemporary European sound science captive.

Tribedi's somatomimetic alphabetics did not develop by being ignorant of post-Kantian European science of sounds. His praise of Helmholtz sometimes verged on veneration; he even compared the latter to a divine "avatar."[73] Yet this did not stop Tribedi from pushing beyond Helmholtz's own formulation. He was able to transcend the Kantian and Helmholtzian frameworks precisely because he was embedded within another rich and vibrant sonic world. He was willing to do this, however, because he was also deeply invested in the political resonances between racial and linguistic histories within nationalist circles in turn-of-the-century Bengal.

Notes

Ramendrasundar Tribedi's ideas are extraordinarily complex and in trying to make sense of them I have benefited enormously from conversations with several colleagues. I would particularly like to thank Alex Csiszar, Michael Gordin, Josephine Hoegaerts, Alix Hui and the two editors of this volume for their generous engagements with this chapter through its various iterations.

1. Thomas R. Trautmann, "Discovering Aryan and Dravidian: A Tale of Two Cities," *Historiographia Linguistica* 31/1 (2004), 33–58, at 34.
2. Thomas R. Trautmann, *Aryans and British India* (New Delhi: Yoda Press, 2008); Tony Ballantyne, *Orientalism and Race: Aryanism in the British Empire* (Basingstoke: Palgrave Macmillan, 2007).
3. Thomas R. Trautmann, *Languages and Nations: The Dravidian Proof in Colonial Madras* (Berkeley: University of California Press, 2006), 21–34.
4. Trautmann, *Languages and Nations*, 35–41.
5. David Samuels and Thomas Porcello, "Language," in *Keywords in Sound*, ed. David Novak and Matt Sakakeeny (Durham, NC: Duke University Press, 2015), 87–98, at 86.
6. Benjamin Steege, "Acoustics," in *Keywords in Sound*, ed. David Novak and Matt Sakakeeny (Durham, NC: Duke University Press, 2015), 22–31.
7. M. Dodson, *Orientalism, Empire, and National Culture: India, 1770–1880* (Basingstoke: Palgrave Macmillan, 2007).
8. Sean P. Harvey, "'Must Not Their Languages Be Savage and Barbarous Like Them?' Philology, Indian Removal, and Race Science," *Journal of the Early Republic* 30/4 (2010), 505–532.
9. Gregory Radick, "Race and Language in the Darwinian Tradition (and What Darwin's Language-Species Parallels Have to Do with It)," *Studies in History and Philosophy of Biological and Biomedical Sciences* 39/3 (2008), 359–370.
10. Romila Thapar, "The Theory of Aryan Race and India: History and Politics," *Social Scientist* 24, no. 1/3 (1996), 3–29, at 5.
11. Ibid.
12. Radick, "Race and Language in the Darwinian Tradition," 365–368.
13. Thapar, "The Theory of Aryan Race," 5.
14. Ibid., 6.
15. Ibid., 7.
16. Ibid., 8.
17. Ibid., 9.
18. Nico Slate, "Translating Race and Caste," *Journal of Historical Sociology* 24/1 (2011), 64–70.

19. Ramendrasundar Tribedi, "Barnasramadharma," *Ramendra-Rachanabali* [Complete Works of Ramendrasundar Tribedi], ed. Brajendranath Bandyopadhyay and Sajanikanta Das, vol. 4 (Calcutta: Bangiya Sahitya Parishad, 1950), 40–49.

20. Ibid., 45.

21. Ibid., 49.

22. Ramendrasundar Tribedi, *Sabda Katha* [Story of Sound] (Calcutta: Sanskrit Press Depository, 1917), 2. All translations are mine, unless otherwise stated. Notably, Tribedi's linking of the origins of language with labor bears resemblance to Karl Bücher's theory about the origin of music in labor. Bücher's theory was popular in nineteenth-century Europe, and it is very possible that Tribedi had encountered it. But I have not yet found an explicit reference in Tribedi to Bücher. I am grateful to Alix Hui for pointing me to Karl Bücher.

23. Ibid.

24. Ibid., 3.

25. Ibid. The essay Tribedi referred to was Rabindranath Tagore, "Bangla Dhwanyatmak Sabda" [Bengali Sonic Souled Words], *Bangiya Sahitya Parishat Patrika* 7 (1307 BE [1900]), 252–259.

26. Trautmann, "Discovering Aryan and Dravidian," 41.

27. Tribedi, *Sabda Katha*, 142.

28. Ibid., 156–159.

29. Ibid., 131.

30. Ibid., 142–152.

31. Tribedi, *Sabda Katha*, 221.

32. Ibid., i.

33. Ibid., 18–20.

34. Ibid., 20–24.

35. Peter McMurray, "Qur'an Alphabetics and the Timbre of Recitation," in *The Oxford Handbook of Timbre*, ed. Emily I. Dolan and Alexander Rehding (New York: Oxford University Press, 2021), 96.

36. Tribedi, *Sabda Katha*, 5.

37. Ibid.

38. Ibid.

39. Ramendrasundar Tribedi, "Taranga" [Wave], *Ramendra-Rachanabali*, vol. 4, 385–388; Ramendrasundar Tribedi, "Sabda Taranga" [Sound Wave], *Ramendra-Rachanabali*, vol. 4, 388–391.

40. Julia Kursell, "Sound Objects," in *Sounds of Science—Schall im Labor (1800–1930)*, ed. Julia Kursell (Berlin: Max Planck Institute for the History of Science, 2008), 29–38.

41. Tribedi, *Sabda Katha*, 10.

42. Ramendrasundar Tribedi, "Pratyaksha, na Anuman" [Perception of Interference], *Ramendra-Rachanabali*, vol. 4, 400–401.

43. Tribedi, *Sabda Katha*, 13–14.

44. Tribedi, "Pratyaksha na Anuman," 401.

45. Ibid.

46. Alexandra Hui, *The Psychophysical Ear: Musical Experiments, Experimental Sounds, 1840–1910* (Cambridge: MIT Press, 2013); Julia Kursell, "'False Relations': Hermann von Helmholtz's Study of Music and the Delineation of Nineteenth-Century Physiology," *Nineteenth-Century Music Review* 19/1(2022), 85–106.

47. Hui, *The Psychophysical Ear*, 58.

48. Ibid., 55–88.

49. Ramendrasundar Tribedi, "Badyajantra" [Musical Instruments], *Ramendra-Rachanabali*, vol. 4, 395–396.

50. Ibid., 398.

51. Ibid., 396.

52. Richard David Williams, "Music, Lyrics, and the Bengali Book: Hindustani Musicology in Calcutta, 1818–1905," *Music and Letters* 97/3 (2016), 465–495, at 471.

53. Ibid., 479.

54. Ibid., 467.

55. Ibid., 484.

56. Krishnadhan Bandyopadhyay, *Geetasutrasara* [Quintessence of Music], 3rd ed. (Calcutta: Nirendranath Bandyopadhyay, 1934), ii.

57. Ibid., xi.

58. Amanda Weidman, "Voice," in *Keywords in Sound*, ed. David Novak and Matt Sakakeeny (Durham, NC: Duke University Press, 2015), 232–245, at 233.

59. On the "classical" traditions of India, see Janaki Bakhle, *Two Men and Music: Nationalism in the Making of an Indian Classical Tradition* (Oxford, UK: Oxford University Press, 2005); Amanda J. Weidman, *Singing the Classical, Voicing the Modern: The Postcolonial Politics of Music in South India* (Durham, NC: Duke University Press, 2006); Lakshmi Subramanian, *New Mansions for Music: Performance, Pedagogy and Criticism* (New Delhi: Social Science Press, 2008).

60. Joseph T. O'Connell, "Tracing Vaishnava Strains in Tagore," *Journal of Hindu Studies* 4/2 (2011), 144–164.

61. Dipesh Chakrabarty, "Nation and Imagination," *Studies in History* 152 (1999), 177–207.

62. Apurbakrishna Ghosh, *Acharya Ramendrasundar* (Calcutta: Bhattacharya & Sons, 1923), 38.

63. Michael D. Gordin, *Scientific Babel: How Science Was Done before and after Global English* (Chicago: University of Chicago Press, 2015).

64. Praphullachandra Ray and Prabodhchandra Chattopadhyay, *Rasayanik Paribhasa* [Chemical Terminology] (Calcutta: Bangiya Sahitya Parishad, 1912), i–iv.

65. Gyan Prakash, *Another Reason: Science and the Imagination of Modern India* (New Delhi, New York: Oxford University Press, 2000), 49–85; Michael S. Dodson, "Translating Science, Translating Empire: The Power of Language in Colonial North India," *Comparative Studies in Society and History* 47/4 (2005), 809–835.

66. Here it is worth noting that the clear hitching of a very specific view of the past to the creation of a terminology for the future undermines the overly sharp distinction some scholars wish to make between Ray's "science" and his "antiquarianism."

See Pratik Chakrabarti, "Science, Nationalism, and Colonial Contestations: PC Ray and his Hindu Chemistry," *Indian Economic and Social History Review* 37/2 (2000), 185–213.

67. Praphulla Chandra Ray, *A History of Hindu Chemistry from the Earliest Times to the Middle of the Sixteenth Century A.D.*, vol. 1 (Calcutta: Prithwis Chandra Ray, 1902), xxxvi.

68. Tribedi, *Sabda Katha*, 163.

69. Ibid., 162–163.

70. Ghosh, *Acharya Ramendrasundar*, 1–4; Ashutosh Bajpeyi, *Ramendrasundar Jeeban Katha* [The Story of Ramendrasundar's Life] (Calcutta: Gurudas Chattopadhyay & Sons, 1923), 1–31.

71. Ramendrasundar Tribedi, *Pundarikakulakirtipanjika* [Genealogy of the Pundarik Family] (Calcutta: Hindu Machine Press, 1900).

72. Gordin, *Scientific Babel*; Marwa Elshakry and Carla Nappi, "Translations," in *A Companion to the History of Science*, ed. Bernard V. Lightman (Chichester: John Wiley & Sons, 2016), 372–386; Sietske Fransen, "Introduction: Translators and Translations of Early Modern Science," *Translating Early Modern Science*, ed. Sietske Fransen, Niall Hodson, and Karl A. E. Enenkel (Leiden: Brill, 2017), 1–14.

73. Ramendrasundar Tribedi, "Hormman Helomholtj" [Herman Helmholtz], in *Ramendrasundar Rachanasamagra*, ed. Buddhadeb Bhattacharya, vol. 1 (Calcutta: Granthamela, 1957), 209–217.

PART III
MUSICAL ENCOUNTERS

7

Cosmopoiesis

Stories Sung of the Equatorial Gulf of Guinea, 1817

James Q. Davies

Genesis Stories

This chapter proposes a theory of *cosmopoiesis*, a poetics of songful world-making. It suggests how weaving together biocultural environments in song and storytelling might be related to both decolonial struggle and the poetic imperatives of empire building. I ask how a world forms anthropogenically in relation to those who would seek a home in it, or who seek asylum in it. The chapter concerns itself with multiple states of song, or the multiple ways in which a single song might be heard to afford multiple overlapping states. I want to know how, while dependent on its elemental provision, one speaks into or narrates the place of one's medial utterance. I take seriously the power of musical storytelling, not by overvaluing the power of an exceptional case study, but by assessing the ritual force of narrative schemas sung over and over. I counter, that is, the tyranny of Euro-Romantic environmentality with the oratorical power of oft-iterated stories and songs sung locally from within. In my view, struggles over territory are as much battles over competing storytelling traditions as battles over environments. Where is the world for those who travel or are forcibly displaced in it? How have political ecologies been made? *Where* is the place of song?

The image in Figure 7.1 pictures "notes sung" above the sounds of an eight-string *ngombi* harp. This record was made for the lettered colonial archive by Sarah Wallis Bowdich, English naturalist, African explorer, prolific author, and in this instance, phonographer. She heard the harp song in 1817 at a site almost exactly on the equator—in the middle of global things—at the site of a historical node in the transatlantic slave economy serving as conduit for human traffic in the Gulf of Guinea. The harpist-bard's whiteness is observed: he is a person from "Imbeekee" with albinism. Roshanak Kheshti's

James Q. Davies, *Cosmopoiesis* In: *Acoustics of Empire*. Edited by: Peter McMurray and Priyasha Mukhopadhyay, Oxford University Press. © Oxford University Press 2024. DOI: 10.1093/oso/9780197553787.003.0008

Figure 7.1 "Notes sung." T. Edward Bowdich, *Mission from Cape Coast Castle to Ashantee* (London: John Murray, 1819), unnumbered page between pp. 448 and 449, DT507.B67, Bancroft Library, University of California, Berkeley.

writings on the role of white women as song-hunters come to mind, as do her observations on the construction of modern listening, as both a technique of differentiating radically othered subalterns, and as a radically feminized practice.[1]

This is a model transcription. Bowdich, or rather her husband Thomas Edward, since she acted as his ghost writer, is frequently credited for the fidelity and authenticity of the work, which served the extractive logics of myths of colonial encounter. Sarah Bowdich herself admitted merely that "every notation must be far inadequate," and that the poetic narration she heard resisted her attempts to re- or deterritorialize it.[2] That said, the Bowdich ethnographies have been hailed as the first to penetrate the musical interior of any West African musics, what musicologists call "The Music Itself." Kofi Agawu, in his *The African Imagination in Music*, for example, extols these records for being the first in European history to deal "not only with the external morphology of instruments," but also to record actual "musical elements."[3] In multiple prose narrations allied to the printed transcription reproduced here, Bowdich described the harp song—performed by an enslaved person with albinism living amongst Myènè-speaking Mpongwe people—as a hyper-poetic oration of genesis or initiation myths involving the birth of the world. Bowdich called it "an oratorio."[4]

In what follows, I present multiple ways of reading Bowdich's transcription of the harp song "along the grain" of the archive of colonialism.[5] Using shipping documents, maps, and letters, I examine the geopolitical struggle over the resources of a territory off the Gabon Estuary, by proposing comparative ways of narrating the harpist's performance: first, as a "rainforest acoustemology," since the musician was allegedly procured in the deep equatorial interior; second, as the sounds of the circum-Atlantic trade in the enslaved; and finally, as the supposed expression of the vestige of an original whiteness preserved by this white-skinned harpist-singer at the heart of a "blackening" climate. The chapter presents several possible ways of animating and experiencing this equatorial environment in sound, alongside several competing ways of ranking the human in relation to each political ecology.

One intention is to offer counternarratives to the *Heart of Darkness* archetype, by writing against white encounter stories, ones that stage originary scenes of contact between primitive nature and penetrating civilization. The harpist's poetic improvisation occurred as part of the complex meeting of the enslaved, slave trader, and naturalist-scientist (as they were referred to in the colonial archive). Bowdich found herself in Central Africa as an agent for the African Committee of the Company of Merchants; the singer was inscribed as "the property of Rassondji," a trader with circum-Atlantic interests in Liverpool, New York, and Caen. The alienating effects of racial capitalism, as we shall see, necessitated the transformation of economic relations that themselves perpetuated transformations in the experience and production of natural acoustic environments. The Central African tropics prove useful to my multiple genesis stories because it was under the most biodiverse of conditions that climate was deemed, at least in the imagination of the African Committee, to be most inhuman. In such torrid climates, given this performance's association with the history of the triangular trade, the cause of humanity itself was thought to be under violent geotechnical construction.

I take as axiomatic Achille Mbembe's claim in his *Critique of Black Reason* that "there is no domination without a cult of spirits."[6] The *ngombi* harp has traditionally appeared at the heart of colonial things, mythologized as the first and most sacred instrument of creative genesis. It is often said by those studying harp morphology and migration that this southwestern-most example of the African harp belongs to an antediluvian family of arched lyres that can be seen in the pictographic rock art at the Ennedi Plateau in Chad and the Tassili n'Ajjer cave paintings in Algeria, as well as many even more antiquated Egyptian sources. In white European mythology, the hand-held lyre has long symbolized imperial wandering and misplacement.[7] For centuries, it has carried the idea of civilization across forbidden thresholds. Its magic has remade worlds and overcome death, in ways definitive of heroic crusader narratives and their attendant Orphic foundation myths. Narratives about suffering whiteness and lyric power have not only buttressed superstitions about musico-aesthetic abstraction. The strings of Orpheus's harp will resonate again at the site of a now-forgotten trading depot I will soon describe. The circulation of alienated sounds followed the transit of abstracted persons and other traded "raw materials" in a contested spiritual climate.

Further, I concur with Mbembe that "blackness and race have constituted the (unacknowledged and often denied) foundation of what we might call the [African] nuclear power plant, from which the modern project of knowledge—and of governance—has been deployed."[8] The aim of this chapter is to tell stories that invert dominant narratives about the centrality of metropoles and the irrelevance of peripheries. It is to show how Equatorial Africa was maintained as a nuclear site for the European knowledge and energy economy. In 1817, events unfold in the wake of the abolition of human trafficking in British dominions, though not yet in the era of the abolition of slaveholding per se. Sarah Bowdich and her husband were charged to gather official information about this site. The African Committee, having capitalized for so many years on racialized flesh and racialized labor, now sought to reimagine this standing reservoir as a storehouse for massed environmental extraction: for harvesting woods; later, palm oil and latex rubber; and, even later, oil and natural gas. The era of "abolition," uncomfortably, was also an era of eco-colonial expansion, an era that required a vast, strategic restructuring of this storehouse for global biopower and biocapital. This site had long been a primary source of British, French, Spanish, Dutch, and Portuguese wealth. But, from 1817, the milieu itself was identified as a strategic site for environmental extraction, including as a resource for musical knowledge, where nineteenth-century European ideas about musical creativity and expressive freedom could be essentialized, sourced, and regenerated.

The Mission

The image in Figure 7.2 is a map. It was printed, in the wake of the Bowdich expedition, for the African Association, also known as the Association for Promoting the Discovery of the Interior Parts of Africa, a London society devoted as much to the abolition of the trade in enslaved peoples as to circum-Atlantic commercial capitalization. The African Association (1788–1831) should not be confused with the African Committee of the Company of Merchants trading to Africa (1752–1821) that sponsored the Bowdich adventure. Partly because of the Bowdiches' complaints, the government shut down the latter joint stock company in 1821, the African Committee having failed, largely because of booming Fante-Spanish trade, to rescue the Atlantic slave trade for British profit-making.[9]

One way to think of the map fragment is as a cosmogram, an imperial projection imagined as part of the failed colonial attempt to make this gridded, flat, neutralized space real; that is, enclosed, boxed in, and raised to productivity and light. A small one-street settlement, now long since swallowed by the rainforest, is indicated in tiny script as "Naängo," just north of the equator above swamps, colored in. The Bowdiches identified the harpist-musician brought to them as "a slave belonging to Rassondji." Rassondji was the Mpongwe-speaking chief trader at Naängo, which had

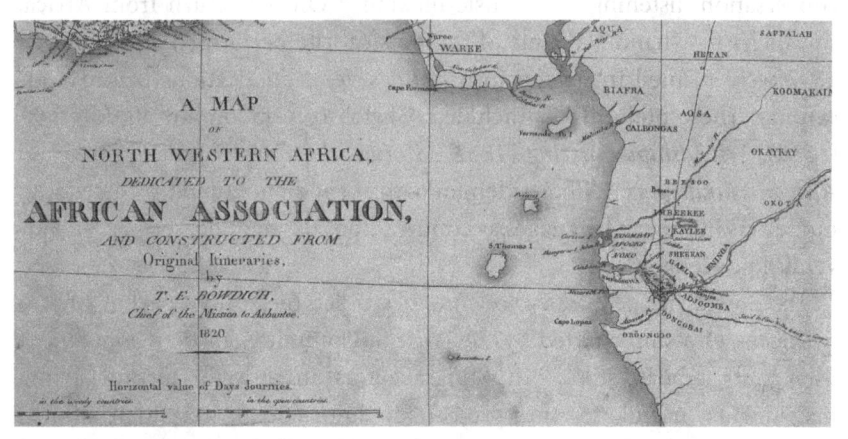

Figure 7.2   Detail of T. Edward Bowdich, *A Map of North Western Africa Dedicated to the African Association* (1820), gallica.bnf.fr, GE C-7798, Bibliothèque nationale de France.

been a staging post for circum-Atlantic slave trading since at least the 1720s. Bowdich was informed that the musician came from the mountain indicated on Figure 7.2 as "Imbeekee." He had been acquired by Rassondji through Kele-speakers or Bakele (marked as "Kaylee") who, Bowdich was informed, were "cannibals." Historians since François Ngolet recognize the ethnonym "Bakele" as an invented identity (from the Ongom verb *U-kelekwe* meaning "those who are suspended, those who no longer have roots") concocted by colonialists, Bowdich being the first to use "Kaylee," to redefine a pre-colonial "Ongom" symbolic consciousness.[10] It was at Naängo—in this reportedly most inhospitable, purportedly uncivilizable, and abject of moral climates—where Sarah Bowdich heard and recorded the harp song.

Who was Bowdich? John Keats described the twenty-six-year-old author-scholar, not without condescension, as a "beautiful little sylphid woman."[11] Alexander von Humboldt and other servants of global enlightenment at the Institut de France knew her well. Illustrious French naturalist Georges Cuvier "received her as a daughter" at the Jardin des Plantes in Paris during several periods of intensive study in the early 1820s, where she had access to his extensive library and collections.[12] Sarah was also a pianist.[13] In her middle years, she was associated with perhaps the most cultivated musical circle in Europe. The diary of the wife of Ignaz Moscheles records her as a regular at the composer's home in London, a haven for Anglo-German conversation, listening, and music-making.[14] On her return from Africa, Bowdich's first-hand accounts of the musical rite performed at Naängo in 1817 were printed in several forms and several publications before mid-century. These publications included "Sketch of Gaboon and its Interior" (1819), *Friendship's Offering* (1833), *Stories of Strange Lands* (1835), and *African Wanderers* (1846), written for a mix of audiences and translated into numerous European languages as contributions to scientific, serious, and juvenile knowledge.[15]

The Bowdiches penetrated to what they called the "rudest part of Africa" by means of a ship charted by the African Committee of the Company of Merchants. Aboard the Lord Mulgrave was an array of territorializing instruments useful to the project of bureaucratic respatialization— "instruments for determining the latitude and longitude of places," thermometers, barometers, chronometers, astronomical equipment, logbooks, and so on. The ship's ledger of extra freight, now preserved in the National Archives of the United Kingdom, lists an onboard pianoforte in the itemized record of cargo, no doubt for Sarah's use. These tools served an array of techniques that served colonizing orders of perception, orders that would be gridded over the rainforest. The tactic, useful as much to cartography as sonic transcription, was to deploy inscriptive devices to fill up empty space, after the fact of erasure. Such were the contextualizing practices of biopolitical government, ones that involved not so much a way of getting about the forest, as a way of managing or enclosing it from above—working to negate the power of environment itself by naming names on whited-out spaces on paper.[16]

The Bowdich mission was to gather the testimony of slaves and traders to determine "the geography, history, language, natural resources, and the moral and local state of the nations of the interior of western Africa."[17] Another goal was "to become intimately acquainted with the interior of Africa, and to tranquillize it; to take the first great steps towards commercial intercourse and civilization."[18] This mission of tranquillization would involve bringing to light the riverine trade routes of the interior, and testing the so-called "Congo hypothesis" (later proved false) that "the Gaboon River" (actually an estuary) might veer into the Ogooue, and thence into the Congo, Niger, and Nile. In addition, the Bowdiches would "collect the remains of Arabic literature as may exist," Sarah's husband being a philologist of Islamicate languages.[19] The Bowdiches were amongst the first to claim that the languages and music of sub-Saharan Africa could be traced back to the prehistoric source culture of ancient Egypt, as part of the quest for the lost (white Hamitic) roots of civilization.[20]

The Bowdiches spent nine weeks off Naängo gathering information, while the African Company negotiated the trade of a supercargo of ebony and barwood. For a sense of the climatic threat, consider that, on this voyage alone, several sailors including the first mate, the carpenter, and even one of Sarah's children, died of malaria: literally "bad air." Six years later, Sarah's husband would also be killed by "land breezes" farther north off The Gambia. Sarah herself was forced to return to London by 1830 to make a living off the London literary market. Besides ships and all the rest, perhaps the most important imperial technology for overcoming this climatic environment in the long term—an achievement basic to colonialization—was quinine, made possible after the isolation of the Andean plant *quina-quina* by French apothecaries in the 1820s. Even then, Equatorial Africa remained one of the most purportedly malarial, racializing, and pathologized climates known to Enlightenment man.

Sarah Bowdich pronounced herself to be "the first white woman that had ever visited the Gaboon," a claim that served the market for encounter anthropography back home.[21] Yet the inhabitants at Naängo were anything but "encounterable." Their first-hand knowledge of Europe far outstripped European knowledge of the territory of the Gulf. English, French and Portuguese were widely spoken.[22] At the time, Mpongwe-speakers used 60-foot vessels equipped with masts and sails capable of carrying eight to ten tons of cargo, and up to 80 men.[23] Rassondji may have been bedridden in 1817, in ways that Sarah interpreted as a sign of his people's climatic degeneration. But he had also traveled widely in his youth, having visited Liverpool, where he maintained lifelong financial interests.[24] At least two Mpongwe-speaking traders introduced to the Bowdiches had spent their adolescence, for upwards of eight years, in France, one, named Richard, being raised in Caen.[25] European furniture and dress was common, as when the Bowdich party was greeted by the brother of Rassondji, in a long brown greatcoat and a cocked hat. Known to the English as Tom Lawson, this trader was the same whom one historian speculates had been educated in New York, "as part of an understanding made with English slave traders."[26] Sarah Bowdich found this brother of Rassondji to be "mild," "respectable," and "gentlemanly," in ways that frustrated the arc of her heroic explorer narrative.[27]

The story went that one stormy night in 1817, Bowdich and her husband were invited to dinner at Lawson's (with knife and fork at table), after which a musician was brought into "the middle of the room, which was lighted by a large torch stuck upon a pole and composed of sweet-smelling gums tied up in palm leaves."[28] The musician was allegedly acquired by Rassondji during war. In his hand, the harpist-musician carried an eight-stringed *ngombi* harp, which the Bowdiches would be amongst the first Europeans to record and study. It was an instrument of "full, harmonious, and deep tone." The *ngombi*'s design was typical of what later-century French-American explorer Paul Du Chaillu would call, describing a Kele-associated statue rather than a musical instrument, "a monstrous and indecent figure of wood of the feminine sex." The resonator of anthropomorphic forms of the harp represented a woman's body, the soundboard her skin (here covered in goatskin), the sound-hole her sexual organ, the neck her spine, and the strings her intestines—as per descriptions by leading ethnomusicological authority on the instrument, Pierre Sallée.[29] Sarah Bowdich, who inspected and later played the *ngombi* for an eavesdropping Mpongwe audience, observed similarly. "The figure head, which was well curved," she wrote, "was placed at the top of the body, the strings were twisted round long pegs, which easily turned when they wanted tuning, and, being made of the fibrous roots of palm wine tree, were very tough and not apt to slip." "Both [the musician] and the harp," Bowdich confirmed, "came far from the interior."[30]

Narration I: The Breath of the Forest

There are multiple possible ways to narrate this performance. One way would be to adopt a "rainforest acoustemology" after Steven Feld and interpret the harp song as an emanation of the spirit of the forest—even as the first music of the forest.[31] If Pierre Sallée and ethnographers of the so-called "*Bwiti* cult" are right, what Sarah Bowdich witnessed was an invocation of the sacred wind that purportedly first animated the world.

The term *Bwiti* invokes plural meanings. According to precolonial historian and linguist Kairn Klieman, ethnographic evidence suggests that *Bwiti*-inspired initiation societies originated in the forest world of the Kele- and forager Seke-speaking peoples.[32] The cult of *Bwiti* is now recognized as one of the three official religions of Gabon, practiced there by the late-arriving Tsogo-speakers, having purportedly been birthed amongst now remnant Kele-speakers and other "forest people." It may be defined as a set of practices dedicated to the veneration of first-comer ancestors or spirits of the land. One meaning, Klieman writes, might be derived "from the standard reconstruction of [*-yìtí*] as a proto-Bantu noun meaning 'tree' or 'medicine.'" It is also possible that the term *bwiti* (from *bu-yiti*) refers to "the one/spirit/entity who calls," the musician-visionary having invoked the procreative powers of the ancestors, by stirring the strings of the *ngombi*.[33]

Sallée speculates that the Gabonese *ngombi* was originally forged in encounters between those Kele- and Seke-speakers, as well as other "bush peoples" (that is, so-called "pygmies," which recent scholarship has shown is and was an invented European category).[34] Bowdich herself sourced these sounds deeper within the forests, amongst a mythic white tribe of "Mbiki." (Without mentioning "Albino Tribes," in 1853, missionary James L. Mackey described the "Mbikoo" as a scattered people of once-numerous nomadic "bushmen" decimated by the slave trade and roaming "a belt of country from the Muni southward to the Gaboon" in the area of the Noya river.)[35] Whatever the primal source from whence it sprung, the *ngombi* of "Mbeekee" was held to awaken the spirits of the forest.[36]

According to the oral tradition of Tsogo-speakers, an inland peoples later intimate with the harp, the instrument originated with Kele-speakers, the same "forest people" whom Bowdich stigmatized as "cannibals." For Sallée, the evidence of "the music itself" suggests the truth of Kele-speaking origins. The disenfranchisement of these now near-extinct anthropophagists, who have supposedly inhabited these forests for millennia, he suggests, is audible in the death motives and sadness of traditional harp-song lamentation. Sallée quotes the nineteenth-century explorer Du Chaillu, who marveled at the "almost always plaintive airs" of a "savage and treacherous people."[37] The sounds of the Bakele harp, for Sallée, conjures something of the dying spiritual traditions of their threatened existential ecology.[38]

In this narration, that pole in the center of the room incarnated the aboriginal Edenic tree, by which, according to *Bwiti* genesis myths, the first people descended to earth. As such, these *batwa* were "the people that fell from the sky."[39] The arch of the harp was made from the flexible wood *kuta*; the aerial cords of the *roang* (*géoko*) palm and the resonator of the *raphia obanza*. Its aerial fibers extended upward manifested a kind of umbilical cord connecting earthly residents, who imagined themselves as tenants of the forest, to the primordial-creative world-process that sustained it. In the terms of *Bwiti* genesis myths, the harp sounded the original vibrations of the forest's limitless creativity, animating a music attuned to the immersive soundscapes of the equatorial ecology. The energies emanating from her resonator were a narcotic, inhaled with the psychoactive fumes of tree barks to produce altered psycho-physical states, characteristic of *ngombi* initiation rites.[40] The vitality of these sounds, in other words, at once represented a medicine breathing powers of transformation into the world, and the verdant energies of the life-giving rainforest.

Thus was the anthropomorphic sculpture that Bowdich saw carved into the resonator of the harp. To extrapolate Klieman's argument, in *Bwiti*-derived mythologies, the female form of the instrument bore the breath of life, whilst her bloated belly bore procreative pneumatic power. The first ancestor and "mother, origin of all things," her large belly and cheeks were no abstraction. They symbolized the blowing out of air, evoking associations "between breath (wind, air) and the original creation, for many West African genesis accounts consider human life to have been engendered through the sacred breath, or 'wind' of God."[41] In *Explorations and Adventures in Equatorial Africa* (1858), Du Chaillu printed an image of a "Harp of the Bakalai [Bakele]," the Bakele harp being a more angular instrument without the humanoid carving at its shoulder. This harp appeared above a detailed description of a life-size wooden idol of a "cloven-footed" woman venerated at the large Kele-speaking center at "Njali-Coudié" (far to the south near modern-day Ivanga) which was "situated in the very hilly country between the Ofoubou [Ofubu] and Ovenga [Doubanga] Rivers." Du Chaillu reported that this powerful fetish with copper eyes—this statue with "one cheek painted red, and the other yellow"—was named "Mbuiti."[42] No doubt he meant for his Bakele harp to be an object charged by a similar spirit, and "the rainforest a sacred place, one that houses ancestral and territorial spirits that serve as intercessors to *-yambé, the 'first spirit' and 'first creator' of all things."[43] The source of those sounds heard at Naängo in 1817, in such listenings, was to be found deep within the forest. It was to be found amongst the swollen-bellied "first men."

Narration II: Transatlantic Sounds

A second way to narrate the harpist-singer's performance is by withdrawing from the "sacred trees" and returning to the open trading waters of the estuary at Naängo. At the edge of the rainforest, the slave's "extraordinary vociferations" appear less an inspiration of Bakele-Pygmy origin than an act of allochthonous Mpongwe creation. Our second narration imagines transatlantic sounds, human trafficking, and sonic circulation oriented around a powerful trading empire centered at Naängo.

In 1851, the aged Rassondji himself offered an oral history of his coastal people to yet another American missionary, Rollin Porter. Porter painted a picture of inexorable decline since the heyday of Rassondji's father, since it reinforced the missionary's conviction of the need for "salvation." Not long ago, Porter ventriloquized, "the Mpongwes lived far back in the bush; and it used to be thought that if one of them saw the salt water, he would soon die."[44] The first occupants at the Estuary, according to Rassondji, were the "Divwas"/Ndiwas, who were reportedly extinct but for a single individual living with Tom Lawson.[45] Following Ndiwa-speakers, Mpongwe groups were purportedly also dying by the 1840s, as were Seke-speakers, who had "literally sold themselves out as slaves." Indeed, according to Porter, every wave of race flooding in from the interior had succumbed—one by one—to the same climatic-degenerative state.[46] The swamps purportedly drained these once noble migrants of their virility.

The European slave trade was a likelier cause; yet, if the Bowdiches were critical of the Naängan's capacity for "indigenous music," this imagined deficiency owed little to climatic conditions. Rather, the musical inferiority of coastal latecomers owed to the ways in which they appropriated and revitalized *Bwiti* myth such as to advance the politico-religious concerns of the transatlantic trade in enslaved peoples. The Bowdiches, in fact, claimed that Mpongwe-speakers themselves were only musical to the extent that they forced subordinated peoples to make music for them, coastal music being "very inferior to that I have before noticed."[47]

This second narration imagines that the poetic cartography established at Naängo was not animated by the earth spirits of *Bwiti*-inspired practice, as invoked by forest-dwelling Bakele groups. Instead, it recounts, after Klieman, that, in "*Mwetyi*-inspired societies," late-on *batwa* were water spirits (often coded white) understood to inhabit estuaries, creeks, rivers, lakes, ponds, and oceans.[48] For Klieman, the powers of ancestral water spirits arose amongst coastal settlers as a way for authorities such as Rassondji's to legitimize territorial precedence. The movement of these white spirits, in other words, functioned to animate ethnic linkages along the flow of oceanic trade routes radiating towards and outwards from Naängo. To maintain triangular flows from Europe to the Americas, new creation stories were required to connect those who owned the land with those who had been marginalized from it. As such, coastal aristocracies expropriated and invented an aboriginal *Bwiti* mythology (which was then turned back on the interior) in order to establish kinship systems useful to the relational structures of economic exchange. According to what Kopytoff called "a principle of precedence," Bantu populations throughout sub-Saharan Africa separated themselves out from imagined "first-comers," that is, those who took precedence over the environment because their ancestors were supposedly buried first in the land.[49] An appropriation of the powers of "the first men," that is, proved foundational, not only to coastal genesis myths, but to coastal acts of empire- and circum-Atlantic world-making.

More than this, Klieman claims, groups engaged in ocean trade imagined *batwa* not in the abstract, as wooden figurines or invisible spirits of the forest. Instead, "the people from the sky" were personified. Klieman cites a process of ideological rejuvenation by which *Bwiti* sources were appropriated in the politico-religious terms of *Ombwiri/Mwiri* institutions—the prefix "–om" generally denoting embodied human beings. Thus, a new cast of flesh-and-blood subjects was birthed into this world, a primordial *batwa* to be enslaved, bought, and sold to British, French, Spanish, or Portuguese masters. Such subjects were objectified in the humanoid anthromorphic harp so characteristic of late-comer *Ombwiri/Mwiri* practice—in contradistinction to the plain so-called Bakele harp. The word *batwa*, that is, became a stigma affixed to individuals and groups absorbed, or better invented by resident "latecomer" populations. The bodies of "bush peoples" were thus reimagined as a kind of resource or "detritus" to be harvested from the interior. True, disenfranchised individuals were feared for their deep spiritual knowledge. True, they were afforded special powers, charged with mysticism, and granted a spiritual birthright to the environment. Yet, they were also captured by client Mpongwe-speakers, ostracized and driven to the inner reaches, which is to say that these abject "pygmy" people were always-already mythic, even as they were invented. These forest beings were stigmatized as at once human and non-human, gods and slaves, according to the synoptic genesis narratives of how the world came to be. This is to say that the figure of the "slave" presented to the Bowdiches in 1817 was just as spiritually charged as the female figure emerging from the sacred harp. At Naängo, both were *batwa*.

The harpist-singer that appeared to Sarah Bowdich, in this narration, was the means by which such "big men" expropriated the enchanted power of the perifluvial forest. Rassondji, who kept him as an enslaved person (according to Bowdich), represented a new type of client-chieftainship seen at the Gabon Estuary in the era of transatlantic slavery, a wizard-like figure (complete with bell) who evoked authority, not only by a ritual appropriation of the powers of territorial spirits, but by literally taking possession of them. In *Mwetyi* ideology, it should be emphasized, *batwa* came from an unspecified, ravaged, and mystic interior. These nomad musicians were without fixed genetic or geographic location. The designation *batwa* might refer to marginalized individuals as diverse as infants born breech or with the umbilical cord around their neck, children who left missing limbs in the netherworld, twins, individuals with sexual bimorphism, those with dwarfism, and persons with albinism. At once feared and venerated, these marginalized bodies were absorbed into latecomer cosmologies that served the territorial imperatives of the white circum-Atlantic trade.

According to Sallée, the power of the *Ombwiri* was amplified in the sounds of the *ngombi* harp and the rush of wind on a waterborne pirogue, a dugout not unlike the one that bore the Bowdiches to Naängo. The shape of the sacred harp itself, in the terms of a genesis myth recorded at the coast by Pierre

Sallée, was an analogy for the "pirogue of life." In *Mwetyi* oral tradition, the shape of the pirogue, thus, could be associated with the shape of female sexual organs, whilst the wind symbolized "the original animating force or 'breath of God.'" It was in a vessel such as this that the first humans were supposed to have journeyed to "the landing stage of world."[50] If you exhibit the *ngombi* in certain way, it is true that it can look like a boat, as in the non-anthropomorphic example pictured in Figure 7.3.

In her vocal transcription (Figure 7.1), Bowdich inscribed these landings perfectly, taking note of a cadential "leading phrase" or "sentence" (as she called it) that finished each "strain." Note, for example, the repeated cadential figures: the two descents from C-(A)-G in the second system, and the four cadential turning figures (A-B-G) in the phrases through the *presto* and *andante* before the "long rapid recitative." These stopping points exemplify what Sallée awkwardly calls a *cadence suspensive*, by which he means melodic formulae sung against patterns spun on strings 2, 4, 6, and 8 of the harp. The remaining odd-numbered cords of the eight-string instrument, meanwhile, help the singer toward more decisive resting points: the *cadence conclusive*. Sallée is rightly reluctant to associate the periodicity of this European

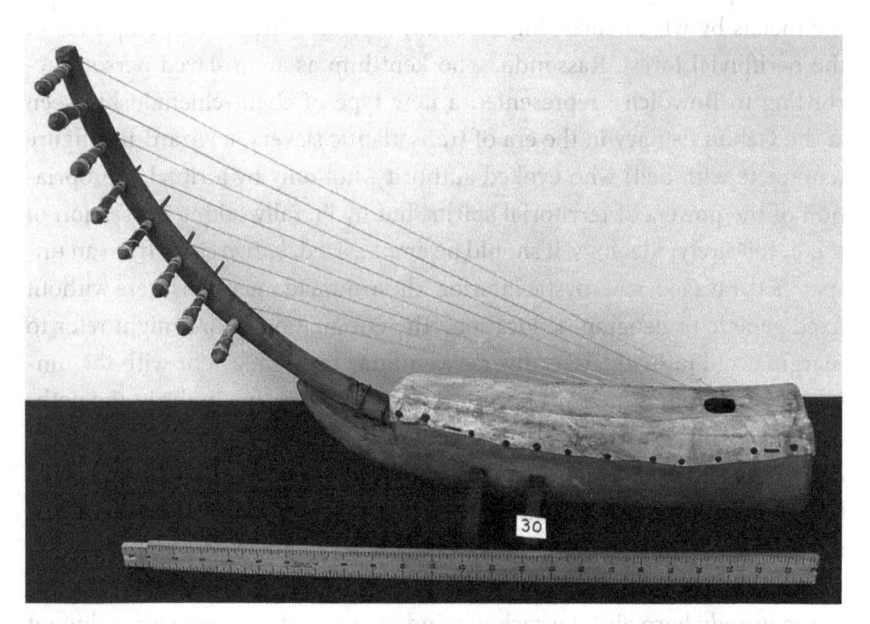

Figure 7.3 *Ngombi* harp collected by Albert Schweitzer, Roderic C. Knight Instrument Collection, Oberlin College Conservatory of Music, Knight-Revision Classification C42.13. Reproduced with permission.

galant style—this improvised ethnolanguage of tension and rest, motion and arrival—with some vaguely Iberian syncretism or some *ancien fond culturel luso-congolais.*[51] The presence of these circum-Atlantic schema, for Sallée, only shroud the genealogy of these "labyrinthine" harp-songs in yet more mystery. The point is that the evidence of this inscription was essentially waterborne or estuarine in provenance. In this tradition, according to Sallée, these cadential arrivals mimic "the action of the wind on the pirogue which, wind from behind, is carried upright and straight ahead [*cadence conclusive*] or, blown to the side, must tack [*cadence suspensive*]."[52]

Oral accounts of how the first men were birthed, Klieman writes, "often relate that humans were 'delivered' to earth in a pirogue, usually traveling on a current of water (amniotic fluids) and shepherded by a sacred wind (breath being the source of life)."[53] The very category of the human, that is, was vouchsafed for those that journey, and narrated in the ways that swept up that bewildered group of enraptured travelers on that stormy equatorial night in 1817. Here, in the rhetorical sweep of the harp sounds, were stories that bound these listeners to trade relationships reaching at once deep into the interior and out far across the sea.

Narration III: White Genius

A final way to narrate this performance would be to plumb white mythologies, to explore kinship systems suitable to colonizing orders of acoustic perception. The whiteness of the harpist, for the Bowdiches, misplaced him as a genius. He was tragically ill-adapted to the climatic terrors to which he was subject. His displacement, for Sarah Bowdich, manifested itself as a divorce of sight from sound. The "unsightliness" of his body vouchsafed the beautiful purity of his music. "Orpheus's lyre," proto-romantic music critic E. T. A. Hoffmann famously declared from Berlin in 1813, opened the portals onto an "unknown realm, a world that has nothing in common with the external sensual world that surrounds him, a world in which he leaves behind him all definite feelings to surrender himself to inexpressible longing."[54] The harpist-singer appeared, in this sense, as a creature lifted free from time and space.

In nineteenth-century white mythology, the spirits of genius were migrant and non-territorial. "He was wholly abstracted," Sarah Bowdich confirmed, "from all around during the execution of his compositions."[55] That is, the terrible isolation of this "maniac," as Bowdich called the singer-harpist, was a sign of his heroic resistance to contingency. His whiteness was a vestige of supposed original whiteness, and his isolation explained his deep immersion in the astonishing music. This vestige of the ancient world, as such, wielded his harp as a weapon against the blackening climate itself.

It was Ptolemy, in first-century Alexandria, who first heralded a "pale, night-dwelling people living on the African continent."[56] A text published under the auspices of the Bowdiches' mentor in Paris scoffed at the myth of a white tribe in the deep Gabonese interior, preferring to medicalize albinism as a pathological disorder. (The clinicalization of albinism as a modern condition, while it worked to free the conundrum from climatic explanations, simultaneously instituted the medical logic that something was wrong with hypopigmentation.) Yet even the Cuvier-endorsed "Supplemental History of Man" (1824) blamed "the albino's" supposed hyper-sensitivity to light on a deficiency in "the coloring principle." "Hence we find the eyelids of these people generally closed," one of Cuvier's disciples wrote, "but in twilight, dusk, or even a close approach to darkness, they see remarkably well."[57] The received wisdom was that their eyes were either possessed of a convulsive motion, or seemed to be "fixed in their heads, like people that lie a dying." Sarah Bowdich observed that the eyes of the harpist at Naängo seemed "small, bright, and of a dark grey" in one version, but also "small and blue, and from seeing imperfectly in the day-time, they were constantly blinking, and had a vacant expression [since] his vision was imperfect in the light." "The light seemed to hurt [his eyes]," she explained, "and their constant quivering and rolling gave his countenance an air of insanity."[58] The *leucaethiop*, purportedly, had no place in the torrid zone.

At the foot of the tree of life, in this third narration, the musician agitated against existence itself. The Enlightenment constructed persons with albinism as the living dead. "Pale as dead corpses," the influential *Encyclopédie* entry read, "their eyes are gray [and it] is said that they see only in moonlight like owls."[59] The analogy to "bats and owls" was partly derived from Olfert Dapper, who also compared their flesh to "the skin of a dead corpse."[60] The *homo nocturnus*, according to Enlightenment consensus, were said to come into their own by night, taking bloodthirsty revenge on those who persecuted them by day. "Notwithstanding their being thus sluggish and dull in the day-time," one old story quoted by such explicitly humanitarian nineteenth-century ethnologists as James Cowles Prichard (1813), "yet when moon-shiny nights come, they are all life and activity, running abroad into the woods, and skipping about like wild bucks, and running as fast by moon-light."[61]

These myths about "white tribes" were remarkably persistent. As late as 1861, French navy officer and explorer Jules Braouezec printed a map indicating the country of "nomadic albino tribes named Bakouï" across the Crystal Mountains. He claimed to have seen "two or three" of this "small-sized people," who were called "Akowa" by the Mpongwe, and had "woolly red hair and eyebrows, albino color eyes, and pale yellow skin."[62] (The words *Akowa, Bakouyi, Bakoya, Baka*, as well as a host of related names, are now generically affixed to so-called "pygmies.")[63] It is revealing that white autochthons were invented first, and in ways contiguous with the later "invention of the pygmies" "as a distinct racial category and then as a global stratum or frozen moment in human physical and social evolution."[64] An "albino paradigm," here, elides uncomfortably with a "pygmy paradigm" such as to buttress narratives about development, genesis, and Hamitic myths about original whiteness.[65]

Sarah Bowdich was struck how the musician, blinking against the world, seemed to push past the affordances of his instrument, to the extent that its crude materials were transcended:

> The running accompaniment served again as a prelude to a loud recitative, uttered with the greatest volubility, and ending with one word, with which he ascended and descended, far beyond the extent of his harp, with the most beautiful precision. Sometimes he became more collected, and a mournful air succeeded the recitative, though without the least connection, and he would again burst out with the whole force of his powerful voice in the notes of the Hallelujah of Handel. To meet with this chorus in the wilds of Africa, and from such a being, had an effect I can scarcely describe, and I was lost in astonishment at the coincidence. There could not be a stronger proof of the nature of Handel, or the powers of the negro.[66]

Bowdich, that is, heard universal Handelian genius, and a powerful expression of the proof of the theory of original whiteness, the Hamitic myth that, as Voltaire once characterized Malpertuis's position: "Blacks are a race of whites blackened by the climate."[67] As we have seen, persons with albinism had long been an obsession for such Enlightenment thinkers as Buffon and Cuvier, given the challenge they posed to race-and-climate theories. The idea was that, since all humankind was originally white, and were apparently still born white, their complexions darkened only after exposure to the corrupting powers of climate. The music of genius is configured, in this narration, as a technology of isolation, alienation, and deep immersion. The harpist-singer, this vestige of the ancient world, as such, had heroically held out for millennia against the malarial effects of the climate, wielding his harp as a weapon against the forest. His appearance was a sign of hope, so the Bowdiches surmised, for the prospects of future civilization, borne on the back of this strange idea of a vestigial whiteness at the heart of the forest.

Conclusion

I have wandered several times off track, but only to show how much the sounds of the sacred harp, which Sarah Bowdich saw under the hands of an enslaved musician, provided a kind of raw material for multiple competing ways of narrating cosmic birth. The Orpheus of Imbeekee, for all involved, was a bard of sacred cosmopoietic force. In the multiple narrations I have sketched, the single performance of this orator-harpist was said to mediate the life-giving breath of the forest, the embodied *batwa* of transatlantic ritual, and the lost spirits of dissevered white genius. I have argued that these competing spiritual powers established the environments to which the earwitnesses gathered at Naängo were subject. The harp-song not only evoked experiences of dependency or resistance in relation to these disputed cosmologies. These sounds called into existence the very spiritual condition of acoustic surroundings. In each genesis narrative, the harpist told of the frontiers of relational worlds, even the birth of those worlds.

More than this, these ways of storying the environment were the very means by which participants and listeners traded kinship alliances with each other. The context of performance, as we have seen, was not an empty or neutral space for circulating false superstition, *pace* white ideology. The very medium of utterance was a dense spirit-filled domain subject to continual anthropogenic transformation—as much for Europeans as Africans—where divisions of labor were imposed, where the scale of ecological and economic exploitation was set, and where the potentialities of empire were laid out. I have countered ideas about metropoles and hyperperipheries by arguing that Equatorial Africa was a nuclear site for the sonic production of environmental and musical knowledge, the strategic marginalization and historical erasure of such sites as Naängo notwithstanding. I have claimed that the occasion of the harpist's improvised fantasy provided a kind of staging post from which to renew power structures, patterns of commercial exchange and mutual enrichment, as well as to establish relations of alterity and domination. My determination has been to take the elemental force of the stories told by ritual actors seriously, and to pay attention to the world-making power of the spirits that jostled to narrate this territory.

Notes

Parts of this chapter appear in James Q. Davies, *Creatures of the Air: Music, Atlantic Spirits, Breath, 1817–1913* (Chicago: University of Chicago Press, 2023). Reproduced with permission of University of Chicago Press.

1. Roshanak Kheshti, *Modernity's Ear: Listening to Race and Gender in World Music* (New York: New York University Press, 2015).

2. T. Edward Bowdich, *Mission from Cape Coast Castle to Ashantee* (London: John Murray, 1819), 451.

3. Kofi Agawu, *The African Imagination in Music* (New York: Oxford University Press, 2016), 72–73.

4. Sarah Wallace Bowdich Lee, "A Visit to Empoöngwa; or a Peep into Negro-Land," *Friendship's Offering: A Literary Album* (1833), 294–304; Mrs. Lee, "A Visit to Empoöngwa," *Stories of Strange Lands: And Fragments from the Notes of a Traveller* (London: Edward Moxon, 1835), 309–336.

5. Ann Laura Stoler, *Along the Archival Grain: Epistemic Anxieties and Colonial Common Sense* (Princeton, NJ: Princeton University Press, 2009).

6. Achille Mbembe, *The Critique of Black Reason* (Durham, NC: Duke University Press, 2017), 128.

7. For Orpheus in empire, see Olivia Bloechl, "On Colonial Difference and Musical Frontiers: Directions for a Postcolonial Musicology," *Native American Song* at the *Frontiers* of *Early Modern Music* (Cambridge, UK: Cambridge University Press, 2008), 1–31; Vanessa Agnew, *Enlightenment Orpheus: The Power of Music in other Worlds* (Oxford, UK: Oxford University Press, 2008); Nicholas Till, "Orpheus Conquistador," *Opera Indigene: Re/Presenting First Nations and Indigenous Cultures* (Farnham, UK: Ashgate, 2011), 15–30.

8. Mbembe, *Critique of Black Reason*, 2.

9. See T. E. Bowdich, *The African Committee* (London: Longman, 1819); Ty M. Reese, "'Eating' Luxury: Fante Middlemen, British Goods, and Changing Dependencies on the Gold Coast, 1750–1821," *William and Mary Quarterly* 65/4 (2009), 851–872.

10. François Ngolet, "Inventing Ethnicity and Identities in Gabon. The case of Ongom (Bakele)," *Revue française d'histoire d'outre-mer* 85/32 (1998), 5–26, at 9.

11. In a January 3, 1819, letter; see *The Letters of John Keats: 1814–1821*, ed. Hyder Edward Rollins, vol. 2 (Cambridge, UK: Cambridge University Press, 1958), 28.

12. Mrs. R. Lee (formerly Mrs. T. Ed. Bowdich), *Memoirs of Baron Cuvier* (London: Longman, 1833); "Mrs. Lee's Memoirs of Cuvier," *Monthly Magazine* 4/2 (1833), 159–178, at 160.

13. Lee, *Stories of Strange Lands*, 177.

14. Charlotte Moscheles, *Life of Moscheles: With Selections from his Diaries and Correspondence*, trans. A. D. Coleridge, 2 vols. (London: Hurst and Blackett, 1873), 1: 265–266.

15. Mary Orr, "Women Peers in the Scientific Realm: Sarah Bowdich (Lee)'s expert collaborations with Georges Cuvier, 1825–33," *Notes and Records of the Royal Society* 69/1 (2014), 37–51.

16. "Lord Mulgrave: A soft-bound ledger of the ship," British National Archives, Kew, 1816. T70/1220/2.

17. T. E. Bowdich, "Prospectus of an Expedition into Africa," *Quarterly Journal of Science, Literature, and the Arts* 9 (1820), 428–430, at 430.

18. T. E. Bowdich, *The African Committee* (London: Longman, 1819), 18.

19. "Mr Thomas Edward Bowdich and Mrs Sarah Bowdich," MS Archives of the Royal Literary Fund, Registered case 13/465. Paris, May 13, 1822.

20. T. Edward Bowdich, *Essay on the Superstitions, Customs, and Arts Common to the Ancient Egyptians, Abyssinians and Ashantees* (Paris: J. Smith, 1821), 390.

21. Bowdich Lee, *Friendship's Offering*, 295.

22. "American Board of Commissioners for Foreign Missions," *The Missionary Herald, Containing the Proceedings of the American Board of Commissioners for Foreign Missions* 39/6 (1843), 229–240, at 231.

23. Karl David Patterson, "The Mpongwe and the Orungu of the Gabon Coast, 1815–1875: The Transition to Colonial Rule" (PhD dissertation, Stanford University, 1971), 57.

24. Henry Hale Bucher, "The Mpongwe of the Gabon Estuary" (PhD dissertation, University of Wisconsin–Madison, 1977), 123.

25. Bowdich, *Mission from Cape Coast Castle*, 423. "Affaire de jeune nègre fils du prince du Gabon, pris sur le navire anglais la Junon," Archives nationales d'outre-mer, Sénégal et côtes d'Afrique, sous-série C⁶ (1588/1810), FR ANOM COL C⁶ 1-35 (1809), 24. Patterson, "The Mpongwe and the Orungu," 106.

26. Bucher, "The Mpongwe of the Gabon Estuary," 197–198.

27. Lee, "A Visit to Empoöngwa," 318.

28. Lee, *Stories of Strange Lands*, 320.

29. See Pierre Sallée's ethnographic film *Disoumba: Liturgie musicale des Mitsogho du Gabon central* (Le Centre national de la recherche scientifique, 1969), and Pierre Sallée, "L'arc et la harpe: contribution à l'histoire de la musique du Gabon" (PhD dissertation, Université de Paris X, 1985), 66, 77. These words, "l'idole est un monstreuse et indecent figure de bois, du sexe féminin," are a description of a statue made by Kele-speakers, in Paul Du Chaillu, *L'Afrique sauvage: nouvelles excursions au pays des Ashangos* (Paris, Michael Lévy, 1868), 258.

30. Bowdich, *Mission from Cape Coast Castle*, 450; Lee, *Stories of Strange Lands*, 321.

31. Steven Feld, "A Rainforest Acoustemology," in *The Auditory Culture Reader*, ed. Michael Bull and Les Back (New York: Berg, 2003), 223–239.

32. Julien Bonhomme, *Le Miroir et le Crâne: Le parcours rituel de la société initiatique Bwete Misoko (Gabon)* (Paris: CNRS Éditions—Éditions de la Maison des Sciences de l'Homme, 2005).

33. Kairn A. Klieman, "Of Ancestors and Earth Spirits: New Approaches for Interpreting Central African Politics, Religion, and Art," in *Eternal Ancestors: The Art of the Central African Reliquary*, ed. Alisa LaGamma (New York: Metropolitan Museum of Art, 2007), 33–61, at 49.

34. Roger Blench, "Are the Africa Pygmies an Ethnographic Fiction?" in *Challenging Elusiveness: Central African Hunter-Gatherers in a Multidisciplinary Perspective*, ed. Karen Biesbrouck, Stephen Elders, and Gerda Rossel (Leiden: CNWS, 1999), 41–60. For more fictions still, see Steven Feld, "The Poetics and Politics of Pygmy Pop," in *Western Music and Its Others: Difference, Representation, and Appropriation in Music*, ed. Georgina Born and David Hesmondhalgh (Berkeley: University of California Press, 2000), 254–279.

35. James L. Mackey, "Journal of a Tour in Western Africa (1853)," *Journal of Presbyterian History* 40/2 (June 1962), 113–118, at 116.

36. France Cloarec-Heiss, "Les harpes: ce que leur nom révèle," and Gaetano Speranza, "Les harpes," in *La parole du fleuve: harpes d'Afrique centrale*, ed. Philippe Bruguière and Gaetano Speranza (Nanterre: Cité de la musique/musée de la Musique, 1999), 35–47, at 40–41; 59–94, at 90; also 280, 360.

37. Paul B. Du Chaillu, *Explorations and Adventures in Equatorial Africa* (New York: Harper, 1861), 432. Pierre Sallée, "L'arc et la harpe," 75.

38. Ibid., 24.

39. Kairn A. Klieman, *"The Pygmies Were Our Compass": Bantu and Batwa in the History of West Central Africa, early times to c. 1900 C.E.* (Portsmouth, NH: Heinemann, 2003).

40. See, for example, James W. Fernandez and Renate L. Fernandez, "'Returning to the Path': The Use of Iboga(ane) in an Equatorial African Ritual Context and the Binding of Time, Space, and Social Relationships," *Alkaloids: Chemistry and Biology* 56 (2001), 235–247.

41. Klieman, "Of Ancestors and Earth Spirits," 51.

42. Du Chaillu printed what Sallée calls "a precisely-drawn image of a harp observed under the hands of the Kele" in "L'arc et la harpe," 66. Chaillu, *Explorations and Adventures*, 339.

43. Klieman, "Of Ancestors and Earth Spirits," 38.

44. Patterson argues, on the basis of available clan genealogies, that Naängo was settled only around 1700–1725. See Patterson, "The Mpongwe and the Orungu," 67.

45. Patterson claims that powerful Ndiwa traders originally settled amongst the "pygmy" first peoples around two hundred years earlier. One legend has it that they were "birthed from the earth" at the estuary; others report that, by 1698, the Ndiwa were decimated after a century of Dutch attacks. See Annie Merlet, *Le pays des trois estuaires, 1471–1900* (Libreville, Gabon: Centre Culturel Français, 1991), 14.

46. "Gaboon: Letter from Mr. Porter, October 1, 1851," *The Missionary Herald, Containing the Proceedings of the American Board of Commissioners for Foreign Missions* 48/3 (1852), 83.

47. Bowdich, *Mission from Cape Coast Castle*, 449.
48. Christopher J. Gray, *Territoriality, Ethnicity, and Colonial Rule in Southern Gabon 1850–1960* (Bloomington: Indiana University, 1995), 164.
49. Igor Kopytoff, "The Internal African Frontier: The Making of African Political Culture," in *The African Frontier: The Reproduction of Traditional African Societies*, ed. Igor Kopytoff (Bloomington: Indiana University Press, 1987), 1–86, at 53.
50. Sallée, "L'arc et la harpe," 218.
51. Ibid., 413.
52. Ibid., 218. See also Philippe Bruguière, "La harpe du Gabon, pirogue de vie," in *La parole du fleuve: harpes d'Afrique centrale*, ed. Philippe Bruguière and Gaetano Speranza (Nanterre: Cité de la musique/musée de la Musique, 1999), 151–155.
53. Klieman, "Of Ancestors and Earth Spirits," 52.
54. E. T. A. Hoffmann, "Beethovens Instrumentalmusik," *Zeitung für die elegante Welt* 13/ 246–7 (1813), 1964–1967, 1973–1975.
55. Lee, *Stories of Strange Lands*, 320.
56. Andrew S. Curran, "Rethinking Race History: The Role of the Albino in the French Enlightenment Life Sciences," *History and Theory* 48 (October 2009), 151–179, at 153.
57. Georges Léopold C. F. D. Cuvier, *The Animal Kingdom, with Additional Descriptions by E. Griffith and Others* (London: Whittaker, 1827), 157.
58. Bowdich, *Mission from Cape Coast Castle*, 450.
59. "Negroes, white" (*Negres blancs*), *The Encyclopedia of Diderot & d'Alembert Collaborative Translation Project*, trans. Pamela Cheek (Ann Arbor: Michigan Publishing, University of Michigan Library, 2003), http://hdl.handle.net/2027/spo. did2222.0000.027, accessed January 1, 2024.
60. See Curran, "Rethinking Race History," 154–155.
61. James Cowles Prichard, *Researches into the Physical History of Man* (London: John and Arthur Arch, 1813), 20.
62. Jules Braouezec, "Notes dur les peuplades riveraines du Gabon," *Bulletin de la Société de Géographie* (May/June 1861): 345–359, at 356.
63. Judy Knight, "Relocated to the Roadside: Preliminary Observations on the Forest Peoples of Gabon," *African Study Monographs* suppl. 28 (2003), 81–121.
64. Chris Ballard, "Strange Alliance: Pygmies in the Colonial Imaginary," *World Archaeology* 38/1 (2006), 133–151; Julien Bonhomme, Magali De Ruyter, and Guy-Max Moussavou, "Blurring the Lines: Ritual and Relationships between Babongo Pygmies and their Neighbours (Gabon)," *Anthropos* 107/2 (2012), 387–406.
65. For an intellectual history of the so-called pygmy paradigm, see Kairn A. Klieman, "Pygmy Paradigm," "*The Pygmies were our Compass*," 3–34.
66. Bowdich, *Mission from Cape Coast Castle*, 451.
67. Voltaire, *Des singularités de la nature* (London, 1768), 98–99, quoted in Curran, "Rethinking Race History," 172.

8

Listening to Korea

Audible Prayers, Boat Songs, and the Aural Possibilities of the US Missionary Archive

Hyun Kyong Hannah Chang

Choson, the Land of the Morning Calm: A Sketch of Korea (1885) offers a corpus of knowledge about Korea.[1] As was common in nineteenth-century European and North American surveys of the non-Western world, this monograph of 530 pages gave an account of a place little known in North America and Europe through the lenses of topography, climate, religion, customs, and history. Its author, Percival Lowell (1855–1916), was a polymath from a wealthy Massachusetts family and a Japanologist with a secondary interest in Korea, a country that was separated from Japan by a strait roughly 100 kilometers wide. For Lowell, who had a lifelong interest in the intersection of ancient religions, planetary science, and the occult, it was only natural to be drawn to the "Far East," long imagined in the West as a mysterious site of antiquity.[2]

Lowell's prolific work on Korea was the result of his three-month foray into the country from one of his trips in Japan in the 1880s. In Lowell's exposition of Korea, stillness figured as a repeated theme. He was most likely taking a cue from the name of the then-ruling dynasty of Korea "Chosŏn" (朝鮮), which can be translated as "the Beauty of the Morning." Generalizing this appellation associated with the Korean court, he articulated aural and visual descriptions of stillness, positing it both as an essential trait of Koreans and a metonym for Korea's condition of lying outside history. He wrote:

> The sun rose for them in the peaceful splendor that wraps the morning hours there even to this day, and the sunbeams fell into the valleys between the hills and nestled on the land. "Morning Calm" they called it; and it seemed not so much a name as its very essence. The drowsy quiet of the spot

Hyun Kyong Hannah Chang, *Listening to Korea* In: *Acoustics of Empire*. Edited by: Peter McMurray and Priyasha Mukhopadhyay, Oxford University Press. © Oxford University Press 2024.
DOI: 10.1093/oso/9780197553787.003.0009

lulled them to rest, and they fell asleep, passed away. They were in the world,
yet it was to them as if it had passed away. And so they slept on for ages.[3]

Lowell used the emblem of stillness to exclude the Korean people from the
trajectory of a supposedly progressing history. In his reading, stillness had
impeded Koreans from joining the march of time: "They were in the world,
yet it was to them as if it had passed away. And so they slept on for ages."[4]
Moreover, Lowell maintained that this stillness had become the "very essence" of Korea—or, as he put it in another moment in the book, "preeminently the characteristics of the race."[5]

The recourse to acoustic emblem evident in Lowell's work was not uncommon in North American accounts of Korea and the larger Pacific Asian
world in the nineteenth century. The emergence of such accounts registered
expanding North American interests—economic, political, religious, military, and cultural—in the circum-Pacific.[6] In the case of Korea, the majority
of the North Americans who arrived there from the late nineteenth century
to the early twentieth were Protestant missionaries. By the 1910s, several
hundred missionaries were stationed in Korea. As I have written elsewhere,
US Protestant missions in Korea unfolded in the particular context of locally
experienced imperialisms. Japan's military aggressions in Korea, starting in
the mid-nineteenth century, culminated in Japan's colonial annexation of
Korea in 1910. The sense of crisis that this had caused among Koreans aided
the North American Protestant mission, itself part and parcel of US expan-
sionism in the Pacific world.[7] Japan's annexation of Korea framed the Anglo-
American evangelists as possible allies to the Koreans; the oppression of
Koreans under the colonial regime made them highly receptive to Protestant
rituals.

Just like Percival Lowell, North American missionaries, too, were fond
of using sonic descriptors to explain Koreans to themselves and to the
Anglophone world. But what they thought was worthwhile to record was
different. Where Lowell noted silence, the missionaries in Korea recorded
an abundant acoustic life. In their writings, which I call the missionary archive in this chapter, we find traces of vocalizations of Koreans of various
backgrounds—shamans, peasants, laborers, scholars, and children—as well
as instrumental music played by street bands and court musicians. These
records form an acoustically-attuned archive consisting of published and
unpublished sources. Many of these descriptions were passing comments
in longer pieces about local life; some belonged to essays written exclusively

on the topic of Korean music. As portrayed in this archive, the streets of Korea were animated by bands whose instruments included a "shrill, fife-like, wailing instrument"[8]; common laborers such as farmers, horsemen, and boatmen sang in ways that "would be impossible to represent with our staff and notes"[9]; boys who gathered in village schools called *sŏdang* recited Confucian texts in "a little sing-song melody"[10]; mourners at funerals wailed, "not gentle or smothered sobs, but open-mouthed howlings."[11] The night was disrupted by noise as well, whether by women who beat clothes in coordination with wooden ironing sticks, by the shamans who "beat their tom-toms and drums and utter[ed] their peculiar calls,"[12] or by Christians who wept and loudly confessed their sins. In contrast to Lowell's thesis of acoustic fixity, the missionaries also wrote about changes in local sonic practices, some of which were instigated by the missionaries themselves.

The multiplicity of sonic descriptions in the writings of US Protestant missionaries in Korea signals that these expatriate North Americans had a degree of familiarity with Korea that the likes of Lowell simply did not have. Indeed, given the nature of the missionary profession, many of them had to learn Korean and interact with Koreans on a daily basis. Some female missionaries or wives of missionaries were even privy to the more private domains occupied by Korean women. However, notwithstanding their intimacy with local life, their knowledge of Korea was also mediated by the epistemologies of modern/Western empires, wherein listening played a major role in "the constitution of acoustic ontologies and knowledges"[13], and by a particular Anglo-American practice of imperialist evangelism. In particular, I draw attention to two different ways of listening to Korean vocalizations that emerged from the missionary archive. One of these involved applying Western-centric imperial dichotomies (such as civilized/heathen, rational/emotional, and correct/incorrect) to Korean vocalizations. This form of listening rested on the conceptualization of vocal practice as an object of conversion and linked authentic Christian faith to the supposed universality of North American culture. Another way of listening, which conceptualized vocal practice as an object of folkloristic analysis, projected romantic and essentialist ideas about Korean alterity onto Korean vocal practice. I argue that both forms of listening, despite their oppositional outlook, were powered by an ingrained practice of listening that assumed Korean vocalization as an audible site of interiority.

This chapter examines the interrelation of listening and knowledge in the archive pertaining to North American missionization in Korea from the nineteenth to the early twentieth century. It gives a glimpse into what the North American missionaries heard and listened to in Korea, while situating this listening itself in the ideologies of North American imperialism and evangelicalism. To this end, the first section examines the general shape, dynamics, and motivations of this missionary archive. The second and third sections look at a variety of missionary representations of Korean vocalization in the activities of praying and singing, and argue that these representations—what amounted to aurally mediated knowledge of Koreans—rested on assumptions of audible interiority. The construction of the objects of listening involved in this process shaped notions of what is valid Korean Christian vocal practice and what is not. The final section briefly considers the issue of agency regarding Korean voices depicted in the missionary archive.

The Dynamics of the US Protestant Missionary Archive

Writing had long been central to the work of Christian overseas missions, but it was an especially prized activity for Protestant missionaries from the United States in the late nineteenth century. The vast body of texts that resulted from their evangelization around the world belonged to different genres, from minutes of meetings, reports to the mission board, and novellas in English, to dictionaries, grammar books, and secular textbooks in other languages. The missionaries' commitment to writing ran parallel to increasing interest and capacities in publishing sectors in the United States. Their writings were published not only by Protestant organizations and presses but also, depending on the genre, by secular presses such as Fleming H. Revell Company, which was devoted to travel writings and other forms of imperial knowledge at the turn of the century. Moreover, missionization typically entailed setting up one or more printing shops in the "field." This allowed the North Americans to print materials in English for the expatriate community, which also included diplomats and traders, as well as religious and secular materials in local scripts.[14]

The missionary archive in Korea comprised three modes of writing, each with its own purpose. First, there were record-keeping documents, such as minutes of meetings and reports to the mission society headquarters. These were primary ways in which the missionary organizations managed themselves, in a manner that Max Weber called rationalization.[15]

Second, there were texts that contributed to the documentation of Korea and Koreans. Written by missionaries for Christian or secular publications, these texts supplied cultural characterizations of the Korean people through descriptions of rituals, kinship, and beliefs, or what Ann Laura Stoler terms the "production of social kinds."[16] Many of them appeared as descriptive essays in English-language journals published in Seoul such as *The Korean Repository* (1892–1898), *The Korea Review* (1901–1906), and *The Korea Mission Field* (1905–1941), while some appeared as ethnographic notes from the field in *The Missionary Review of the World* (1878–1939), meant for globe-trotting American missionaries. The documentation of local life also abounded in single-authored memoirs, surveys, and fiction written for a broader Anglo-American Protestant readership at home.[17] Third, the missionary archive includes Christian literature in Korean vernacular and mixed (classical Chinese and Korean vernacular) scripts for circulation within different groups of Koreans. This literature encompassed multiple projects of translating the Bible and the hymns, initiated at the denominational level as well as by individual missionaries.[18] Bible and hymnal translations were complemented by tracts and pamphlets, such as *T'yŏllo ryŏktyŏng* (1895), a translation of *The Pilgrim's Progress*.[19]

As a whole, the body of texts that constitute the missionary archive gives us a glimpse into the dynamics of North American knowledge-making in the age of imperialism and imperialist evangelization. This archive is a testament to the ways in which writing served as a technology of selfhood for missionaries. Writing (and publishing) was an affective mechanism through which many missionaries expressed and performed their understanding of themselves, not just as the "civilized" of the world but also as self-sacrificing individuals fighting to save the soul of the pagan world, whether the audience was fellow evangelists, lay readers at home, or the "natives." In other words, the act of writing was strongly connected to the moral economy of self-affirming humanitarianism that had characterized the nineteenth- and early-twentieth-century United States.[20] This strand of humanitarianism was powered not only by the Christian belief of salvation but also by the missionaries' consciousness of the growing secular power of the United States in the world. This consciousness underpinned their unrelenting conviction in the superiority of "American" values including capitalism and their advocacy of these values in foreign lands.

Within the US Protestant missionary archive, self-narration often sat within a structure of moral economy that was poised between the ethnographic impulse characteristic of imperial knowledge collection and the Protestant epistemology of conversion. In Korea, as elsewhere, this narrative structure was especially visible in expository work that took up the task of explaining Korea to readers in the Anglophone world. Authors of this genre described a range of world-making practices through which they experienced Korea in vivid acoustic and visual detail, from weddings and funeral rites to shamanic rituals and familial drama, only to fold the local teleologically into the Protestant trajectory of "darkness-to-light" transformation. Thus, even when these practices were introduced with striking exactness and portrayed almost with a sense of amazement, they were ultimately cast as local customs to overcome within the tale of "pagan" Koreans becoming "civilized" Christians with the help of self-sacrificing missionaries. For example, Annie L. Baird's *Daybreak in Korea: A Tale of Transformation in the Far East* (1909), a mishmash of fiction, ethnography, and morality tale, provided detailed, sensory descriptions of commoner women's experience in a Korean village, including those vilified by the missionaries, such as shamanic rituals.[21] This evident desire to explain the local for the Anglophone readers is ultimately arrested by the imperative of Christian conversion: the female protagonist "Bo Pai" becomes a Christian as the result of the work of a female missionary ("Mrs. Missionary"); this transformation entails the renunciation of those practices so carefully illustrated by the missionary author.

Beyond saviorism, which was common to both nineteenth-century imperialism and Protestant missions, evangelicalism also drove the penchant for self-expression that characterized the Protestant missionary archive. A powerful ideology within Anglophone Protestantism since the early nineteenth century, evangelicalism privileged signs of personal authenticity and encouraged individuals' public statements of interior religious convictions in spoken and written forms. As such, it championed the interpolation of the religious into the narratives and textures of secular life more than those Christian missions that traded exclusively in fixed liturgical texts. Crucially, the evangelical demand for an exteriorized account of oneself also explains in part why the missionaries were listening to Koreans: to listen to Koreans was to know the truth that lay in their interior realm.

In sum, the imperatives that structured the missionary writings—the ethnographic impulse to know the local, the urgency of conversion, and the evangelical emphasis on confessional practice—reinforced the assumption of audible interiority within this archive. The missionaries consistently treated listening as a technology for measuring the Koreans' moral character, innate attributes residing in the interior domains, and, in the case of converts, the authenticity of conversion. In this sense, listening was one important condition of making sense of Koreans.

Listening to Korean Prayers

The most classic instance of the connection of knowledge and listening involved the missionaries' attunement to Christian Koreans' loud, improvised prayers. These vocalizations became objects of missionary archiving beginning in 1903, appearing in journals such as *The Korea Mission* and *The Missionary Review of the World* as well as reports to the headquarters. At least several dozens of these published items were witness accounts of large congregations of Koreans praying loudly in hopes of forgiveness. Such prayers were parts of revival meetings organized by missionaries in conjunction with emerging Korean pastors, and these events were well-attended not least due to the widespread dispossessions caused by foreign military campaigns in Korea, including the Sino-Japanese War (1894–1895) and the Russo-Japanese War (1904–1905). One account of Koreans' prayers was penned by J. Robert Moose, a Methodist stationed in Seoul. In this piece from 1904, Moose reports that during a special "ten day meeting in Chat-Coal Church," an impassioned lecture and prayer by the missionary Robert Hardie led Koreans in attendance to make loud and spontaneous confessions:

> This was a most wonderful meeting in which conviction for sin was so deep that it led to many most disgraceful confessions and restitution of stolen goods. Many of our people were brought to know for the first time what sin and forgiveness really mean. . . . Too often it has been the case that our converts to Christianity in this country have had only a conversion of the head, while the heart remained ignorant of the cleansing power of the Holy Spirit.[22]

Moose's account presents two refrains in the missionary writing on prayers: spirituality measured by the intensity of speech and the connection of this heightened vocality to the act of repentance.

The archive tells us that what Moose called "the cleansing power of the Holy Spirit" was even stronger in Pyongyang and the surrounding areas in northern Korea, which had become the hub of the US Presbyterian mission in Korea by the late 1890s. Leading missionaries in this region, including William M. Baird, Graham Lee, James S. Gale, and William B. Hunt, marveled at the outpouring of spoken words that they had witnessed among congregations of Koreans in the 1900s. For example, in a lengthy description of what came to be known as the Pyongyang Revival of 1907, which evidently drew upwards of 1,500 Koreans, Graham Lee wrote, "Man after man would rise, confess his sins, break down and weep, and then throw himself to the floor and beat the floor with his fists in a perfect agony of conviction."[23] Just like Moose, Lee noted that many Koreans disclosed offenses involving the transgression of property ownership and economic transaction. For example, he highlighted an "Elder Chu," who "began in a broken voice and could hardly articulate, so moved was he." Chu "confessed to . . . misuse of funds" among other deeds.[24]

These representative accounts suggest that the missionaries understood Koreans' prayers to be a kind of audible portal into the converts' hearts— that is, a way of knowing what the converts really thought and believed. In this sense, the prayers were a site of discipline and power through which the missionaries sought to confirm whether the Koreans had internalized Christian notions preached at the pulpit. And the ample citations of stealing and the "restitution of stolen goods" in the missionaries' records of Korean confessions indicate that the benchmark of Protestant conscience for the North Americans was the honoring of private property.

Besides the confessed sins, missionaries thought it worthwhile to observe and record the intense emotionality that manifested in the participating Koreans' speech and bodily gestures, as the quotes suggest. In particular, those who arrived in Pyongyang and the surrounding northern provinces in the 1890s and 1900s recorded animated qualities that they witnessed in the meetings. These qualities, dismissed as "shamanic" by elite Korean Christian notables[25], had much to do with the social history of northern Korea.[26] For most of the Chosŏn dynasty period (1392–1897), this region had been characterized by vibrant commoner-centered modalities and rituals, including shamanic prayers and incantations and a weak conformity to neo-Confucian orthodoxy. The Christianity that emerged partly from this legacy—a loud, confessional, and spiritual Christianity—was embraced by the likes of Lee, Baird, and Gale as a very welcome change from the upper-class cultures in Seoul, the national capital. This also explains why these influential missionaries promoted Kil Sun Joo, a Daoist disciple-turned-Protestant and a blind pastor in Pyongyang, as a touchstone of Korean

Christianity in the 1900s. As portrayed in the missionaries' accounts, Kil's sermons, full of theatrical, improvised demonstrations, had the power to incite loud confessional prayers among the Korean congregants. In the words of Graham Lee, Kil made the congregation "cr[y] out with a desire to confess their sins" and "thr[o]w themselves to the floor in a perfect agony of weeping."[27]

It is not an exaggeration to say that the attraction to an audible confessional religiosity among a number of key missionaries mobilized the notion that northern Koreans were the real subjects of Korean Christianity, over and against Koreans in the capital, who had initially been the targets of proselytization. William Baird, for one, idealized Pyongyang's Christians as a "people enjoying an experimental knowledge of Christ" and suggested that their faith was more authentic than those in Seoul, many of whom were from elite backgrounds. As Baird put it in a personal letter, among this class of Koreans in Seoul who frequented churches and mission schools, "the demand [. . .] is largely for an English education." He refused to play into this notion of Christian education: "It is not my idea of a mission school that its chief work is to train up interpreters and office seekers."[28] For Baird and likeminded missionaries, the religiosity that marked commoner-centered churches in Pyongyang was deemed to express "a Korean viewpoint" and was called "vernacular."[29]

In sum, a number of leading missionaries in Korea idealized an alterity that resonated with their preconceived evangelical ideas of the individual voice, emotional confessions, and audible interiority. For them, fiery speech was evidence of spiritual authenticity that flowed from one's heart. The missionary listening evident here was not an inconsequential element of early Korean Christianity, but rather, as Korean church historians note, the very reason why a religious ethos associated with early-twentieth-century Pyongyang became idealized and eventually came to be considered the hallmark of Korean Protestantism.[30]

Listening to Koreans Singing

The missionary archive tells us that singing in Korean churches was a more contentious subject than praying. This is because the vast majority of North American missionaries who went to Korea (and elsewhere) held the belief that singing was an indispensable part of Protestant worship and had a fixed definition of what counted as proper Protestant vocal music. They held strong convictions about the universality and superiority of their worship music, particularly Anglo-American four-part hymns, and were eager to "entrain (auto-)listening and vocal behavior"[31] among the Koreans so that they could sing in the same way. This reflects a colonial desire which, as Kofi Agawu argues in the context of African musical life, led to the European missionaries' export of "tonal thinking."[32]

By the 1890s, there were at least three different Korean-language hymnals in circulation, each reflecting the work of different missionaries. The prefaces of these hymnbooks acknowledge the help of Korean assistants, but they were almost never credited by name. The three known hymnals were used in three emerging Protestant epicenters in Korea during this time: *Ch'anmiga* (1892) was used among Methodists in Seoul, *Ch'anyangga* (1894), among Presbyterians in Seoul, and *Ch'ansŏngsi* (1895), among Presbyterians in Pyongyang.[33] In all three versions, the lyrics of selected North American hymns were translated and metrically adjusted to form Korean verses. Two of the three editions were text-only publications, in which each Korean-script hymn was annotated with the information of the sourced North American hymn, such as its incipit (e.g., "Praise God from whom all blessings flow"), the name of the tune (e.g., "Old Hundred"), and the poetic meter (e.g., L.M. standing for long meter). Only *Ch'anyangga* included Western staff notation. These editions eventually combined and culminated in a single interdenominational hymnal with staff notation in 1908, *Ch'ansongga*. This authoritative version influenced all subsequent hymnals with minimal challenges or resistance, and as such it offered the archetype of tonal thinking for millions of Koreans who visited the church throughout the twentieth century, whether for faith, food, or friendship.

That translated North American hymns were indiscriminately issued in the first decades of missionization suggests that most missionaries arrived in Korea with little concern that what they called "music" might have been incompatible with pre-existing local modalities of listening and singing. The missionary archive, marked by observations of Koreans "making a noise"[34] when singing hymns, imparts patronizing judgments that evaluated the "natives" based on their ability to sing imported hymns. In the words of missionary J. D. Van Buskirk: "If you have been to a Korean church service and heard their enthusiastic but very futile attempts to sing our hymn-tunes, you may be ready to say there is no music in them."[35] For others, the inability of Koreans to sing the hymns was a horrific unpleasantry that they had to bear in their overseas work. For example, Paul L. Grove described the first time he listened to Koreans sing a North American hymn as follows: "My spirits drooped, and as I looked into the future, I shrank, for I saw there some of the agony that would come to me as a result of enforced listening to, and participation in just such heinous offences against the laws of harmony."[36]

However, the archive also tells us that the eagerness to reproduce North American music with Korean lyrics was at times curbed or contested. Several missionaries, especially those who had accumulated time and experience in the field, began to examine their taken-for-granted ideas about what should and could be sung by Protestant Koreans. Thus, we can see in the archive the coexistence of zealous calls for the continued "cultivation of the voice and ear"[37] of Christian Koreans with self-reflexive thought on why it was that some Koreans found it undesirable or difficult to sing and listen to Protestant hymns. For example, Grace Harmon McGary recognized that unison singing, the main form of congregational singing that the missionaries attempted to recreate amid Christian Koreans, did not exist in Korean cultural life. She wrote that the only comparable form was the mnemonic songs used in village schools, which boys sang to memorize Chinese characters for the study of Confucian classics.[38] Eli M. Mowry, the now-legendary architect of the choral music movement in Korea's first Christian college, noted how four-part singing, for which there was no direct counterpart in Korean music, could be displeasing to Korean ears: "One man once said after hearing our college quartet that only one of them could sing and that if the rest had kept still it would have been a pleasure to hear it. Another man at another time on hearing a chorus of about 30 voices said that it was a thing worth running away from."[39] It is in these accounts that we see some missionaries starting to pay attention to how Koreans listened to North American music.

Missionary relativism also turned up in commentaries on issues of scale and prosody. For example, more missionaries came to recognize that the pervasive presence of half steps in North American source materials was an impediment for many Koreans. For some missionaries, this incompatibility demanded a more rigorous musical disciplining of Koreans in a range of Christian meetings (e.g., services, Bible study meetings, revival meetings); for at least one missionary (Paul L. Grove), this was a problem that the worship leaders could work around by relying on a handful of melodies in the hymnal that had no or negligible half steps.[40] Alexander Pieter, a missionary with experience of text-setting in Korean, also raised the problem of iambic meter, the default prosody of North American hymns, placing the accent on the second syllable. Since "Korean words have the accent on the first syllable," the use of iambic settings in Korean-language hymnals meant that "the fundamental law of meter has been frequently transgressed" from the perspective of Korean speech.[41]

However, the missionaries' recognition of such incompatibilities was seldom fed back into the repertory. This was not only because Western tonal music was the official stance of the mission, but also because this admission simply came too late: all signs suggest that the hymns with the "imperfect" prosody and scale were already used widely among Korean congregations by 1910, regardless of the question of whether the Koreans were singing correctly or not. Instead, the awareness of particular attributes of Korean songs pivoted toward a romantic idea of audible Korean alterity in the minds of some missionaries. At odds with the image of North American evangelists condemning non-Western difference, this idea considered Korean vocal music to be a site of true Korean identity. In particular, improvised songs by commoners—the idealized subjects of Korean Protestantism, as we saw above—or work songs by laborers such as horsemen, farmers, and boatmen were objects of fascination. Consider, for example, J. D. Van Buskirk's description of himself listening to horsemen's songs:

> [...] the horseman, who had trudged all day by my side while I rode, struck up an air. It would be impossible to represent it with our staff and notes; it did not have the intervals my ear felt it ought to have, but there was a real tune with weird intervals and long trills and all the strains in a haunting minor key. He improvised his words to make comments on passing scenes or to carry on conversation with his companion horsemen, and they occasionally answered with the same tune. It was very simple melody and poorly sung but it gave utterance to a glad heart in a way that touched my Western "tenderspot." It is a tune we in Korea all hear and that none of us foreigners can imitate.[42]

Buskirk's account demonstrates a mix of judgment and admiration commonly found in exoticism. He felt that the horsemen's singing was incorrect (e.g., "weird intervals") and "poorly sung," but despite this lack of "correct" or "well-sung" qualities (or, because of this lack), he found the singing deeply moving.

Van Buskirk was not the first to listen like a folklorist. Homer B. Hulbert, a missionary-cum-diplomat and one of the most celebrated missionaries in Korean Church history, defended the way Koreans listened and sang by employing the nature/culture lens that had shaped European colonial encounters with the Other. In an article from 1896, which was one of the earliest treatises on Korean vocal music in the English language, Hulbert invoked "the more artificial western ear" to point to the apparently more natural way in which Koreans listened to their environment. He literally compared Koreans to nonhuman animals: "Why should they 'keep time?' There is no analog for it in nature. The thrush does not keep time; and the skylark, that joy of Korean waste places, cares naught for bars and dotted notes."[43] This move ascribed Korean essence to the Korean body and constructed an immanent link between this body and nature. Here we have one formulation of the modern/Western epistemology of alterity, which, through a claim to aurally mediated knowledge, positioned the other "nearer the passionate origins of speech/song."[44]

Such romantic ideas of audible Korean alterity were not uncommon in missionary writings, even though they almost never led to attempts to re-package Christianity in the domain of vocal music, given the institutional commitment to North American styles. But we can turn to "Boat Song / Pae ttŏ na kanda" (Figure 8.1) for an example of how Korean alterity was and could be represented in missionary-created Christian vocal music in the Korean language. "Boat Song" was one of several dozens of songs included in A Book of Songs / Ch'yanggajip (1915), a collection of secular and religious songs edited by Annie Baird (wife of William Baird) and Louise Becker, two American women who were teaching in Christian schools in Pyongyang in the early 1900s.[45] All of the songs in this book were in Korean language and carried two titles, one in English and another in Korean. The majority of the songs were borrowings of Euro-American melodies ("Lightly Row," "Battle Hymn of the Republic," etc.). Others, like "Boat Song," were new compositions by Paul L. Grove, who was known in the missionary community for his musical talent. Elsewhere, I have written about the complex conditions surrounding the publication of A Book of Songs[46]; here, I emphasize that it was a musical project associated with the coterie of northern Korea-based missionaries who were committed to "vernacular Christianity," rather than a secular, globalist one. Most likely, it circulated widely in Christian and para-Christian institutions such as churches, schools run by missionaries, and Sunday schools, given the respect that Annie Baird commanded as a pedagogue, author, and translator.[47]

Figure 8.1 "Boat song," *A Book of Songs* (1915), Independence Hall of Korea.

Figure 8.1a

"Boat Song" was an exercise in representing an idealized Korean oral tradition within a North American hymnal style (Figure 8.1).[48] Boat songs were a type of improvised song sung by boatmen while they transported people and goods in boats, a form of labor that was being replaced in the late nineteenth century with the introduction of modern water transportation by Japanese, American, and British businesses. In "Boat Song," we can see a medley of strategies of musical orientalism, including some widely used tropes. The song uses a pentatonic melody (with one B-flat in m. 6 falling outside the D minor pentatonic collection) and occasional parallel voice leading (e.g., m. 15), two techniques for suggesting equivalences between distinct cultures in the minds of musical orientalists. Other attributes appear to want to conjure up the speech-like quality of the Korean boat songs: the use of the unison melody in the first four measures; the flourishes in mm. 2 and 4; accents on the first syllable (i.e., trochaic pattern); and the inscription of non-lexical utterances "*ehi*" and "*ehiya*." "Boat Song" also features regional speech, thereby adding a touch of local color. It uses northern Korean orthography, self-consciously different from that which was used in the national capital, and at least one word—"*mabaram*" in the third verse, which means "south wind"—was drawn from the argot of northern fisherman.

We can even venture to posit a kind of cosmological elision in the making, with the lyrics and the accompanying illustration (Figure 8.1a) evoking sea-crossing, a metaphor for a spiritual journey in Korean Buddhist cosmology.

> Translation:
> The boat is leaving, *ehi* the boat is leaving
> From the port of ruin the boat is leaving
> *Ehiya* our savior is the boatman
> When the storms of life rise, there is no worry
> *Ehi* let's trust our lord

"Boat Song," for all its limits as a song in the hymnal mode, is a rare but marked moment in the archive that casts doubt on the missionary community's categorical treatment of Western music as the proper object of Christian transmission. It seems that by evoking a local practice, "Boat Song" and a few other neo-traditional musical efforts grappled with the possibility of re-tuning Protestant singing to musically audible "Korean-ness."[49] However, given the changing profiles of sonic and acoustic life in Korea from the late nineteenth century (as discussed below), this 1915 experimentation points toward some missionaries' nostalgia toward what is authentically Korean—that is, a modern folkloristic imagination that linked identity to an origin.

It is worthwhile to note that there is nothing in the Korean-language Christian archives that indicates that songs like "Boat Song" (*A Book of Songs*, 1915) were in fashion among the Koreans themselves. In other words, constructing "Korean" Christian music was a belated preoccupation of some missionaries. On this front, it is interesting to note an announcement in the Christian weekly *Guriseodo Hoebo* (Christian News) from 1913. In it, the missionary creators of *A Book of Songs* ask Korean readers to send in "Eastern" hymns, a request that was most likely made with the songbook project in mind. The missionaries required that Koreans send in verses that "use Eastern poetic form, not Western." They added: "the melody should be an Eastern one, not Western. You may compose the poetry so that it can be recited in a prosody used in Korea, or you may use a regional dialect."[50] The evident intention to divest Western influence suggests the artificiality of "Boat Song" as a "Korean" Christian song. It also suggests that by 1913 many Korean Christians were well versed in Western music and that they were living in a pluralistic world.

Can Christian Koreans Speak?

As I have shown so far, representations of Korean vocalization in the missionary archive were strongly mediated by the ideology of sameness and difference internal to North American imperialist evangelization. In this final section, I ask: how can we, as historians in the early twenty-first century, conceptualize the Korean voices captured in the archive in light of the missionaries' mediation? To borrow Spivak's phrasing: can Christian Koreans speak?

Given the power dynamics inherent in the building of the missionary archive, we might instead move to contemporaneous writings by Christian Koreans as an alternative site in which to search for the voices of Koreans. But this move, too, presents complications. From the late nineteenth century to the early twentieth, Korean-language Christian materials by either Korean or North American authors were curated and printed through missionary publishing houses. In addition to the missionaries' material, financial, and infrastructural sponsorship, this body of materials closely followed the contents and ethos of North American Protestantism. These signs of reproduction make it tempting for us to claim that it is impossible to find Korean voices even within documents penned by Christian Koreans themselves. However, I suggest that this claim holds true only if we theorize the "Korean voice" in the framework of oppositional qualities such as resistance, insubordination, or unique style, which in some sense only extend modernity's binaries. Rather, what we crucially know from the Christian Korean archive is that the interests of Christian Koreans were not always same as those of the missionaries. To illustrate this claim, here are two examples.

First, Korean-language Christian publications suggest that a number of Christian Koreans were interested in repurposing the missionaries' vocal-ritual practices as a tool to convert Koreans into modern national(ist) subjects in the wake of Japan's imperialization. Some early endeavors of this kind unfolded via *The Independent / Tongnip Sinmun* (1896–99). This bilingually-titled newspaper was printed by a Methodist missionary publisher in Seoul and directed by the dynastic official-turned-independence activist Sŏ Chep'il (Philip Jaisohn) alongside missionary advisers. *The Independent* published a number of nationalist verses with minimal reference to Christianity that were meant to be sung to particular hymn tunes in the translated hymnals. *The Independent* also published pieces about mass meetings in which such patriotic hymns were sung. These accounts are notable for highlighting the expediency of the hymnal genre. For example, in the following report, not only hymns but also the Christian ritual of public prayer are connected to a narrow nationalistic aim, rather than to Protestant piety:

> Yesterday at Mohwagwan, Christians in Seoul celebrated the birthday of the Emperor. About a thousand people gathered and sang patriotic hymns [. . .] They prayed for the advancement of learning, knowledge, and the law so that Korea can become like other countries [. . .] [They prayed] for love among the Koreans to deepen so much that if one Korean were to be humiliated or put in trouble by a foreigner, the people of the entire nation would rise to the support of the victimized as if it were they who were mistreated.[51]

This kind of secular interest among some Christian Koreans was so persistent that it disturbed and divided the missionary community during its first decades in Korea. Here, recall William Baird, who decided to move out of the capital because he could not stomach the likes of Sŏ Chep'il.

Second, the Korean Christian archive is marked by a general lack of interest in constructing a specifically *Korean* Christian vocal repertory, an interest that preoccupied at least a subset of the missionary community. On some level, this lack is a symptom of Korean Protestantism's uncritical assimilation of North American universalism and the corollary dismissal of indigenous practices. However, I suggest that we can also take the dearth of interest in a specifically *Korean* form of Christianity as an indication of the widespread transformations that swept many parts of the non-Western world in the second half of the nineteenth century. In Korea, this period was marked by a radical geopolitical unmooring. The Sino-Japanese War (1894–1895) and the Russo-Japanese War (1904–1905), fought on Korean territory over the question of Korea's sovereignty, left a cultural void by weakening the country's centuries-long connection to the Sinocentric order that had shaped pre-modern and early-modern East Asia. More broadly, the intrusion of Russian, Japanese, British, and American interests had left many parts of the country in a state of uncertainty. The entry of multiple foreign forces, which generated not only anti-colonial movements but also fluid forms of trans-national affiliation,[52] heralded a changing soundscape, rather than guaranteeing the continuity of autochthonous sonic traditions. When considering just how much was changing in Korea and Northeast Asia during this time, there is nothing particularly surprising about the embrace and accumulation of new songs among Korean Christian communities. These songs, the majority of which were in the style of North American songs, encompassed not only the missionary-edited hymns and songs discussed above but an increasing number of adaptations and compositions by Koreans after 1900.

Conclusion

North American missionaries' writings about and for Koreans say as much about the expatriates as they say about the land and the people they sought to know. In other words, their depictions of Korean vocalizations were not the objective narratives that they purported to be. From the missionary archive emerge two apparently opposite ways of listening which were mediated by nineteenth-century imperialist epistemologies. One aural orientation wanted to control, discipline, and re-tune the "native" voices, while another desired to hear Korean alterity. The idea of audible interiority was the linchpin that linked these outwardly oppositional forms of listening. The notion that the voice was an unmediated channel for what lies in people's innermost realm predisposed missionary ears to the sentiment that they could "hear" the essence, identity, and truth of people in distant lands.

It seems that the self-affirming nature of the missionary community did not hurt its chances in Korea. The history of modern Korea tells us that due to geopolitical circumstances, the religion planted by the North Americans became one of the most popular religions in the twentieth century and arguably the most popular one during the post-Korean War decades. Yet, with the exception of Nicholas Harkness's study of the intimate link between European-style classical singing and the aspirations of South Korean Protestant institutions, Anglophone studies of Korean musical cultures have offered very little on Protestantism in Korea.[53] The dearth of attention to what turned out to be a vibrant and multifaceted phenomenon speaks to the long-lasting legacy of the very essentialism that I have critiqued. By and large, the objects of Korean music scholarship were assumed to be those that sounded and looked different from the Western ones. While what counts as valid Korean music has been changing in the last ten years or so with the global rise of Korean popular music, notions of authentic Korean traditions had been a strong undercurrent in the study of Korean music in and outside Korea for the better part of the twentieth century.

When we turn attention to the archive of religious and secular documents by Christian Korean authors, we find a wide-ranging body of music and discourses about music that do not align with either the missionaries' double-edged insistence or the tradition-centered legacy of music studies. How do we write about these unmarked materials, which do not contain the kinds of affect and allegiance that would earn them a place in the pantheon of Korean traditions, but which would tell us more about the micropolitics of everyday life? Records of sonic transformation and multiplicity in this corpus highlight the inauthentic beginnings of the twentieth century in imperialist histories of the late nineteenth century. It is within these records that we might find a way to tell stories about the agency of the Korean people.

Notes

This work was supported by the Core University Program for Korean Studies of the Ministry of Education of the Republic of Korea and the Korean Studies Promotion Service at the Academy of Korean Studies (AKS-2023-OLU-2250003).
1. Percival Lowell, *Choson, the Land of the Morning Calm: A Sketch of Korea* (Boston: Ticknor and Company, 1885).
2. For more on Percival Lowell, see David Strauss, *Percival Lowell: The Culture and Science of a Boston Brahmin* (London and Cambridge, MA: Harvard University Press, 2001). Also, on Lowell and the politics of sonic emblems in the Korean context, see Katherine In-Young Lee, "Dynamic Korea: Amplifying Sonic Registers in a Nation Branding Campaign," *Journal of Korean Studies* 20/1 (2015), 113–147.
3. Lowell, *Choson*, 7.
4. Ibid.
5. Ibid., 10. The description of Korea as peaceful, asleep, and quiet reverberated with a lineage of early modern and modern Western thought that perceived the "Far East" as mystical and archaic. In turn, this lineage was shaped by associations of the "Far East" with Buddhism, Confucianism, and the imagined ideogrammatic (versus phonetic) time of the Sinosphere.
6. See, for example, David Brody, *Visualizing American Empire: Orientalism and Imperialism in the Philippines* (Chicago: University of Chicago Press, 2010); Mari Yoshihara, *Embracing the East: White Women and American Orientalism* (New York: Oxford University Press, 2003).
7. See Hyun Kyong Hannah Chang, "Singing and Praying Among Korean Christian Converts (1896–1915): A Trans-Pacific Genealogy of the Modern Korean Voice," in *The Oxford Handbook of Voice Studies*, ed. Nina Sun Eidsheim and Katherine Meizel (New York: Oxford University Press), 457–474. Also see Danielle Kane and Jung Mee Park, "The Puzzle of Korean Christianity: Geopolitical Networks and Religious Conversion in Early Twentieth-Century East Asia," *American Journal of Sociology* 115/2 (2009), 365–404.

8. James Gale, *Korea in Transition* (New York: Eaton & Mains, 1909), 71.

9. Ibid.

10. E. M. McGary, "Music in the School," *Korea Mission Field* 11/4 (1915), 103–104, at 104.

11. Gale, *Korea in Transition*, 71.

12. Horace Allen, "Some Korean Customs: The Mootang," *Korea Repository* 3/4 (1896), 163–165, at 163.

13. Ana María Ochoa Gautier, *Aurality: Listening and Knowledge in Nineteenth-Century Colombia* (Durham, NC: Duke University, 2014), 34.

14. See, for example, Sung-Deuk Oak, *The Making of Korean Christianity: Protestant Encounters with Korean Religions 1876–1915* (Waco, TX: Baylor University Press, 2013), 221–270; Hong-Yu Gong, "Hymnals and Hymnody in Late Qing and Early Republican China," *Journal of Music in China* 6/2 (2016), 213–238.

15. Max Weber, *The Protestant Ethic and the Spirit of Capitalism*, trans. Talcott Parsons (New York: Charles Scribner's Sons, 1958).

16. Ann Laura Stoler, *Along the Archival Grain: Epistemic Anxieties and Colonial Common Sense* (Princeton, NJ: Princeton University Press, 2009), 53.

17. See, for example, Lillias Horton Underwood, *Fifteen Years Among the Top Knots* (New York: American Tract Society, 1904); Gale, *Korea in Transition*.

18. See Oak, *The Making of Korean Christianity*, 221–222.

19. Ibid., 107–110.

20. On this topic, see Julie Ellison, *Cato's Tears and the Making of Anglo-American Emotions* (Chicago: University of Chicago Press, 1999); Thomas L. Haskell, "Capitalism and the Origins of the Humanitarian Sensibility, Part 1," *American Historical Review* 90/2 (1985), 339–361.

21. Annie L. Baird, *Daybreak in Korea: A Tale of Transformation in the Far East* (New York: Fleming H. Revell Company, 1909).

22. J. Robert Moose, "Report of the Seoul Circuit," *Minutes of Annual Meeting of the Korean Mission of the Methodist Episcopal Church, 1904* (Seoul: Methodist Publishing House), 39–42, at 41.

23. Graham Lee, "How the Spirit Came to Pyeng Yang," *Korea Mission Field* 3/3 (1907), 33–37, at 34.

24. Ibid., 35.

25. See Kenneth Wells, *New God, New Nation: Protestants and Self-Reconstruction Nationalism in Korea, 1896–1937* (Honolulu: University of Hawai'i Press), 38.

26. See Sun Joo Kim, ed., *The Northern Region of Korea: History, Identity, and Culture* (Seattle: University of Washington Press, 2010).

27. Lee, "How the Spirit Came to Pyeng Yang," 37. Kil became such an emblematic, beloved, and legendary figure among these missionaries and the larger missionary community in general that he was featured on the cover of the largest Anglophone mission journal, *The Missionary Review of the World*, in 1907.

28. William Baird, "Educational Report," 1899.

29. Ibid.

30. In-ch'ŏl Kang, *Han'guk ŭi kidokkyo wa pan'gong chuŭi* [Korean Protestantism and Anticommunism] (Seoul: Chungsim, 2007).

31. Nina Sun Eidsheim, "Race and the Aesthetics of Vocal Timbre," in *Rethinking Difference in Music Scholarship*, ed. Olivia Bloechl, Melanie Lowe, and Jeffrey Kallberg (Cambridge: Cambridge University Press, 2015), 338–365.

32. Kofi Agawu, "Tonality as a Colonizing Force," in *Audible Empire: Music, Global Politics, Critique*, ed. Ronald Radano and Tejumola Olaniyan (Durham and London: Duke University Press, 2016), 334–355.

33. For more details, see Hyun Kyong Hannah Chang, "A Fugitive Christian Public: Singing, Sentiment, and Socialization in Colonial Korea," *Journal of Korean Studies* 25/2 (2020), 291–323, at 294–295.

34. E. M. Mowry, "Korean Church Music," *Korea Mission Field* 11/4 (April 1915), 107–110, at 109.

35. J. D. Van Buskirk, "Old Korean Music," *Korea Mission Field* 11/4 (April 1915), 100–102, at 100.

36. Paul L. Grove, "Adequate Song-Books," *Korea Mission Field* 11/4 (April 1915), 110–113, at 110.

37. McGary, "Music in the School," 104.

38. Ibid., 102.

39. Mowry, "Korean Church Music," 109.

40. Grove, "Adequate Song-Books," 111; McGary, "Music in the School," 109.

41. Alexander A. Pieters, "Translation of Hymns into Korean," *The Korea Mission Field* 11/4 (April 1915), 113–116, at 115.

42. Van Buskirk, "Old Korean Music," 100.

43. Homer Hulbert, "Korean Vocal Music," *The Korean Repository* (February 1896), 45.

44. Gary Tomlinson, *The Singing of the New World: Indigenous Voice in the Era of European Contact* (Cambridge: Cambridge University Press, 2007), 14.

45. Annie Baird and Louise Becker, eds., *Ch'yanggajip, A Book of Songs for Social and Other Occasions* (Kyŏngsŏng: Chosŏn Yasogyo Sŏhoe; P'yongyang: Yasogyo Sŏwŏn, 1915).

46. See Chang, "A Fugitive Christian Public," 297–307.

47. That a second revised edition of this book was published in 1920 also suggests that *A Book of Songs* was received enthusiastically.

48. This song uses four-part harmony and the standard 16-measure verse-refrain structure of North American hymns. It makes a standard tonal move, starting in D minor, moving to its relative major (F major), and finally returning to D minor.

49. These included Kil Sun Joo's Protestant *P'yongbuk Susimga* (a type of Korean folksong) in 1912 and James Gale's *Yŏn'gyŏngjwadam* (Gospel as Sung) in 1923.

50. "Syang ŭl talgo mojipham" [A contest with award], *Yesugyo hoebo*, January 28, 1913, 1.

51. "Nonsyŏl" [Editorial], *Tongnip Sinmun*, September 3, 1896, 1.

52. See, for example, Yumi Moon, "From Periphery to a Transnational Frontier: Popular Movements in the Northwestern Provinces, 1896–1904," in *The Northern Region of Korea: History, Identity, and Culture*, ed. Sun Joo Kim (Seattle: University of Washington Press, 2010): 181–215.

53. Nicholas Harkness, *Songs of Seoul: An Ethnography of Voice and Voicing in Christian South Korea* (Berkeley: University of California Press, 2014).

9

Listening through the Operatic Voice in 1820s Rio de Janeiro

Benjamin Walton

I begin with a sonic absence: in April 1827, a music critic in Rio de Janeiro reminisced about the operatic performances at the city theater of the Spanish-born tenor, Pablo Rosquellas, a few years earlier. Rosquellas would plant himself in a heroic stance, the critic recalled, before throwing back his head and opening his mouth into a wide "O." Then, to quote directly: "He indicated by a parabolic movement of his hand, and in sublime silence, the shape the notes would have followed had he decided to make them heard."[1]

It may have seemed a good solution for a musician like Rosquellas, as a part-time singer trained first as a violinist, and also active as a composer, entrepreneur, and impresario, when faced with the intricate passagework of the Rossinian *bel canto* repertoire that had recently come to dominate the Rio stage. But given that Rosquellas had left Rio in 1824 to stage the first performance of a complete opera in the newly independent republic of Argentina—an occasion that would later see him anointed the "father of opera in Buenos Aires"—it's tempting to read more into the later recollection of his strategic voice loss in Rio.[2] Rosquellas, after all, played a key part in marketing Italian opera as luxury product to an audience well aware of its prestige among elite audiences in London and Paris. Imported opera, in these terms, could sit alongside other novelties shipped in from Europe—the jewelry, evening gowns, cognac, wallpaper, looking glasses, armchairs, dressing tables, and other fancy goods—that flooded South American markets at the time.[3] Opera as luxury item, meanwhile, merged smoothly with opera as beacon of civilizational progress, thereby availing itself of a discourse of social improvement through theater introduced to South America during the late eighteenth century under colonial rule, but quickly repurposed by the new republics of Argentina, Uruguay, Chile, and Peru, as well as by the empire of Brazil, following its declaration of independence from Portugal in 1822.

Benjamin Walton, *Listening through the Operatic Voice in 1820s Rio de Janeiro* In: *Acoustics of Empire.*
Edited by: Peter McMurray and Priyasha Mukhopadhyay, Oxford University Press. © Oxford University Press 2024.
DOI: 10.1093/oso/9780197553787.003.0010

In this context, the aural space that Rosquellas left open can speak eloquently to the central role of fantasy in shaping the experience of attending opera in Rio, through which the projection of an imagined ideal could substitute for the actual sound of a singer's voice, and thereby leave the operatic fantasy intact. After all, while there were numerous ways for expectations of early nineteenth-century transatlantic opera to be thwarted, from theaters thick with cigar smoke and scrappy orchestras to inappropriate costumes and shaky scenery, it was the operatic voice that most conclusively demonstrated the instability of opera as either luxury commodity or as civilizational instrument: celebrated for its superiority to other forms of vocal production, yet so liable to disappoint, and to collapse the desired difference between opera and other forms of vocal production.[4]

Recent scholarship on the explosion of Italian opera across post-colonial South America has tended not to dwell on such instability, with the result that there is a notable degree of critical consensus from the early nineteenth to the early twenty-first century about opera's potential to reinforce the lines drawn and redrawn between categories such as civilization and savagery, or music and noise. As Cristina Magaldi describes:

> Imperial Rio de Janeiro was captive in the international deluge of opera, a striking phenomenon that was a predecessor to twentieth-century globalization. As a major force in European colonialism, opera is said to have been more enduring than any military glory. For opera was experienced, transmitted, and perceived as emblematic of European culture, embodying the idea of civilization, urban life, modernity, and financial and cultural power.[5]

Opera, as a consequence, forms a key part of the larger history of art music in postcolonial South America. As Thomas Turino writes: "The use of European-styled music and performance contexts and the importation of European composers and artists were a means of maintaining the cultural prestige of the criollo elites and a means of marking distinction from other social groups *within* the state, that is, Indians, African Americans, mestizos, and mulattos."[6]

It is easy enough to find statements from the time to support such diagnoses, whether extolling the virtues of opera to improve local conduct and commerce, or in policing the boundaries, real and symbolic, between the interior of the theater and the outside world.[7] Take this description, for instance, which appeared in a Rio journal in October 1827, a few months after that reminiscence of Rosquellas:

> While Rossini's music enchants a brilliant group of spectators at the Théâtre Impérial, assembled in a decorated hall with all the ornaments of the richest architecture, some Indians, reunited in a forest on the same latitude, a few hundred leagues from the civilized capital of the empire, dismember the limbs of a lost traveller, to the discordant sound of a cow's horn that serves as a trumpet.[8]

The starkness of the divisions here might seem to invite little further comment; and still less so once pointed out that this commentary appeared, as does my opening description of Rosquellas's performance, within a local francophone journal, linguistically targeted at an audience of elite locals and foreign residents.[9] As Roberto Schwarz concluded in his influential commentary on imperial Brazil's imitative culture: "It is not copying in general but the *copying of one class* that constitutes the problem."[10]

Yet with the ideological contours of Italian opera's migration beyond Europe set so firmly in place in historical and theoretical terms, I am interested here in moving beyond a simple restatement of the general entanglement of the composite phenomenon called opera within the European colonial project. Instead, I want to consider what we might find by listening past the confident oratory of operatic civilizing *and* past its equally confident later critique, in pursuit of the local reverberations of opera—as idea, problem, genre, experience, repertory, site for vocal display and vocal disappointment—in a fractious political and social environment such as Rio in the 1820s. By mixing the sounds of opera, real and imaginary, into the city's contested acoustic geographies, I suggest we can understand more about opera's multivalent role within that environment, as well as about the environment itself. If such a move can also contribute to an ongoing recent impetus to explore the overlaps between opera studies and sound studies in new ways—through rendering the sturdy walls of the opera house more porous and the operatic voice less distinct from other vocal activities—so much the better.

There is something more at stake here, however, in trying to interpret operatic culture in Rio at that time. Put simply, I contend that the best way to complicate some of the stark binaries of the time is through attention to a wide range of discourses, from visitors and residents, that dealt both with sounds from within the opera house and without, even as many writers strove to hold them apart. More specifically, these discourses lead us to confront the place of operatic production in the context of slavery, in the city with the largest enslaved population in the Americas, and at a time when an anticipated ban (however partial in practice) led to a huge increase in numbers of enslaved men, women, and children docking in Rio at exactly the time of an explosion of operatic activity. As a result, contemporary writings on slavery intersect with writings on opera not only in their structural reliance on opposed categories such as noise and music or human and non-human, but also in their preoccupations with voice (imported trained European operatic voices still being a novelty at the time) and, most tellingly, with real or metaphorical acts of violence. This final subject, I will argue, so present in descriptions of the sounds of Rio, most especially in relation to the many forms of violence practiced on the enslaved, also seeps into discussions of theatrical activity and operatic criticism in a variety of forms. As striking, though, is the refusal to draw parallels between, say, the violence witnessed in the streets and the violence enacted (often for comic effect) on stage in some of the best loved works from the time, several of which also depicted slavery. To understand opera in Rio at this time, then, involves not just engaging with the new wave of operatic criticism that emerged in the mid-1820s, but reading this criticism with an ear both to its resonances with other contemporary writings, and also to its silences.

Rio in the years of Pedro I, from 1822 to 1831, where he was first regent and then from 1826 emperor, offers a particularly rich focus for such a study, for various reasons. The translocation of the Portuguese court to the city in 1808 by Pedro's father, João, in flight from Napoleon's invading army, brought with it an unprecedented gravitational shift of colonial power that included in 1813 the construction of a grand new theater modeled on Lisbon's São Carlos, and the import of singers from Italy soon afterward.[11] It also entailed a self-conscious theatricalization of court life in its new Brazilian setting that sought to blur the lines between spectacle and power.[12] The subsequent transition to independence in 1822, however psychologically momentous, in certain respects amounted to little more than a royal succession, along with a straight transfer of power from Portuguese elites to Brazilian. And the close connection between empire and opera continued, not least thanks to Pedro's strong musical enthusiasms, while the theater—rebuilt after a fire in 1824—remained spacious enough when it reopened in 1826 (as the Teatro São Pedro de Alcântara) to hold a large and sometimes raucous audience in the stalls,

along with the well-dressed, well-to-do and (supposedly) well-behaved patrons in the boxes. The continued importance of the theater throughout the
period, meanwhile, came not only from its function as a social and artistic
hub, but also through its role as the honored location for events of high political drama around independence, and as a key venue for ongoing national
festivals.[13]

During this period, theatrical performances also became a focus for attention in a newly liberated press that grew from a single newspaper under
Pedro's father João, to fifteen competing publications in Rio alone by 1828.[14]
And for the later researcher, it is the contents of these new journals that
most vividly underscore Rio's reputation at this time as an unusually noisy
city: by turns irascible, polemical, unrestrainedly libelous, and remarkably
intimate in their detailing of the minutiae of daily urban life. In their pages,
meanwhile, the rhetoric extolling the civilizational capacities of opera was
sometimes advanced, but just as often tested, ridiculed, or turned inside out.
Polemics were launched in favor of spoken theater over opera, or else arguing
for national performers over Italian, for serious opera over comic, or for one
singer over another, in a way that seems to mix the noise of the performances
themselves with the noise of the arguments waged around them. At the same
time, the supposed civilizing potential of opera is often invoked with frus-
tration or even despair, in an attempt to counter the reality of a more tumul-
tuous daily reality. A report in September 1827, for example, lamented the
indecent cries and "unbearable uproar" ("*uma algazara insoportavel*") from
the audience in the stalls, while another a few months later emphasized that
the theater should be a place to foster moral behavior and national edifica-
tion, but instead just filled the pockets of foreign singers.[15]

These kinds of debates, echoing at high volume across the pages of journals
of the time, could be employed at the time as evidence of civilization in themselves through their circulation as newsprint. A dialogue printed in the *Jornal
do Comercio* in October 1828, for instance, quoted one person proposing
newspapers as the "infallible thermometer of civilization" and of the relative
importance of nations. England defeated Napoleon, this writer suggested, because of the quality of its newspapers, while Brazil had gained independence
from Portugal thanks to the fact that only one solitary government journal
was published in Lisbon.[16] Three months later, another paper reprinted as
its cover story an article from a French journal comparing the populations of
the different continents to the number of their newspapers, drawing an explicit comparison between a noisy, multivocal press and a civilized society.[17]

Papers could also be read aloud to interested audiences at street corners, thereby giving voice to heated arguments in print in theatricalized form.

Travelers arriving in Rio at the time noted, on occasion, the activities of the press, both in terms of numbers of journals and the ferocity of their personal attacks.[18] Yet the noise of the Rio newspaper world, whether taken to indicate the cut and thrust of a nascent public sphere or the unseemly public settling of private scores, was for those newly arrived in the city easily drowned out by the immediate acoustic environment.[19] As in so many other places, impressions of this environment were obsessively taxonomized in the extraordinary quantity of travelogues written by the wide range of European and American visitors (sailors, soldiers, scientists, merchants, and so on) who stopped off in Rio, typically en route elsewhere, whether by sea or by land. These in turn added to the discursive volume of words written about the city, capitalizing on the growing thirst for travel literature.[20]

Before taxonomy, though, came undifferentiated clamor. The German botanists Johann Spix and Carl Friedrich von Martius, for instance, arrived in Rio around 1817 and described "a confused unheard-of discord, which is perfectly stunning to the stranger."[21] Similarly, the German mercenary Eduard Theodor Bösche described being subject on his arrival in Rio in 1825 to "a terrible noise and such a hellish concert that in the first few hours, as if numb in all senses, no sensible thought can come about."[22] But it never took long for travelers to start breaking this noise down to its constituent parts. When the blind British traveler James Holman in 1829 failed to hear a sermon at the English Chapel one Sunday morning, for instance, the offending noises came specifically from street vendors outside hawking their wares, and from the notorious grinding din of huge wooden ox carts, with ungreased axles, which to another writer, the Pennsylvanian Henry Brackenridge, sounded "like the gates on their hinges of Milton's Pandemonium."[23] Other frequently highlighted sounds included the cannon and artillery fired on the arrival of new boats into harbor, church bells tolling for national celebrations, and the fireworks let off day and night during the religious festivals that were frequent enough for Robert Walsh— the Irish chaplain whose sermon Holman had been straining to hear—to claim that during his time in Rio in 1828–1829 he "rarely went out into any street, or at any hour in the day or evening" without hearing "some report crackling over my head."[24] These sounds could be supplemented by military music, funeral processions, barber musicians, wedding bands, and so on.[25] And in some cases, this emphasis on Rio's noise came no doubt in part from the shock of arriving in a busy port after weeks at sea, as well as from the fact that for many writers the city often came near the beginning of a longer voyage, therefore concentrating particular attention on anything striking to the ear of a traveler in pursuit of the exotic.

But there was another reason for the emphasis on the noisiness of Rio: above all, the sounds of the city consisted of the sounds of slavery, in an urban context where the presence of a huge enslaved population, with more arriving by sea on a regular basis, served for many European and North American travelers as the single dominant characteristic of what was "far and away the busiest slave port in the world in the nineteenth century," at its very busiest time.[26] When the British explorer Charles Brand visited in 1827 en route to Peru, for example, and described a scene of "continued noise and uproar," it originated from the enslaved carrying heavy burdens through the streets, chanting as they went.[27] Plenty of other writers were as insistent as Brand on categorizing songs of the enslaved as part of the city's noisescape, whether by merging them with the sound of the chains that shackled enslaved people together,[28] or by means of contrast, such as the juxtaposition of a rec- itation that came "with the charm of music" from a local school, "amidst the din of less grateful sounds, and the monotonous and barbarous song with which the slaves cheer themselves."[29]

Walsh attempted another form of juxtaposition, sketching out four encounters with Afro-Brazilians over the course of his first hours in the city, as a demonstration of the degradation wrought by slavery. As a re- sult, he depicted the enslaved in the streets as "chattering the most inartic- ulate and dismal cadence as they moved along," while a regiment of black soldiers played "sweet and agreeable music of their leader's own composi- tion" to accompany the funeral of a colonel. Next, the mainly free black men and women selling food and other goods in the streets and from small shops quietly demonstrated for Walsh their decorum and respectability; and fi- nally, another funeral taking place in a church was led by solemnly chanting priests, one of whom was black.[30] Separate from such didactic parables, Walsh elsewhere demonstrated a fascination with the musical practices of Afro-Brazilians, providing a transcription of one chant that he heard "every day, and in almost every street in Rio," and classified by him as a "national song," though his attempts to find out the meaning of the words were met with silence.[31] He was also one of several writers to detail as closely as pos- sible different forms of Afro-Brazilian musical practices, instruments, and dances.[32]

Such a level of attention is unsurprising, in an urban context where the population of Afro-Brazilians, however unreliably classified at the time, outnumbered European descendants by two to one, with record imports of new slaves through the late 1820s in advance of a legislated ban that came into force in 1830; and where Afro-Brazilian musical gatherings tended by necessity to take place outdoors.[33] The European fascination with slave music, though, often involved some kind of tuning out of the extreme violence routinely practiced against the enslaved population in favor of something more picturesque. The London businessman Alexander Caldcleugh, for example, was one of several writers to insist that "without wishing it to be inferred that they lead an enviable life, nobody can affirm, on seeing them singing and dancing in the streets, that they are wretched and continually pining over their unhappy fate."[34] And a German soldier, Carl Schlichthorst, who served in the Brazilian army in the mid-1820s as part of a European regiment created to fight in the ongoing war with Argentina, tapped into longstanding racial stereotypes in casting the apparent happiness of the singing and dancing slaves against the supposedly melancholic, sensual, solemn, and suspicious character of the (white) Brazilians.[35] For these writers, then, the enslaved population became more audible the more "musical" their activities became, and that musicality was itself determined by the distance from visible markers of enslavement. By contrast, those suffering most from enslavement produced sounds deemed least human, such as the "miserable wretches chained together by the neck" described by Henry Brackenridge, who "made a kind of harsh noise not unlike that made by a flock of wild geese."[36]

Just as the operatic activities and audience behaviors reported by the Rio press invoked an imaginary spectrum of theater's civilizational potential, so the musical practices of the Afro-Brazilians could be positioned along an equally ideological spectrum of musicality, with noise at one extreme and virtuoso musical expressivity at the other. Sometimes, as with Walsh's parable, the gradations along the scale would be determined by proximity to enslavement, with those enslaved deemed most noisy, yet least able to produce music to be appreciated by European ears; for others, such as the English merchant John Luccock, who lived in Rio for a decade from the time that the Portuguese court arrived in 1808, it would be exactly reversed, shaped instead by a writer's degree of moral horror at the overwhelming presence of slavery in Rio, with those most sympathetic to the enslaved also the most receptive to the musical performances they encountered while walking through the streets of the city.[37] At certain points, meanwhile, these two scales of noisiness—the civilizational and the moral—became overlaid, thereby creating an unexpected meeting point between those deemed most civilized, namely the European merchants and elites, and those deemed by some writers as the most musical: the enslaved.

This intersection was made possible thanks to a guiding idea, expressed by numerous non-Brazilian commentators, of Rio lacking in the sort of elite sociability that defined a functioning public sphere. The perceived absence of sociability, on a European or North American model, exhibited by upper-class Brazilians, and by an absence of women in the public sphere more generally, appeared to stand in marked contrast with the society of republican Buenos Aires down the coast, capital of the new Argentinian republic (at that point named the United Provinces of the Río de la Plata). The botanist Charles Bunbury, for instance, declared that by comparison with Rio, Buenos Aires "is neater, cleaner, better built, better paved, and infinitely less noisy."[38]

In terms of social interactions, then, Rio became for visitors at once oppressively noisy *and* problematically silent, in a public context where, as Henry Brackenridge claimed in 1820, "there is yet, in fact, no public."[39] The Brazilian elites, in this context, became voiceless, lacking in the eloquence required of true civilization.[40] John Luccock went so far as to suggest that the songs of the slaves "gave a cheeriness to the streets which they would otherwise have wanted, for the whole population seemed tongue-tied";[41] while another writer proposed in the early 1830s that it was instead the rich foreign merchants who gave life to those same streets as they passed by in their carriages, again in contrast to the perceived silence of the upper-class Brazilians.[42]

At stake here are different registers of imported urban hubbub, whether from the enslaved, imported against their will from Africa, or from the merchants and musicians who chose to travel from Europe. And a sensitivity to the various ways in which noise became figured within the environment of urban Rio brings us back to the unstable role of operatic performance here. Put simply, opera was supposed to provide "good" noises: the noises that best embodied the values of European civilization. These noises could be separated from the noises of the city outside both by the walls of the theater, and by the process of being wrapped up and insulated within the smooth platitudes of operatic criticism, which served to witness and validate the spectacle that had taken place, before broadcasting the existence of opera in Brazil through the export of journals along international shipping routes.

Yet in practice this process was undermined at every point, whether through the shortcomings of performers or behavior of audiences at the opera, by the role of the theater as public space, by the varieties of discourse employed by feuding newspaper critics, or simply by the fact that there was no single, stable object called "opera," whose sonic imprint could be reliably reproduced wherever it traveled, much less reliably separated from all the other noises within the "porous city" of Rio.[43] At the same time, the beloved Rossinian repertory to which Pablo Rosquellas silently gestured with his expressive arm movement, itself carried within it a similar instability. On the one hand, it was undeniably the musical sounds that during the 1820s defined European upper-class operatic experience. Yet on the other, the Rossinian style had routinely been decried by its many critics around the operatic centers of Europe as itself nothing more than noise, overloaded with percussion and brass, and in its facile virtuosity paying no attention to the meaning of the words being sung.[44]

Of course, operatic failure at the time could easily become just one more way to restate some of the familiar assumptions of difference between Europe and the tropics. Take John Macdouall, a British Navy clerk who spent time in Rio on the way to and from Patagonia in 1826 and 1827, and who described the singers at the opera house as "generally the refuse of the Italian Opera on the continent."[45] Or take the opera-loving Parisian botanist Victor Jacquemont, stopping over in Rio in 1828 en route to India, who declared in 1828 that "a detestable Italian company, with a still more execrable orchestra, murder Rossini three times a week."[46] The only similarity with opera in Paris, he suggested, was the ostentatious boredom shown by the upper-class members of the audience.

For all their world-weary disdain, however, the violence of some of the vocabulary used by both writers here is striking: opera singers as refuse; and opera, embodied in the figure of Rossini, actually murdered onstage. Taken together with some of the more polemical language employed in local newspapers to describe operatic performance, such imagery suggests that one way for us to bring the sounds of opera into closer contact with the sounds of the city might be to focus more closely on such discursive violence, not least in the context of the extreme (and extremely public) levels of violence inflicted on the enslaved population, as reported by numerous travelers, in sight or in earshot, through the sounds of acts of punishment and the agonized responses that they caused.

A caveat seems important here: I am not in any way suggesting a literal comparison between the real and life-threatening violence practiced against those enslaved in Rio with the rhetorical extremes sometimes employed against opera singers in the city. Rather, I am proposing that one way to hear past or through the operatic experience as cordoned off from life beyond the theater is to attend to the discursive traces of violence in the accounts of theatrical life in Rio at the time; and equally to attend to their absences, through the attempt to insulate opera within the theater walls.

Look back, for example, to that bald juxtaposition quoted near the beginning of this chapter between the rarefied evening at the Teatro São Pedro and the imagined dismemberment of a traveler by members of an indigenous tribe, to the sound of a cow horn a few hundred leagues away. Juxtapose this, in turn, with a description a few months later, of one visiting Italian opera singer to Rio having a voice so unpleasant that it seemed to have "nothing human in it," and to evoke images of a witches' sabbath.[47] Next, set this alongside the account of a traveler from 1833, who reached for the same image of a witches' sabbath on witnessing a group of slaves in Rio singing and dancing by firelight.[48] Or read the response from a supporter of the singer with the allegedly inhuman voice, lashing out at the reigning castrato in Rio, declaring him an "anthropomorphic animal."[49] The original critic answered back, declaring that had the singer made her debut, as she had wished, in Rossini's *Semiramide*, pregnant women present would have risked miscarriage, since the experience of hearing her voice would have been worse than hearing Astolfo's horn: a reference to the magic horn in Ariosto's *Orlando Furioso*, which caused all who heard it to flee in terror.[50]

Such examples could be multiplied, and with each one the distance between the gilded opera house and those native tribes dismembering the lost traveler to the sound of their own terrifying horn shrinks, and the more moderate critical rhetoric needed to ensure their separation grows less secure. Eventually it becomes unclear whether the figures of those distant, jungle-dwelling Indians serve as a cipher for the external world that constantly threatens the theater as hermetic space, or instead as a cipher for operatic performance itself, with the dismembered traveler as the (European?) fantasy of Italian opera, embodied in Jacquemont's synecdochic appeal to the figure of "Rossini," cut to pieces and murdered.

Similar conclusions emerge from a consideration of the context in which accounts of the opera in Rio appear. Jacquemont, for instance, notes not just the murder of Rossini in the theater, but also the way that the square outside the theater during the performance had the air of a military camp, consisting of not less than three hundred to four hundred carriages and a thousand or so mules or horses, along with several hundred domestic slaves.[51] And he also provides a disturbing vignette of an episode on the smartest shopping street of the city, the rua Ouvidor, lined with shops selling imported luxury goods from Paris, which is recounted like a scene from a grotesque comic opera, despite the seriousness of the events described:

> There is a road inhabited almost exclusively by the French, who sell items of clothing and fashion. [. . . Middle and upper class Brazilians] press together on the thresholds of these establishments for the pleasure of seeing these Parisian faces. Some drunken Blacks, who march in the middle of the road, sing their monotonous African psalmody. The Whites that they offend beat them; from there, scenes of violence, cries, murders sometimes; the guard that arrives, commanded by a stupid Black man, perhaps drunk himself, who deliberates over whether to arrest or not to arrest; in the midst of this tumult, a light carriage, hitched to two horses driven by a coachman, and often preceded by a man on horseback who carries a torch in his hand, arrives at a trot in these overcrowded roads, while from the other side some cavalry men arrive, returning to their barracks, and whose horses almost fall at each moment on an irregular and slippery road surface.[52]

For Jacquemont, who would later interpret various aspects of his travels onwards from Rio to India through an explicitly operatic lens,[53] the stores stuffed full of fancy goods seem here to serve as a stand-in for the gilded opera house, while the Brazilian window-shoppers are like those in the opera boxes, paying more attention to the displays around them than to the miserable drama unfolding on stage. Macdouall effects a similar move in his own account, slipping across a page or two from a description of his night at the opera, where he notes with surprise the presence of "some very gloomy and ochre countenances in the interior," to a visit he made to the Rio slave market, only to find the slaves "are seated like the audiences in the pit of a theatre . . . chatting to each other with such a peculiarity of wild gesture and tone."[54]

At points such as these, the boundaries so painstakingly policed at the time—and so carefully curated ever since—between opera and non-opera, music and noise, singing on stage and singing in the streets, begin to crumble:[55] not in the way intended by Jacquemont and Macdouall, however, as proof that no real civilization on the model of Paris or London could exist in Rio in the first place; but instead toward a continuum of sonic activities inside and outside the theater that could be productively applied in thinking about opera anywhere it was performed during this period.

The idea of such a continuum was itself present at the time (and has remained so ever since), but in a relatively benign form, following an imagined progression from inside the theater outward. In this version, in Rio and elsewhere, Italian opera in the 1820s spreads from operatic stage to upper-class drawing-room piano, to church, to balls, and then out into the streets, played by military bands or even obtaining a sort of folk-like status. In the case of Brazil, the Italian style is then preserved as a marker of nation in the form of the national anthem, written in 1831 by Francisco Manuel da Silva, as an impeccable homage to the Rossinian sound world. This story can be traced through the wealth of advertisements in the local press detailing operatic arrangements for sale, alongside lists of imported musical instruments, and invitations to sign up for music lessons taught according to Parisian methods. It is another part of the civilizational tale, in other words, and appears to offer ways to engage with the operatic fantasy (or commodity) unmediated by erratic opera singers. And to be sure, it is a fascinating story in its own right, and a significant part of the larger narrative of the history of European art music in Brazil in the nineteenth century, which gains its strength by looking beyond the standard venues of elite performance. Yet it is also a story that risks veering toward the picturesque, reviving a much older fantasy of operatic osmosis whereby the innate charms of Italian opera allow Rossini's music to spread through city streets and the whole world beyond through some mystical power, far removed from the throats of actual singers.[56]

As an alternative, I want to propose something less easy to idealize, by looking from the outside in. In musical terms, this would involve a clearer acknowledgment of opera's pairing with dance on the Rio stage (as in Paris), frequently including dances associated with Afro-Brazilians repurposed by French ballerinas into their performances.[57] It would also require setting white elite attendance at the opera alongside white elite attendance at the singing and dancing of the enslaved population that would take place on Sundays in the outskirts of Rio.[58] Further, it would entail foregrounding the fact that performances at the opera house inevitably replicated some of the tensions outside, still traceable in the reports of abusive shouting from the theater pit whenever Afro-Brazilian stagehands entered to move the scenery during a production. One visitor wrote to a local paper that he found it hard to believe "in a court as civilized as this," that "it is a custom adopted by people of education to whistle and shout in the most discordant way" whenever the scenery was changed.[59]

And what of the Rossinian repertoire itself? After all, the piece Jacquemont described as enacting the murder of Rossini was none other than *L'italiana in Algeri*, one of the composer's most popular comic operas, with a plot concerning Italians traveling to an "uncivilized" land, defined largely by its reliance on enslavement, and with a sovereign who rules through violence. It was the most popular opera of the period in Rio, and sparked the city's first diva war, as journalists sparred over the virtues of the incumbent prima donna, Teresa Fasciotti, and an incomer, Elisa Barbieri, with one accusing Fasciotti of "a true musical assassination."[60] But most strove for a calmer tone, and the review of Barbieri's debut in the title role of Isabella in the *Écho de l'Amérique du Sud* took care to celebrate Barbieri's performance in uncontroversial and "European" terms, describing the brilliance and flexibility of her voice, the style of her acting, and her perfect combination of Italian vocal talent and French gestural skills. The reviewer also praised the theatrical management for their good work in employing her, and for such an excellent production, with fine and appropriate costumes.

Since the opera was already familiar, meanwhile, no plot summary was deemed necessary. And perhaps no one present reflected on any possible resonances between the comic threats of violence to the enslaved characters voiced on stage ("have him impaled at once"), and the real threats of violence carried out each day in the streets outside. Certainly there seems to be no link made in any of the surviving reviews, nor in the accounts of any of the travelers like Jacquemont who witnessed the opera on stage. Perhaps to make any such link would have seemed risible. Yet faced with such an absence of interpretation, we might return once again to Rosquellas's eloquent silence and see it as symbolic of the challenges to this day of holding fast to an imaginary operatic ideal. At the same time, it offers an invitation to catch the alternative silences that lurk behind the easy understandings both of the time and since, about how and what opera signified, and an invitation to attend to some of the sounds that the potent fantasy of opera would always seek to drown out, but that actual performance could so easily amplify.

Notes

1. "Théâtre impérial," *L'Indépendant*, April 28, 1827.
2. Vicente Gesualdo, *Historia de la música en la Argentina*, vol. 2, *La independencia y la época de Rivadavia, 1810–1829* (Buenos Aires: Libros de Hispanoamérica, 1978), 164.
3. See Benjamin Orlove, *Allure of the Foreign: Imported Goods in Postcolonial Latin America* (Ann Arbor: University of Michigan Press, 1997), and Arnold J. Bauer, *Goods, Power, History: Latin America's Material Culture* (Cambridge, UK: Cambridge University Press, 2001).
4. See Benjamin Walton, "Italian Operatic Fantasies in Latin America," *Journal of Modern Italian Studies* 17/4 (2012), 460–471.
5. Cristina Magaldi, *Music in Imperial Rio de Janeiro: European Culture in a Tropical Milieu* (Lanham, MD: Scarecrow Press, 2004), 36.
6. Thomas Turino, "Nationalism and Latin American Music: Selected Case Studies and Theoretical Considerations," *Latin American Music Review* 24/2 (2003), 169–209, at 179. Emphasis in original.
7. See, for instance, *Jornal do Commercio*, "Miscellanea. Theatro," October 1, 1828, which argues for the importance of theater for Brazilian business interests, and calls for the establishment of a Brazilian national theater; or the letter from "A Subscriber" in the same paper on January 28, 1829, referring to theater's beneficial influence on "customs, civilization and . . . commercial interests" (*"os costumes, a civilisação, e os . . . interesses commerciaes"*).
8. *L'Écho de l'Amérique du sud*, October 3, 1827: "Tandis que la musique de Rossini enchante au Théâtre Impérial une brillante société de spectateurs rassemblés dans une salle décorée avec tous les ornements de la plus riche architecture, des Indiens, réunis dans une forêt placée sous la même latitude, à quelques vingtaines de lieues de la capitale civilisée de l'empire, dépècent les membres du voyageur égaré, au son discordant d'une corne de bœuf qui leur sert de trompette."
9. On the place of French journals in Rio at this time see Isabel Lustosa, "Henri Plasson et la première presse française au Brésil (1827–1831)," *Médias19*, <www.medias19.org/index.php?id=23758>, accessed January 1, 2023.
10. Roberto Schwarz, "Brazilian Culture: Nationalism by Elimination," *Misplaced Ideas: Essays on Brazilian Culture* (London: Verso, 1992), 1–18, at 11. Emphasis in original.
11. See Rogério Budasz, *Opera in the Tropics: Music and Theater in Early Modern Brazil* (New York: Oxford University Press, 2019).
12. On the theatricalization of Rio life with the arrival of the court see (for the reign of João VI) Jurandir Malerba, *A Corte no exílio: Civilização e poder no Brasil às vésperas da Independência (1808 a 1821)* (São Paulo: Companhia das Letras, 2000). For the reign of Pedro I from 1823, and Pedro II from 1831 Hendrik Kraay, *Days of National Festivity* (Stanford, CA: Stanford University Press, 2013).
13. See, for instance, Maria Graham, *Journal of a Voyage to Brazil, and Residence There, During Part of the Years 1821, 1822, 1823* (London: Longman etc., 1824), 65, on the operatic performances that formed part of the declaration of independence in 1822;

or on the operatic celebrations for the return of Pedro from Bahia in April 1826 see Kraay, *Days of National Festivity*, 42–44.

14. Robert Walsh, *Notices of Brazil in 1828 and 1829*, 2 vols. (London: Frederick Westley and A. H. Davis, 1830), 1:426. See also William M. Wisser, "Rhetoric and Riot in Rio de Janeiro, 1827–1831" (PhD dissertation, University of North Carolina at Chapel Hill, 2006); and on the effect of this explosion of journalism on theatrical and operatic criticism, see Luís Antônio Giron, *Minoridade crítica: A ópera e o teatro nos folhetins da corte* (São Paulo: Ediouro, 2004), 72–102.

15. *Gazeta do Brasil*, September 12, 1827; *Aurora fluminense*, December 21, 1827.

16. *Jornal do Comercio*, October 21, 1828; the dialogue is reported as one overheard in a pharmacy, and framed through a comparison between the state of journalism in Rio and Buenos Aires.

17. *Aurora fluminense*, January 2, 1829. The article was reprinted from the *Journal d'éducation et d'instruction*, and compared a total of 2,142 journals published in Europe with the twenty-seven it said were published in Asia, most founded by Europeans.

18. See Walsh, *Notices of Brazil*, 1:426–35.

19. For a recent account of nineteenth-century Rio as soundscape as heard by German travelers, see Hans-Jakob Zimmer, *Wie klingt es im "Paradies"? Deutschsprachige Reiseberichte als Quellen zur Musikgeschichte Brasiliens im 19. Jahrhundert* (Bielefeld: Transcript-Verlag, 2019), 129–222.

20. See Paulo Berger, *Bibliografia do Rio de Janeiro de viajantes e autores estrangeiros, 1531–1900*, 2nd ed. (Rio: SEEC, 1980).

21. Johann Baptist von Spix and Karl Friedrich Philipp von Martius, *Travels in Brazil, in the Years 1817–1820*, 2 vols. (London: Longman etc., 1824), 1:142.

22. Eduard Theodor Bösche, *Wechselbilder oder Reisen und Abentheuer in Brasilien.* (Hamburg: Hoffmann und Campe, 1836), 236.

23. James Holman, *A Voyage Round the World*, 4 vols. (London: Smith, Elder and Co., 1834), 2:64; H. M. Brackenridge, *Voyage to Buenos Ayres, in the Years 1817 and 1818* (London: Richard Phillips and Co., 1820), 63.

24. Walsh, *Notices of Brazil*, 1:377.

25. On barber musicians, see in particular José Ramos Tinhorão, *História social da música popular brasileira* (Lisbon: Editorial Caminho, 1990), 155–175, and Peter Fryer, *Rhythms of Resistance: African Musical Heritage in Brazil* (London: Pluto, 2000), 140–141.

26. Zephyr L. Frank, *Dutra's World: Wealth and Family in Nineteenth-Century Rio de Janeiro* (Albuquerque: University of New Mexico Press, 2004), 23.

27. Charles Brand, *Journal of a Voyage to Peru* (London: Henry Colburn, 1828), 13.

28. Captain Henry Webster, *Narrative of a Voyage to the Southern Atlantic Ocean*, 2 vols. (London: Richard Bentley, 1834); 1:42: "The streets resound with the echo of their uncouth song and the rattling of their chains."

29. Charles Samuel Stewart, *A Visit to the South Seas*, 2 vols. (London: Henry Colburn and Richard Bentley, 1832), 1:68. On the tendency of visitors to South America in this period to categorize foreign sounds as (non-human) noise, see in particular Ana

María Ochoa Gautier, "Of Howls And Pitches," *Aurality: Listening and Knowledge in Nineteenth-Century Colombia* (Durham, NC: Duke University Press, 2014), 31–76.

30. Walsh, *Notices*, 1:135–40.

31. Walsh, *Notices*, 2:185.

32. See also Clarke Abel, *Narrative of a Journey in the Interior of China, and of a Voyage to and from that Country, in the Years 1816 and 1817* (London: Longman etc., 1818), 13–14; Carl Schlichthorst, *Rio de Janeiro wie es ist* (Hanover: Hahn'schen Hofbuchhandlung, 1829), 183ff. Other relevant accounts are quoted and summarized in Mary Karasch, *Slave Life in Rio de Janeiro, 1808–1850* (Princeton, NJ: Princeton University Press, 1987), 232–249; Carlos Eugênio Líbano Soares, *A capoeira escrava e outras tradições rebeldes no Rio de Janeiro, 1808–1850*, 2nd ed. (Campinas: Editora UNICAMP, 2002); and Eneida Maria Mercandante Sela, *Modos de ser, modos de ver: viajantes europeus e escravos africanos no Rio de Janeiro (1808–1850)* (Campinas: Editora UNICAMP, 2008).

33. In 1821 there was an estimated population of over 86,000 in Rio, including 40,000 slaves (Karasch, *Slave Life in Rio de Janeiro*, 62); Walsh (*Notices*, 1:463–465) estimated a population of 50,000 enslaved from a total population of 150,000 in 1828. The Anglo-Brazilian anti-slave treaty came into effect in March 1830, though the traffic in slaves continued until 1850. In anticipation of the treaty, numbers of ships carrying enslaved people were unusually high during the final years of the 1820s, rising from 31,327 between June 1826 and May 1827 to 57,097 between June 1829 and May 1830; see Herbert S. Klein, *The Middle Passage* (Princeton, NJ: Princeton University Press, 1978), 76.

34. Alexander Caldcleugh, *Travels in South America*, 2 vols. (London: John Murray, 1825), 1:83.

35. Schlichthorst, *Rio de Janeiro wie es ist*, 185.

36. Brackenridge, *Voyage to Buenos Ayres*, 120.

37. John Luccock, *Notes on Rio de Janeiro* (London: S. Leigh, 1820), 108.

38. Frances Horner Bunbury and Katharine Horner Lyell, ed., *Memorials of C.J.F. Bunbury*, Vol. 1, *Early Life* (1891; reprinted Cambridge, UK: Cambridge University Press, 2011), 104.

39. Brackenridge, *Voyage to Buenos Ayres*, 119.

40. On the importance of eloquence to theories of civilization within the nineteenth-century South American context, see Ochoa Gautier, *Aurality*, 18.

41. Luccock, *Notes on Rio de Janeiro*, 109.

42. Furcy de Brémoy, *Le Voyageur poète, ou Souvenirs d'un français dans un coin des deux mondes* (Paris: Furcy; Pillet aîné, 1833), 139–140.

43. See Bruno Carvalho, *Porous City: A Cultural History of Rio de Janeiro* (Liverpool, UK: Liverpool University Press, 2013).

44. On Rossini as producer of excessive noise see Benjamin Walton, *Rossini in Restoration Paris: The Sound of Modern Life* (Cambridge, UK: Cambridge University Press, 2007), and Emanuele Senici, *Music in the Present Tense: Rossini's Italian Operas in Their Time* (Chicago: University of Chicago Press, 2019), 117–123.

45. John Macdouall, *Narrative of a Voyage to Patagonia and Tierra del Fuego* (London: Renshaw and Rush, 1833), 22.

46. Victor Jacquemont, *Letters from India*, 2 vols. (London: Edward Churton, 1834), 1:40.

47. *L'Indépendant,* April 28, 1827.

48. *Memorials of C. J. F. Bunbury*, Vol. 1, 91, entry of August 30, 1833: "It was by far the strangest scene I ever witnessed; there was a good number of blacks, men and women, dancing by firelight in a kind of outhouse, and what with the irregular red gleams of the fire on their uncouth figures, the darkness of the rest of the buildings, the extraordinary contortions of the performers, the strange wild monotonous chant and violent clapping of hands, it gave me more the idea of a witch's sabbath than anything I ever saw." Alongside the evident racialized tropes employed by Bunbury here, it also seems worth highlighting the proximity—familiar from other travelers' texts (and from operatic criticism of Rossini)—of ostensibly incompatible musical descriptors of a chant both "wild" and "monotonous."

49. *L'Indépendant*, May 3, 1827.

50. Ibid.

51. Victor Jacquemont, *Voyage dans l'Inde pendant les années 1828 à 1832*, 4 vols. (Paris: Firmin Didot frères, 1841–1844), 1:57–58.

52. Jacquemont, *Voyage dans l'Inde*, 1:39. "Il y a une rue habitée presque exclusivement par des Français, qui y vendent des objets de mode et d'habillement. [... Les Brésiliens de condition moyenne et relevée] se presse sur les trottoirs de ces maisons pour le plaisir de voir ces figures parisiennes. Des Nègres ivres, qui marchent au milieu de la rue, chantent leur monotone psalmodie africaine. Les Blancs qu'ils froissent, les battent; de là des scènes de violence, des cris, des meurtres quelquefois; la garde qui arrive, commandée par un Noir stupide, ivre peut-être lui-même, et qui délibère si elle arrêtera ou n'arrêtera pas; au travers de ce tumulte, une voiture légère, attelée de deux chevaux menés par un postillon, et précédée souvent d'un homme à cheval qui porte une torche à la main, arrive au trot dans ces rues encombrées où débouchent par l'autre côté quelques cavaliers qui retournent à leur caserne, et dont les chevaux manquent de s'abattre à chaque instant sur un pavé inégal et glissant."

53. See, for example, his depiction of his meeting with the Great Mogul of Delhi in terms of the absurd "Kaimakan" scene in Act 2 of Rossini's *L'italiana in Algeri*, described in Benjamin Walton, "*L'italiana* in Calcutta," in *Operatic Geographies: The Place of Opera and the Opera House*, ed. Suzanne Aspden (Chicago: University of Chicago Press, 2018), 130–131.

54. Macdouall, *Narrative of a Voyage*, 21, 26.

55. On the employment of these categories, see Ochoa Gautier, *Aurality*, 42–8.

56. See, for example, Giuseppe Carpani's "Intorno alla musica di Gioachino Rossini," *Biblioteca italiana* (June 1822), 287–318; 302–303: "[Rossini's music] readily makes the circuit of the earth, touches on every shore, and enters every port . . . in simple and naked beauty, like another Venus, it glides along the surface of the ocean, and subjects the land to its irresistible attractions."

57. See, for instance, Schlichthorst, *Rio de Janeiro wie es ist*, 185; Joseph Friedrich von Weech, *Reise über England und Portugal nach Brasilien*, 3 vols. (Munich: Auer, 1831), 1:353–354.

58. See Thomas H. Bennett, *A Voyage from the United States to South America* (Newburyport, MA: Herald Press, 1823), 12: "Large groups . . . assemble on Sundays in the suburbs of Rio, to sing and dance and revel. The construction of their musical instruments, their *music* itself, and the varied dance and gesture of these Africans, never fail to attract the attention of hundreds of the white inhabitants." Emphasis in original.

59. *El Spectador brasileiro*, "Correspondencias," May 9, 1827: "com tudo não posso accreditar que em huma Corte tão civilisada como esta, seja costume recebido pelas pessoas de educação de assobiar, e gritar do modo mais discordante quando se appresentão na Scena os criados para remover as mezas, cadeiras etc."

60. *L'Écho de l'Amérique du sud*, 25 July 1827: "C'est un véritable assassinat musical!"

10

Ethnography and Exoticism in Nineteenth-Century France

Sindhumathi Revuluri

Let's begin in Paris, at the Musée du Quai Branly.

Standing in the middle of the museum, one is confronted with a transparent glass tower full of musical instruments.[1] Striking in its sculptural aesthetic, the display is nonetheless disorienting to those attuned to sound, since the instruments remain silent. The centrality of musical instruments to the architecture of the museum and its viewing experience, as well as the centrality of the questions of sound, silence, and organization, makes a certain kind of sense—and perhaps sends a message about what is being communicated by the museum, however unintentional. Furthermore, in displaying sounding objects in a silent way, the tower invites imagination that seems grounded in realism but cannot be confirmed, denied, or contextualized through relevant sensory (touch or hearing) evidence.

The newly renovated museum opened in 2006. A major accomplishment of former French president Jacques Chirac, the Musée was a response to a call by over three hundred artists and intellectuals to have a space in Paris dedicated to non-European art. While the building itself is new, the collections are largely not: the Musée du Quai Branly combines the collections of the former Musée national des Arts d'Afrique et Oceanie (National Museum of African and Oceanic Arts) and the Musée de l'Homme (Museum of Man) under one roof. With the merger of these two collections also came the combination of oversight between the Ministry of Culture and the Ministry of Education, making explicit that the provenance of the museum's objects stemmed both from ethnological missions and displays of art.

Much of what can be said about the Quai Branly can be said of the challenges of building and designing museums and specific exhibits. Fixing objects in time and space, creating narratives of how pieces fit together, honoring their materiality and functionality, making their display educational but not

Sindhumathi Revuluri, *Ethnography and Exoticism in Nineteenth-Century France* In: *Acoustics of Empire*.
Edited by: Peter McMurray and Priyasha Mukhopadhyay, Oxford University Press. © Oxford University Press 2024.
DOI: 10.1093/oso/9780197553787.003.0011

voyeuristic—these are common tropes among museum curators. And as Lydia Goehr has eloquently argued, in what she calls the "imaginary museum of musical works," they are common in histories of music, too.[2] Yet the charge of such questions in the case of the Quai Branly is all the more sharp given the explicit attitude of the museum toward displaying cultural difference. The mission of the two predecessors, as well as the explicitly stated mission of this new entity, was to focus on art or objects from elsewhere. Though not a nineteenth-century institution, the Quai Branly continues in the tradition of museums established in the colonial period as places of curated collections. Its imperial impulse to display the spoils of power is obvious, even as it works to intellectualize that impulse. The privileging of material culture from Africa, Asia, and the southern Americas, while seemingly celebratory, serves to differentiate those objects from European traditions which are not to be found in this museum. So while it is a site to celebrate archaeological and anthropological accomplishments and thought, it also serves the function of orientalizing the cultures that come under its ethnographic scrutiny.

Critiques of the museum follow at least partly from this premise, but they also suggest that there are ways of embarking upon the display of otherness that would not rehearse tropes of marginalization. As one critic put it, the Musée du Quai Branly got it "brow-slappingly [wrong]."[3] Though not specified, I can imagine the criticism applying in particular to the display of musical instruments. Enriched by multimedia installations, the display is nonetheless quite removed from musicality, with instruments suspended in time and space. In a sound studies framework, this gesture could produce something transcendent by highlighting the materiality of sound, the arbitrariness of display, or the possibility of echoes and acousmêtres.[4] But in the museum and in the glass tower are the legacies of musicology, too. The stillness and silence evoked in that display, not to mention the obvious artifice of organization, suggests that those instruments left undisciplined could never produce real, orderly music, only raucous, random sound and noise. That is among the reasons why the display is so problematic. While these instruments and the cultures that bore them should have access to abstraction, in the context of the Musée, they absolutely do not because the display is not in their voice. They are further alienated through decontextualization and silencing of their origins and their musicality without access to a narrative of their own.

I begin with the Musée du Quai Branly because I believe it vividly illustrates the practices of ethnography and exoticism and their interplay.[5] I offer it partly as a provocation—both of silent displays of sounding objects and of the conditions of knowledge production. Made all the more politically, ethically, and morally challenging given the historical power differentials at play—in this case legacies of colonial conquest and its lingering effects despite explicit decolonization—the museum participates in practices of both ethnography and exoticism.

In this essay, I use these two key terms—ethnography and exoticism—to untangle a thread of musicology's imperial origins. In musicology's disciplinary history, the two are usually seen as opposites—definitely not friends—and even as undoing one another. Ethnography, at least as it is construed today, is the study of a community via deep engagement and often participant observation. As a key tenet of cultural anthropology, ethnography values the voices of its subjects, and in its ideal form, allows them to speak for themselves and even to "talk back." Exoticism, by contrast, usually refers to a system of representation by which a culturally removed Other is spoken for by a privileged subject. Its connotation is often, though not always, negative, not least because of the power dynamics with which it has been associated. Historically, those in power have done the speaking, those represented have been subjugated, and the resulting portraits have not been particularly complimentary. Further complicating their relationship and setting up their potential incompatibility is the way in which each has been affiliated with different disciplinary stances, historically and contemporaneously: ethnography began and remains a common methodology in the qualitative social sciences; exoticism is a system of representational aesthetics that is invoked in analyses of fictional texts and works of art in a variety of media. Though sound studies tends not to dwell in the narrative and hermeneutic the way that some strains of historical musicology do, in thinking about exoticism in particular it is critical to remember that the very idea of "sound" is politicized in the historiography of music studies because of how the concept of sound was and is used to establish the boundaries of music (as sound's ordered, inherently and internally meaningful counterpart) and those who are allowed to make it.

Despite these foundational differences, I would like to suggest that at key historical moments, ethnography and exoticism were born of the same ideology, twins separated at birth and sharing key DNA, if different fingerprints. This may seem like a radical or less radical claim, depending on your own scholarly interests. It is important to me because I see the link between ethnography and exoticism as a key to understanding the emergence and persistence of certain hierarchies of knowledge in contemporary scholarly study of a diverse array of musical genres, practices, and expressions. I would like to suggest that un-obscuring their twin birth might force us to reflect on some uneasy parts of our own disciplinary histories and presents. This perspective is inspired by a dynamic outlined by Edward Said in his seminal *Orientalism*: "that European culture gained in strength and identity by setting itself off against the Orient".[6] At various points in this chapter, I will read methodologies, disciplines, and cultures as participating in oppositional power dynamics, hoping along the way to call attention to some of the less visible and underdiscussed structures and values that guide inquiries in well-established areas of study.

My own historical orientation within musicology tends toward the long nineteenth century, so I will present a few cases that illustrate the implications of the claim that I have just laid out. The first two of these cases, from Julien Tiersot and François-Joseph Fétis, respectively, reflect on scholarly practices of the nineteenth century and musicology's inheritances from them. I offer the third by way of conclusion; it will reflect on a particular piece of music, its complex historiography and reception history, and issues of taste as they intersect with cultural representation. Through these three cases, I hope to engage the contemporary subdisciplines of ethnomusicology, music theory, and historical musicology in a conversation about shared origins, assumptions, and values. Furthermore, I hope to explore how an embedded ideology of difference shapes music, musical thought, and musical historiography in ways that both reflect and form colonial dynamics in the nineteenth century and beyond.

Musicology and *Orientalism*

In the context of the acoustics of empire, I am very aware of my training as a historical musicologist. In that discipline's history, most scholarship that deals with representational media or markers of otherness, most notably musical exoticism of the eighteenth to the twentieth centuries in opera, ballet, musical theater, and some programmatic instrumental works, relies on the work of Edward Said in *Orientalism*. Said's name is so prevalent in that body of scholarship that one could come to think that by reading this corpus, one had all but absorbed Said's thinking. Yet there is something largely un-satisfying about the conclusions drawn in the musicological work about representations of difference: much of it boils down to a distinction between fact and fiction, using Said to bolster the claim that as expressions of the im-aginary, the musical works in question abided by a different logic than other musical works or than documentary evidence.[7]

Indeed, reading Said directly produces other conclusions entirely. He suggests that discourse about the Orient is governed by Orientalism and that therefore also knowledge about the Orient is governed by Orientalism. Crucially, he does not make a distinction between fiction and documentary evidence (a point that may be particularly salient in a visitor's experience at the Musée du Quai Branly, where its origin story brings these strands to-gether and such boundaries remain blurry at best). Similarly, methodology does not make or break a document's Orientalist stance—whether pursued in the spirit of critique, textual analysis, or anthropological understanding, Said suggests that all utterances about the Orient participate in the same dis-course. In more contemporary de-colonial work, such ideas are the premise for thinking about colonial epistemologies and what is truly possible in the realms of theory and historiography.[8] While Said does not necessarily de-center Eurocentric ways of knowing, his reminder about the conditions of knowledge production forms an important precursor to the call from subal-tern studies, and post- and decolonial studies, to provincialize Europe.

Though in what follows I fix my gaze firmly on European expressions of knowledge and art, I aim to remind us of the ways in which encounters with otherness resonated through all forms of musical knowing, making, and being. Instead of a novel subject that inspired European greatness, I seek to center the foreign in the making of the European, and through this process, rethink some of the foundational tenets of musicology, including that of the work-concept and its related hermeneutics. If I were writing here only for musicologists, I would ask: What would happen if we shifted our focus in musicology from musical works to musical knowledge? If we broaden our understanding in such a way, what might we find in our documentary ev-idence that could serve as an alternate pathway to the more well-trodden ground of musical exoticism? And what might we make of the interplay be-tween the documentary and the imaginative, the space in which Said says Orientalism takes shape?

For the audience of this volume, which I imagine includes scholars of sound and those who are broadly interdisciplinary in their approach to the aural and the context of empire, further questions are begged: What might a history of musical thought that is shaped by such interplay say to today's sound studies? What are the acoustics we mean, who can hear them, and how might they operate past the political life of any given empire?

I think there may be some uncomfortable truths—more or less obvious depending on your disciplinary affiliation and point of study—that emerge from such questioning. In my own realm, these come down to something relatively basic: that ways of knowing are shaped by much more than those who wield them and own them and push them forward. I ask: What would happen if we shifted our focus from works to knowledge? And the answer is both simple and unsettling: frames of reference would shift, centers would drift, and focus would change, likely revealing our values and priorities in ways that we may not wish to have laid bare.

It is with these questions and a spirit of shifting, drifting, and changing in mind that I wish to visit some examples from France in the long nineteenth century.

Early Ethnography: Julien Tiersot

Even before the self-reflexive turn in anthropology, before the subsequent anthropological turn in ethnomusicology, and indeed, before ethnomusicology was a discipline in its own right, travelers, scholars, artists, and writers explored other places, cultures, peoples, and music. Many of these investigations fall under the broad rubric of ethnography, despite not practicing the very nuanced approach of today's eponymous activity. (As just one example, participant-observation was not a tenet of these early efforts, nor was a self-reflexive approach to what was found.) But the self-named ethnographies of the nineteenth and twentieth centuries are documentary efforts, capturing information in writing. Similar to Said's examples in *Orientalism*, these works, while communicating musical information, exhibit patterns of hierarchal and relational definitions, embedded biases, and judgments of sophistication and civilization.

I would like to offer a close reading of a few opening lines from a relatively progressive volume by Julien Tiersot (1857–1936), a critic, writer, scholar, and librarian. Tiersot is perhaps best known for his work with French folk song, including multi-volume works cataloguing songs from each of the French provinces. But he also was inclusive in his subject matter: he not only wrote biographies of Gluck and J. S. Bach, but also published transcriptions of "exotic" musics from the Parisian World's Fairs, and a two-volume *Notes d'ethnographie musicale* that covered music of East and South Asia, the Middle East, and North America, published in 1905 and 1910.[9] The first volume collects articles on a wide range of musical practices primarily from Japan, China, and India, some of which Tiersot encountered himself (through their presence in France), while others he acquainted himself with via travelogues, personal accounts from others, and published works. All of the essays originally appeared as columns in the Parisian musical newspaper, *Le Ménestral*, and their address suggests an audience with a grounding in Western musical theory, particularly notions of harmony and meter. The second volume, also collected columns, follows a different trajectory. Rather than an overview and tour, it delves in-depth into the musical practices of Native Americans. Information and analysis in the second volume seem to be derived entirely from secondary sources, as there does not seem to be much corroborating evidence of Tiersot's own interaction (nor does he presume this). The approach is not necessarily cohesive—his work is not an intervention in today's scholarly sense—and the methodology varies from place to place and over the essays. Yet it is also fair to say that his work is unusually thorough for the time, including a bibliography of extant secondary literature and a number of transcriptions throughout and in an appendix.

Given his positioning as someone aware of the sound worlds around him, Tiersot offers a provocative jumping-off point for what might be seen as fixed values and an understanding of "music" at the time. In his second volume, he clearly states that ethnography is a science based on numerous and repeated observations—the latter a tenet that still holds for most definitions of ethnography today. Yet at the same time, Tiersot's core musical and intellectual perspective cannot be in doubt. He begins the first volume with the following paragraph:

> The history of music at the end of the nineteenth century has made notable progress. It would not have been possible without including the study of non-European musics. Though quite different from what our race has been working on for centuries, it is nonetheless worth our hearing. That these arts are inferior to our own must be admitted upfront and without question. Nothing is more natural than this truth: Europe, having always been the cradle of human civilization, will naturally be home to a musical

practice far superior to what people of other parts of the world could ever attain.[10]

As an opening paragraph to a book about the music of foreign places, there is much to say about it, especially as it represents the tone of both volumes. My analysis is not an attack on nineteenth-century perspectives or values. (For one, I don't think it would be very useful to visit historical documents with the intention of pointing out the ways in which they may not align with our politics. Second, for whatever we may find almost laughable about the arrogance of this writer's confident assessment of European greatness, he took the time to travel and to learn about and engage with the musical practices of faraway places at a uniquely progressive level—not something that could be said for all of his contemporaries, including his colleagues at the Paris Conservatoire where he was librarian.) Despite this caveat, it should be relatively easy to see how Tiersot's work falls within Said's understanding and assessment of Orientalist discourse, especially with respect to the assumptions and values that create filters for the evidence in question. Not simply in what Tiersot reports about musics of the world, but in the question: *What can he even hear as music per se?* I am not suggesting that the answer to this is knowable, but rather that considering it might remind us that the limits of Tiersot's own hearing influence what is said and what judgments are passed.

Ultimately, the other lesson I would like to offer by reading Tiersot through Said is not about the Orientalism of early ethnography but about the similarities between the tone of Tiersot's work and the stances of musical exoticism of the same period. In the discipline of musicology, scholars have mostly corralled works that engage in displays of foreign difference into a small pen of musical exoticism, arguing that they follow their own logics of representation, they have their own conventions of sound and spectacle, and that they have spurious—but nonetheless present—connections to authentic practice.[11] Almost nobody believes—or at least is willing to argue—that staged musical exoticism was documentary or received as "real." And indeed, its fictional or imaginative categorization has rescued its creators and audiences from charges of full-on racism or prejudice. After all, could anybody possibly have believed such things about these people? This was only entertainment and different rules apply.

Even if you are not willing to take such a generous stance about musical works that traffic in exoticism—that is, even if you believe we should read them critically and informed by postcolonial discourse—I think it is fair to assess scholarship on the whole body of such works as invested in the binary between truth and fiction, real and imagined. If this is the case, however, then works like Tiersot's would be seen as the antithesis to *Carmen* and *Lakmé*—the objective corrective to the subjective imagination. Yet, for those interested in colonial epistemology, the distinction between fiction (in the form of an exoticist opera) and objective documentary evidence (in the form of published ethnographic notes about Native Americans) is much less important than the systems of power each betrays.

The suggestion that there are commonalities in stance and manners of representation across the genres of scholarship and composition should not be so surprising, given the colonial context in which all of these cultural products emerged, and takes us squarely back to Said's core argument. He makes plain a belief that all work was conditioned by its political time but that even as learning and scholarship moves forward to more progressive stances that can identify and correct deep biases, Orientalism, as a discourse, retains certain key elements.[12] For him, the distinction in genre (between scholarship and composition, for example) matters far less than the political climate in which it was created and the shared aspects of identities of the creators. For decolonial scholars like Walter Mignolo, what is even more revelatory is that decades of scholars and scholarship have declined to see this connection, instead reproducing the very dynamics of the subject they claim to analyze critically.[13]

There is another key term in Tiersot's opening paragraph worth mentioning: history. Just as scholarly knowledge has sometimes been understood as exoticism's antithesis (or its antidote?), so, too, have history and ethnography been cast in opposing roles. Tiersot's acknowledgment not just of history but of the "history of music" is a remarkable inclusion here. He invokes it not as an inert entity but as a scholarly discipline. When he says that the "history of music" has made progress, he actually means something like the contemporary discipline of musicology. In other words, he is actively recognizing and distinguishing "what happened" from how we write or talk about it. Even if "history" in Tiersot's time would have been a finding-and-gathering kind of mission—one full of answerable questions rather than "how" or "why" ones—it was a major move to acknowledge its life and development.[14]

At the same time, Tiersot engages in several other, less explicit but telling methodological moves. In his mention of Guillaume Villoteau—to him a consolation since Étienne Méhul declined to join an expedition to Egypt[15]—he gestures to a potential lineage of gathering musical information (even as he laments the lack of transcriptions, or better, phonographic records).[16] His description—which seems to consider a transcriber as a mere vehicle, suggesting that a musician could have been replaced by a machine—also implies that foreign musical cultures are knowable via description and transcription, however brief and decontextualized, ending with almost a celebration that the presence of "exotic" musics on French soil is the utmost convenience in engaging in study.[17] The terms of knowing are thus built into these approaches, which are necessarily not concerned with shifting Tiersot's or others' frameworks or contexts—or even physically shifting themselves!—but hearing music and sound from elsewhere through pre-existing models of Western harmony and form.

Furthermore, reference to history and the foreign in the same paragraph was remarkable. (To be clear, Tiersot is not suggesting that these foreign musics have the same history or capacity for history.) That learning about other places would be an asset for the general enterprise of music history was a relatively radical claim. Crucially, however, for Tiersot this "ethnographic" endeavor was related to music history, in that the contemporary study of foreign musics provided insight into the past of humanity[18]—in other words, these so-called primitive cultures were a window onto what Europe might have been, had progress not occurred. In this sense, his ethnography is both history's companion and its opposite: it is paradoxically the study of the past frozen in the present.

Histories of Music: François-Joseph Fétis

When Tiersot talks about "music history" and its progress as being bound to a greater understanding of foreign musics, he may have had François-Joseph Fétis and his *Histoire générale de la musique* in mind.[19] Within disciplines of music today, Fétis is perhaps best known as a music theorist and historian, and perhaps even as one who was unusually culturally sensitive. Through his treatise on harmony and his history of music, he can also be credited with the codification of the scholarly discipline of music history.[20]

Fétis's *Histoire générale de la musique* (1869–1876) was the most comprehensive history of music written in French to date.[21] It is, in many ways, a magnificent work, full of detail and expansive in its geographic reach. Over the course of five volumes, it covers Western music from the ancients to the present day, and it also includes discussion of musics from all over the globe. That said, it is difficult to know exactly how to read Fétis's "music" of the title (or his "general history" for that matter). On the one hand, it is a radical gesture of inclusion to acknowledge that musics from other parts of the world and other times should be admitted into a history that also speaks of more familiar heroes and the present day. On the other hand, once admitted, what is done to those musics bespeaks a familiar hierarchical relationship that, while culturally conditioned and situated, persists in the endurance of his text and its theoretical interventions.

For example, the structure of the five volumes tells a fascinating story, quite apart from the content contained within. Fétis's primary preoccupation was with harmony and tonality.[22] It is perhaps therefore not surprising that his history is organized by musical system. (Discussions of tonality dominate most of the book, even though it is cast—in its title and throughout—as a history of *music*.) The first three volumes follow a geographic organization— moving from the music of one people to the next, in a kind of spiral that eventually lands close to Europe and those most often claimed as legitimate European ancestors (e.g., Greece). The fourth volume shifts from a purely geographic to a functional perspective, discussing music of the Church in the East and in the West. When we shift to Europe halfway through the fourth volume, however, it is suddenly history all the way: now all the chapters and sections are divided by *time* (century and decade).

My observations about the work's structure are compatible with, and perhaps even endorsed by, Fétis's claims throughout that the musics of inferior races are stuck in the past and are not capable of changing. Apart from this general observation, Fétis also makes connections to this idea through specific musical details, with particular emphasis on harmony and tonality, as well as capacity for change and progress, as the sign of modern practices. Any music that does not exhibit these qualities, then, is not thoroughly modern. That French (and other European) musics have progressed to tonality, while other musics have not, is a sign to Fétis not of a different musical system, but of a necessarily lesser and incomplete one.[23] As Jean Littlejohn has discussed thoroughly in her dissertation, Fétis linked the history of music to the history of people via their tonal and harmonic systems.[24] In making these claims, he draws on the theories of Arthur Comte de Gobineau, whose *Essai sur l'inégalité des races humaines* ("Essay on the Inequality of Human Races") forwarded a scientifically-based racial classification and insists upon race as the originator of all history.[25] In other words, the structure of Fétis's study was very much in line with contemporary French intellectual approaches to race, evolution, and progress, the latter being a particular preoccupation of colonial French thought.

Despite these rather overt discussions of human difference via music, we do not generally call texts like Fétis's multi-volume history "exoticist"—in large part because the information transmitted is more easily categorized as "objective" than fictional. Indeed, Fétis's transcriptions and descriptions are not technically incorrect—that is, they do not include mistakes that we could easily correct with today's knowledge. It is therefore tempting to read Fétis only for information: after all, few comprehensive histories of European musical practice include sounds and thought from other parts of the globe.

Similarly, we may wish to read Tiersot only for the musical information contained within: we do not have many accounts from the early twentieth century of the musical practices of Native Americans, and certainly many of those that do exist have very little in the way of transcription. We could look to Tiersot's work as ethnography and glean valuable insights from it, especially since he cites other scholars and published works, and his writing grows out of a relatively long-term engagement with a foreign musical culture.

But I need hardly say that the manner in which the musical and historical material is presented affects our reading of that information in problematic ways. These two issues of information and narrative are so deeply intertwined that any suggestion of reading with a filter—one that separates the more exoticist claims from the "facts"—is impossible. Instead, we must learn to read for what Said calls the "latent" Orientalism of these texts.[26] Not all statements of values will be as explicit as Tiersot's opening paragraph or Fétis's racial categorizations—and certainly when dealing with such clearly stated aims, we must heed them. But even when such flags are not waved, we must still attend to the ways in which individual sections and the text as a whole communicate *multiple messages* at once—that of musical information and that of values.

One critical way in which latent Orientalism plays out in both of these texts—and this is a value we have inherited, whether we like it or not—is the definition of European practice against the foreign. These texts allowed for a seemingly fuller understanding of "foreign" musics, such that the boundaries could be established more concretely. For Tiersot, what was admitted into his ethnographic studies were those musics that were not notated or part of the Western canon. For Fétis, European practice is defined through progress and fully-formed and mature tonality, in contrast to "inferior" systems. Without texts like Tiersot's and Fétis's, European practice had little to ground it and even less to elevate it. Music, in their imagination, needed the discipline of foreign encroachment to be sure it knew its own limits, value, and superiority.

It was reading Fétis that originally inspired my thinking down the path of connections between ethnography and exoticism—not because Fétis was actively involved with either as we define them today. He did not himself travel (as far as I know) or immerse himself in foreign cultures. He also did not engage primarily in the creative act of musical composition, let alone in the representational practices of musical exoticism. But in his *production of knowledge*—and here, that knowledge is simultaneously about Self and Other—he reproduces familiar hierarchies of power and narrates a history that projects the cultivation of the West alongside the primitiveness of the Other.

Certainly, Tiersot and Fétis stand out for their time in their awareness of and engagement with foreign musics. My intention, therefore, is not to single them out for critique, but rather to look at our inheritances from their contributions, meaning not just what they said but how their organizational and knowledge-producing practices cemented certain logics of power that were taken up elsewhere and therefore persist. For both, the tool of transcription in Western staff notation undergirds the ability to make rational claims about ordered sound, almost unnoticed in their commentary or that of later scholars. In the case of Fétis, the embeddedness of ideas of self and other, and their necessary hierarchy, persists in music theory and the study of harmony, which, when used as a tool to understand musical expression writ large and broadly, subsequently exacerbates and amplifies the evaluation of musics as good or bad, primitive or sophisticated.

Ethnography and Exoticism: Stravinsky's
Le sacre du printemps

I turn now to my third case: Igor Stravinsky's *Le sacre du printemps* (*The Rite of Spring*), which debuted, infamously, at the Théâtre des Champs-Élysées in Paris on May 29, 1913. As arguably one of the best-known pieces of the Western canon, it is not necessary to rehearse its history here, but I will share these key details: a production of the Russian troupe the Ballets Russes, *The Rite* was a collaboration between Stravinsky, during his so-called Russian

period, Sergei Diaghilev (the impresario of the Ballets Russes), and the cho-
reographer Vaslav Nijinsky, with sets and costumes by Nicholas Roerich.
The Ballets Russes had established a following in Paris starting in 1909, and
successfully commanded the attention of French audiences in their colorful
productions that often built upon Russian mythology and folklore through
modernist music, dance, and visuals. As scholars have compellingly argued,
their work was, at its core, Russian-for-French-audiences at the same time as
it has—in the moment and in hindsight—proved a cornerstone of modernist
music and dance.[27]

Precisely because of the work's persistence in musicology and because of
its ability to inhabit a historiography of modernism (rather than exoticism),
it is worth poking a bit at how it picks up on threads of ethnography and
exoticism as introduced earlier. For the purposes of this chapter, the point
I would like to home in on is the role of folkloric research in the story of its
genesis. At the heart of the primitivist depictions are a series of ethnographic
details, costume, scene, setting, and music alike. Indeed, much has been
made by scholars of the efforts of Stravinsky to work with Nicholas Roerich,
and their collaborations on many key elements of *The Rite*. As just one example, Roerich conducted extensive research into the history of textiles and
Slavic symbolic ornament in designing the costumes.

Similarly, though Stravinsky characteristically embraced and alternately
denied it, traces of actual folk songs permeate the work. We are lucky to have
a wealth of sophisticated arguments about *The Rite*, and especially about its
folk, primitive, or exotic content, which is in many ways a significant departure from musical exoticism in the eighteenth and nineteenth centuries.[28]
The abstracted way in which the ethnographic and folkloric material was
used has often seemed to rescue Stravinsky (and Roerich and Nijinsky) from
the blunt accusation of "exoticism," and the complex musical processes tend
to make more sense in the context of modernism and its version of neo-
primitivism, both arenas which *The Rite* has come to define.

But the reliance on tradition and authenticity—however conscious or
explicit it may or may not have been—is actually just as embedded in the
power and representational dynamics of exoticism, however objective their
sources and modes of inquiry may seem to be. In other words, it is not in the
transformation of the "originals" that the exoticism is or is not created (as it
might be in other imagined worlds put on stage and in song), but in the nature of the ethnographic research itself: a task that is motivated by finding
and displaying difference. The same is true for so-called auto-exoticism: a

representing of the self, even in a stylized way, that Stravinsky was famous for doing with Russian-ness. If we see exoticism as a practice, then it is not actually Stravinsky's cultural or political citizenship that determines authority or authenticity, but the approach and what is made of the materials.

Given the rise of academic disciplines before and around this time, the recourse to ethnography and folkloric research suggests that a sense of objectivity and reality could be assumed in the arts of textile and architecture (which comes out in the costumes and sets of *The Rite*). (And, put more boldly, it is possible that the appeal to ethnography might have actually *meant* something to audiences.) Yet, as I have been saying throughout this chapter, our contemporary critical apparatus allows us to question what kinds of representations were being preserved and perpetuated through the seemingly innocuous documents on which Stravinsky and Roerich based their research. It may not seem correct to say that *The Rite of Spring* is an ethnographic or authentic ballet, at least not in the sense we use ethnography; the label of exoticism sits a bit more comfortably.

If we were to consider the place of ethnography and authentic artifact in *The Rite* and its historiography even more deeply, we may return to the very assumptions I have tried to challenge throughout this chapter about the real and imagined, the fictitious and the documentary. For audiences in Stravinsky's time and for us now, what power is accorded to the semblance of the objective real in the context of the imagined exotic? What kind of modernity is implied by the appeal to ethnography and its resultant exoticist ballet? And what if the foundational ethnography was itself exoticist?

In other words, there is something to the practice of exoticism: whether the source materials are "real" or imagined, presented realistically or abstracted, there is a shared premise of putting difference on display. I would argue that this has everything to do with the dynamics of Orientalism by which the Self is defined through an interaction with the Other. In the case of *The Rite*, it is the combination of exoticism in a familiar sense and the use of ethnography that might itself be steeped in exoticist dynamics that situates it at the heart of a modernist enterprise: one that Fétis pre-figured, one that defines Tiersot's intellectual enterprise, and one that makes *The Rite* both canonical and exceptional. This is a modernism—at least in one aspect—in which the dynamic of Self/Other is so deeply influential that it is nearly impossible to imagine how to exempt it. Perhaps most critical for the work ahead is to fully see the ways in which this intertwining has shaped the foundations of the discipline of music studies writ broad—historical musicology, ethnomusicology, music theory, and even sound studies.

Underground Selves

There is a chance that many readers imagine these three cases are set up as straw men: contemporary scholarly and musical practice are far removed from these three examples and their stances. Ethnography is so much more refined now that we would never call what Tiersot was doing "ethnographic," and Stravinsky and Roerich's possible "misuse" would be much more transparent in its political aims. None of these examples follow cultural anthropology in participant observation, self-reflexiveness, or any of the other nuances of contemporary anthropological and ethnomusicological practice. Similarly, we would include foreign musics alongside Western music—as we do in textbook vignettes—or give them their own histories, not make them the history of Western practice or a primitive version of European tonality as in the case of Fétis.

Yet we share an attitude with Tiersot and Fétis and even Stravinsky when we engage in an approach premised on difference, however nuanced or self-reflexive. This is true when we attempt to make sense of historical works or contexts only through readings of documents, but it is also true when we make harmony and tonality the basis for studying "music."[29] It is true when we limit the study of certain musical cultures to the domain of ethnomusicology, or when we associate ethnography with space and history with time.

Perhaps these are uncomfortable truths, and perhaps they are familiar. Regardless of the scope you are willing to allow in understanding our inheritances from Tiersot and Fétis and others like them, there is a small but important point I hope to have made: musical exoticism did not exist in a vacuum. There is a danger in focusing too exclusively on "music" as the repository for the kinds of ideas that Said presents in *Orientalism*. The musical works that traffic in it, especially those from the height of British and French imperialism, may often be treated as novelties, but the impulses behind them were entirely common and widespread. They are present not only on the stage but in the academy, in the library, and in the archives that many of us frequent. In other words, exoticism in music is not only in musical works but also in knowledge about music. The acoustics of empire resonate beyond music and sound, and they resonate past (geographically and historically) the edges of empire, too.

When we turn to records like ethnographies, transcriptions, or travelogues, it is thus critical to see them as part of a larger practice of exoticism (as a representational ideology), rather than as its parallel or its inverse. These so-called objective records do not provide a corrective to imagined exoticism. Rather they demonstrate a cohesive Orientalist (in the Saidian sense) approach whereby difference is the governing perspective and penetrates production of both fiction and nonfiction, travelogue and history, music and musicology.

If, as Said argues at length, Europe invented the Orient, then it can also be said the Orient helped to shape Europe. Said's arguments suggest that Europe *used* the Orient—as its antithesis, as a "surrogate and even underground self."[30] Without the Orient and without Orientalism, it would seem, Europe would not be what it is. Though made almost in passing, Said's framing of a shadow, formative Other is almost haunting. Reading closely, it is apparent in his analyses of literature throughout *Orientalism*, that what seems in some cases like imaginative play is actually a potentially darker exercise in self-reflection, and that what is fetishized or mocked externally is in fact part of a deep questioning or fear directed internally. Whether that psychoanalytical approach is productive or not, it remains his critical and almost evergreen intervention that the presence of Orientalism was a non-neutral force in the shaping of European thought. In confronting its generative power in such a way, we are therefore forced to confront values and fears as they exist within us and our intellectual traditions, rather than having the convenience of the fiction of purity and independence from difference writ large.

Said calls this "flexible *positional* superiority," whereby the West never has to lose the "relative upper hand."[31] This certainly emerges in Fétis's ordering of his history, which almost suggests that foreign musics lay the groundwork for European tonality, even if they are then frozen there. For Stravinsky, the transformation of so-called primitive source material sets him apart as a modernist, rather than one of the primitive masses himself.

Musicology, too, relies upon its antithesis, its surrogate and underground self, which, at least in the case of turn-of-the-century France, may very well be the musical practices of foreign places and peoples. This is made explicit in Tiersot and Fétis's writings, and I think it is made quite clear in Stravinsky's ballet, too, where ethnographic components justify the sounds of modernism.

Another thought, one that may occur particularly to readers of this volume, is that perhaps it could be that sound studies could serve as musicology's surrogate—or, more productively, that it works to make visible and audible musicology's surrogates.[32] I raise this cautiously, even as I wonder if this is a set of dynamics that should be perpetuated. I want to linger here for just a moment, though, because I do believe there is value to this reflection, in that the idea of relating the disciplines in this way brings to light hierarchies that exist whether we name them or not. But there is also a danger in that it perpetuates the privileges of a well-established discipline (like musicology) with attendant institutional structures at the expense of inquiries that rely on interdisciplinary movement and collaboration (like in sound studies). It is far from me to say what is the right or appropriate way to approach the question of underground selves at a disciplinary level, but certainly an awareness of the ways in which we—all of us—use others in defining selfhood—disciplinarily, historically, personally, and existentially—bears significant and repeated examination.[33]

The frame of "acoustics of empire" is suggestive and productive for exactly this reason: it forces us to think about what resonates in the chamber of empire, whether we understand its bounds or not. I see empire forming the bounds of what was heard, what *could be* heard, and how music and sound (or even noise) were delineated from one another. In other words, empire is not an overlay to be placed over studies of music and sound; it is, instead, the very foundation on which we have come to understand what we hear.

I would like to return to where I started: at the Musée du Quai Branly. When I first saw the display of musical instruments, I was reminded of what I had read about a gamelan gifted to the French by the Dutch after one of the nineteenth-century Parisian World's Fairs.[34] The gamelan sat in the lobby of the Paris Conservatory—silent and unplayed and an artifact of a fleeting yet powerful encounter with foreignness. Was this a stand-in for Western music's surrogate and underground self, a daily reminder of what it was not?

That display of art and knowledge at the Quai Branly, opened less than twenty years ago, makes for a startling truth about the sacred boundaries still so persistent between Other and Self in French culture. Credited to Jacques Chirac's vision, the Musée du Quai Branly nonetheless sets a tone for French ideas of universalism and assimilation that have direct connections to contemporary debates about immigration and citizenship. Pasts live on in the present, and I wonder what our musicological artifacts—and the ways in which we display, use, and interact with them—say about us.

Notes

1. https://www.quaibranly.fr/en/public-areas/the-musical-instrument-tower/, accessed January 1, 2024.

2. Lydia Goehr, *The Imaginary Museum of Musical Works: An Essay in the Philosophy of Music* (Oxford, UK: Oxford University Press, 1992).

3. Michael Kimmelman, "A Heart of Darkness in the City of Light," *New York Times*, July 2, 2006.

4. There is little to suggest that the Quai Branly is operating via the frameworks suggested by Eliot Bates ("The Social Lives of Musical Instruments," *Ethnomusicology* 56/3 (2012), 363–395) or John Tresch and Emily Dolan ("Towards a New Organology: Instruments of Music and Science," *Osiris* 28/1 (2013), 278–298) or other recent approaches to musical instruments. I read the display in the way I do in large part because of the overall alienation. Where Bates, Dolan and Tresch, and others read against an established grain in their examinations of instruments, there is no grain/context present here to read against, leaving the silence of the instruments all too palpable, rather than unsettling of a familiar power dynamic.

5. I am far from the first musicologist to find the Musée du Quai Branly a compelling site of provocative questions. For example, Tamara Levitz traces lines of history and ways of thinking about the Dogon in France via a specific object and the legacies of colonialism and displays of cultural difference it embodies. See Tamara Levitz, "The Aestheticization of Ethnicity: Imagining the Dogon at the Musée du quai Branly," *Musical Quarterly* 89/4 (2006), 600–642.

6. Edward Said, *Orientalism* (New York: Pantheon Books, 1978), 3.

7. For a thorough overview of scholarship to date—and a response to the framing of musical exoticism in historical musicology—see Ralph P. Locke, *Musical Exoticism: Images and Reflections* (Cambridge, UK: Cambridge University Press, 2009) and Sindhumathi Revuluri, review of "*Musical Exoticism: Images and Reflections*, by Ralph P. Locke," *Journal of the American Musicological Society* 64/1 (2011), 253–261.

8. For example, in the special issue, "Contesting Imperial Epistemologies," *Journal of Historical Sociology* 27/3 (2014), edited by Gurminder K. Bhambra, Robbie Shilliam, and Daniel Orrells, the authors and editors ask about how foundational concepts in their field change when viewed from a lens that does not center the West.

9. Julien Tiersot, *Notes d'ethnographie musicale (Première Série)* (Paris: Librairie Fischbacher, 1905) and *Notes d'ethnographie musicale (Deuxième Série): La musique chez les peuples indigènes de l'Amérique du Nord* (Paris: Librairie Fischbacher, 1910).

10. "L'histoire de la musique, à la fin du dix-neuvième siècle, a fait de notables progrès. Elle ne sera pourtant point achevée avant que, étendant son champ d'action, elle ait compris dans son domaine l'étude des musiques extra-européennes. Bien différentes de celles aux formes desquelles nos races sont accoutumées depuis des siècles, celles-ci n'en sont pas moins dignes d'être écoutées par nous. Que ces arts soient inférieurs au nôtre, concédons-le, ou plutôt affirmons—le tout d'abord. Rien n'est plus naturel que cette vérité: l'Europe ayant toujours été le foyer principal de la civilisation humaine,

il est tout simple que la musique qu'on y pratique ait acquis une supériorité à laquelle n'ont pu atteindre les peuples des autre parties du monde." Julien Tiersot, *Notes d'ethnographie musicale*, 2 vols. (Paris: Fischbacher, 1905), 1:1(my translation).

11. The separation of exoticist works from contemporary repertoire happens more and less explicitly depending on the particular scholar and argument. However, affinities between exoticist works are implied and explored thoroughly, and volumes that purport to treat them as an ensemble—and with their own histories—abound. See, for example, Jonathan Bellman, ed., *The Exotic in Western Music* (Boston: Northeastern University Press, 1998); Georgina Born and David Hesmondhalgh, eds., *Western Music and Its Others: Difference, Representation, and Appropriation in Music* (Berkeley: University of California Press, 2000); and Locke, *Musical Exoticism*.

12. While this is a point elaborated throughout, it is also firmly and clearly explored in the introduction to *Orientalism*, particularly pp. 9–15, as part of exploring the artificial distinction between "pure" and "political" knowledge.

13. In framing a decolonial approach, Mignolo puts the necessary action succinctly: "Delinking means to change the terms and not just the content of the conversation." Walter Mignolo, "Delinking: The Rhetoric of Modernity, the Logic of Coloniality and the Grammar of De-Coloniality," *Cultural Studies* 21/2–3 (2007), 449–514, at 459.

14. For more on the emergence of music history and historiography in Tiersot's time, see Sindhumathi Revuluri, "French Folksongs and the Invention of History," *19th-Century Music* 39/3 (2016), 248–271.

15. Tiersot, *Notes d'ethnographie musicale*, 1:3. The reference is to the French Egyptian Expedition, 1798–1801.

16. "Si le phonographe eût été inventé au temps de la campagne d'Egypte, point n' eût été besoin de faire venir un musicien de Paris: l'instrument soigneusement emballé avec une bonne provision de rouleaux, le tout tenant moins de place dans le fourgons de l'armée que le bagage d'un adjudant,—il n'en eût pas fallu davantage pour faire retentir sur les rives de la Seine et dans les Instituts appropriés, pour transmettre ensuite jusques à nos derniers neveux des vestiges de musiques présumées remonter justques à Sésostris, ou tout au moins avoir charmé les oreilles de Cléopâtre!" Ibid., 4.

17. "Le dix-neuvième siècle ayant supprimé les distances, il est permis de croire que ces interprètes continueront de venir à nous, et que nous pourrons souvent les entendre sans être obliges de nous déranger nous-mêmes." Ibid.

18. This is particularly evident in his thought experiment about hearing the music Cleopatra heard; of course, this is rhetorical and hypothetical, but the emphasis on geographical distance, rather than the passage of time, alludes to a common conflation in his work and in others.

19. François-Joseph Fétis, *Histoire générale de la musique* (Paris: Librairie Firmin Didot Frères Fils et Cie, 1869–1876).

20. François-Joseph Fétis, *Traité complet de la théorie et de la pratique de l'harmonie* (Paris: Brandus et Dufour, 1867).

21. In some ways, the *Histoire générale* parallels Charles Burney's four-volume *A General History of Music* (1776–1789), published in English. Burney's volumes similarly consider various European traditions, their precursors in the music of the ancients, and

questions of church modes and tonality. He does not venture quite as far afield as Fétis, however, who includes Asia and Africa (various regions and to varying degrees of depth and certitude) in his examination.

22. Thomas Christensen's *Stories of Tonality in the Age of François-Joseph Fétis* (Chicago: University of Chicago Press, 2019) is a detailed examination of the rise of the idea of tonality and its nineteenth-century theorization as a response to foreign and provincial encounter.

23. This is an issue taken up more explicitly even in some of Fétis's other works that deal more centrally with harmony. What I find remarkable in the *Histoire générale* is that the subject is meant to be history, with some attention to geographic diversity, yet the fundamental question and method of evaluation remains harmony.

24. Jean Marie Littlejohn, "Fetis's Theory of Harmony in Nineteenth-Century Europe: Historical and Cultural Context of the Principle of Tonality" (PhD diss., Northwestern University, 2004).

25. Arthur Comte de Gobineau, *Essai sur l'inégalité des races humaines* (Paris: Librairie de Firmin Didot Frères, 1853).

26. Said, *Orientalism*, 201–225.

27. Seminal works in this body of scholarship are Lynn Garafola, *Diaghilev's Ballets Russes* (New York: Oxford University Press, 1989) and Richard Taruskin, *Stravinsky and the Russian Traditions: A Biography of the Works through* Mavra (Berkeley: University of California Press, 1996).

28. Key references here are Richard Taruskin, "Russian Folk Melodies in The Rite of Spring," *Journal of the American Musicological Society* 33/3 (1980), 501–543; and the debate between Richard Taruskin and Pieter van den Toorn starting with Taruskin's "A Myth of the Twentieth Century: *The Rite of Spring*, the Tradition of the New, and 'The Music Itself,'" *Modernism/Modernity* 2/1 (1995), 1–26, and followed by van den Toorn's response, "A Response to Richard Taruskin 'A Myth of the Twentieth Century,'" *Music Theory Online* 1/5 (1995). See also Robert Fink, "'*Rigoroso* ($\musEighth$ = 126)': *The Rite of Spring* and the Forging of a Modernist Performing Style," *Journal of the American Musicological Society* 52/2 (1999), 299–362.

29. For an elegant analysis of the implications of tonality as foundational to studies of music, see Kofi Agawu, "Tonality as a Colonizing Force in Africa," in *Audible Empire: Music, Global Politics, Critique*, ed. Ronald Radano and Tejumola Olaniyan (Durham, NC: Duke University Press, 2016): 334–354.

30. Said, *Orientalism*, 3.

31. Ibid., 7.

32. The idea of underground disciplinary selves is not new in music studies but remains a potentially productive avenue of self-reflection. In her article "Sound, Silence, Music: Power," Deborah Wong explores the premise and situation of the discipline of ethnomusicology as a kind of surrogate (my word) to musicology, at the same time as she calls on her colleagues to decenter "music" as foundational and to recognize that this positioning already subscribes to the values of a powerful center. She closes with a gesture to sound, noise, and silence—almost as a way out of the disciplinary power

dynamic at play. Deborah Wong, "Sound, Silence, Music: Power," *Ethnomusicology* 58/2 (2014), 347–353.

33. In Ana María Ochoa Gautier's *Aurality: Listening and Knowledge in Nineteenth-Century Colombia* (Durham, NC: Duke University Press, 2014), she interrogates haunting descriptions of sonic encounter; the opening anecdote of the chapter "On Howls and Pitches" vividly demonstrates Alexander von Humboldt's experience of human differentiation (pp. 31–37). Ochoa Gautier describes it as "sonic perception . . . spread on corporeal difference" (p. 32). She also draws connections to disciplinization and elegantly links the personal with the disciplinary in much the same way I have attempted to with my nineteenth- and twentieth-century French examples.

34. For more context on the gift and the larger project of collection and display, see Jann Pasler, "The Utility of Musical Instruments in the Racial and Colonial Agendas of Late Nineteenth-Century France," *Journal of the Royal Musical Association* 129/1 (2004), 24–76, especially 36. Pasler does not comment on the silence of the instrument, but I read its presence there, and not elsewhere (in practice rooms or concert halls), as highly salient.

PART IV
SILENCE AND ITS OTHERS

11

The Anacoustic

Imperial Aurality, Aesthetic Capture, and the Spanish-American War

Jairo Moreno

> From the blood of our heroes, shed at Santiago and Manila, there shall arise a New Imperialism, replacing the waning Imperialism of Old Rome; an Imperialism destined to carry world-wide the principles of Anglo-Saxon peace and justice, liberty and law.
>
> —John R. Procter, "Isolation or Imperialism"

On September 30, 1898, Major General Fitzhugh Lee, former governor of Virginia and Confederate officer then in the service of the United States Army, attended a motion picture show advertised as the Wargraph at Metzerott Hall, in Washington, D.C. "The general was enthusiastic over the realism of the Cuban war [sic] views," the *Washington Star* reported, and "he pronounced the execution by the Spanish of Cuban prisoners [sic] especially excellent."[1] Under the heading "Stirring Scenes at the War-graph," the *Washington Post* proclaimed, "the old, old, but ever new strains of martial music, the stir and thrill of marching soldiers, the story of national glory and victory, are daily reproduced with startling fidelity by the Wargraph moving pictures at the Metzerott Hall . . . *The Execution of Cuban Prisoners by Spanish Soldiers* [sic] [. . . is] of thrilling interest."[2] As early as March of that year, in the build-up to the formal declaration of war, "cinematograph movies of *The Disaster of the Maine* and *Spanish Artillery* were being shown twice daily (2:30 and 8:15) at Willard Hall," in the nation's capital.[3] In New York City, the week of May 7 offered plenty of similar bills. Folks looking for entertainment could attend the "Sensational Edison Wargraph" at Proctor's on 23rd Street, "Edison's Wonderful War-Scope" at Pastor's, a few blocks downtown, on 14th St., and "Edison War-Graph (New Views)" at the Pleasure Palace on 58th St., where you could "come any time" from 1:30 to 11 p.m. Over at Olympia

Jairo Moreno, *The Anacoustic* In: *Acoustics of Empire*. Edited by: Peter McMurray and Priyasha Mukhopadhyay, Oxford University Press. © Oxford University Press 2024. DOI: 10.1093/oso/9780197553787.003.0012

Music Hall, on Broadway, near 44th St., a new musical awaited its premiere the following week: "War Bubbles: An Original Patriotic Extravaganza."[4] War was very good for entertainment business.[5]

Throughout 1898, the press enthused over the Spanish-American War films, their technology, and their effects on audiences. The trade publication the *Phonoscope* cited a review of a showing at Proctor's by the *New York Journal*, William Randolph Hearst's widely read daily: "'Last night enthusiastic crowds cheered to the echo as they watched the Edison War-Graph throw upon the giant screen the pictures secured of the scenes attending the prosecution of war in Cuba.' Events in films 'gained a significance and reality that no newspaper could produce.'" The crowd said that it was not photography, "it was the real thing."[6]

"The real thing": the expression sums up the complex embodied in the Edison Spanish-American War films.[7] At stake in the nascent technology of motion pictures was the reordering of sense experience, of the experience of others, of history-in-the-making, and of US society itself.[8] The assemblage of technology, perception, representation, and their production and circulation through a set of institutions (print media, technology invention and motion picture production companies, theater exhibitors, spectatorship, and the state) gave these films an ontological allure and captivating power that rendered the intensely mediated conflict as "real" on American soil. This ontological allure, however, was also an ontological lure: the "real" were staged enactments of combat scenes.[9]

Uncannily, "the real thing" was without sound. There was, of course, sound, and lots of it. As Rick Altman has shown, "silent film" was anything but: Raucous audiences vociferated, bands played accompanying music, sound effects were made offstage, all part of the vaudevillian character of showings.[10] But the films, those nodal embodiments of "the real thing" in the assemblage of the war, themselves were "silent," a technical corollary of the fact that the recording and reproducing devices (e.g., the Edison kinetoscope and kinetograph), although noisy in their operation, heard nothing of what they captured visually.[11]

Perhaps this is too obvious, but I wish to argue that this "silence" needs to be conceived of beyond the technological limitations of the apparatus and beyond the "phenomenological" noisiness in theaters. My proposal, modestly theoretical, is for a sonic form that I give the neologism *anacoustic*. Most simply, this form is characterized by an absence of sound in which sound exists as potentiality and where sound *might have been heard*.[12] In phenomenological terms, in the *anacoustic* we see a sonic source but do not or cannot hear its sound. A second proposal, of historical-speculative character, explores the *anacoustic* as a condition of possibility for a particular sensorial engagement with war and violence that marks the entrance of the United States into the theater of imperial warfare, an imperial aurality abetted by the new technology of moving images, its representational wagers, and the institutions involved.[13] I call this sensorial assemblage, which includes but is irreducible to the capture of images by technologies, to the profusion of spectacularized news media reports, or to the perception by viewers of images of war, *aesthetic capture*.

My inquiry into the *anacoustic* and *aesthetic capture* assembles three conceptual spheres: (i) a critique of historical notions of technological inscription of sense perception (hearing and vision) that provide society with a matrix of intelligibility, via the work of James Lastra; (ii) the idea of "cultural techniques," which situates culture at the conjunction of sense faculties, signs, and media technologies, from which emerges a set of conceptual and ontological techniques socially taken to be real; (iii) the notion of "the parasite" (Michel Serres), which understands communication systems as being inevitably disrupted by something inherent to the system itself and as entailing an economy of taking without giving. In this economy, a feedback loop links a filmic apparatus that takes sound away from its source, audiences who take from this a deracinated and anesthetized sense of violence, and an infrastructure of empire (both military abroad and audiences at home) that takes away territory and self-governance from someplace and someone else. By placing cultural techniques in relation to the economy of the parasite, I show their entanglement with empire. I focus on two 1898 films by the Edison Manufacturing Company.

Images

Two particular Edison films focused directly on the combat and violent death of the war. The first is called *Shooting Cuban Insurgents: Spanish-American War*, by Edison employees James Henry White and William Heise (as cameraman), released on July 1898.[14] The film was advertised in *The Phonoscope*:

A file of Spanish soldiers approaches guarding some Cuban prisoners, hatless and shoeless. Officer commands "Halt." They place their miserable victims' faces towards a blank wall and step back four or five paces. The Spanish officer, resplendent in gold lace and buttons, raises his sword. One can *imagine* his commands by his gestures. "Aim" "Fire!" and four poor fellows have joined the ranks of martyrs for the cause of Cuba Libre. Their death struggles are painful to witness. One of them dies hard, so the officer helps him into the next world with his sword.[15]

The second film, *Cuban Ambush*, also by White and Heise, was produced the same month and copyrighted on August 5.[16] Edison's film catalogue remarked on the "fine smoke effects," highlighting the unique and, for its time, impressive capture of moving images by the Company's novel apparatus, the kinetograph. The *Phonoscope* announcement reads:

Concealed in the upper story of a ruined building on a sugar plantation is a party of Cubans, lying in wait for their hated enemy. A scouting party of Spaniards appears through the thick underbrush, led by an officer. They suspect the presence of an enemy, but evidently not concealed above their heads: for not until the Cubans pour forth a sudden volley are the Spaniards conscious that they are ambushed. One falls, the others drop on one knee and fire at random at the upper windows. It is noticeable that the brave Spanish lieutenant moves rapidly close in to the wall, out of range. There is no further shooting, however, as the lifeless forms of the Cubans are still, excepting one, who in his terror jumps from the window, a sheer twenty-foot drop, right into danger instead of out of it. He is quickly dispatched by a shot from one of the Spaniards, aided by a sword thrust by the brave officer.[17]

Gory stuff indeed, and equally titillating and alluring. As Amy Kaplan reminds us, "at the height of the war, these films were so popular that they were repeated every hour around the clock in urban theaters, where the line between the representation of war on the screen and the experience of spectatorship seems to have been fluid."[18] When these two films were made the war had reached its second month—it would end in early August. Even after combat ended, public interest in the films remained high, subsiding only in October 1899, with the production of the final three films dealing with the war, all dedicated to Admiral George Dewey, the designated hero of the US imperial wars in Cuba and the Philippines.

Words

The impact of the moving images of war was entangled with printed press coverage of the conflict, where, before the formal declaration of war, readers had been literally bombarded with jingoistic pro-war messages for weeks.

In a well-documented episode of early US mass media, two influential owner-editors, Hearst in the *New York Journal* and Joseph Pulitzer in the *New York World*, waged a war of their own for supremacy in the medium, both appealing to the possibility of armed conflict with Spain as a strategy to increase sales and readership. In Figure 11.1, a cartoon from the satirical *Puck Magazine* depicts Hearst and Pulitzer as obdurate children play-fighting over toy letter cubes, each claiming war as his own.

This tug of war must be understood in the context of US president McKinley's administration, which sought first a diplomatic resolution to the growing discontent in Cuba over the Spanish governance of the island.

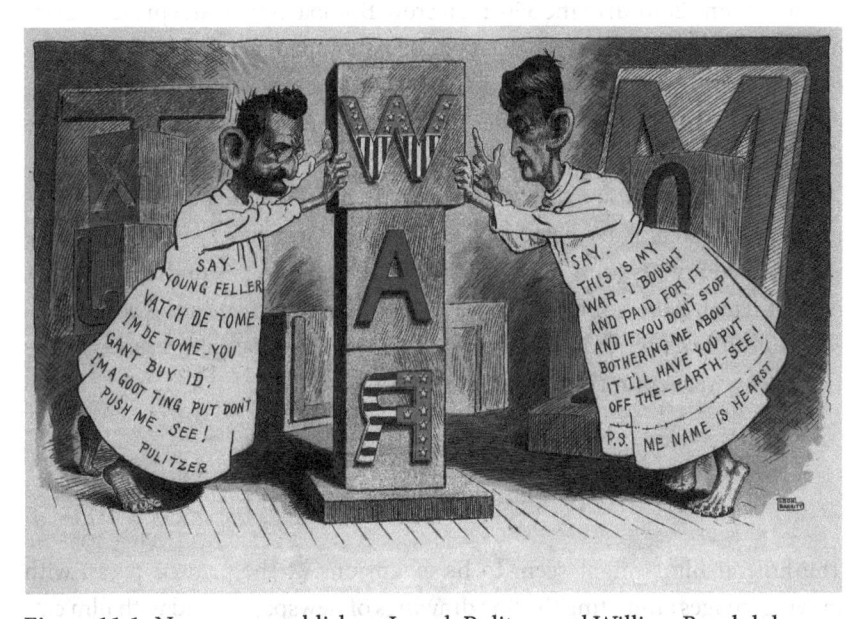

Figure 11.1 Newspaper publishers Joseph Pulitzer and William Randolph Hearst, full-length, dressed as the *Yellow Kid* (a popular cartoon character of the day), each pushing against opposite sides of a pillar of wooden blocks that spells WAR. This is a satire of the Pulitzer and Hearst newspapers' role in drumming up USA public opinion to go to war with Spain. Editorial cartoon by Leon Barritt, *Puck*, June 29, 1898, Library of Congress.

Cuban insurgents had by then waged three previous uprisings against the Spanish Crown: the Ten Years' War (1868–1878), the Little War (1879–1880), and the War of 1895. Active in Florida, New York City, and Washington, Cuban independentists had sought help from the United States. Hawkish actors in government constituted a majority, and the press, led by Hearst and Pulitzer, loudly and relentlessly built public support for direct military intervention. In another *Puck* cartoon, McKinley appears to sit calmly with a letter that reads in part, "the people of the United States have full confidence in your patriotism, bravery, and integrity. They know . . ."—and on the back we see—"you will act justly and wisely, [signed] the decent press." Hearst and Pulitzer hover above McKinley, waving leaflets saying "War, War, War" and "Fight first, investigate afterwards," among other combative slogans.[19] The letter, on a single, foldless page, denotes its public character.[20]

Under the premise of protecting American interests in Cuba, on January 24, 1898, McKinley sent the USS *Maine* battleship to Havana. Twenty-two days later, on the evening of February 15, the USS *Maine* exploded in Havana harbor, killing 266 out of the 350-man crew. Bombastic visual representations of the event spread across the front pages of newspapers (see Figure 11.2).

In the aftermath of this naval disaster, US Congress issued a formal declaration of war on April 25. On June 22, American troops disembarked in Cuba (see Figure 11.3).

In close collaboration with troops from the Cuban independentist movement, the United States helped defeat the Spaniards in a swift and decisive victory, prompting John Hay, the US Secretary of State under McKinley, to characterize the conflict in a July 1898 letter to Theodore Roosevelt as "a splendid little war."[21] The pattern of American imperial presence in the Caribbean was set for the long twentieth century.

"Visual Newspapers"

The Edison films might seem to be extensions of the printed press, with moving images animating the line drawings of newspapers and with film catalog descriptions and press advertisements offering compressed narratives that paralleled war dispatches. Noted Edison scholar and film historian Charles Musser reads the films as "visual newspapers."[22] Indeed, Hearst had correspondents in Florida in the run-up to the war, sent his personal yacht to Cuba, and hired Edison camera operators to cover the conflict. Like the

Figure 11.2 Illustration: Painting by the Chicago firm of Kurz & Allison showing the destruction of the US battleship *Maine* in Havana Harbor, Cuba, with inserts: "Location of the Maine-Havana Harbor," "Recovering the dead bodies," and head-and-shoulders portraits of Admiral Sicard and Captain Sigsbee. Library of Congress, Prints and Photographs Division.

newspaper magnates, Edison too had drummed up the imminence of war. For instance, a description of a film showing the iconic Morro Castle on Havana Harbor remarked how, "in view of probable bombardment, when the old-fashioned masonry will melt like butter under the fire of 13-inch guns, the view is of historic value." As James Castonguay notes, there was "giddy anticipation of real battles," with audiences being informed by a "nineteenth-century belief in photographic objectivity and in the inherent realism of motion pictures."[23]

This, from *The Indianapolis News* (June 6, 1898), captures the spirit of the war at home:

What a marvel, indeed, would be a moving photograph of a duel between two warships, American and Spanish, terminating, of course, in

Figure 11.3 Americans landing at the pier, Daiquirí. *Harper's Pictorial History of the War with Spain,* vol. 2 (New York and London: Harper and Brothers, 1899), 318.

the destruction of the enemy's vessel, exhibited on a stereopticon screen before wildly enthusiastic audiences from Boston to San Francisco. How the enthusiastic American audiences aforesaid would yell if they could see with their own eyes that monument to medievalism, Morro Castle, actually falling into a heap of its own debris before the fire-vomitting [sic] guns of Admiral Sampson's fleet.[24]

In the same article, the correspondent writes how "the history of the war with Spain will be recorded for the benefit of future generations not only in writing, but also in vivid pictorial shape that will appeal to the understanding of the smallest schoolboy."[25]

For Castonguay, newspaper accounts of the war "facilitated the 'receptivity' of early cinema and made Spanish-American War films an especially powerful 'attraction' in the larger 'cinema of attractions.'"[26] Musser believes that "audiences generally acquired prior knowledge of events through a variety of cultural forms . . . vaudeville spectators generally read the papers and could appreciate the films within this context."[27]

The commercial interests of print and other media technologies were very good for war. In perverse synergy, visual media boosted war, and war boosted and consolidated the fledging film industry. These films, recall, were "the real thing," rendering visually information intelligible to adults and children alike by bypassing, it seems, the communicational detours of the written word. These new media poetics ("visual newspapers") and technics and American empire were of a piece.

"Soundless Objects"

Through it all, eyes saw war, but ears heard nothing of it. Or I should say, ears heard through language and reporting narrative. Consider this June 23 dispatch from the *New York World* immediately following the landing of US forces, when, backed by the battleship USS *Texas*, the Americans joined Cuban revolutionaries in attacking the Spanish:

> Fifteen miles west . . . the strategic game opened at 8 o'clock, when Rabi's two thousand Cubans attacked the Spanish forces at Mazzamorra [sic]. The battleship *Texas* at the same time ran close inshore and opened on a block-house back of Cabanas Bay. The Estrella battery opened on the *Texas*, the shots coming near, for the range was short. The *Texas* silenced the battery in forty minutes. . . . Meantime, the Spanish and Cubans became hotly engaged. The fierce fire was heard on Cervera's ships in the harbor and they opened fire on the Cubans on the plateau at Little Bay Julici.

In this account, silence, which only the strepitous racket of gunfire could attain, descends on the battle scene with the enemy annihilated. War, particularly during combat, must have been an acoustically terrifying affair, and silence became, in the dispatch, a metaphor for Spanish death. As Castonguay notes, new combat tactics, such as firing under cover, manifested the increasing power of new weapon technologies and meant that direct combat happened across increasing distances.[28] Destruction was readily visible, as shown in Figure 11.4.

What kind of acoustic was this? As historians of film, perception, sound, and media know, in the phonograph the ear gained the means to inscribe the heard. In contrast, despite rapid advances in photography earlier in the nineteenth century, the eye would not achieve a parallel inscription of the seen. This was not for lack of trying. In a famous 1894 letter, Edison wrote:

Figure 11.4 Stone fort at El Caney, Cuba. Library of Congress, Public Domain Archive.

> In the year 1887, the idea occurred to me that it was possible to devise an instrument which should do for the eye what the phonograph does for the ear, and that by a combination of the two all motion and sound could be recorded and reproduced simultaneously. This idea, the germ of which came from the little toy called the Zoetrope, and the work of Muybridge, Mariè [sic], and others has now been accomplished.[29]

This combination of "all motion and sound" was not to be. Instead, in 1891, led by William Dickson, Edison's team developed the kinetograph, a bulky apparatus able to capture moving images (Figure 11.5). True, Edison's phonographic and photographic work shared in the production of continuity by means of an acceleration of information. The phonograph emerged in part from the desire to speed up telegraphic communication just as the kinetograph sped up single still-image shots. An inventive device, the Kinetograph captured images along a perforated strip of film:[30]

> These perforations occur at close and regular intervals, in order to enable the teeth of a locking device to hold the film steady for nine-tenths of the one forty-sixth part of a second, when a shutter opens rapidly and

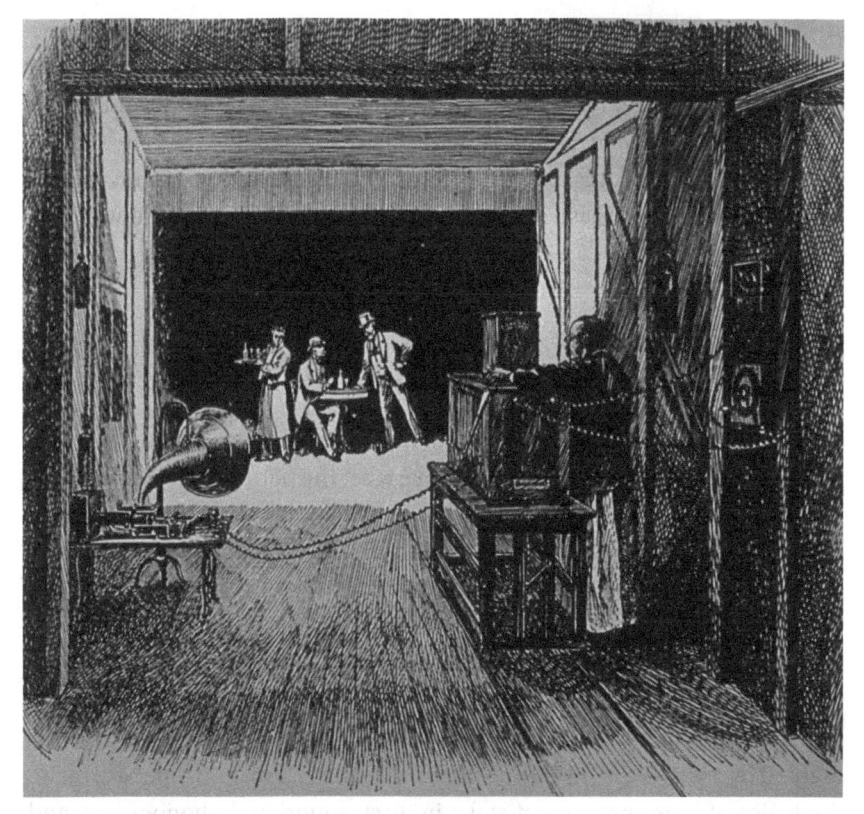

Figure 11.5 Interior of Edison's Kinetographic Theater. *American Medico-Surgical Bulletin* 8/18 (September 15, 1895), 1106, National Library of Medicine Digital Collections.

admits a beam of light, causing an image or phase in the movement of the subject. The film is then jerked forward in the remaining one-tenth of the one-forty-sixth part of a second, and held at rest while the shutter has again made its round, admitting another circle of light, and so on until forty-six impressions are taken a second, or 2760 a minute. This speed yields 165,600 pictures in an hour, an amount amply sufficient for an evening's entertainment, when revolved before the eye.[31]

In a short experimental film made between 1894 and 1895, William Dickson himself famously tried to coordinate the phonograph and the kinetograph. Playing a violin directly into the horn of the phonograph, the sound is barely audible, while two men appear to dance to the music. The challenge of synchronizing recording and playback, itself a corollary of the differences between the speeds of sound and light, would indefinitely defer Edison's dream of bringing eye and ear together: the Edison kinetograph films would remain silent. Writing with his sister Antonia, Dickson would describe Edison's moving image apparatuses as "the taking and reproduction of movable but *soundless* objects."[32] These were the objects that audiences of the war films experienced.

Sound and Image Inscription

Reacting to Edison's 1894 letter, James Lastra wonders what it means to say that the kinetograph would do for the eye what the phonograph had done for the ear; it was not a given that such intermedial relay would be as simple as Edison wished.[33] Answers pivot on Edison's understanding of the representational operations at work in phonography. Edison cast the phenomenon of phonography in terms of capturing sounds previously considered fugitive. Once captured, these sounds could then be reproduced at will, unconcerned with "the original source."[34] Lastra connects this figuration to a particular understanding of writing, à la *Phaedrus*, as a form of inscribed presence marked by the absence of the "speaker." Writing is a major trope organizing the logics of representation at stake in, first, sound and phonography and, second, moving images and cinematography.[35] Before taking on board Edison's understanding of phonography as embodying operations of inscription and storage, with their particular conception of writing, Lastra asks why it might have been so culturally pervasive, what kinds of explanatory power it may have carried and which institutional media conveyed this power, and which material differences it made.[36]

I group these important queries by Lastra under the general rubric of "cultural techniques." I adopt the term broadly to understand the technical production of culture as the intersection of sense faculties (seeing, hearing) and media technologies that harness them (the phonograph, the kinetograph). At this intersection, one tries to observe and absorb how media observe and absorb the world, provided attention is given to how media's "observation" is shot through with some sense of a pre-existent observation, for instance human perception, Lastra *dixit*.[37] As Geoffrey Winthrop-Young puts it, cultural techniques "account for basic operations and differentiations that give rise to an array of conceptual and ontological entities which are said to constitute culture."[38] Edison's wager on writing becomes a wager on the technological capacity to arrest and store for further reproduction evanescent phenomena, with evanescence (or fugitivity, which has slightly more complicated political connotations) emerging as a condition of possibility for phenomena to become perceptible by humans: things that appear before ears and eyes and quickly go. Inscription, as a general term for writing, constitutes, in turn, the techne that helps articulate as culture the intersection of seeing and hearing with the technological capacity to register (or capture) these phenomena. To Lastra's question of cultural pervasiveness, we answer that writing, in Edison, responds to a "cultural" commitment to fixity and unchanging iterability that made writing its preferred form. This helps us understand why, rather than thinking of an impossible intermedial relay, Edison would place the ear and the eye on the same plane of sensorial possibilities and thus on the same realm of "cultural" experience.

Other elements help give writing its allure in dealing with the contingencies of experiences of reality, particularly perception and sensation. Pivoting on the idea (and ideology) of language as a matrix for intelligibility and communicability, writing transfers these to phonography and cinematography, Lastra argues. This transference had its drawbacks, however, for technology could and did exceed human perceptual capacities. Simply put, cameras could "see" too much, exceeding writing as explanatory trope and becoming so objective as to be inhuman; that is, they would be indifferent to what they could capture. As a corollary, because moving image capture could be carried out within this frame of indifference and hypersensitivity, the films could acquire the character of non-arbitrary, non-mediated signs, which is to say not signs at all but rather reality itself.

All the same, Lastra remarks how that experientially impossible "fleeting image made sense if one perceived with the camera," because "embodied looking" was equated with "picture-making."[39] This owed to the other predominant figure for the relation of sense perception, technology, and forms of representation: simulation. The idea combines both the notion that technology transfers to apparatuses what the senses already do—that is, phonographs hear and kinetographs see—and that the materiality of phenomena, be it sound or movement, contains its "own language," as Étienne-Jules Marey put it, such that it "writes" itself. It was a short step to render this as the projection of life itself, life being fundamentally given in motility.[40] Indeed, before the kinetograph, Edison marketed a projector with the name "vitagraph," which would be also called the "wargraph."[41]

We could elaborate further the effect of this disparity on the constitutive artificiality of the sounding moving image, as does Chion, who argues for the audio-visual character of cinematic moving images and observes that any coordination between sound and movement results from a technical intervention to produce synchrony where there is none.[42] This contemporary insight does not invalidate the historical assumption under which Edison and his team were committed to the idea of technologies as media that faithfully inscribed perception. Their protocols of representation attending to both sound and moving image focus on *how* these were inscribed and reproduced, much more than *what* was inscribed and reproduced.[43] For it is in this *how* that the materiality of communication of the apparatus, as described, for instance, by the Dicksons, becomes dialectically knotted with what the medium perceives and inscribes, namely "soundless objects." In the end, materiality and affect as well as perception and signification fold into one another to produce a *what*. This is how moving images produce what I am calling "ontological allure," such that, for audiences, they become a soundless reality but "the real thing" nonetheless. As a "thing," the moving image becomes an irresistible ontological lure.

The "Real Thing"

From the perspective of cultural techniques, this "real thing" results from what Bernhard Siegert calls "operationalizing distinctions in the real."[44] That said, for the medium and for audiences the "real" is not quite the same thing.

Consider first the medium. Different from an ontological stance in which, for instance, object and image belong to distinct realms that are then brought into proximity by representation, as a medium, the kinetograph would perform the work of hybridizing the moving object/moving image pair in a singular form—for example, "movable but soundless objects." It is important to note that the medium performs this operation by intersecting with a field of perception for which there is no a priori distinction between moving object and moving image simply because the moving image as such does not exist to perception before the operationalizing distinction the kinetograph makes. Indeed, "cultural techniques are based on the transition from nondistinction [sic] to distinction and back."[45] The nature of this transition "back" to nondistinction is tricky, however. It requires that we understand the medium as drawing distinctions while escaping them itself.[46] This transparency of the technical apparatus, then, makes it possible for the medium to simply render things as they are, remedying the paradox that media be both in-between and immediate. As Castonguay argues, the Edison films gave "Americans for the first time unmediated access to real history in the making . . . film history can simply be intuited even 'by the smallest school boy,' offering a transparent window to the world."[47] This "transparency"—which emerges only after technology has introduced first a distinction between human perception and machinic perception—exemplifies the "operational distinctions in the real" at the heart of cultural techniques.

Here we move past Lastra's analytic of representation, because, put otherwise, the "operationalizing distinction" of inscription and simulation cannot be inscribed or simulated itself: the kinetograph sees the moving image. And what might begin as a circuit involving technology, signs, and perception folds into and consolidates as the cultural form "the moving image" or "real history in the making." Any such cultural form, of course, partakes in chains of communication, information, and signification that are material through and through. This helps explain the meaning of "the real" for the medium: it does not refer to an indexed reality exterior and objective in relation to the distinction it first makes. Rather, it refers to how, within the sphere of the medium, the old Lacanian non-linguistic, non-signifying Real existing in excess of the Symbolic domain of culture and the subject-forming domain of the Imaginary comes to inhabit the core of culture.[48]

The "real" for audiences, most simply, is the consolidated cultural form experienced as "the real thing," something that signifies, communicates, and informs, something that, abetted by institutional networks, circulates across material and symbolic realms as it helps constitute those audiences as believers, consumers, and enjoyers, and, in our case, patriots and jingoists besides.

Aesthetic Capture

Cultural techniques constitute modes of aesthetic affordance. Much in their operationalizing distinctions (and eventual return to non-distinctions) is a function of how technologies are both made possible *and* limited by the materialities of communication and media—sound and light, celluloid film and wax cylinders, but also cinematic techniques such as camera placement, movement, lighting, editing, and *mise-en-scène*. Noël Burch, for example, has shown how pre-1909 spectators remained in a position of exteriority to the images they saw, a position that will shift to the imaginary centering of a sensorially isolated spectator.[49] By these lights, it might have mattered little or nothing that audiences could not hear the rifles gunning down the Cuban prisoners, exterior as they remained from the *mise-en-scène* precisely because of the absence of sound. Plus, there was plenty of sonic stimulus in the theaters, which were sometimes displaced from the wargraph, for instance, into different venues. "When the United States was once again plunged into armed conflict with the Spanish-American War," Altman notes, "musical battle recreations became even more popular."[50] Here is the synopsis accompanying a Fourth of July, 1903, performance in Montana of "The Cuban War, or the Fall of Santiago":

> War is threatened, remonstrance of the nations. Uncle Sam's ultimatum. Approach of the troops. Parting scenes. All aboard for the South. A Southern scene. Life on the ocean. Rocked in the Cradle of the Deep. Hornpipe. Taps. Night on Southern waters. "To Arms." Pursuit of the enemy: The majestic squadron. "Commence Firing." Battle scene. Fall of Santiago. It's [sic] grim and dread horror. Its magnificent triumph. Victorious America. The land of the free.[51]

Despite this and similar displacements that sonically supplemented the "silence" of the war film, other elements conjured up possible voicings in the firing line scene. Recall the off-handed way the catalogue describes "Shooting Insurgents," for example: "One can *imagine* [the Spanish officer's] commands by his gestures. 'Aim!' 'Fire!'" This constitutes most obviously a prompt to vivify the voice accompanying human gestures, imputing sounds to images. But it also appeals to what some regard as a human perceptual predisposition to link visual gestures to "imagined" sound, an instance of "audiovisual coupling" that cognitively privileges hearing and sight as a sensorial pair, embodied here also in the way that even Spanish officers would be heard as if speaking in English, the language of the spectators.[52] Additionally, there was a reported predisposition (or receptivity, as Castonguay puts it) to come to see the films as the phenomenal realization of what audiences had read and spoken about in a public sphere brimming with conversation about the war. In short, there were sufficient elements to think that the soundless moving images might have compelled some sound.

For Burch, though, the kinetoscope's lack of synchronous sound produced "an intolerable contradiction in the context of these [Edison's] aspirations to the faithful reproduction of Life," adding to the radical exteriority of the spectator.[53] Thus, we have a tension between the cognitive predisposition of Chion's audiovisual coupling and Burch's technical-cultural interpretation of the historical spectator. But regardless, we also have the irrevocably tacit complicity of audiences with war violence, partly an effect of the power of the "cinema of attractions" to capture audiences by means of shock and surprise, images rendered in the purity of spectacle. The anacoustic, in my view, reveals a friction between the cognitive and the technical-cultural. But the anacoustic also resides in that friction, consolidating itself as cultural technique. For it matters more how it enables a space of sonic abstraction, an absolute space freed of the particularities that might tether sound to place and place to event, a space, furthermore, in which temporality would come to pass without resonances or sonic traces, at all. This operation of abstraction produces a particular form of relationality in which the space of both the moving images and the viewing becomes inured to the grim horror of imperial warfare. Hereby, time is trapped in the specificity of the event while space becomes atomized.[54]

We might argue that none of these considerations matter. After all, the films were staged and therefore there were no events, and thus no original time-space of their occurrence. This, however, would ignore a powerful poietic force at play in the films and the anacoustic. Namely, that they inscribe and store something for which there was no precedent. In a way, there is no sense in speaking of fakery. The films and their anacoustic character are mimetic in the best sense of the word: they participate in the production of originals, not, as certain Platonic traditions would have it, merely in their reproduction.[55] And while they appear at a time in which, as Lastra puts it, "culture [is] coming to grips . . . with the boundary between the real and the represented," they are successful in their mimetic production of originals because of this questioning.[56] I would go even further to suggest that perhaps there is no greater "operationalizing distinction" at play than the rendering of the real-fictional distinction as non-distinct. As a corollary, if the films inscribe and store anything, it is, so to speak, a future in which war will remain a soundless affair for those at a distance. That is, the anacoustic forms part of a new system of aesthesis under which US society would experience its many wars in the century that followed. This is in line with the classical Benjaminian "aesthetization of politics" in which media, in Susan Buck-Morss's elaboration of Benjamin, function in part as an anesthetic for a sensorium confronting new shocks of modernity.[57] But it is also part of how, in the production of this system, US society also produces new material conditions for its existence.[58] Key to these conditions is the idea that, as Amy Kaplan has argued, US empire operated in the entanglement of the state with a world that it did everything to keep at bay, a world often seen and all too rarely heard.[59] This entanglement is anacoustic.[60]

Anacoustic

I began by defining the anacoustic phenomenologically, as the aural relation in which one sees the object but does not hear its sound. This definition holds, but there is more. For one, although it applies to the medium and the audience, this definition only partially explains the "operationalizing distinctions" that produce it in the first place. One might understand the "deafness" of the kinetograph exclusively as a technological contingency or even failure and as part of a particular narrative in which cinema would eventually catch up to the acoustic realities that saturate the world it produces. But the anacoustic is no failure. It is the condition of possibility for the production of a relationship to acoustics specific to imperial conflict: Namely, the existence of a non-distinction between the sounding and non-sounding world such that "soundless objects" come to be the way things are. At home, war will be precisely and unquestionably that, anacoustic.

The reach of the anacoustic will be determinant for US society's experience of war, silently accompanying its imperial adventures throughout the twentieth century and well into the twenty-first. To begin assessing this reach, I borrow from Michel Serres: The anacoustic is parasitical. For Serres, the parasite refers to the disruptive noise and static in any communication (from the French meaning of the word), to the idea of an uninvited guest, and to an entity that takes without giving.[61] Essential to any relation, particularly exchanges across incommensurable orders, and to the formation of any system, the parasite would be that in the medium that disrupts what it could yet do—that is, the parasitic "noise" in the system I have outlined is the *elimination* of noise, and of audible sound altogether.[62] In our case, and as Edison hoped, this would correspond to disrupting the capture and inscription of sounding moving objects while producing an acoustic domain in which things are seen without being heard (i.e., the anacoustic) and a system in which spectators inhabit that domain and engage it as "the real thing." At the same time, as if feeding off the technological contingencies of the kinetograph, the anacoustic filters out the noise of war. This, in turn, also performs the parasitical operation of taking without giving: Taking sound away from its objects, it mutes the noise of both the dominant and the dominated and prevents the disruption of the communication and information of the war as it must reach its target audience. The disruptive character of the parasite intercepts one relation (between objects and sounds) in order to produce another (between soundless objects and audiences). In this, the anacoustic takes from events their sonic dimension and gives nothing but their images, what Serres wittily calls "abuse value." The anacoustic is *analytic*, the result of a parsing out of things from which it takes something (like Siegert's passage from non-distinction to distinction). But it is also *paralyzing*, interrupting the normal functioning of an order.[63] And as Steven D. Brown notes, it is *catalytic*, forcing its host to act differently, inaugurating for the host—here, US civil society and the state—a "new form of communication," or as Serres puts it, "a new system."[64] One can see how the "abuse value" that attends to the medium extends to the ways in which spectators take in images of imperial war while giving nothing back in return to the events themselves or the people and places depicted (even if fictionally) in them. For empire, "abuse value" is of the essence.

The story of the anacoustic is a story of the materiality of communication assembling technological and perceptual affordances, cultural techniques, and economic-commercial interests, and it is also and most obviously a story of the politics of representation in which the synergies of the state and civil society produce modes of relation to the world through media propaganda and its corollary affective energies. The anacoustic affords a view of empire as a cultural technique that produces a devastating non-distinction in US society between mass mobilization and necropolitics. That is, the anacoustic enables the emergence of producing a violent presence and a presencing of violence ("real history in the making," as the *Indianapolis News* put it) in and through which the necropolitics of empire quietly unfolded. Achille Mbembe, from whom I borrow the term "necropolitics," writes that, "in the future, part of the task of empire will consist in transforming the real into fiction and fiction into the real," part of a "mass mobilization of images, a key part of the deployment of a violence that seeks purity."[65] This future, as I proposed, began when cultural techniques consolidated in the non-distinction of the unheard-seen, and the parasitic character of this anacoustic relation became an unquestionable communicational and informational system. The future of empire was inscribed then and stored for further abuse. It helped foster an imperialism in the Caribbean and beyond, inconceivable without the entanglements of the anacoustic's peculiarly quiet but deadly aurality.

Notes

1. *Washington Star*, October 1, 1898. The film in question, *Shooting Captured Insurgents: Spanish-American War*, was produced by the Edison Company earlier that year. The United States formally declared war with Spain on April 25, 1898, and the warring countries signed a treaty on December 10, 1898. Armed hostilities in Cuba, however, took place between February and August of 1898. Lee's report follows the end of hostilities, as a kind of victory ode.
2. *Washington Post*, October 6, 1898.
3. Robert K. Headley, *Motion Picture Exhibition in Washington, D.C.: An Illustrated History of Parlors, Palaces, and Multiplexes in the Metropolitan Area, 1894–1997* (Jefferson, NC: McFarland & Company Inc., 1999)
4. Advertisements compiled together in an article by Mark Twain, "About Play-Acting," *Forum* 26 (September 1898–February 1899), 143–151.
5. The intimate bonds between the entertainment world and the military constitute a central theme in technology studies, from sound and visual technologies to the most recent digital domains. See, among others, Friedrich Kittler, *Gramophone, Film, Typewriter*, trans. Geoffrey Winthrop-Young and Michael Wutz (Stanford, CA: Stanford University Press, 1999); Paul Virilio, *War and Cinema: The Logistics of Perception* (London and New York: Verso, 1989); Geoffrey Winthrop-Young, "Drill and Distraction in the Yellow Submarine: On the Dominance of War in Friedrich Kittler's Media Theory," *Critical Inquiry* 28/4 (2002), 825–854; Martin van Creveld, *Technology and War: From 2000 B.C. to the Present* (New York: Free Press, 1991); Manuel de Landa, *War in the Age of the Intelligent Machines* (New York: Zone Books, 1992). Historical research on the connection between the Spanish-American War and the media and entertainment business includes Robert C. Allen, "Vaudeville and Film 1895–1915: A Study in Media Interaction," PhD dissertation, University of Iowa, 1977; Rick Altman, *Silent Film Sound* (New York: Columbia University Press, 2004); James Castonguay, "The Spanish-American War in United States Media Culture," in *Hollywood and War: The Film Reader*, ed. J. David Slocum (New York: Routledge, 2006), 97–108, available at http://chnm.gmu.edu/aq/war, accessed March 1, 2023; Richard Harding Davis, "Our War Correspondents in Cuba and Puerto Rico," in *Dispatches from the Front: News Accounts of American Wars, 1776–1991*, ed. Nathaniel Lande (New York: Henry Holt and Company, 1995), 157–165; Robert Eberwein, "'Hearing' the Music in War Films," in *A Companion to the War Film*, ed. Douglas A. Cunningham and John C. Nelson (Malden, MA: Blackwell and Wiley, 2016), 6–19; Amy Kaplan, *The Anarchy of Empire*

in the Making of U.S. Culture (Cambridge, MA: Harvard University Press, 2002): J. Stanley Lemons, "The Cuban Crisis of 1895–1898: Newspapers and Nativism," *Missouri Historical Review* 60/1 (1965): 64–65; Gerald F. Linderman, "The Popular Press and the War," in *The Mirror of War: The Spanish-American War and American Society*, ed. Gerald F. Linderman (Ann Arbor: University of Michigan Press, 1974), 148–173; Charles Musser, "American Vitagraph: 1897–1901," *Cinema Journal* 22/3 (1983): 4–46; Charles Musser, *The Emergence of Cinema: The American Screen to 1907* (Berkeley: University of California Press, 1990); Charles Musser, *Before the Nickelodeon: Edwin S. Porter and the Edison Manufacturing Company* (Berkeley: University of California Press, 1991); Charles Musser, *Edison Motion Pictures, 1890–1900: An Annotated Filmography* (Gemona del Friuli Italy: Giornate del Cinema Muto, 1997); Dylon Lamar Robbins, "War, Modernity, and Motion in the Edison Films of 1898," *Journal of Latin American Cultural Studies* 26/3 (2017), 351–375; Robert Sklar, *Movie-Made America: A Cultural History of American Movies* (New York: Vintage Books, 1994). The intertwining of new media and war is examined in various essays in Gavin Williams, ed., *Hearing the Crimean War: Wartime Sound and the Unmaking of Sense* (New York: Oxford University Press, 2019). The Crimean War saw the birth of embedded journalism.

6. "Cuban War Pictures," *The Phonoscope: A Monthly Journal Devoted to Scientific and Amusement Inventions Appertaining to Sound and Sight*, 2/4 (April 1898), 7.

7. Of the Edison Company's films produced in 1898–1899, 42 percent were dedicated to the Spanish-American War. Musser, *Edison Motion Pictures*, 379. Besides the Edison Company, the American Mutoscope & Biograph Company, founded by former Edison employee William Dickson in 1895, the Lubin Manufacturing Company, and Chicago-based producers William Selig and Edward Amet, working separately, also made war films, as did the French filmmaker/producer Marie-Georges-Jean Méliès. I am aware of the reductionist character of a history of phonography that focuses on Edison at the expense of many others. I identify him and his associates as part of a more complex assemblage within which the Company's films stand in for the general synergies between the state and institutions in civil society, particularly corporations. Edison is less important as an inventor of individual devices, such as the kinetoscope, in which he saw no intrinsic significance, than he is as a manager of consumption and circulation who "saw the marketplace in terms of how images, sounds, energy, or information could be reshaped into measurable and distributable commodities." Jonathan Crary, *Suspensions of Perception: Attention, Spectacle, and Modern Culture* (Cambridge, MA: MIT Press, 1999), 31–33.

8. This argument follows the incisive analysis by James Lastra, *Sound Technology and the American Cinema: Perception, Representation, Modernity* (New York: Columbia University Press, 2000).

9. As Robert Sklar puts it, "Fabrication was, of course, the point." And yet, "the film medium," he adds, "showed itself capable of re-creating extreme moments of life and death for an audience safe in auditorium seats," citing the example of Edison's 1898 *Shooting Captured Insurgents*. Sklar, *Movie-Made America*, 22. Charles Musser notes that re-creations were nonetheless advertised as authentic. Musser, *The Emergence of Cinema*, 247.

10. Rick Altman, *Silent Film Sound*. Emily Thompson writes of kinetoscopes, individual viewing units located in nickelodeon halls: "Kinetoscopes were viewed amid the clatter and din of the amusement parlor, and the earliest theaters to project motion pictures were just as noisy and chaotic. Emily Thompson, *The Soundscape of Modernity: Architectural Acoustics and the Culture of Listening in America, 1900–1933* (Cambridge, MA: MIT Press, 2002), 256.

11. In Michel Chion's provocation, silent cinema was "deaf." Michel Chion, *Film: A Sound Art*, trans. Claudia Gorbman (New York: Columbia University Press, 2009). (Incidentally, across Romance languages, the expression for silent cinema is mute cinema.) At the speed of forty-eight frames per second, the kinetograph was noisier and used a lot more film than the Lumière brothers' *Cinématographe*, which photographed and projected at the speed of sixteen frames per second. Friedrich Kittler, *Optical Media: Berlin Lectures, 1999*, trans. Anthony Enns (Malden: Polity, 2010), 161.

12. The extensive bibliography on the Spanish-American War films makes no mention of the absence of sound's relation to the violence portrayed. This absence is taken for granted. One exception is Michael Gaudio, who comments on the disconnect experienced by viewers of the kinetoscope seeing the *Sioux Ghost Dance*, an 1894 film from the Edison Company: "Even with that mechanical noise in their ears, along with the background sounds of the nickel-in-the-slot phonographs that were typically found in kinetoscope parlors, the earliest viewers of *Sioux Ghost Dance* would have experienced a disconnection of the optical from the auditory, as they saw bodies in motion but did not hear them." The dance would have been seen live in traveling shows by many viewers, however; not so the war in Cuba. Michael Gaudio, *Sound, Image, Silence: Art and the Aural Imagination in the Atlantic World* (Minneapolis: University of Minnesota Press, 2019), 141, also available at https://manifold.umn.edu/read/52146297-52a2-43ca-bb54-37996fc589f9/section/165195cc-1aa2-4500-83e6-e9825782ffac#ch06, accessed March 1, 2023. On sound and war more generally, or "belliphonics" (Daughtry), see, among others, J. Martin Daughtry, *Listening to War: Sound, Music, Trauma, and Survival in Wartime Iraq* (New York: Oxford University Press, 2015); Jim Sykes, "Ontologies of Acoustic Endurance: Rethinking Wartime Sound and Listening," *Sound Studies* 4/1 (2018), 35–60; Steve Goodman, *Sonic Warfare: Sound, Affect, and the Ecology of Fear* (Cambridge, MA: MIT Press, 2010). The differences between the anacoustic and Goodman's "sonic warfare," with its focus on "logistics of imperception (unsound)" (p. 9) and the subsonic should be clear.

13. American musicians around the same time and involved in postwar Cuban occupation engaged in another form of imperial aurality; namely, hearing Afro-Cuban music through US understandings of musical Blackness. As I argue below, imperial aurality is profoundly shaped by the contradictory capacity of US society to see and listen to a world that it conquers while keeping it outside of its own perceptual orbit. See Jairo Moreno, "Jazz, the Archive, and U.S. Empire," in *Audible Empire: Music, Global Politics, Critique*, ed. Ronald Radano and Tejumola Olaniyan (Durham, NC: Duke University Press, 2016), 176–213.

14. *Shooting Captured Insurgents* (Edison Manufacturing Company, 1898), https://www.loc.gov/item/00694305/, accessed March 1, 2023.

15. *The Phonoscope: A Monthly Journal Devoted to Scientific and Amusement Inventions Appertaining to Sound and Sight* 2/11 (November 1898), 15. Emphasis added.

16. *Cuban Ambush* (Edison Manufacturing Company, 1898), https://www.loc.gov/item/00694185/, accessed March 1, 2023.

17. *The Phonoscope* 2/11 (November 1898), 15.

18. Amy Kaplan, "The Birth of an Empire," *PMLA* 114/5 (1999), 1068–1079, at 1069.

19. This image is available from the Library of Congress: https://www.loc.gov/pictures/resource/ppmsca.28685, accessed March 1, 2023.

20. Contrary to the sealed missives of yore which might suggest governmental intrigue before they became *raison d'état*, as Bernhard Siegert notes, this public document is this *raison*, indexing the power of public but corporate media to inflect governance. Bernhard Siegert, *Relays: Literature as an Epoch of the Postal System*, translated by Kevin Repp (Stanford, CA: Stanford University Press, 1999), 30–32.

21. For details on the manner of combat collaborations between US and Cuban troops, see O. O. Howard, "The Conduct of the Cubans in the Late War," *The Forum* 26 (September 1889), 153–156.

22. Musser, "American Vitagraph," 43; Allen, *Vaudeville and Film*, 139.

23. Castonguay, "The Spanish-American War," excerpt online at https://chnm.gmu.edu/aq/war/recep1.htm, accessed March 1, 2023.

24. "Photos of the Conflict," *Indianapolis News*, June 6, 1898. Cited in Castonguay, "The Spanish-American War."

25. Ibid.

26. Castonguay, "The Spanish-American War." "Cinema of attraction" is Tom Gunning's well-known notion that early cinema (1895–1906) consisted mainly of "the harnessing of visibility, [an] act of showing and exhibition" largely unconcerned with plot or narrative. Tom Gunning, "The Cinema of Attraction: Early Film, Its Spectator and the Avant-Garde," *Wide Angle Journal* 3/4 (1986), 63–70, at 63–64.

27. Musser, "American Vitagraph," 43.

28. Castonguay, "The Spanish-American War."

29. Thomas Edison, Caveat 110, October 8, 1888, filed October 17, 1888, patent records, NjWOE, cited in Musser, *The Emergence of Cinema*, 64. See also the well-known citation in Antonia Dickson and W. K. L. Dickson, "Edison's Kineto-Phonograph," *Cassier's Magazine: Engineering Illustrated* 7 (November 1894–April 1895), 145–156, at 145.

30. As an aside, recall that Edison worked as a telegrapher during the American Civil War.

31. Dickson and Dickson, "Edison's Kineto-Phonograph," 146.

32. Antonia Dickson and William Kennedy-Laurie Dickson, *History of the Kinetograph, Kinetoscope, and Kinetophonograph* (New York: Albert Bunn, 1895), 8.

33. Lastra, *Sound Technology and the American Cinema*, 16. See also Tom Gunning, "Doing for the Eye What the Phonograph Does for the Ear," in *The Sounds of Early Cinema*, ed. Richard Abel and Rick Altman (Bloomington: Indiana University Press, 2001), 13–31.

34. In 1878, Edison uses the term "captivity" "without regard for existence or non-existence of the original source." Lastra, *Sound Technology and American Cinema*, 19, citing Thomas Edison, "The Phonograph and Its Future," *North American Review* 126 (May–June 1878), 527–536.

35. Lastra, *Sound Technology and the American Cinema*, 20.

36. Ibid.

37. This draws from Berhard Siegert, in "Entrevista a Bernhard Siegert (Interact #20: Mecanologia), Parte 3," https://www.youtube.com/watch?v=nIYUHB_x3cE, accessed March 1, 2023. The influence of second-wave systems theory, particularly the work of Niklas Luhmann as well as a key precursor, Michel Serres, is evident here. On Siegert and Serres, see Reinhold Martin, "Unfolded, Not Opened: On Berhard Siegert's *Cultural Techniques*," *Grey Room* 62 (2016), 102–115; on Serres and Luhmann, see Cary Wolfe, "Bring the Noise: *The Parasite* and the Multiple Genealogies of Posthumanism," and "New Introduction to the New Edition," in Michel Serres, *The Parasite*, trans. Lawrence R. Schehr, with a new introduction by Cary Wolfe (Minneapolis: University of Minnesota Press, 2007).

38. Geoffrey Winthrop-Young, "Cultural Techniques: Preliminary Remarks," *Theory, Culture and Society* 30/6 (2013), 3–19, at 5.

39. Lastra, *Sound Technology and the American Cinema*, 55.

40. The reference is to the French physiologist's zoetrope and his experiments with bodies in motion, as well as his *chronophotographe*, which Edison saw in France. The work of photographer Eadweard Muybridge, particularly his zoopraxiscope, projecting successive phases of movement-of-image series, was also key to Edison's development of the kinetograph. See Lastra, *Sound Technology and American Cinema*, 29, 42.

41. Another projector, by the American Mutoscope Company, founded by Dickson, was called the "biograph."

42. Michel Chion, *Audio-Vision: Sound on Screen*, with a foreword by Walter Murch, ed. and trans. Claudia Gorbman (New York: Columbia University Press, 1994).

43. Lastra, *Sound Technology and the American Cinema*, 10.

44. Bernhard Siegert, *Cultural Techniques: Grids, Filters, Doors, and Other Articulations of the Real*, trans. Geoffrey Winthrop-Young (New York: Fordham University Press, 2015), 14.

45. Siegert, *Cultural Techniques*, 14.

46. This is not the place to address the signal transition from discrete images to continuous moving images that lies at the heart of film: "Individual frames of the film stood beautifully still during the sixteenth of a second in which they were recorded or observed, while all further transport between the individual frames fell precisely to the pauses in between [. . . since then,] film has been a hybrid medium that combines analog or continuous single frames with a discontinuous or discrete image sequence." Kittler, *Optical Media*, 162.

47. Castonguay, "The Spanish-American War."

48. This is Kittler's famous and polemical argument, except that here no domain or sensory modality is tethered to a medium (Kittler's triads are: Real/Gramophone/Sound; Imaginary/Film/Images; Symbolic/Typewriter/Writing).

49. Noël Burch, *Life to Those Shadows*, trans. Ben Brewster (Berkeley: University of California Press, 1990).

50. Altman, *Silent Film Sound*, 49.

51. Ibid.

52. Audiovisual coupling—"the treatment of hearing and sight as enjoying a privileged relationship of complementarity and opposition among the other senses"—has a correlate in the "audiovisual"—"the simultaneous representation or inscription of the visible and the audible." Michel Chion, *Sound: An Acoulogical Treatise*, trans. and with an introduction by James A. Steintrager (Durham, NC: Duke University Press, 2016), 150.

53. Burch, *Life to Those Shadows*, 33.

54. For Patrick Loughney, the films helped "orient audiences to the geographical locations where international actions were taking place." Patrick Loughney, "Movies and Entrepreneurs," in *American Cinema, 1890–1909: Themes and Variations*, ed. André Gaudreault (New Brunswick, NJ: Rutgers University Press, 2009), 66–90, at 83.

55. See Daniel Villegas Vélez, "Mimetologies: Aesthetic Politics in Early Modern Opera," PhD dissertation, University of Pennsylvania, 2016. This reading of mimesis draws from Derrida and Lacoue-Labarthe.

56. Lastra, *Sound Technology and American Cinema*, 66.

57. Walter Benjamin, "The Work of Art in the Age of Mechanical Reproduction," *Illuminations*, trans. Harry Zohn, ed. Hannah Arendt (New York: Schocken, 1969), 217–252; Susan Buck-Morss, "Aesthetics and Anaesthetics: Walter Benjamin's Artwork Essay Reconsidered." *October* 62 (Autumn, 1992): 3–41.

58. See also Lastra, *Sound Technology and American Cinema*, 5–6.

59. See Kaplan, *Anarchy of Empire*. I would be remiss to ignore that the category of "historical spectatorship" is far more complex than my reading might suggest. Castonguay maps parts of the United States such as Boston where patriotism was less jingoistic than in, say, New York. He shows the complexity of the North-South divide and notes critiques of the idealization of proletariat audiences at the time. Feminist scholarship has studied the shifting character of the public sphere for women who attended theaters, although their pro- or anti-war stances remain unknown. Race, which is, like gender, explicitly foregrounded but "unsaid" in the films, influenced how audiences "saw," for instance, Cubans, or Black American soldiers shown in several other Edison films. Castonguay, "The Spanish-American War." On gender, see Constance Balides, "Making Dust in the Archives: Feminism, History, and Early American Cinema," PhD dissertation, University of Wisconsin, Milwaukee, 1993; Constance Balides, "Scenarios of Exposure in the Practice of Everyday Life: Women in the Cinema of Attractions," *Screen* 34/1 (1993), 19–39; Miriam Hansen, *Babel and Babylon: Spectatorship in American Silent Film* (Cambridge, MA: Harvard University Press, 1991); Miriam Hansen, "Early Cinema—Whose Public Sphere?" in *Early Cinema: Space-Frame-Narrative*, ed. Thomas Elsaesser (London: British Film Institute, 1990), 228–246; Miriam Hansen, "Early Cinema, Late Cinema: Transformations of the Public Sphere," in *Viewing Positions: Ways of Seeing Film*, ed. Linda Williams (New Brunswick, NJ: Rutgers University Press, 1994), 134–152; Judith Mayne, *Cinema and*

Spectatorship (New York: Routledge, 1993); Judith Mayne, *Private Novels, Public Films* (Athens: University of Georgia Press, 1988); Judith Mayne, *The Woman at the Keyhole: Feminism and Women's Cinema* (Bloomington: Indiana University Press, 1990). On race, see Amy Kaplan, "Black and Blue on San Juan Hill," in *Cultures of United States Imperialism*, ed. Amy Kaplan and Donald E. Pease (Durham, NH: Duke University Press, 1993), 219–236.

60. See Rey Chow's notion of entanglement: "linkages and enmeshments that keep things apart; the voidings and uncoverings that hold things together." Rey Chow, *Entanglements, or Transmedial Thinking about Capture* (Durham, NC: Duke University Press, 2012), 12.

61. Michel Serres, *The Parasite*, trans. Lawrence R. Schehr, with a new introduction by Cary Wolfe (Minneapolis: University of Minnesota Press, 2007).

62. Thanks to Peter McMurray for making this point.

63. Steven D. Brown, "Michel Serres: Science, Translation and the Logic of the Parasite," *Theory, Culture and Society* 19/3 (2002), 1–27, at 16.

64. Ibid.; Serres, *The Parasite*, 52.

65. Achille Mbembe, *Critique of Black Reason*, trans. and with an introduction by Laurent Dubois (Durham, NC: Duke University Press, 2017), 4–5. See also Achille Mbembe, *Necropolitics*, trans. Libby Meintjes (Durham, NC: Duke University Press, 2011).

12

pēē ä wēē, an Outrageous Clatter, and Other Sounds of Acclimatization

Alexandra Hui

Another undesirable alien . . . It multiplies rapidly, and moves in large flocks, makes an outrageous clatter and delights in devouring young, green crops.

—*Hattiesburg American*

Nay, I'll have a starling shall be taught to speak
Nothing but "Mortimer," and give it him,
To keep his anger still in motion.
  —Hotspur, William Shakespeare, *Henry IV* (Part I. Act i. Sc. 3)

The story goes something like this: on a cold day in March of 1890, Eugene Schieffelin—compounding chemist, avocational birder, amateur artist, Shakespeare enthusiast—made his way to New York City's Central Park. He carefully set a series of bird cages down on the slushy ground and then, one by one, opened the cage doors. Cautiously at first, the birds fluttered out. Then, boldly, they began to chatter and strut. They were beautiful birds, simultaneously inky black and iridescent in the morning light. They would survive the winter. And their offspring would survive the next. And in this way, those sixty European starlings (*Sturnus vulgaris*) released by Schieffelin would eventually spread across the entire continent; the current North American starling population is directly descended from this release.[1] Schieffelin's act is regularly offered as the quintessential example of a misguided late nineteenth-century effort to bring all the birds in William Shakespeare's writings to America.[2] From repeated references in popular media to academic publications to internal government management agency reports, the Schieffelin story and his Shakespearean motivations have taken on the status of lore.[3]

Alexandra Hui, pēē ä wēē, *an Outrageous Clatter, and Other Sounds of Acclimatization* In: *Acoustics of Empire.*
Edited by: Peter McMurray and Priyasha Mukhopadhyay, Oxford University Press. © Oxford University Press 2024.
DOI: 10.1093/oso/9780197553787.003.0013

But the story isn't true. Or rather, in its retelling, it has changed. For one, Schieffelin was not the first to release birds of the Old World on the American continent. Documentation of deliberate releases dates back to the 1840s.[4] Nor was March 6, 1890, the first time Schieffelin himself had liberated European species on US soil. The American Acclimatization Society, of which Schieffelin was president, had been releasing birds since 1877 with the express goal of acclimating foreign species that would be "useful or interesting."[5] Further, no evidence has been found that concretely links Schieffelin's love for the Bard to his bird introduction efforts.[6] Over the following century, the American public and various governmental agencies tasked with resource management understood Schieffelin's release of the birds to be, in turn, a celebrated civilizing exercise, vilified for unleashing agricultural and ecological disaster, or neutralized as a charming cautionary tale.

The evolution of the European starling's immigration story prompts a more general question of whether sounds themselves could acclimate. In this chapter, I aim to determine when the starling stopped sounding like a *European* starling. Examining print media, United States Department of Agriculture (USDA) reports, and the writings of ornithologists can give us a sense of what the starling sounded like and how that sound changed over time. Or rather, how and why the *hearing* of the bird's sound changed over time. Historian Peter Coates has drawn out the intersecting representation and reception of immigrant flora, fauna, and humans. He is especially interested in how the language of relocation—*immigrant, alien, stranger, foreigner, nonnative, non-indigenous, invader,* and *exotic*—points to a phenomenon of humanizing animals, and naturalizing humans.[7] Likewise, musicologist Rachel Mundy argues that the story of modern sonic culture cannot be fully understood without animal musicalities.[8] That is, we can only know our sonic selves by better comprehending the framework through which we make sense of the sounds of the non-human. Tracing out the acclimatization of the starling's sound offers a framework to think about the mechanisms through which turn-of-the-century naturalism and agricultural science contributed to cultural assumptions about human difference. Further, by tracing out the evolving efforts to manage the expanding starling population through sound, I show how human sounds were used to colonize shared human–nonhuman spaces. These sounds of abatement, along with the sounds of modern, industrialized agriculture became, in a way, interchangeable with the sounds generated by the bird itself.

Warwick Anderson has declared the nineteenth century to be "a century of acclimatization."[9] The concept of *acclimater*, first introduced at the end of the eighteenth century reflected a growing interest in the process by which species might adapt to new climates. Anderson and others have shown how by the 1830s, the deliberate and systematic *acclimatisation* of species was a project of French and English scientists.[10] Correspondingly, this interventionist theory of acclimatization gave scientific credibility to the systematic exploitation of the flora, fauna, and peoples of the colonies. These organisms were constructed as simultaneously alien and available as scientific objects but also for the "economic gain, literary suggestion, and popular entertainment" efforts of European imperialism.[11]

Certainly, the colonial powers moved plants and animals around during the early years of their expansion.[12] Menageries, aviaries, and zoos had long been repositories of aristocratic collecting impulses that can similarly be dated to the fifteenth century. It was in the nineteenth century, though, that the project of imperialism and science dovetailed in new ways.[13] In 1854 Isidore Geoffroy Saint-Hilaire founded the *Société zoologique d'acclimatation* and then the *Jardin d'acclimatation* to study and promote the acclimatization and study of productive species in France. That same year, the *Akklimatisations-Verein* was established in Berlin. In the next decade, the Acclimatisation Society of the United Kingdom was established in London and then Amsterdam, Brussels, and Moscow also followed suit. These societies were sites in which the demonstration of metropolitan control over the colonies—or more generally, human control over nature—was acted out and reinforced alongside and intertwined with the practice of science.

Provincial centers and colonial capitals like Algiers, Melbourne, and Christchurch also established acclimatization societies. In these locations, however, species often flowed the other direction, from the metropole to the periphery, often in the form of livestock varieties. Historian Thomas Dunlap has argued that the systematic introduction and acclimatization of European flora and fauna to the colonies was motivated by aesthetics, nostalgia, and, to a lesser degree, the desires of sport hunters.[14]

But the introduction of the European starling was met by the American public with suspicion. Almost immediately, the European starling was understood to be a troublesome invader, in part due its noisy roosting behavior. Dunlap explains that, compared to New Zealand or Australia, the individuals in the United States that could afford to import species from Europe at the end of the nineteenth century were reading John Burroughs's and John Muir's vivid descriptions of the American landscapes as well as a well-established home-grown tradition of natural history and ornithological writing. That is, by the end of the nineteenth century, Americans did not necessarily, for example, long for the sounds of European songbirds. Very few saw—and heard—the introduction of the starling to the North American continent as the creation of what Alfred Crosby has termed a "neo-Europe."[15] Rather than follow Crosby's concept of the movement of organisms as deliberate and accidental consequences of European colonization, what he termed the "Columbian Exchange," the starling's story—its sounds, especially—hews closer to that of late nineteenth-century human immigrants.

The Calamity of an Ornithological Vacuum

In 1871, the American Acclimatization Society of New York City received its charter. Cincinnati, Ohio; Cambridge, Massachusetts; and Portland, Oregon, soon followed. The Cincinnati Acclimatization Society expressly sought to introduce all useful, insect-eating birds "as well as the best singers."[16] And indeed when the Cincinnati group introduced European robins, wagtails, skylarks, starlings, sparrows, thrushes, blackbirds, redwings, nightingales, various finches, siskins, tits, and crossbills to the wealthy Cincinnati enclave of Burnet Woods, the society's president, Andrew Erkenbrecher, described the woods as resonating "with a melody of thanksgiving never heard before and probably never heard since."[17] The Cincinnati Society of Natural History soon criticized the Cincinnati Acclimatization Society for introducing imbalance to the country's animal and vegetable life, insisting that energies should be focused on preserving the habitat of local species, and nature would "provide effectually against the calamity of an ornithological vacuum."[18]

Had Erkenbrecher and his compatriots heard an ornithological vacuum? Or did their actions contribute to one? Erkenbrecher had immigrated to Ohio from Germany. The founder of Portland, Oregon's Society for the Introduction of Useful Song Birds into Oregon, one C. F. Pfluger, was also a German immigrant. The Portland Song Bird Club, as the Society was commonly known, also spent several thousands of dollars in 1889 and again in 1892 to release thrushes, crossbills, siskins, finches, starlings, European robins, linnets, skylarks, woodlarks, mockingbirds, nightingales, and chickadees. The birds were imported directly from Germany and England to winter in a large enclosure before being released in the spring.[19] Apparently thousands of curious locals visited the birds before their release, and the Society recouped some of its costs by charging admission.[20]

Who were these people that visited the caged migrants? Were they also recent European transplants, like the leaders of the most active acclimatization societies?[21] We should consider whether the sounds of these immigrant birds were familiar to these visitors or not. Even if these were familiar sounds, they would have been juxtaposed against the hearer's auditory memory as well as mediated by the new setting; the sounds of a childhood were now flitting about in a large cage on the edge of a smallish Oregon town, muffled by constant drizzle.

If the nineteenth century was a century of acclimatization, it was also a century in which the sounds of nature were first systematically collected and documented, especially in the United States.[22] Naturalists such as Simeon Cheney, F. Schuyler Mathews, and Henry Oldys, documented their soundscapes, especially bird vocalizations, with musical notation.[23] By the 1930s, ornithologists sought to replace musical notation with a system that was not limited by the Western tuning system. For example, Aretas Saunders developed a graphic notation technique, culminating in his 1935 *Guide to Bird Songs*, that he believed better captured the birds' sliding between pitches.[24] Arthur Allen and Albert Brand were at the same time refining a method for recording bird vocalizations in the field using film, to be analyzed as a graphic document but also transferred to phonograph disc for ear-training.[25] The potentially changing sound of the starling is part of a larger narrative of the professionalization of ornithology as well as the growing public interest in birding.[26] It is also part of the growing scholarship on the history of sound collecting and archiving, which now increasingly intersects with media studies and the history of science and technology.[27]

The Sounds of Citizenship

In 1895, British naturalist William Henry Hudson explained that the merit of the starling's song "lies less in the quality of the sounds he utters than in their endless variety. . . . He will sometimes ramble on for an hour, whistling and warbling very agreeably, mingling his finer notes with chatterings and cluckings and squealings, and sounds as of snapping the fingers and of kissing, with many others quite indescribable."[28] At dusk, tens of thousands of the birds would fly in sweeping, rising visual rhythm, a breathtaking phenomenon now called a murmuration. Following the nightly dance, the flock descended into a greatly amplified clatter as each bird established its roost: "For an hour longer the wood is filled with an indescribable noise—a tangle of ten thousand penetrative voices, all together whistling, chattering, scolding, and singing."[29] This was the sound of the European starling in the Old World at the end of the nineteenth century.

In 1902, Ernest Harold Baynes, a birder who spent his early childhood in northern England, investigated an unfamiliar bird in the apple tree of a yard in Stamford, Connecticut. As he made his way up the tree he heard "a familiar but half-suppressed, rattling call . . . it was with great gladness that I recognized her as the starling, the old friend of my boyhood."[30] We might take this brief story as (thin) evidence that over several generations, the species' sound had not changed in the interim. Or that this individual human immigrant's auditory memory had not changed. Or both.

For the first couple years after the 1890 release, Schieffelin's birds had stuck pretty close, spotted no further than the outer boroughs of New York City. Then they were found on Long Island. In 1898, the *Buffalo Commercial* reported the bird in Buffalo. Already in 1897, Frank Chapman included the starling in his field guide (considered the first modern field guide).[31] He explained that it had been recently introduced and appeared to favor living uptown, most especially the eaves of the Museum of Natural History. Over the next twenty years they were found in Philadelphia, Boston, and Baltimore. Then Bessemer, Michigan, and Fort Wayne, Indiana. By 1937 they occupied every state east of the Mississippi River.[32] Ten years later they had made it over the Rocky Mountains, across the desert, and to California.

Even prior to Schieffelin's release, many were concerned about the introductions of European birds on new continents. Recall that the Cincinnati Society of Natural History cautioned that the introduction efforts of the Cincinnati Acclimatization Society was, "zoologically speaking, a wrong one, and that its application [was], in many instances, absolutely harmful, economically considered."[33] In 1891 *Littell's Living Age* offered a harsher judgement titled, "Some Evils of Acclimatization."[34] The piece focused on the cascade of disastrous events following the introduction of rabbits in Australia and the mongoose in Jamaica but also highlighted the introduction of birds in the United States. The work of acclimatizers, "usually

with the most beneficial intentions," but without consideration of the ultimate results of their actions, had effected "an enormous amount of evil."[35]

Recall that 1882 was the year the Chinese Exclusion Act was signed into
US law. The Act, which prohibited the immigration of all Chinese laborers,
was the culmination of nearly fifty years of efforts to restrict the immigration of a specific ethnic group. The Immigration Act of 1924 codified a series
of maneuvers of the intervening forty years to ban the immigration of non-
white peoples as well as limit, through a quota system, specific groups of
Europeans (Italians, Greeks, Poles, Slavs, and Eastern European Jews). In his
essay, "Eastenders Go West: English Sparrows, Immigrants, and the Nature
of Fear," Peter Coates analyzes the "eco-jingoism" of the "Sparrow War" to
argue that one of the ways in which Americans "have come to know nature is through nationality."[36] Introduced species making harsh, unfamiliar
sounds, and pushing out locals, functioned as a straightforward metaphor
for immigration. Or, in the case of late nineteenth-century rumors that
Italian immigrants ate songbirds, both newly-arrived humans and birds were
portrayed as attacking the local songbird population.[37] Coates describes the
Lacey Act of 1901 as a "sparrow exclusion act" of sorts.[38]

The Lacey Act, of course, applied to starlings as well, regulating their introduction, prohibiting their transportation across state lines, and empowering
the US Secretary of the Interior to restore vanishing native game and birds.[39]
Though less frequently than for the English sparrow, American newspapers
described the European starling as an alien invader as well. A 1910 article,
"Invasion of the Starling," for example, described the bird as "perhaps a del-
egate from the horde of foreign invasion sent to spy upon the land of the
sons of Eli."[40] A 1917 article on the enemies of house birds stated that the
European starlings must be "condemned for their pernicious interference
with native house birds."[41] Another example: in a 1924 notice titled, "Another
Undesirable Alien," in the *Hattiesburg American*, the starling was a "fellow-
alien" of the English sparrow.[42] Since its introduction, the article explained,
the starling had reproduced rapidly and targeted crops as it expanded westward. Additionally, the large flocks made "an outrageous clatter."

There was a flurry of coverage of the Secretary of Agriculture's 1910 ban
on the European starling, as well as the mongoose, the English sparrow, and
fruit-eating bats.[43] The sub-headline in the *Evening Star* ticked off the bird's
crimes: "Bird Imported from Europe an Undesirable Citizen/His Habits
Here Are Bad. . . Like English Sparrow, He Changed Mode of Life in Land
of Liberty."[44] In December of 1914, the same newspaper ran the headline,

"Grave Charges Against the European Starling," before explaining that while the USDA had recently found the birds to be helpfully insectivorous and not a threat to grain crops, the authors believed the bird maintained habits that could not "be overlooked in an estimation of his character."[45] "A European invasion has always been the nightmare of alarmists," they continued, "and never more than today, when all Europe is at war and seemingly couldn't invade the United States."[46] And yet much of the Northeastern Seaboard woke "to the shrill war-cry of bands of starlings." Additionally, the bird ate small fruits, threatening the orchardist and competing with native birds. Thus, they concluded, "the starling will have to go, even if the democratic administration doesn't believe in a protective tariff."[47]

Starlings were a noise nuisance in the city but in the country, they were seen as a threat to farmers' livelihoods. The birds were charged with eating young cherry, apple, and sweet corn crops and spreading disease among livestock, supposedly costing American agriculture hundreds of millions of dollars in damage annually.[48] In 1916, in an effort to determine the economic value of the European starling in the United States, the Bureau of the Biological Survey (part of the USDA) commenced a study of the contents of starling stomachs, supplemented by a survey of observed behavior distributed to birders, horticulturists, and farmers in regions with high starling populations.[49] After examining the contents of over 2,500 starling stomachs and finding mostly insects and wild fruit, the USDA declared the birds' food habits "to be either beneficial to man or of a neutral character."[50] In the bimonthly USDA Radio Service program, "Uncle Sam's Naturalists," several spots between 1929 and 1933 were devoted to defending the starling as beneficial. When judged by their food habits alone, these "immigrants" were, according to USDA scientists' scripts, "not bad citizens."[51]

But they were also, the USDA radio script acknowledged, "gangsters." They roosted in enormous flocks where they were least welcome, likely driving out local birds in the process.[52] During the fieldwork portion of its study, the USDA scientists observed a large roost of starlings and grackles. For nearly an hour, nearly eight thousand birds gathered, making an "incessant din—the starlings with their variety of whistles and rasping notes" that eventually quieted with nightfall. At the first light of day, the birds "would break out with a volume of song that terminated abruptly the slumbers of all light sleepers in the vicinity" as they departed in search of food.[53]

In the 1921 re-issue of his *Field Book of Wild Birds and Their Music*, Schuyler Mathews explained that the starling, because his notes "are an indescribable jumble of mixed tones including a few sweet whistles," is scarcely a singer.[54] He continued: "there is the twang of the jews'-harp [sic], the squeak of a rusty gate-hinge, the cluck of the hen, and the rattle of a wire spring in his tones— one can scarcely call them tunes!" For most of the other species in his guide, Mathews included a representation, sometimes several, of the bird's sounds in musical notation. It was not worth attempting such a thing for the starling, he explained, since his voice lacked distinct intervals. The bird was a polyglot with a language all his own, unmatchable by any sounds we know: "Being English, his song is a possible rendering of Thomson's 'Come gentle spring'; but to the American ear his tongue is hopelessly twisted."[55] Americans could not understand the starling's sound because he was foreign-born.

There were others, however, who attempted to naturalize the bird. The esteemed ornithologist, Frank Chapman, declared in 1925 that the European starling was an American citizen.[56] The American-born descendants of Schieffelin's release now numbered in the millions. Nature, Chapman noted, "has accorded him his 'papers' and he exercises all the privileges of citizenship."[57] He explained that the bird's impressive abundance was due to the fact that it occupied an empty ecological niche. He devoted most of his article to qualifying and defending the case against the starling's food habits (they eat more harmful insects than crops), competition with other species (mostly just isolated incidents in which flocking behavior can overwhelm other species), and impact on human life (again flocks' noise, poop). He ended with an invocation of the immigrant roots of most American citizens, whose forebears arrived by the Mayflower or Mauritania. The birds were also Americans. And, as such, they were "not only the products but expressions of their environments."[58]

The bird gained more public defenders by the 1930s even as it began to rapidly spread across the Great Plains. Marcia Bready, for example, devoted significant discussion in her study, *The European Starling on his Westward Way*, to the advanced musical abilities of the starling, most evident in its adherence to the diatonic scale.[59] In his regular column, "This and That," for the Washington D.C. *Evening Star*, Charles Tracewell defended the starling's persistent pursuit of unnecessary refinements as humanlike, explaining that the starling was "an essentially human bird."[60] In response to subsequent letter-writers describing the bird as an ugly nuisance that should be advertised as good to eat in order to reduce their numbers, Tracewell referred to the work of ornithologist R. W. Shilling, explaining that, first, there is not nearly enough meat on a starling for it to make a good foodstuff and second, the starling was a wonderful example "of all life to accommo-date itself to its environment."[61] In 1935, *The Eureka Mirror*'s coverage of the 1934 USDA Circular on the Japanese beetle in the United States was titled: "Disreputable Starling Enemy of Jap Beetles."[62] The short summary of the bird's insectivorous ways was followed with what was described as a Japanese proverb: "The heron's a saint when there are no fish about." Perhaps the enemy of one's enemy was not necessarily a friend, and some ambiv-alence about the (disreputable) starling remained. "Starling Seeks New Country to Conquer," the title of the *Midland Journal*'s announcement of the bird's arrival in North Dakota in September of 1935, was especially well-turned to exploit both ambivalence toward the starling and more general geopolitical anxieties.[63]

But, as Rachel Carson pointed out in the following decade, the starling was there to stay. The question was then whether it should still be regarded as an alien or be concluded "that his successful pioneering and his service in insect destruction entitle him to American citizenship."[64] This discourse surrounding the starling's status as immigrant highlights shifts in Americans' understanding of citizenship.[65] Both Chapman and Carson noted that the starling was comfortable in, and possibly even preferred, human-built environments. Carson charmingly described the starling as a commuter-in-reverse that ventured from the city into the countryside each morning to earn his bread.[66]

According to a 1943 analysis of Christmas bird count numbers since the bird's 1891 introduction, starlings spread faster across the prairie.[67] The spe-cies followed modern, industrialized agricultural techniques. Where there were big farms, there were big flocks of starlings. So by the middle of the twentieth century, the bird had been proven not guilty of agricultural damage and was instead celebrated as a helpful consumer of insect pests. In large numbers, roosting starlings remained a noisy annoyance but not a significant economic threat. Following World War II, complaints about roosts declined, likely a product of the refinement of urban abatement techniques. Similarly, systematic studies by various government agencies and wildlife ecologists determined the species was far more likely to eat insects than crops, and thus more of a help than a pest. Farmers no longer heard the low hum of an eve-ning murmuration as a menace. The modern tractor with closed cab, by the way, can expose the operator to noise levels of about 85 decibels. A combine harvester gets close to 100 decibels. Cab-less tractors, sounds of a workshop, grain dryers, chain saws, and even pig squeals can get above 100 decibels.

Only a very large murmuration of starlings would be louder than a modern workaday farm.

The Sounds of Abatement

The starlings' sounds became interchangeable with human-made sounds. The birds were introduced by humans. They were—and continue to be—meaningful to humans because of their agricultural impact and strike danger (more on this later). If the sound of the starling indicated the presence of the bird, then so did the sound of combine harvesters, tractors, and so on. And vice versa. We might consider their sounds to be interchangeable. Over the course of the first half of the twentieth century, simultaneous to the acclimatization of the bird's song, the sounds of starling abatement began to populate the landscape, bound to the presence (in an effort to create absence) of the starling.

Roman candles (120 decibels), bells, shotgun blasts (170 decibels), and in one case, rockets attached to teddy bears, were used in the first decades of the twentieth century to deter starling roosts.[68] The USDA offered alternative techniques to prevent roosting—hanging wire screens, eliminating ledges, trimming trees—but maintained that startling flocks with sound was the most effective means of reducing nuisance roosts.[69] Though limited by safety considerations in urban areas, "shooting with powder and shot" was the most frightening measure, according to the USDA.[70] Success required vigilance, up to six successive nights in a row, always when the birds first arrived in early evening and continuing until after dark. Blank shells—if the safety of humans or other, federally protected species, was a concern—were also reasonably effective, as was an acetylene "flash gun."[71]

Even if the eight-thousand-bird roosts were an "incessant din," surely the regular cacophony of fireworks or gunfire was just as noisy. More recently, propane-powered cannons have been used to remotely produce bird-disturbing explosions (150 decibels). Across the arc of starling abatement techniques of the long twentieth century, I want to underscore how noisy all these programs were. Silencing starlings was anything but quiet. Most of these techniques sought to startle and harass the birds with sound. As was already known in the 1920s, though, the effectiveness of these sounds quickly declined as the birds became accustomed (acclimated?) to the disruptions and subsequently ignored them.[72] But when these technologies were effective, these sounds replaced those of the starlings. A chorus of squawks and buzzes might indicate an expansion of the species' range but hot on their stubby tails was a series of additional sounds, from banging cans to fireworks to the blast of shotguns. The human-made sounds of abatement—sometimes justified by economic imperatives, sometimes not—overwhelmed the sounds of starling murmurations, the undulating flocks in flight. And in this way, sound was employed to re-assert human control in shared spaces.

On October 4, 1960, Eastern Air Lines Flight 375, a four-engine propellor Lockheed Electra, took off from Logan airport in Boston. Only seconds after takeoff the plane struck a cloud of starlings and crashed into Boston Harbor. Only ten of the seventy-two individuals on board survived, making it the deadliest bird strike in American aviation history. Two weeks later, another Eastern Airlines flight struck starlings on the runway but was able to safely stop. The pilot described the sound of the birds hitting the front of the airplane as resembling machine gun fire, "Just brrrrummm!"[73]

This "brrrrummm!" of plane strikes was a new cause for concern. Passenger air travel increased exponentially following World War II, both in frequency and geographical reach. Airstrips with regular national carrier service penetrated rural spaces. Bird strikes currently cost the civil aviation industry nearly $937 million per year and have been credited with 255 fatalities in the last twenty-five years alone.[74] Low-flying jets, by the way, can emit sounds as great as 100 decibels.

The now century-old technique of frightening the birds with sound remains the main strategy for preventing bird strikes at airports, still with shotguns, sometimes with air cannons. In 2013, several researchers at the College of William and Mary investigated an alternative protocol of disturbing birds with silence. The team performed a series of experiments using nonlinear ultrasonic parametric arrays that overlapped with the frequency of starling vocalizations.[75] Ghazi Mahjoub's lab found that the use of this "sonic net" reduced bird presence in a given feed area by 46 percent. Further assessment confirmed that the sonic net disrupted the ability of the birds to respond to alarm calls. The researchers suspect that the inability to communicate, most especially the inability to hear alarm calls, motivated the birds to move on to different feeding areas. In the following year, John Swaddle's lab performed another series of experiments with a modified speaker setup at an active airfield near Newport News, Virginia.[76] Point counts before and during the four-week deployment of the sonic net, varying the volume from 65 to above 80 decibels, resulted in up to an 82 percent reduction in bird presence. Both of these experiments built on earlier ecological studies that showed that human-generated sounds, such as road or machinery noise, displaced and/or decreased the fitness of bird species, especially when the sounds' frequencies overlapped with that of the birds.[77] Mahjoub and Swaddle's labs sought to mobilize these observations into a deterrent technology, replacing the sound of a starling murmuration or the "brrrrummm!" of a collision with a disruptive sound that humans heard as silence. The ethics of adding so much sound to an environment that the individuals of this gregarious and social species can only stand around blinking at each other is an open question.

Mortimer: Mimicry as Curse

The sound of the starling has also at times been heard as human speech. In Shakespeare's *Henry IV, Part 1*, the starling's imitation skills were used by Hotspur as a curse upon the King. The bird was to follow him about, repeating "Mortimer" to keep him enraged. The starling's mimicry skills could exacerbate an underlying anxiety. Likewise, Plutarch wrote that, because of the bird's ability to learn to talk, they could be "patrons and advocates on behalf of other creatures."[78] In what ways can the starlings, through their mimicry, articulate the human experience of immigration at the beginning of the century? Tracing out the changing discourse on the starling as mimic also helps us understand one of the underlying anxieties around immigrants to America: authenticity. Rey Chow's application of Walter Benjamin's discussion of the power of mimesis in sonically producing similarity and community between things to a sociopolitical framework, I think, helps us draw further connections between starling sounds and the immigrant experience.[79] To name something was a form of mimesis for Benjamin. For Chow, to name some-*one* (an objectification process not unlike documenting and defining the extent of the "starling problem"), establishes a boundary zone in which slippage between the sounds and accents and syntax of immigrant and non-immigrant, native- and non-native speakers, authentic and inauthentic languaging, is possible. At the end of the nineteenth century, the starling was critiqued as a poor mimic, not nearly so skilled as the mockingbird. Then the species was credited with credibly stealing the sounds of native birds, thereby displacing them, and was attacked for destroying local bird populations. By the end of the twentieth century, the starling was celebrated by neuroscientists as a model mimic, and like a good citizen, contributed its skills to the noble project of science. This evolving judgement of the starling's mimicry corresponded to the shifting status of the bird from outside invader to helpful pest-gobbling citizen and from an "outrageous clatter" and "incessant din" to—in the case of the sonic net study sites—completely silent. Had the starling truly acclimated or just gotten better at mimicking American sounds? Had they become native speakers or had the ears of listeners changed?

Many ornithologists in the first decades of the twentieth century debated the nature of mimicry, which was bound up in a larger discussion about human language acquisition.[80] Related also were various efforts to ascribe true mimicry skills to various species, from the mockingbird to the black-capped warblers to starlings. Recall, for example, that Mathews insisted that the starling was a polyglot but not a mimic.[81] Charles Townsend believed the species' powers of mimicry varied greatly between individuals.[82] Further, he believed that the ability of at least some starlings to mimic American birds was evidence that their imitation came from individual mimicry rather than an inherited repertoire.[83]

The British ornithologist Hudson suspected that the starling's imitation abilities were overstated and perhaps even nonexistent. Instead, the variety and range of the birds' sounds were so great that it was possible to recognize the calls of other birds in the chatter.[84] Chapman too suspected that the starling's reputation for skilled mimicry was something closer to a case of hearing what one was listening for. What birders were alleging to be imitation might instead be, Chapman continued, "resemblances between the starling's natural notes and those of the American bird they recall."[85]

Chapman found the starling's ability to mimic to be a betrayal of sorts. He explained the thrill of seeing a smudge on the horizon heralding the arrival of spring only to realize that it was not, in fact, a flock of wood pewees but a flock of starlings. It was a "mimetic travesty" he said.[86] There were ecological implications to be sure, as starlings potentially displaced these birds both physically and sonically. But where did the travesty of mimesis lie? Chapman resented the "intrusion" of the starling's "strange notes" in the spring chorus, especially its imitation of the wood pewee in February, far too early for that bird to be in New York.[87] Chapman's concern is representative of birders in the early twentieth century, generally. They worried that the starling would supplant native songbirds both through their aggressive behavior and mimicry—skillfully imitating the plaintive "pee-a-wee" whistle of the wood pewee, the bluebird, cowbird, bobwhite, and chickadee.[88] The starling could also don the auditory mask of the beloved songs of the catbird and brown thrasher.

In his popular 1935 sound-based field guide, *A Guide to Bird Songs*, Aretas Saunders explained that the starling, since its arrival in America, had learned to imitate nearly forty species of American bird.[89] In his graphic representation of the starling's song (see Figure 12.1), Saunders included hash marks, ascending and descending lines, timbral descriptors such as "squeaky" and "clear, loud whistle," onomatopoeia ("hāy ēē ō-ō-ō" or "hay whēēo!"), and "Imitation of the Cowbird" and "Imitation of the Wood Pewee." Saunders built the voices of other species directly into the voice of the starling. This would in turn, I would argue, inform how the starling would be heard by birders using Saunders's guide in the field. To an ornithologist training from Saunders's guide, the "pee-a-wee" of the starling would not be heard as acclimatization to the North American soundscape but as theft.

There is some anthropocentric slippage here. Birders worried the mimicked sounds were replacing the original, authentic sounders. USDA scientists described the starling as "a mimic par excellence" that fooled observers who——as remains often the case—depended on sound alone to identify a bird.[90] But it was the *human* ears that were tricked. The starlings were not necessarily fooling other species with their mimicry. Indeed, the USDA report determined that while individual starlings may take over specific dooryard nests, they did not threaten entire species on the continent; nor, by extension, the soundscape.[91]

If ornithologists began the process of objectification through their documentation of the bird's sound at the end of the nineteenth century, linguists

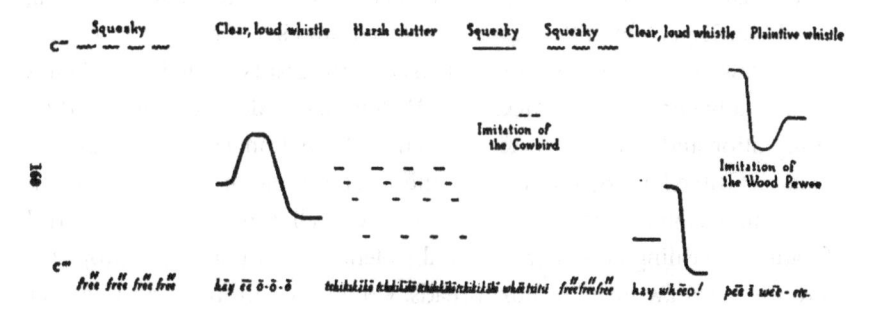

Figure 12.1 Portion of a song of the starling. Aretas Saunders, *A Guide to Bird Songs*, 160.

and cognitive scientists have recently rendered the bird's mimicry skills into a scientific object. Neurophysiologist Timothy Gentner recently demonstrated that starlings were able to recognize song patterns far better than tamarins (Chomsky, Hauser, and Fitch's research object), and at least as capably as the psychology undergrads at the University of California, San Diego.[92] The ability to recognize acoustic patterns accurately through the use of syntactic rules is considered necessary to be able to produce new utterances that are comprehensible to other members of the same community.[93] That is, the capacity to classify acoustic sequences is critical for convincing mimesis. So, a century after leading ornithologists dismissed the starling as a mediocre imitator, the bird is now the model species for understanding mimesis.

Conclusion

Schieffelin's starling release was not linked to Shakespeare until 1948, in Edwin Way Teale's *Days Without Time: Adventures of a Naturalist*, again without evidence. Schieffelin's story was made quaintly colonial precisely as decolonization was underway and precisely when the threat of the European starling—to crops, to the soundscape—appeared to be neutralized.[94] "Murmuration" has described grumbly, low utterances since Chaucer. The term has been ascribed to starling behavior since the fifteenth century— "A murmeracion of stares" in William Caxton's *Hors Shepe & G.*—but was only re-embraced and popularized in the middle of the twentieth.[95] It seems more than coincidental that the story of the starlings' release on the continent was made charming and the sound of the enormous flocks undulating on the wing was made romantic at the same time. In 1948, the enormous influx of Europeans seeking permanent residence in the United States following World War II prompted the passage of the country's first refugee and resettlement law. In 1952, the exclusion of Asian immigrants to the United States was formally ended by the McCarran-Walter Act. A decade later, the 1965 Immigration and Nationality Act ended the 1924 national origin quotas.

Harriet Ritvo has argued that both the successes and the failures of North American acclimatization efforts undermined belief in the human control of nature, revealing an underlying ambivalence about that larger project.[96] Here we can draw together our threads. Could the European starling ever acclimate to sound like—to be—an American? By the mid-twentieth century the USDA granted the bird clemency, declaring the species economically valuable. Birders had ecological concerns that the starling would push out native birds, but auditorily, they could not necessarily distinguish one from the other. And if the rapid decline in media coverage of starlings by the 1940s is any indication, once techniques for preventing starling roosts became effective, the public appeared to lose interest in the birds and their spread. So, to answer my initial question of whether sounds could acclimate, I think we have arrived at a partial answer at least. The sound of the starling became indistinguishable from native sounds. The European starling could be mistaken for the wood pewee. Or, to push my point about the colonization of non-human spaces a bit further, the sound of the European starling can be—was—eventually interchangeably heard with the sounds of the spread of American cities, of the growth of industrialized farming, of the expansion of passenger air travel. The sound of acclimatization was as dependent on the hearer's as the sound's source.

How do hearers acclimate to new sounds? This chapter has covered some possible examples of the process: through the sonic domination of human–starling shared spaces by human sounds; through the retelling of histories with threats neutralized (immigrant-makes-good stories); and through the objectification of the unsettling quality of inauthenticity. What about the acclimatization of the starling's sound itself? The sound of a starling was: an agreeable whistling and warbling, a murmuration, an outrageous clatter, a combine harvester, a shotgun firing, a spluttering jet engine, other more beloved birds, and silence.

Notes

I would like to thank Scott Wooley, recent graduate of Mississippi State University Department of History PhD program, for his assistance researching this paper, Brian Dorr and Ron Johnson of the United States Department of Agriculture (USDA) for their extended tutorial on European starling management techniques when we were supposed to be registering voters, and the ERC-funded "Sound and Materialism in the 19th Century" project at Cambridge University for funding the fruitful workshops and conferences that led to this edited volume.

1. This claim flies in the face of some conventional assumptions about population genetics. Despite the small gene pool of the original sixty birds Schieffelin released, the subsequent population is remarkably—spectacularly, really—robust.

2. Old World actors had been performing the Bard's plays in the New World since 1752, when Lewis Hallam's London Company of Comedians began to travel regularly to Virginia. By the middle of the nineteenth century, American-born Shakespeareans

fueled the expansion of the reading and watching of Shakespeare's plays and an American interpretation. By the end of the nineteenth century, Shakespeare had been made American. Alden Vaughan and Virginia Vaughan, *Shakespeare in America* (Oxford, UK: Oxford University Press, 2012).

3. In the last ten years alone, the Shakespeare lover's actions have been mentioned in *Smithsonian Magazine*, *Scientific American*, the BBC, the Library of Congress blog, *Medium*, and *Aeon* essays. "Eugene Schieffelin and Shakespeare's Birds" is Bad Idea #14 on the Human Echoes YouTube Channel.

4. John Phillips, *Wild Birds Introduced or Transplanted in North America*, Technical Bulletin no. 61 (Washington, D.C.: United States Department of Agriculture, 1928).

5. American Acclimatization Society, New York, *Charter and By-Laws of the American Acclimatization Society* (New York: G. W. Averill, 1871), 5; The bird-releasing activities of the AAS are summarized in "American Acclimatization Society," *New York Times*, November 15, 1877, 2.

6. For some discussion of the lack of evidence of Schieffelin's Shakespearian motivations see Peter Coates, "Eastenders Go West: English Sparrows, Immigrants, and the Nature of Fear," *Journal of American Studies* 39/3 (2005), 431–462; and Harriet Ritvo, "Going Forth and Multiplying: Animal Acclimatization and Invasion," *Environmental History* 17/2 (2012), 404–414.

7. Peter Coates, *American Perceptions of Immigrant and Invasive Species: Strangers on the Land* (Berkeley: University of California Press, 2006).

8. Rachel Mundy, *Animal Musicalities: Birds, Beasts, and Evolutionary Listening* (Middletown, CT: Wesleyan University Press, 2018).

9. Warwick Anderson, "Climates of Opinion: Acclimatization in Nineteenth-Century France and England," *Victorian Studies* 35/2 (1992), 135–157.

10. Anderson, "Climates of Opinion"; Thomas Dunlap, "Remaking the Land: The Acclimatization Movement and Anglo Ideas of Nature," *Journal of World History* 8/2 (1997), 303–319; Michael Osborne, *Nature, the Exotic, and the Science of French Colonialism* (Bloomington: Indiana University Press, 1994); Ritvo, "Going Forth and Multiplying"; Douglas Weiner, "The Roots of 'Michurinism': Transformist Biology and Acclimatization as Currents in Russian Life Sciences," *Annals of Science* 42/3 (1985), 243–260.

11. Anderson, "Climates of Opinion," 136–137.

12. Alfred Crosby, *The Columbian Exchange: Biological and Cultural Consequences of 1492* (Westport, CT: Greenwood Publishing Company, 1972); Alfred Crosby, *Ecological Imperialism: The Biological Expansion of Europe 900–1900* (Cambridge, UK: Cambridge University Press, 1986).

13. Warwick Anderson, *Colonial Pathologies: American Tropical Medicine, Race, and Hygiene in the Philippines* (Durham, NC: Duke University Press, 2006); Warwick Anderson, "From Subjugated Knowledge to Conjugated Subjects: Science and Globalization, or Postcolonial Studies of Science?" *Postcolonial Studies* 12/4 (2009), 389–400; Projit Bihari Mukharji, *Nationalizing the Body: The Medical Market, Print and Daktari Medicine* (London: Anthem Press, 2009); Michael Osborne,

"Acclimatizing the World: A History of the Paradigmatic Colonial Science," *Osiris* 15 (2000), 135–151; Marissa Petrou, "Apes, Skulls, and Drums: Using Images to Make Ethnographic Knowledge in Imperial Germany," *British Journal for the History of Science* 51/1 (2018), 69–98; Suman Seth, "Putting Knowledge in its Place: Science, Colonialism, and the Postcolonial," *Postcolonial Studies* 12/4 (2009), 373–388; Harriet Ritvo, "Zoological Nomenclature and the Empire of Victorian Science," in *Victorian Science in Context*, ed. Bernard Lightman (Chicago: University of Chicago Press, 1997), 223–253; Andrew Zimmerman, "Adventures in the Skin Trade: German Anthropology and Colonial Corporeality," in *Worldly Provincialism: German Anthropology in the Age of Empire*, ed. H. Glenn Penny and Matti Bunzl (Ann Arbor: University of Michigan Press, 2003), 156–178.

14. Dunlap, "Remaking the Land," 307–308.

15. The European starling was also introduced to Australia, Tasmania, New Zealand, and South Africa. Here I refer to Alfred Crosby's concept of "neo-Europes" in his *Ecological Imperialism*.

16. Quoted in Coates, *American Perceptions of Immigrant and Invasive Species*, 35.

17. Quoted in Christopher Lever, *They Dined on Eland: The Stories of Acclimatisation Societies* (London: Quiller Press, 1992), 186.

18. "Proceedings of the Society," *Journal of the Cincinnati Society of Natural History* 4/4 (1881), 341–343.

19. Or at least a December 8, 1907, notice in the Portland *Oregonian* about a later release said as much. Quoted in "Editorials," *Condor* 10 (January 1908), 52.

20. Simeon Cheney, *Wood Notes Wild: Notations of Bird Music* (Boston: Lee and Shepard, 1892), 182–184.

21. The 1928 USDA report on non-native bird species describes the twenty-year period beginning in the late 1860s in which European songbirds were introduced "largely through the enthusiasm of German-American bird fanciers and various cage-bird clubs." Phillips, *Wild Birds*, 4.

22. John Bevis has documented much of this impulse to collect and imitate birdsong in his *Aaaaw to Zzzzzd: The Words of Birds: North America, Britain, and Northern Europe* (Cambridge, MA: MIT Press, 2010).

23. Cheney, *Wood Notes Wild*; F. Schuyler Mathews, *Field Book of Wild Birds and Their Music* (New York: G. P. Putnam's Sons, 1904/1921); Henry Oldys, "Parallel Growth of Bird and Human Music," *Harper's Monthly* 105 (1902), 474–478; Henry Oldys, "The Music of Bird Songs," *Harper's Monthly* 113 (1906), 723–729; Henry Oldys, "Music of Man and Bird," *Harper's Monthly* 114 (1907), 766–771; Maurice Thompson, *By-Ways and Bird Notes* (New York: John B. Alden, 1885); Maurice Thompson, *Sylvan Secrets, and Bird-Songs and Books* (New York: John B. Alden, 1887); J. Williams, "The Study of Bird Songs," *Condor* 4 (1902), 12–14.

24. Aretas Saunders, *A Guide to Bird Songs: Descriptions and Diagrams of the Songs and Singing Habits of Land Birds of Northeastern United States* (New York: D. Appleton-Century Co., 1935).

25. Joeri Bruyninckx has shown how the acceptance of these sound-recording techniques—and sound recordings as scientific objects—as an authoritative and

reliable way to study wildlife was anything but simple. Joeri Bruyninckx, *Listening in the Field: Recording and the Science of Birdsong* (Cambridge, MA: MIT Press, 2018).

26. Mark Barrow, *A Passion for Birds: American Ornithology after Audubon* (Princeton, NJ: Princeton University Press, 2000); Thomas Dunlap, *In the Field, Among the Feathered: A History of Birders and their Guides* (Oxford, UK: Oxford University Press, 2011); Daniel Lewis, *The Feathery Tribe: Robert Ridgway and the Modern Study of Birds* (New Haven, CT: Yale University Press, 2012).

27. Erika Brady, *A Spiral Way: How the Phonograph Changed Ethnography* (Jackson: University Press of Mississippi, 1999); Brian Hochman, *Savage Preservation: The Ethnographic Origins of Modern Media Technology* (Minneapolis: University of Minnesota Press, 2014); Carolyn Birdsall and Viktoria Tkaczyk, eds., "Listening to the Archive: Sound Data in the Humanities and Sciences," special issue, *Technology and Culture* 60/2 supplement (2019).

28. William Hudson, *British Birds* (London: Longmans, Green, and Co., 1895), 155.

29. Hudson, *British Birds*, 156.

30. Ernest Baynes, "Bird Immigrants," *New Haven Morning Journal and Courier*, February 15, 1902.

31. Frank Chapman, *Handbook of Birds of Eastern North America* (New York: Appleton, 1897), 259.

32. Leonard Wing, "The Spread of the Starling and English Sparrow," *Auk* 60/1 (1943), 74–87.

33. F. Langdon, "Introduction of European Birds," *Journal of the Cincinnati Society of Natural History* 4/4 (1881), 342–343.

34. "Some Evils of Acclimatization," *Littell's Living Age* 189 (1891), 823–824.

35. "Some Evils of Acclimatization," 824.

36. Coates, "Eastenders Go West." Coates borrows "eco-jingoism" from David Matless, *Landscape and Englishness* (London: Reaktion Books, 1998). Presently, some scientists are reckoning with the way in which such terms as "invasive," "exotic," and "non-native" perpetuate cultural assumptions of difference and xenophobia. See Mark Woods and Paul Moriarty, "Strangers in a Strange Land: The Problem of Exotic Species," *Environmental Values* 10/2 (2001), 173–191; and Robert Colautti and Hugh MacIsaac, "A Neutral Terminology to Define 'Invasive' Species," *Diversity and Distributions* 10/2 (2004), 135–141.

37. Coates, "Eastenders Go West," 457.

38. Ibid., 452.

39. The Lacey Act was used in its early years to crack down on illegal hunting. Now it is predominantly used to control the illegal importation of organisms.

40. "Invasion of the Starling," *Washington Herald*, November 6, 1910. This same phrase was used again in "Starling Invasion in the City of Elms," *San Francisco Call*, December 27, 1910.

41. "Enemies of House Birds," *Connecticut Western News*, May 3, 1917.

42. "Another Undesirable Alien," *Hattiesburg American*, February 23, 1924.

43. "Starling is Barred," *Evening Star*, April 7, 1910; "Ban Placed on European Starlings," *Daily Capital Journal*, April 29, 1910; "Invasion of the Starling."

44. "Starling is Barred."
45. "Grave Charges Against the European Starling," *Evening Star*, December 8, 1914.
46. Ibid.
47. Ibid.
48. David Pimental, Lori Lach, Rodolfo Zoniga, and Doug Morrison, "Environmental and Economic Costs of Nonindigenous Species in the United States," *BioScience* 50 (2000), 53–65.
49. The *Evening Journal* explained that the USDA determined the value of an organism to society by examining its stomach. "Birds Must Feast on Bugs to Get Uncle Sam's Approval," *Evening Journal*, February 3, 1915.
50. E. Kalmbach and I. Gabrielson, *Economical Value of the Starling in the United States*, Bulletin No. 868, (Washington, D.C.: United States Department of Agriculture, 1921), 59.
51. "With Uncle Sam's Naturalists" script, released May 9, 1930, *USDA Radio Service* (1930), 2. US Department of Agriculture, National Agricultural Library. Available on archive.org: https://archive.org/details/withunclesamsnat1930unit/page/n61/mode/2up, accessed February 1, 2023.
52. Ibid.
53. Kalmbach and Gabrielson, *Economical Value of the Starling*, 54.
54. Mathews, *Field Book of Wild Birds*, 276. The original edition did not include the starling, but in 1921 Mathews expanded his original text and added several birds.
55. Mathews, *Field Book of Wild Birds*, 276.
56. Chapman, "The European Starling as an American Citizen," *Natural History* 25/5 (1925), 480–485.
57. Ibid., 480.
58. Ibid., 484.
59. Marcia Bready, *The European Starling on his Westward Way* (New York: Knickerbocker Press, 1929), 58–80.
60. Charles Tracewell, "This and That," *Evening Star*, November 13, 1936.
61. Charles Tracewell, "This and That," *Evening Star*, November 29, 1940.
62. C. Hadley, *General Information About the Japanese Beetle in the United States*, Circular No. 332 (Washington, D.C.: United States Department of Agriculture, 1934). Newspaper coverage of the report ran in several newspapers that fall, all titled, "Disreputable Starling Enemy of Jap Beetles." The *Eureka Mirror* (November 1, 1935) is the only one to include the Japanese proverb.
63. "Starlings Seek New Country to Conquer," *Midland Journal*, September 27, 1935.
64. Rachel Carson, "How about Citizenship Papers for the Starling?" *Nature Magazine* (June–July, 1939), 317–319.
65. Peder Roberts and Dolly Jørgensen, "Animals as Instruments of Norwegian Imperial Authority in the Interwar Arctic," *Journal for the History of Environment and Society* 1 (2016), 65–87; Dolly Jørgensen, "Rethinking Rewilding," *Geoforum* 65 (2015), 482–488.
66. Carson, "How about Citizenship Papers for the Starling?," 317.
67. Wing, "Spread of the Starling and English Sparrow," 78.

68. "City at War on Starlings," *New York Times*, July 29, 1914.

69. E. Kalmbach, *Suggestions for Combating Starling Roosts*, Wildlife Research and Management Leaflet BS-81 (Washington, D.C.: United States Department of Agriculture, 1937). The USDA also described several methods for the lethal destruction of starling flocks through shooting, trapping, gassing, or poisoning but did not recommend these as worth the money or time.

70. Ibid., 6.

71. Ibid., 6–7.

72. George Linz, H. Jeffrey Homan, Shannon Gaulker, Linda Penry, and William Bleier, "European Starlings: A Review of an Invasive Species with Far-Reaching Impacts," in *Managing Vertebrate Invasive Species: Proceedings of An International Symposium*, ed. Gary W. Witmer, Will C. Pitt, and Kathleen A. Fagerstone (Fort Collins, CO: USDA/APHIS Wildlife Services, National Wildlife Research Center, 2007), 378–386.

73. W. H. Jenkins's testimony in 1961 Civil Aeronautics Board hearings, quoted in Michael Kalafatas, *Bird Strike: The Crash of the Boston Electra* (Waltham, MA: Brandeis University Press, 2010), 59.

74. John R. Allan, "The Costs of Bird Strikes and Bird Strike Prevention," in *Human Conflicts with Wildlife: Economic Considerations: Proceedings of the Third NWRC Special Symposium*, ed. Larry Clark et al. (Fort Collins, CO: National Wildlife Research Center, 2000), 147–153; Travis DeVault, Bradley Blackwell, and Jerrold Belant, eds., *Wildlife in Airport Environments: Preventing Animal-Aircraft Collisions through Science-Based Management* (Baltimore: Johns Hopkins University Press, 2013); J. Thorpe, "100 Years of Fatalities and Destroyed Civil Aircraft Due to Bird Strikes," in *Proceedings of the 30th International Bird Strike Committee* (June 25–29, 2012), Stavanger, Norway.

75. Ghazi Mahjoub, Mark Hinders, and John Swaddle, "Using a 'Sonic Net' to Deter Pest Bird Species: Excluding European Starlings from Food Sources by Disrupting their Acoustic Communication," *Wildlife Society Bulletin* 39/2 (2015), 326–333.

76. John Swaddle, Dana Moseley, Mark Hinders, and Elizabeth Smith, "A Sonic Net Excludes Birds from an Airfield: Implications for Reducing Bird Strike and Crop Losses," *Ecological Applications* 26/2 (2016), 339–345.

77. Clinton Francis, Catherine Ortega, and Alexander Cruz, "Noise Pollution Changes Avian Communities and Species Interactions," *Current Biology* 19/16 (2009), 1415–1419; Clinton Francis, Catherine Ortega, and Alexander Cruz, "Noise Pollution Filters Bird Communities Based on Vocal Frequency," *PLoS ONE* 6/11 (2011), e27052; Sarah E. Goodwin and W. Gregory Shriver, "Effects of Traffic Noise on Occupancy Patterns of Forest Birds," *Conservation Biology* 25/2 (2011), 406–411; Georg Klump, "Bird Communication in the Noisy World" in *Ecology and Evolution of Acoustic Communication in Birds*, ed. Donald Kroodsma and Edward Miller (Ithaca, NY: Cornell University Press, 1996), 321–338.

78. Plutarch, *Plutarch's Morals*, vol. 5, corrected and revised by William Goodwin (Boston: Little, Brown and Co., 1905), 188–189.

79. Rey Chow, *Not Like a Native Speaker: On Languaging as a Postcolonial Experience* (New York: Columbia University Press, 2014).

80. Lloyd Morgan, *Animal Behavior*, 2nd ed. (London: E. Arnold, 1908); Donald Dickey, "The Mimetic Aspect of the Mocker's Song," *Condor* 24/5 (1922), 153–157; Charles Townsend, "Mimicry of Voice in Birds," *The Auk* 41/4 (1924), 541–52; Charles Witchell, *The Evolution of Bird-Song, with Observations on the Influence of Heredity and Imitation* (London: A. and C. Black, 1896).

81. Mathews, *Field Book of Wild Birds*, 276.

82. Townsend, "Mimicry of Voice in Birds," 544.

83. Townsend inquired of an English birder whether his Old World starlings ever made a sound similar to the eastern wood pewee; the birder confirmed they did not. Townsend, "Mimicry of Voice in Birds," 543–544.

84. Hudson, *British Birds*, 155–156.

85. Chapman, "The European Starling as an American Citizen," 485.

86. Ibid., 484.

87. Frank Chapman, "Editorial," *Bird-Lore* 2/2 (1909), 91. Similar concerns can be found in May Cooke, *The Spread of the European Starling in North America (to 1928)*, Circular No. 40 (Washington, D.C.: United States Department of Agriculture, 1928).

88. The starling was also known to mimic the red-winged blackbird, grackle, field sparrow, flicker, blue jay, Carolina wren, and English sparrow. Kalmbach and Gabrielson, "Economical Value of the Starling," 9; Saunders, *A Guide to Bird Songs*, 159–161.

89. Saunders, *A Guide to Bird Songs*, 160.

90. Kalmbach and Gabrielson, "Economical Value of the Starling," 9.

91. Ibid., 58.

92. Timothy Gentner, Kimberly Fenn, Daniel Margoliash, and Howard Nusbaum, "Recursive Syntactic Pattern Learning by Songbirds," *Nature* 440/7088 (2006), 1204–1207.

93. Charles Hockett, "The Origin of Speech," *Scientific American* 203 (1960), 88–111; Noam Chomsky, *Syntactic Structures* (Berlin: de Gruyter, 1957).

94. The study, viewing, and performance of Shakespeare was also being decolonized, as it were, in this period. New York City's Shakespeare in the Park program, for example, was established by Joseph Papp in 1954 to offer free performances in Central Park, embracing diverse ethnicities, accents, and interpretations by actors, in order to increase the accessibility of Shakespeare's works.

95. The earliest reference to the flocking of starlings is apparently in William Caxton's printing of John Lydgate's *Hors Shepe & G.* [The Horse, the Sheep, and the Goose] in the 1470s. See "murmuration," no. 2, *The Oxford English Dictionary*, vol. 6, L-M (Oxford, UK: Oxford University Press, 1978 [1933]), 774.

96. Ritvo, "Going Forth and Multiplying," 8–9.

13

Gandhi's Silence

Faisal Devji

Si, quand le peuple sufissamment informé délibère, les Citoyens n'avoient aucune communication entre eux, du grand nombre de petites différences résulteroit toujours la volonté générale & la délibération seroit toujours bonne.

If citizens deliberate when adequately informed and without any communication among themselves, the general will would always result from the great number of slight differences, and the resolution would always be good.

—Jean-Jacques Rousseau, *The Social Contract*
(1762, Book II, Section 3)

Democracy is very often linked with voice, speech, and communication, just as tyranny is defined by silence and obedience. Yet silence also lies at the heart of freedom, represented in democratic practice by the secret ballot.[1] As an institutional form the secret ballot is meant to guarantee the voter's anonymity as well as liberty from the undue influence of external forces. But it possesses another dimension as well, one which has to do with the coincidental character of the democratic majority. If such majorities are to reflect anything more than the identity, organization, and prejudice of the largest or most powerful social groups, they must be composed of voters who have arrived at their decisions independently and so in silence.

Democratic majorities are constituted by a logic of coincidence, with the general will understood as a statistical average rather than a social identity. Its legitimacy depends upon this will representing the decisions of a range of social identities brought together for a number of sometimes incommensurable reasons. However far the working of elections falls from this logic, it remains the only justification for democracy as a political form. But this

Faisal Devji, *Gandhi's Silence* In: *Acoustics of Empire*. Edited by: Peter McMurray and Priyasha Mukhopadhyay, Oxford University Press. © Oxford University Press 2024. DOI: 10.1093/oso/9780197553787.003.0014 means the voice, speech, and communication that make democracy possible can also endanger it by unduly influencing voters. Their decisions are then deprived of autonomy and integrity far more insidiously than through bribery or threats, with the elimination or ritualization of silence destroying the individual's very capacity for freedom.

At issue is the character of political debate as a kind of *rehearsed conversation*, one in which social identities and passions are mobilized to prevent the formation of a statistical average by way of silent, solitary, and even ignorant decisions. While under ideal conditions (for someone like Jean-Jacques Rousseau, as suggested above) interests are meant to cancel each other out precisely in order to produce such an average, their institutionalization in decision-making bodies, from juries and unions to political parties and parliaments, accomplishes the opposite. It is not social identities that are themselves problematic, but rather the party structure that appropriates them to create collective passions. For the political party produces pre-digested arguments and talking points in which individual reasoning is not only set aside for its voters, but actively forbidden among their representatives as well.

How might the individual freedom upon which democracy depends be protected from its collective form? In an essay of 1943 titled *On the Abolition of all Political Parties*, Simone Weil took Rousseau at his word in arguing that parties undercut the basis of democracy by eliminating the silence within which individual freedom is alone possible.[2] Quite apart from giving voice to collective passions that replace the general will by a social majority, the party's polemical structure entails its unconcern with the truth, justice, or goodness on which the individual conscience is meant to deliberate in the public interest. Its constant competition against rivals means that the party turns all such ends into means to augment its own power, in a desire for growth that knows no limits because it acknowledges no other end.

Weil claimed that under these conditions, even the truth offered by political ideology is subordinated to the party's desire for limitless expansion and becomes incidental to it. Truth, justice, and goodness are thus removed from political decisions even as ideals. This puts all those involved with them into various degrees of mendacity and bad faith. Her solution was to abolish political parties, which she saw as obstacles to freedom whose extreme manifestations were to be found in the party-structures of communism and fascism. Instead, Weil recommended that loosely organized intellectual circles should be formed around journals, to provide venues for political debate in a way that reinstated the individual and so public interest at the basis of political life.

While she does not seem to have realized the party's role in protecting its members from the organized violence of their opponents, Weil might well have judged this function in a Gandhian way, by noting how it replicates in itself the very enemy it is founded to fight and thus perpetuates its evil. Remarkably like him in her focus on nonviolence, manual labor, fasting, and truth as a form of divine grace incalculable in its distance from all instrumentality, Weil was also preceded by Mohandas K. Gandhi as a critic of democratic institutions. In his manifesto of 1909 entitled *Hind Swaraj*, or *Indian Home Rule*, Gandhi inveighed against parliamentary democracy, famously describing the so-called Mother of Parliaments in Westminster as a sterile woman and a prostitute.

With these patriarchal metaphors, Gandhi sought to describe the way in which parliament operated only with the spur of outside pressure, indifferent as to whether this took the form of popular demands or the blandishments of a wealthy few. At the same time, it was placed under the control of changing masters, in the shape of the prime minister and his cabinet, who bought loyalty by the inducements of wealth, honors, and influence. Forced to abide by party discipline, its members were in thrall to these changing leaders, who were themselves concerned solely with the expansion of their power. In such a system, whose stability relied upon the ritualization of conflict along party lines, neither truth, justice, goodness nor indeed the public interest were served except by accident.

As for the voter's freedom of conscience and judgment, whose deliberations were necessarily silent, it was drowned out by a purely partisan political debate in parliament and the press:

> To the English voters their newspaper is their Bible. They take their cue from their newspapers which are often dishonest. The same fact is differently interpreted by different newspapers, according to the party in whose interests they are edited. One newspaper would consider a great Englishman to be a paragon of honesty, another would consider him dishonest. What must be the condition of the people whose newspapers are of this type?[3]

The competition set up by parliamentary democracy produced stability at the expense of truth and so freedom, which could only lose meaning without the former.

Instead of seeing the alternation of governments in a democracy as demonstrating the political freedom it promised, Gandhi understood it as an example of inconstancy that was itself mechanical:

> These people change their views frequently. It is said that they change them every seven years. These views swing like the pendulum of a clock and are never steadfast. The people would follow a powerful orator or a man who gives them parties, receptions, etc. As are the people, so is their Parliament.[4]

Rather than blaming the English for this state of affairs, Gandhi attributed it to the link between parliamentary democracy and industrial capitalism, or what he called modern civilization, whose "true test lies in the fact that people living in it make bodily welfare the object of life."[5]

But modern civilization failed to satisfy bodily wants, and not only because it was made possible for a few at the expense of the many. Also important was the fact that its desire was insatiable and led to a limitless expansion no different from that which Weil argued marked the thirst for power in party politics. Indeed, the two were linked in the growth of capital, industry, and empire. Gandhi described this desire in the language of addiction and saw it resulting in the destruction of the subject whose freedom democracy was meant to seek: "It is eating into the vitals of the English nation. It must be shunned. Parliaments are really emblems of slavery. If you will sufficiently think over this, you will entertain the same opinion and cease to blame the English. They rather deserve our sympathy."[6]

Simone Weil, we have seen, sought to rescue the silent freedom of democracy's subject from the cacophony of collective passions and the social majorities they produced by abolishing political parties. Gandhi also thought that parliamentary democracy, and the modern civilization to which it was tied, resulted in the destruction of subjective freedom. But despite his harsh criticism of it, he worked with a political party and did not seek to abolish parliamentary democracy. He did suggest that the Indian National Congress dissolve itself once its work was done with the achievement of independence in 1947, but only so that other kinds of parties could emerge to take stock of a new situation which no longer required the existence of a single anti-colonial organization.

His Master's Voice

If Gandhi precedes Weil in his criticism of voice in parliamentary democracy, his views also hark back to earlier suspicions about it that go back to

Rousseau and even before. But during the nineteenth century it was the real and potential expansion of the franchise in England that gave rise to new anxieties about the independence of voice in political life. It was ostensibly to protect the liberty of this voice that voting rights were restricted to adult males, property owners, and the educated. These qualifications made for overlapping but not identical groups, whose eligibility to vote was determined by the gravity of their voices. For it was thought that only such men possessed the requisite investment in, responsibility for, and knowledge about their society to be entrusted with its governance.[7]

The reasoning behind such exclusions, in the name of guaranteeing both the freedom and therefore meaningfulness of an individual's political voice, remained the same even when some alteration to these qualifications was made. Thus, men of little or no property and education, or women of greater age, would be included in the electoral rolls once they were deemed to have assumed control over their own voices. Like slaves in ancient times, however, and prisoners in some countries even today, those defined as children still cannot have a say in the laws that govern them, and for the same reasons that had once been used to exclude women or the poor, to say nothing of non-white or colonized populations.

But the inclusion of new categories of people into the practices of political representation led to another nineteenth-century anxiety, which had to do with the possibility of a majority drowning out the dissenting voices and interests of minorities, whether defined by birth, wealth, religion, or political views. We have seen this anxiety in Weil's suspicion of collective passions. The prospect of such a tyranny of the majority produced many ideas to have the minority heard, of which John Stuart Mill's proposal in his 1861 *Considerations on Representative Government* is one of the most famous.[8] Mill suggested adding together the votes of constituencies defined not merely by territory but by issues, which would allow minorities the chance to represent themselves by their total number.

Both these liberal anxieties, to ensure the independence and meaningfulness of political voice by a process of exclusion, and to allow for the representation of minorities amidst the uncertain passions of a more undifferentiated electorate, achieved perhaps their starkest manifestation in British India. Voting there was severely restricted by all the qualifications described above from the time it became available to Indians early in the twentieth century.[9] And while Mill's efforts to represent minorities made little headway in England, the most fulsome project ever to do so was launched in India. This was a system of joint and separate electorates that guaranteed the election of Hindu and Muslim legislators in areas where each community comprised a minority.

The debate over political voice in India was defined not so much by the desire to gain or recover it as to endow it with meaning. For it was typical of British administrators to dismiss Indian demands for a say in their government as being the unrepresentative claims of self-interested elites, the coerced and irresponsible voices of their ignorant followers, or the oppressive desires of a caste or religious majority. "Voice" in this situation was a mark not of freedom but slavery and the childish immaturity of those not yet ready to govern themselves. In a reversal of conventional thinking, it was often silence that became the sign of political maturity and power in the empire, with voice understood as the womanly expression of powerlessness.

Gandhi's views about voice and silence must be understood in the context of these nineteenth-century debates, whose terms, I want to argue, he went on to radicalize rather than reject altogether. The Mahatma's advocacy of silence, in other words, has everything to do with the twin anxieties of voice in the liberal imagination of empire: it had to be meaningful and to stand against the tyranny of the majority. These virtues were nowhere better revealed than in the character of the Englishman as empire-builder. In his essay, *The Intimate Enemy: Loss and Recovery of Self Under Colonialism*, Ashis Nandy describes how British ideas of masculinity were formed in imperialism, and I want to dwell upon some of them here.[10]

The image of a strong and silent hero laboring to do his duty by those in his care has become a stereotype, one whose imperial context is made clear in locutions like Rudyard Kipling's "white man's burden." Important about this figure is the fact that his actions are defined by their silence, not least because they represent a duty that is necessarily unilateral, in that he can have no politically meaningful conversation with those among its objects who are not his equals. Colonial subjects, in other words, can speak in petitions and pleas, providing the state with opinions to which it responds not by way of a dialogue, but as a favor and following a consideration in which they play no role. The relationship of ruler and ruled in imperialism is silent because it is conceived of as a moral and not a political one, with the former's duty requiring the latter's education but not representation. This is how silence comes to constitute freedom.

A good example of such a character is to be found in Thomas Carlyle's *Past and Present*, itself a forerunner of Gandhi and even Weil's criticisms of industrial capitalism with its cult of mammon and utility without moral ideals. In his chapter on "The English," Carlyle defines his countrymen's national character by their silence: "Of all the nations in the world at present, we English are the stupidest in speech, the wisest in action."[11] Comparing the English to the Romans in their love of silence, matched as he thought it was by their building of empires, Carlyle pours scorn on facility of speech being a sign of powerlessness among the Greeks in ancient times as the French in his own.

For Carlyle the powerlessness of voice is represented by animals, with India's monkeys if not people serving as the exemplars of voluble impotence: "Nay, of all animals, the freest of utterance, I should judge, is the genus *Simia*: go into the Indian woods, say all Travelers, and look what a brisk, adroit, unresting Ape-population it is!"[12] The awkward silence and even stupidity of the stereotyped Englishman, John Bull, is what Carlyle treasures: "Nature alone knows thee, acknowledges the bulk and strength of thee: thy Epic, unsung in words, is written in huge characters on the face of the Planet—sea moles, cotton-trades, railways, fleets and cities, Indian Empires, Americas, New-Hollands; legible throughout the Solar System!"[13]

In a chapter titled "Democracy," Carlyle goes on to argue that only when the heroic duty of deeds done in silence falters, does the politics of institutions take over: "Hence French Revolutions, Five-Point Charters, Democracies, and a mournful list of *Etceteras*, in these our afflicted times."[14] Here, then, is another criticism of parliamentary democracy for which silence is crucial. While Gandhi was partial to Ruskin's and Tolstoy's style of anti-modern radicalism more than to Carlyle's, we shall see how he transformed imperial ideas of silence and freedom, speech and deeds, majority and minority into a quite novel vision of democracy in which the politics of mastery is replaced by the power of renunciation.

Freedom from Mediation

Gandhi, like Carlyle and also Weil, wanted to recover the subject's freedom in non-institutional ways, by foregrounding silence in the making of a moral subject. He placed silence alongside fasting, celibacy, and other practices which sought to limit the multiplication of insatiable desires and the ever-growing forms of consumption they promoted. Yet silence had its own role to play in this menu of renunciations, because it addressed not only the body's integrity and moral agency, but specifically that of the mind, or rather its thought and judgment. Gandhi's focus on controlling the senses has led historians to interpret it as a form of disciplining rather than liberating the body, especially the bodies and voices of India's poor.

This is the argument Ranajit Guha makes in the only political analysis of Gandhi's silence, which is otherwise considered a purely spiritual phenomenon. Guha's analysis appeared in an essay titled "Discipline and Mobilize," with its clear reference to Michel Foucault's book *Discipline and Punish* on the making of a carceral society in modern Europe.[15] In it he described Gandhi's repeated efforts to curb the din and clamor of the unruly crowds that greeted their Mahatma when he first shot to fame after the First World War. The problem with their adulation was its appropriation of Gandhi within a logic of resistance very different from what he was himself propounding. The newly-minted Mahatma had to wrestle the ownership of his own movement from the very masses he was meant to have mobilized. And he worked hard to interrupt the sheer noise that constituted the language of popular protest in order to discipline and channel it into a politics where such movements were interrupted by negotiations with the colonial state.

For Guha, then, silence served as the name given to Gandhi's interruption and subsequent mediation of popular protest in the national movement. This is an interesting interpretation, particularly in its attribution of discipline, unlike with Foucault himself, to a non-state and indeed anti-state movement. But Guha does not pursue the implications of Gandhi's deployment of discipline against the colonial state. Instead of asking how his version of discipline might have subverted or eventually assisted the state's own, Guha leaves the reader with a romantic vision of popular protest derailed by a man with no access to its repressive arsenal. He never considers the possibility that the "mobocracy" Gandhi criticized in such clamor might represent the nineteenth century's tyrannical majority or Weil's collective passions.

In any case, Gandhi was a harsh critic of mediation, as we have already seen from his views of parliamentary democracy as a structure of political representation. He thought voice and speech were forms of mediation in their own right. In *Hind Swaraj*, for example, Gandhi inveighed against doctors and lawyers as, in effect, agents of the colonial state. This state represented the ultimate form of mediation as a neutral third party, there to arbitrate between Indians rendered into partisan interests.[16] He described doctors as purveyors of commodities from the pharmaceutical industry meant to alienate patients from their own bodies in another instance of addiction. Lawyers, for their part, existed not to resolve conflicts but to increase the state's power by imposing a peace that needed constant enforcement between the rival interests it relied upon and therefore had to maintain.

Such forms of mediation, of course, represented both the manner in which the colonial state operated as well as its justification, with Gandhi advocating their circumvention in unmediated relations between Indians who should no longer be defined as antagonistic interests. Language played a role in all the instances of mediation I have described, especially the highly technical kind used for legal and medical communication. But it became crucial in certain types of conflict, of which the mounting controversies over proselytism in the 1920s took pride of place, especially among Hindus and Muslims in North India but also including Christian missionary activity directed toward both groups throughout the country. Rather than seeing these disputes as the problematic inheritance of pre-modern identities, Gandhi argued, we should understand them as the utterly modern products of liberal politics, which had turned religious communities into interests and therefore constituencies. Interest here is defined by a capitalist understanding of property as some advantage whose possession constitutes the political as much as economic identity of any group or individual. Proselytism, in other words, became controversial for the first time in this manner because it was thought to be an attempt not at challenging a religious claim to truth but instead augmenting the electoral or political power of one group over another, in much the same way as parties operated to diminish the real or potential majority of their rivals.

Addressing the violence that accompanied accusations from Hindus, Muslims, and Christians of predatory missionizing by their religious rivals, Gandhi suggested stopping not conversion itself but its mediation in language. To be true to the ideals of their own faiths, he argued, missionaries should serve as their best representatives in refusing to lie about, unfairly criticize, or run down the religions of others. In doing so, they would also serve humanity by conducting their charitable works in silence and thus drawing converts by the sheer force of their example rather than through unseemly and invariably untruthful polemics. In a 1931 speech to Christian missionaries in London, for example, he said:

> The idea of converting people to one's faith by speech and writings, by appeal to reason and emotion and by suggesting that the faith of his forefathers is a bad faith, in my opinion, limits the possibilities of serving

humanity. . . . Religion is like a rose. It throws out the scent which attracts like a magnet and we are drawn to it involuntarily.[17]

Speech and indeed language itself, in other words, betrayed religious truth like all other truth by mediating it in argument and collective passion. And while Gandhi was concerned here with missionaries in particular, his criticism held true of persuasion as an important part of political practice more generally. As a fundamental liberal virtue, this kind of argumentation had already come under attack from both the left and the right as a disingenuous form of bourgeois discussion, one incapable of advancing any real change.[18] These ideologues sought to cut liberal debate short by creating facts on the ground either in acts of empire-building, as with Carlyle, or of revolutionary violence as with Lenin. Gandhi, however, reimagined persuasion in sacrificial terms, by offering up the sight and sometimes even spectacle of speechless acts as the most effective demonstration of their truth.

In order to manifest itself, therefore, political as much as moral or religious truth had to disavow voice for action and sound for sight, in a way that was both linked to and yet quite different from a political thinker like Lenin's theorization of revolutionary action as a force for change. While privileging the visible over the audible as a modality for truth, Gandhi also lent it olfactory form, as a fragrance which drew the potential convert to itself involuntarily. In other words, he conceived of neither the audible nor the visible as pure forms, since one could include the sense of smell and another the written word as an amalgam of sight and sound. It was the interpretive and so mediating function of language itself that he distrusted, one for which silence served as an antonym.

The unmediated visibility that Gandhi prized as a modality of truth turned persuasion from an aural to an ocular practice, but one which left its viewer in charge of interpreting and deciding on what she or he saw—a metamorphosis or conversion, to use religious terms, in which silence lost its autonomy and was mediated by sight as a negative form. And while this logic seems to countermand Gandhi's emphasis on unmediated relations, it does conform to his propensity for negative forms more generally, of which non-violence, non-possession, and non-cooperation are the most famous. Unlike the kind of mediation that characterized the colonial state, which produced rival interests as positive forms requiring arbitration, silence mediated by sight renounced all positivity and could only be known by its absence. Even by their grammatical structure, after all, virtuous terms like "nonviolence" did not enjoy a positive existence but were defined, negatively, by their evil opposites.

Silence allowed for unmediated relations because of its negative form. Unlike the ability to speak or reason, which constituted one of the classical definitions of the human species, silence did not depend on the logic of either shared capacities or the biological similarities that in Gandhi's view served only to fragment humanity into various kinds of hierarchies. Indeed, the imperative to unify the human race through language and reason not only ended by dehumanizing those among its members who were seen as being unreasonable and beyond persuasion, it also drew an absolute separation between one species and another. It was silence or the inability to communicate through language, then, which made moral relations between humans and animals possible.

The context for Gandhi's reflections on inter-species relations was provided in his time by the violent controversies between Hindus and Muslims over cow-slaughter. Grappling with these conflicts, Gandhi sought to expand and reinterpret the Hindu injunction to protect cattle to not only human but all animal life. He saw in cow-protection humanity's effort to go beyond itself, and in a 1921 article in his journal, *Young India*, emphasized the unilateral and voiceless character of this demand: "The appeal of the lower order of creation is all the more forcible because it is speechless."[19] Without either identifying animal with human life or requiring the kind of contractual reciprocity in their relations that was strangely expected among human beings, Gandhi based such relations on the very absence of similarity and similitude.

As with his views on conversion, which we have seen turn out to be about the problem of liberal persuasion more generally, Gandhi's understanding of cow-protection was also about the liberal values of reciprocity and contract. In his view, of course, such values were made possible by the colonial state as a neutral third party, there to mediate between its subjects construed as political interests. But as we have seen, Gandhi thought these relations to be unworkable and deeply violent in the hierarchies they set up. He was fascinated by what moral (and thus political) relations might look like if they were not founded in what he thought was the transient and unequal agreement of a contract. The controversies over cow-slaughter allowed Gandhi to imagine relationships unmediated by language in another way.

In an article of 1924 in *Young India*, he came close to attributing language to the cow:

The cow is the purest type of sub-human life. She pleads before us on behalf of the whole of the sub-human species for justice to it at the hands of man, the first among all that lives. She seems to speak to us through her eyes: "you are not appointed over us to kill us and eat our flesh or otherwise ill-treat us, but to be our friend and guardian."[20]

Yet crucial here is the fact that this appeal is not only voiceless, but unknowable and thus calls for the unilateral interpretation and moral judgment of human beings. As in the relations between species, Gandhi thought that relations among human beings, too, should be marked by an acknowledgment of their fundamental incommunicability and therefore silence.

The Truth Outside

As we have seen when discussing its negative mediation by visibility, silence for Gandhi is by no means linked to secrecy or the concealment of inner life. On the contrary, it makes for unmediated relations marked by absolute transparency. It is voice, in other words, that creates the impression if not illusion of secrecy, and so hypocrisy, by inevitably concealing the very truth it seeks to express. While Simone Weil was concerned with protecting the inner life from collective passions and rehearsed speech, Gandhi seemed, at first glance, to want to expose this fundamentally silent life by rescuing it from the mediation of voice. But a closer look reveals that his attitude toward the inner life was nominalist or premised upon its radical ignorance of an invariably external and therefore divine truth.

Gandhi was concerned not only by the kind of noise that overwhelmed the moral as well as political subject from the outside, but equally with protecting the inner life from the random or uncontrolled thoughts and fantasies that threatened to undo it from within. As he writes in his autobiography of 1930: "My hesitancy in speech, which was once an annoyance, is now a pleasure. Its greatest benefit has been that it has taught me the economy of words. I have naturally formed the habit of restraining my thoughts. And I can now give myself the certificate that a thoughtless word hardly ever escapes my tongue or pen."[21]

And this also meant defending the subject's outer world from its inner conflicts.

Gandhi's weekly days of silence represented this dual form of preservation, both of the subject and against it, which he describes frequently in passages such as this: "Experience has taught me that silence is part of the spiritual discipline of a votary of truth. Proneness to exaggerate, to suppress or modify the truth, wittingly or unwittingly, is a natural weakness of man, and silence is necessary in order to surmount it."[22] In effect, the inner life and its outer world were inextricably connected to one another, with neither able to claim autonomy for itself. The subject's freedom, therefore, had to be continuously disciplined so as not to become self-possessed, while at the same time being protected from the noise of external mediation.

Silence functioned, in other words, as a double-edged sword, one that made the truth visible outside and even against the subject as much as for it. What kind of selfhood did this entail, and how might we understand the freedom of its inner life? Perhaps we can find out by looking further at Gandhi's autobiography. Not surprisingly, the book is haunted by an authorial anxiety about its self-aggrandizing genre as a memoir, one that some of Gandhi's friends told him was peculiar to the West. More interestingly, they suggested it may mislead readers not by any mistake in the Mahatma's telling, but because he might change his views in the future.[23] This indicates that the text was conceived not as the account of some uniquely individual life, but as an instruction to others in the form of a warning as well as a model.

Gandhi repeatedly emphasizes the generic quality of his experiments by arguing that they could be understood and even undertaken by a child, seeing as they were the efforts of a man as weak and fallible as any other. Because it consistently reduces its author's individuality in this way, the text can even be described as anti-biographical in nature, and Gandhi himself impugns its biographical veracity:

> I know that I do not set down in this story all that I remember. Who can say how much I must give and how much omit in the interests of truth? And what would be the value in a court of law of the inadequate *ex parte* evidence being tendered by me of certain events in my life? If some busy-body were to cross-examine me on the chapters already written, he could probably shed much more light on them, and if it were a hostile critic's cross-examination, he might even flatter himself for having shown up "the hollowness of many of my pretensions."[24]

Reading through the *Autobiography*, one is also struck by how anti-psychological it is. Gandhi does not appear to be very interested in motives or intentions, whether his own or those of others, and in some sense his narrative can be read as the account of a purely external and even accidental causality. The confessional element in the text has deluded readers into mistaking it for a narrative of Gandhi's inner life rather than an act of ritual exposure, but even its most famous instances argue the opposite. The story is often cited of how Gandhi left his father's deathbed to sleep with his wife, during which time his parent died and inspired in his guilty son the first thought of rejecting sex.[25] While the psychological motivation here seems clear, it is far too obvious and, indeed, followed up by a quite different notion.

The child born from this illicit encounter, Gandhi tells us, died soon afterward as a punishment for its father's guilt. We should not dismiss this idea as a superstition "unfair" to both the child and its mother. Coming from such a sophisticated thinker, we might understand it as a deliberate effort to externalize causality in such a way as to make it fundamentally unknowable. As part of his attempt to de-individualize the moral actor, Gandhi not only rejected an inner life for himself by refusing all privacy, he also sought to destroy the ego so as to have it replaced by the truth that for him was entirely external, objective, and so divine. While some of this truth might be known, other parts of it could neither be concealed nor communicated: "There are some things which are known only to oneself and one's Maker. These are clearly incommunicable. The experiments I am about to relate are not such."[26]

The ignorance, or rather incommunicability and therefore silence, at the heart of the *Autobiography* turns many of Gandhi's biographical anecdotes into fortuitous ones, his escape from various moral dangers attributed to causes whose very externality makes them providential rather than intentional. Here, for instance, is his commentary on an awkward experience with a prostitute as a young man:

> I sat near the woman on her bed, but I was tongue-tied. She naturally lost patience with me, and showed me the door, with abuses and insults. I then felt as though my manhood had been injured, and wished to sink into the ground for shame. But I have ever since given thanks to God for having saved me. I can recall four more similar incidents in my life, and in most of them my good fortune, rather than any effort on my part, saved me.[27]

Radical Ignorance

If Gandhi is so intent on the externality of truth, it is because he understands that we cannot be fully cognizant of all the factors that go into the making of any act. Sexual knowledge, for instance, he attributes to the incommunicable "memory" of a previous life, saying of his first experience of it: "The impressions of the former birth are potent enough to make all coaching superfluous."[28] He also rejects knowledge and so its voicing and communication as a criterion of moral action on egalitarian grounds, for this would turn the wealthy, powerful, and educated into the most moral of agents. The *Autobiography* is replete with instances of the unknowable in statements like "We can also see that judging a man from his outward act is no more than a doubtful inference, inasmuch as it is not based on sufficient data."[29] While visibility, particularly that of nonviolence, can persuade or convert its enemies, then, its unmediated and negative character means that it cannot become an object of knowledge in its own right. This is what makes persuasion an act of faith and so moral agency on the part of its recipient.

Because a man's inner life was not apprehensible to the outside observer, he had to be dealt with on the basis of what we might call radical ignorance. Gandhi is ignorant of his own wife's inner life, saying that "Kasturba herself does not perhaps know whether she has any ideals independently of me. It is likely that many of my doings have not her approval even today. We never discuss them. I see no good in discussing them."[30] And he also expresses ignorance of his own motives, for example when reflecting upon his advice urging mill-workers on strike in Ahmedabad in 1918 to honor the pledge they had given him:

> The mill-hands had taken the pledge at my suggestion. They had repeated it before me day after day, and the very idea that they might now go back upon it was to me inconceivable. Was it pride or was it my love for the labourers and my passionate regard for truth that was at the back of this feeling—who can say?[31]

Given the radical ignorance at the heart of all human endeavors, how might it be possible to act morally without depending upon voice, speech, and so knowledge? By committing oneself to a principle almost as a kind of wager and out of ignorance, something that for Gandhi took the shape of a vow. In his student days in London, the future Mahatma had been saved from drink and women by the vow he had made to his mother, though it had not been based on any knowledge or proof about the virtue of abstinence. And in South Africa, Gandhi had justified wearing a charm put around his neck by his mother for no other reason than another such vow, which he describes in a conversation with a Quaker friend who was urging him to discard it:

> He saw, round my neck, the Vaishnava necklace of Tulasi-beads. He thought it to be superstition and was pained by it. "This superstition does not become you. Come, let me break the necklace."
>
> "No, you will not. It is a sacred gift from my mother."
>
> "But do you believe in it?"
>
> "I do not know its mysterious significance. I do not think I should come to harm if I did not wear it. But I cannot, without sufficient reason, give up a necklace that she put round my neck out of love and in the conviction that it would be conducive to my welfare. When, with the passage of time, it wears away and breaks of its own accord, I shall have no desire to get a new one. But this necklace cannot be broken.[32]

The vow, then, was in some sense arbitrary, but saved from self-indulgence by its permanent and sacrificial character. And while it sometimes took verbal or written form, the vow could also be silent as it often was for Gandhi. It compelled moral action by a decision that might well produce its proof in subsequent experience but was initially baseless:

> The importance of vows grew upon me more clearly than ever before. I realized that a vow, far from closing the door to real freedom, opened it. Up to this time I had not met with success because the will had been lacking, because I had had no faith in myself, no faith in the grace of God, and therefore, my mind had been tossed on the boisterous sea of doubt.... "I believe in effort, I do not want to bind myself with vows," is the mentality of weakness and betrays a subtle desire for the thing to be avoided. Or where can be the difficulty in making a final decision?[33]

The "subtle desire" Gandhi refers to in the quotation above shows that he was not unaware of the complex motivations of inner life, but the point was to allay these by resort to the world outside. Having turned himself into a moral agent by the purely external means of a vow and in the absence either of knowledge or its communication, Gandhi was bound to deal with other moral actors in the same way. And he did so by ignoring their inner lives and taking them at their word—or rather testing them by it and so forcing moral life to the surface in a kind of nominalism not unfamiliar to the lawyer in the Mahatma.

Speech or voice, therefore, had to be deprived of all hidden or multiple meanings and understood literally. This did not, however, make its meaning singular in character, since Gandhi frequently read different meanings into words that could bear more than one interpretation. But this legalistic mode of reading did not presume any hidden depths to such words either, understanding them, instead, as being capacious enough to allow for multiple meanings in a purely technical way and not even by reference to any authorial intention.

The *Autobiography* offers a good example of this understanding of language when Gandhi gave his own words a meaning he had never intended. Having forsworn milk from his diet as an animal product that he thought only fed the passions, Gandhi was faced during a serious illness with the necessity of increasing the protein content of his diet. Since he couldn't, of course, take any meat, Kasturba convinced him to drink goat's milk, as his vow to give up animal protein had referred only to cow's milk. This was clearly a ruse, but Gandhi accepted it, writing that: "The memory of this action even now rankles in my breast and fills me with remorse, and I am constantly thinking how to give up goat's milk. But I cannot yet free myself from the subtlest of temptations, the desire to serve, which still holds me."[34]

Rather than revealing anything about the subject, then, language was to be used against it as a kind of external force shaping or keeping it true to itself. It was deployed like legal testimony in some sense, but decidedly not so as to expose the subject's inner life and motivation. The familiar Gandhian aphorism, "My life is my message," may not actually have been uttered by him, but remains nevertheless true to the Mahatma's thought, since the message in question is conceived not as a verbal or written communication so much as the evidence provided by life itself. The message, in other words, has been deprived of its linguistic form and subordinated to or tested against the silent visibility of a life that Gandhi's autobiography is meant to do little more than expose to scrutiny and judgment.

Such an emptying out of the subject bewildered Gandhi's enemies, whose chief accusation against him has always been hypocrisy, with Churchill famously calling the Mahatma the world's most successful humbug. These enemies have from Gandhi's own days to the present been driven by an urge to find the inner motive or secret that informed his actions, refusing to lend his words or acts any credence in their own right. Because he took words at face value, however, the Mahatma for his part only asked his interlocutors to be true to them. This resulted in a competition where the one truest to himself might convert the rest by his integrity and without requiring any prior agreement as to aims and ideals, something we have already seen in Gandhi's views on proselytization.

This made moral action a kind of wager, even if Gandhi thought that the true follower of nonviolence would always win. Yet it was not simply the inability to know as a kind of failure that defined Gandhi's morals, which would give them an entirely passive character. Instead, he saw the truth as being external in nature and therefore divine, because it could never be fully known. And the individual's task was to find this truth at the cost of his inner life because it constituted his only reality and at the same time tied him to a world beyond himself:

> I think it is wrong to expect certainties in this world, where all else but God that is Truth is an uncertainty. All that appears and happens about and around us is uncertain, transient. But there is a Supreme Being hidden therein as a certainty, and one would be blessed if one could catch a glimpse of that Certainty and hitch one's wagon to it.[35]

God and Good Government

It is typical of Gandhi that he defines God in such a way that He can be understood either theologically or epistemologically. In either case, the externality of His truth becomes evident in and through the moral subject, whose selfhood it in fact destroys or makes object-like. The "in-dweller," "spirit," "conscience," or "inner voice" that speaks through Gandhi is quite external to him. In the following passage, his editor Tridip Suhrud provides the Gujarati equivalent of the Mahatma's English phrasing in square brackets, to show how the most intimate portion of the self is in fact the most foreign:

> I write as the Spirit [dweller within] moves me at the time of writing. I do not claim to know definitely that all conscious thought and action on my part is directed by the Spirit [dweller within]. But on an examination of the greatest steps that I have taken in my life, as also of those that may be

regarded as the least, I think it will not be improper to say that all of them were directed by the Spirit [dweller within].[36]

The inner life of the moral self, in other words, cannot fully recognize the foreign reality of which it is constituted. But rather than serving as an example of the self's failure, the externality of this truth is in fact the only connection that the individual possesses with his neighbors as much as with God. One way of putting it would be to say that the Mahatma understands the subject as being determined by factors outside itself, and it is these factors that link it with other subjects and make social life possible. The possession of one's truth therefore takes the form of a dispossession: "The seeker after truth should be humbler than the dust. The world crushes the dust under its feet, but the seeker after truth should be so humble himself that even the dust could crush him. Only then, and not till then, will he have a glimpse of the truth."[37]

Whatever inspiration this way of thinking might have drawn from ancient or medieval ideas of the religious life, far more crucial is the modern context in which Gandhi articulated it. Rather than some kind of uninterrupted tradition, the Mahatma's vision of moral selfhood was both produced by and deployed against the nineteenth-century individualism that made autobiographies possible. In its Gujarati original, the title of Gandhi's book, rendered into English as "The Story of My Experiments with Truth," reads something like "Truth's Experiments" (*satya-na prayogo*), in which it is not the Mahatma who is the subject but instead truth. Rejecting the spirituality that emerged as a reaction against what used to be called bourgeois individualism only to reinforce it, Gandhi's autobiography audaciously seeks to tell the story of truth's experiments with the self it both sustains and destroys.

What does all of this have to do with the link between silence and freedom with which I began this essay? Let us recall that Simone Weil had traced the ruination of democracy to its abandonment of ideals like truth, justice, and goodness. It was the externality of such ideals to the rehearsed speech of party politics that was crucial in limiting the latter's reach. The individual's freedom, in other words, was premised upon these ideals, which alone made political judgment in the public interest possible. They could be instrumentally deployed by parties backed by ascribed social identities, of course, but nevertheless represented ends in their own right rather than power as a means turned into an end in the form of limitless desire. Abolishing political parties was Weil's way of preventing such an eventuality.

While not going so far as to recommend the abolition of political parties, despite his severe criticism of parliamentary democracy, Gandhi also sought to reinforce the individual's moral agency. And he did so through the prescription of silence over speech. But rather than protecting the subject from outside influence and so reifying the individual as a purely autonomous being, silence here worked as a form of internal discipline that protected the outside world as well. It was meant, additionally, to open the individual up to the externality of truth, which in Gandhi's view was another name for God. And this implied that human beings were not brought together by any shared quality like speech and reason, nor a biological one like race or reproduction, but only in their openness to quite alien and metaphysical figures such as truth, justice, and goodness.

To be workable, therefore, democracy required the existence of a subject outside or beyond its own loquacious logic. What became of words and voice in this vision? They were reduced to pure artifice and deprived of any authenticity in the revelation of a subject's inner truth. This did not stop communication, just as Gandhi did not cease to read and write during his days of silence, but it did displace and discipline speech as the privileged revelation of inner life. Words and language served as external constraints to test, limit, and shore up this subject, whose truth Gandhi described in his autobiography as being founded on a presupposition:

> I have not seen Him, neither have I known Him. I have made the world's faith in God my own, and as my faith is ineffaceable, I regard that faith as amounting to experience. However, as it may be said that to describe faith as experience is to tamper with truth, it may perhaps be more correct to say that I have no word for characterizing my belief in God.[38]

It is not that the knowledge or experience of God is so ineffable as to be beyond words, but that it functions wordlessly by virtue of its absence or negative form as a presupposition. God here represents nothing but the silence that for Gandhi destroys the self while opening it up to the externality of its own truth, and on this basis its relations with others as well. A revelation of emptiness rather than any concealment of being, silence made freedom possible in the very stop it put to the false and often violent mediations of speech, showing that social and even inter-species relations rested on a quite different foundation. And while his ideas might seem arcane, they are no more so than those of Rousseau's that Weil cites in her description of the general will. We have seen, indeed, that Gandhi applied them to the most concrete and quotidian problems, from conversion to cow-slaughter.

Systematic though they were, Gandhi's views cannot be understood as constituting some kind of dogma or truth in their own right. After all, he repeatedly disclaimed any access to such verities, and was equally regular in describing his ideas and practices as a set of experiments. And it is as experiments open to the trial and judgment of others that we should also consider his way of thinking and analysis. Indeed, Gandhi's entire theory of nonviolence might be seen as a gigantic thought-experiment, in which he deliberately reversed conventional formulations to produce sometimes startling results. The theatrical character of these reversals is probably not accidental, with the Mahatma preferring silence over speech, ignorance over knowledge, and even the possibility of violent conflict over mediation.

Incapable of guaranteeing the truth, Gandhi's experiments nevertheless made surprising revelations possible, and in doing so allowed for the subject's moral transformation out of a sovereign decision lacking its own proof. We have seen this in his advocacy of the vow as a decision that produced a truth rather than being derived from one. This made truth, like justice and goodness, crucial to the subject's inner life, while yet refusing to validate them in the form of a doctrine meant for others. Like the missionaries urged to propagate their religion silently, Gandhi's moral subject was also meant to test the results of his endeavors against those of his rivals. Such a theater of competition represented perhaps the highest form of political debate, but one that could only be seen in everyday life rather than heard in parliament.

Notes

1. For some recent discussions of voice and silence in and as political activity, see Sophia Dingli and Thomas N. Cooke, ed., *Political Silence: Meanings, Functions and Ambiguity* (Abingdon and New York: Routledge, 2018); a recent special issue of *Critical Review of International Social and Political Philosophy* on "Silence in Political Theory and Practice" (24/3 [2021]), ed. Mónica Brito Vieira; Laura Kunreuther, "Sounds of Democracy: Performance, Protest and Political Subjectivity," *Cultural Anthropology* 33/1 (2018), 1–31; and Amanda Weidman, "Voice" (232–245) and Ana María Ochoa Gautier, "Silence," in *Keywords in Sound*, ed. David Novak and Matt Sakakeeny (Durham, NC: Duke University Press, 2015), 183–192.

2. Simone Weil, *On the Abolition of All Political Parties*, trans. Simon Leys (New York: New York Review of Books, 2013).

3. M. K. Gandhi, *Hind Swaraj or Indian Home Rule* (Madras: G. A. Natesan and Co., 1921), 19.

4. Ibid., 19–20.

5. Ibid., 21.

6. Ibid., 25.

7. For a classic statement of these concerns, see William Blackstone, *Commentaries on the Laws of England*, ed. David Lemmings (Oxford, UK: Oxford University Press, 2016), vol. 1: *Of the Rights of Persons*, ch. 2 ("Of the Parliament"), 142–181. See also Eric J. Evans, *Parliamentary Reform in Britain, c. 1770–1918* (Abingdon and New York: Routledge, 2000.

8. John Stuart Mill, *Considerations on Representative Government* (London: Parker, Son, and Bourn, 1861).

9. See Ornit Shani, *How India Became Democratic: Citizenship and the Making of the Universal Franchise* (Cambridge, UK: Cambridge University Press, 2018).

10. Ashis Nandy, *The Intimate Enemy: Loss and Recovery of Self Under Colonialism* (New Delhi: Oxford University Press, 1988).

11. Thomas Carlyle, *Past and Present* (London: Chapman and Hall, 1843), 215.

12. Ibid., 213.

13. Ibid., 216.

14. Ibid., 288.

15. Ranajit Guha, "Discipline and Mobilize," in *Subaltern Studies VII: Writings on South Asian History and Society*, ed. Partha Chaterjee and Gyanendra Pandey (Delhi: Oxford University Press, 1992), 69–120.

16. M. K. Gandhi, *Hind Swaraj*, ch. 10 ("The Condition of India: The Hindus and the Mahomedans"), ch. 11 ("The Condition of India: Lawyers"), and ch. 12 ("The condition of India: Doctors"), 37–44.

17. M. K. Gandhi, "Conference at the Missionary Society in London," October 8, 1931, in *Collected Works of Mahatma Gandhi*, vol. 48 (New Delhi: Publications Division, Ministry of Information and Broadcasting, 1984), 122.

18. Two classic examples are V. I. Lenin, *State and Revolution* (New York: International Publishers, 1932 [1918]), and Carl Schmitt, *The Crisis of Parliamentary Democracy*, trans. Ellen Kennedy (Cambridge, MA: MIT Press, 1985 [1923]).

19. M. K. Gandhi, "Hinduism," *Young India*, October 6, 1921, 6.

20. M. K. Gandhi, "Notes," *Young India*, June 26, 1924, 6.

21. M. K. Gandhi, *An Autobiography or The Story of My Experiments with Truth*, introduced with notes by Tridip Suhrud, trans. Mahadev Desai (New Delhi: Penguin, 2018), 139.

22. Ibid., 140. This comment is part of an entire chapter, "Shyness My Shield," on Gandhi's hesitation and occasional failure to speak, especially in public settings. He recounts, "I hesitated whenever I had to face strange audiences and avoided making a speech whenever I could." He then continues with the passage quoted above about his hesitancy in speech. Ibid., 139.

23. Ibid., 45.

24. Ibid., 442.

25. Ibid., 91–93.
26. Ibid., 46.
27. Ibid., 83.
28. Ibid., 65.
29. Ibid., 323.
30. Ibid., 440.
31. Ibid., 664–665.
32. Ibid., 321–322.
33. Ibid., 343.
34. Ibid., 699.
35. Ibid., 403.
36. Ibid., 441. Gandhi goes on to explain that even silence or non-utterance from his inner voice may convey meaning: "I, therefore, wonder for a moment whether it might not be proper to stop writing these chapters. But so long as there is no prohibition from the voice [dweller] within, I must continue the writing." Ibid., 442.
37. Ibid., 48.
38. Ibid., 441.

Afterword

Sound in the Imperial Archive

Elleke Boehmer

The phonetics of Bengali in late colonial India. Istanbul street cries. The "outrageous clatter" of European birds acclimatizing in new North American environments. Gasoline-fueled traffic noise in turn-of-the-century Cairo. The "anacoustic" films of the 1898 Spanish American War. The shamans, peasants, and court musicians we hear chorusing through the "acoustically attuned archive" of 1890s Korea. The African heartbeats pulsing through white doctors' stethoscopes in colonial South Africa. The nineteenth-century world, much of it under some form of empire, was many things to many people, but one thing it was not, was silent, as the contributors to *The Acoustics of Empire* resoundingly show. At certain points, the prevailing sounds may have been melodious; at others, stentorian, harsh, jarring; at others, again, hushed and implicit, yet still *there*, part of the scene or the atmosphere, often insistently so. In general, though, these sounds were various and constantly varying, and, above all, they were pervasive, pluri-centered and multi-tongued.

Against the widely accepted yet superficial impression that the visual provides the most accessible portal we have into the imperial past—sound always by its nature "dying away"—the colonial experience wherever we may care to look was never quiet. And hence, if we are to build a properly historical sense of empire both on the ground and in the round, its sounds, if we can tap into them, are powerfully suggestive. To take just one example as a guiding symbol: even as Mohandas Gandhi in his roles as Mahatma and nationalist leader meditated, went on hunger strike, and kept silence, as Faisal Devji evokes in his chapter, the surrounding streets of Poona or Delhi would have been filled with the clatter of traffic and the chatter of passing voices. If we can reimagine this hubbub, we may be able to recreate something of the India of Gandhi's heyday, and hence construct or reconstruct an analytic

Elleke Boehmer, *Afterword* In: *Acoustics of Empire*. Edited by: Peter McMurray and Priyasha Mukhopadhyay, Oxford University Press. © Oxford University Press 2024. DOI: 10.1093/oso/9780197553787.003.0015 narrative of his politically charged moment and the part that he played within it, at a time when the rapidly modernizing world he both protested against and theorized was only getting louder.

In their different ways, the essays in *Acoustics of Empire* all demonstrate that the sounds of empire—their timbre and rhythm, their concentration and density, their transmission and reception—provide fine-grained, evocative ways of understanding more about imperial power: its modes of imposition and dissemination, its spread, and its unevenness. Wherever in the world these case studies are set, they outline from their different regional and geographical vantage points a wider heuristic sensorium than we previously thought we had available with which to analyze empire. Together, the essays speak eloquently to the salience of the acoustic dimension for thinking critically and in depth about colonial experience. They use sound to clarify what it means, for example, when colonial infrastructures changed and became more embedded within cultures. Indeed, as does Gavin Steingo, they point out that the "rationalization of sound" could itself operate as a means of colonial control. Or, as Nazan Maksudyan observes, quoting Emily Thompson, if a soundscape is "simultaneously a physical environment and a way of perceiving that environment," then it can be used as a diagnostic or historiographic lens, "a culture [that is] constructed to make sense of that world."[1]

True, the acoustics of the past are not always immediately get-at-able or even comprehensible to the present-day researcher. The diffusive, pervasive, and boundary-crossing properties that make sound such an immersive and interesting medium also render its capture and representation challenging, especially when compared to the longer-lasting media found in visual and physical archives. For a start, most societies in the colonial and postcolonial world lacked accurate recording devices until very recently, and so most audio records of empire will tend to be somewhat unreliable, if available at all. The book's essays in their different ways take pains to address this challenge: this question of what we hear from the past and how it comes to us. Verbal description and musical annotation can in many cases give some impression of, say, street cries, court music, or even birdsong. However, even then, notational conventions and compositional techniques change radically over time, as do musical instruments and technologies. We don't always quite know what we are hearing or listening out for in the archive. The past sounds that are being described will not necessarily match how the same things sound today.

Another area that mounts resistance to our listening back relates to perspective. As the essays further show, our sonic realities are also subjective and impressionistic, always dependent on point of view, including, importantly, proximity to the sound source, even when we are dealing with relatively modern media of recording and transmission. The fact is that each of us processes sound and sound-memories for ourselves, no matter how near in space or distant in time they may be. Soundscapes are further impacted by cultural and social values and perceptions. For example, as Alexandra Hui discusses, the non-indigenous starlings introduced to the nineteenth-century United States for the European allure and "Shakespearean" beauty of their song came to be heard very differently over time. As the birds were increasingly seen as foreign migrants and even pests, they were also, by and by, perceived as less songful. Therefore, even if certain auditory channels can help to structure and even smooth away "the profusion of sensory information in the world," it remains difficult to "tune out" subjective perception entirely.[2] In this respect, too, as when we deal with unreliable records, creative and adaptative means of tuning into the past's auditory dimensions are required.

In her environmental study, *Weak Planet*, Wai Chee Dimock uses the suggestive metaphor of rogue data activity on the internet to theorize how interpretation, whether auditory or not, always meets with interference, such as we find, for instance, in the domain of world literature, as when classic texts are translated, reworked, and "cascaded" across cultural and linguistic borders.[3] The confusing "sonic theater" and "built-in interference and distortion" that Dimock diagnoses in respect of literary rereading and reinterpretation can be ascribed also to the acoustic environments of empire, with their many polyglot textures, their partially if not wholly undecodable noises, their recalcitrant material and social realities. Her metaphor of rogue activity applies in particular, perhaps, to the resistances such environments can mount to the project of auditory reception and interpretation itself. An exemplary instance of such interference presents itself from the 1890s, when the communications network of the telegraph spread incrementally across the world. For, even as messages were disseminated more quickly across the oceans, via undersea cables, seemingly bringing different parts of the world closer together, these technologies at the same time, by the same token, also intersected very different cultural experiences. At times, this intersection amplified dissonance and multiplied opportunities for misrecognition between countries and communities, just as much as it brought an improvement in communications, in some cases even more so.[4]

The integrative powers of music and rhythm, as well as related sonic media like chanting and street crying, could work to counteract such disharmony. Songs and poems, as forms of patterned and customized sound, in many cases offered a particularly potent antidote to the interferences and confused cascading that beset imperial soundscapes. As Carl Dalhaus explains, the interpretation of poetry no matter how popular or tub-thumping it may be (and perhaps especially then), depends on subtly persuasive "sounding phenomena."[5] Small wonder therefore that poetry and song were fundamental to the creation of what might be called imperial atmosphere in the British colonial world. Tunes, refrains, and rhymes animated the imperial nursery, the parade ground, the route march, the charity gala, the company ballroom, the classroom. The transfer and exchange of song and verse provided highly effective sonic and mnemonic channels also for the creation, amplification, and propagation of imperial feeling.[6] As Jason Rudy observes, perhaps no genre is more interwoven with the lives of nineteenth-century Britons in the empire than ballads and lyrics, including the circulation of jingoist lyrics in newspapers.[7] Rousing poetry as well as Christian hymns served as effective rallying media for transmitting imperial values around the "British" globe and drumming up patriotic emotion. Revealingly, when Robert Baden-Powell ran out of copy while writing his primer *Scouting for Boys*, he filled up the remaining empty space—the "silence"—with song scripts like "The Maple Leaf Forever" or "Vitae Lampada" as exercises for scouts to sing and perform.[8]

If, in the past, poems and songs served to communicate imperial values and inspiration, so, too, in the present, they continue to give us a good diagnostic sense of empire's sonic disseminations. It is further testimony, if more were required, for the critical importance of imperial acoustics. Rudy explains that poetry, whether through direct plagiarism or creative rewriting, allowed its settler colonial makers and readers to adjust to their strange new contexts in the empire while at the same time maintaining nostalgic and other affective bonds with Britain. Poetry offered an emotional see-saw between these different worlds, at once tuning into the new environment and subtly tuning out from the now irretrievable old world. Yet, whatever its role, structured sound was always a ubiquitous emollient—the same as we arguably find also in bird song, street chanting, and even the study of phonetics.

Therefore, even though sound cultures are difficult to recreate, and even though we cannot know for certain what the school children or congregations of Perth, Pune, Pretoria, or Palembang heard when they recited or sang, we can to some extent reimagine these acoustic domains through the frameworks of their verse. It is here that the technology of genre, the resonances and resurrections afforded by rhyme and rhythm, for example, become especially dynamic. Through these patterns we are able to track the role that auditory form played in figuring and re-figuring the imperial status quo.

Each one of the essays collected here provides an acoustic supplement to empire, some device through which to enhance our ability to think or imagine it. Together they explore the ways in which cultures and generations were kept interconnected via the medium of sound. We learn about how the auditory mediated ideas about empire (as grand, worthwhile, impressive, or as transitory, fallible, uncertain), and about how to understand empire through sound (as global, diffusive, emotion-driven, and so on). The sonic opened up to colonizer and colonized alike structures of feeling, repositories of cultural value, and technologies of global transmission. As such, acoustic devices supplied sensitive affective registers for how colonial identities could be posited and propagated, and also, crucially, preserved.

Notes

1. Emily Thompson, cited in Nazan Maksudyan, chapter in this volume.
2. Kate Wakeling, "Scattered System," *TLS* (December 18, 2020), 37.
3. Wai Chee Dimock, *Weak Planet: Literature and Assisted Survival* (Chicago: Chicago University Press, 2020), 27–29.
4. Elleke Boehmer, "Circulating Forms: The Jingo Poem at the Height of Empire," *English Language Notes* 49/1 (Spring 2011): 11–28. See also Alejandra Bronfman, chapter in this volume.
5. Carl Dahlhaus, *Studies on the Origin of Harmonic Tonality*, trans. Robert O. Gjerdigen (Princeton, NJ: Princeton University Press, 1990). See also David Toop, *Sinister Resonance: The Mediumship of the Listener* (New York: Continuum, 2010).
6. Boehmer, "Circulating Forms," 11–28.
7. See Jason R. Rudy, *Imagined Homelands: British Poetry in the Colonies* (Baltimore: Johns Hopkins University Press, 2017), 14: "Poetry—specifically genres like sentimental verse—became for colonial societies a crucial mode of engagement with the work of settlement as well as, more rarely, a mode of critique." See also Rudy, *Imagined Homelands*, 110.
8. Robert Baden-Powell, *Scouting for Boys* [1908], ed. Elleke Boehmer (Oxford, UK: Oxford University Press, 2004), Part VI.

Index

For the benefit of digital users, indexed terms that span two pages (e.g., 52–53) may, on occasion, appear on only one of those pages.

Tables and figures are indicated by *t* and *f* following the page number